TH

£10·99

THE ENCYCLOPEDIA OF
SUPERSTITIONS

Edited and revised by
Christina Hole

Helicon

First published in 1948
Revised and enlarged edition 1961
Reprinted 1969 (twice), 1975
This version first published 1980 by
Hutchinson & Co (Publishers) Ltd

This version reprinted in paperback 1995 by
Helicon Publishing Ltd
42 Hythe Bridge Street
Oxford, OX1 2EP

ISBN 1–85986–093–1

British Cataloguing in Publication Data

A catalogue record for this book is available from the British Library

Printed in Great Britain by
The Bath Press Ltd, Bath, Avon

Acknowledgement

The work on which this present book is based was originally devised by Edwin and Mona A. Radford. Struck by the universal interest of the subject and by the lack of any comprehensive catalogue of English folklore, as apart from the many excellent books dealing with individual aspects, they spent four years in collecting and verifying all the superstitions they could trace. The extent of the revision and enlargement involved in this new edition, confided by the authors to Miss Christina Hole as a leading folklore specialist, is a token of the vast growth of our knowledge of this field of study in recent years.

Foreword

THE SUPERSTITIONS listed in this book have all been found to exist in one part or another of the British Isles. Some still flourish there, and others did so until comparatively recently. The majority are not, of course, confined to these islands. Many are universal, springing from hopes and fears common to the whole human race, and most exist in similar or slightly different forms in various parts of the world. Only a very few are peculiar to England, Scotland, Wales, or Ireland. Nevertheless, all are British in the sense that they are, or were, a part of our traditional belief.

Considerations of space have, unfortunately, made it impossible to include detailed comparisons with foreign variants. A really comprehensive survey of that nature would be a work of immense value to students of human thought and history, but it would require a volume, or more probably, several volumes, far larger than this one. It is hoped, however, that this short list of British examples, arranged in alphabetical order, may serve as an introduction to a wider study of the subject, and as a handy reference book for those who wish to know something of the superstitions of their own country.

Since superstitions are by their nature irrational, it may be asked why time should be spent in studying them. There is, in fact, a very good reason for doing so, quite apart from the intrinsic interest of the subject. Superstitions are the living relics of ways of thought much older than our own, and of beliefs once strongly held but now abandoned and forgotten. Properly understood, they shed light on the history of our race, and help us to understand the thought-processes of our remote ancestors, and our own deeply buried roots. Absurd as some of them now seem in the light of present knowledge, all were serious in their beginnings. The study of their origins and later modifications is therefore richly rewarding because it reveals not only the fears and desires of the past, but also the hidden springs of many modern ideas and prejudices.

Present-day superstitions are fragmentary remains of forgotten faiths, rituals, and systems of thought, left behind when these faded from human minds, as small pools are left behind by the receding tide. Time, and the disappearance of the religion or philosophy that gave them birth, have made them meaningless, and therefore irrational, but have not always deprived them of the power to influence men's lives. When we touch wood to avert

7

A

ADDER

The adder, the only venomous snake found in Great Britain, has always been feared by country people, not only because it is in fact dangerous, but also because it was once thought to be a creature of ill-omen. To meet one and let it live brought bad luck, a belief which has often resulted, and still does, in the unnecessary slaughter of harmless snakes mistaken for it. A live adder on the doorstep of a house was a warning of death for someone living in that house. On the other hand, to kill the first one seen in Spring was lucky; the man who did so would triumph over all his human enemies during the coming season.

A widespread country tradition says that adders, like other snakes, cannot die before sunset, however badly injured they may be. According to some, however, they can be killed outright if they are struck with a stick of ash-wood. They hate the ash and will always avoid it, so that a man carrying a branch in his hand, or wearing a circlet of ash-twigs in his hat, is safe even in the most snake-infested wood.

Charms were often used to destroy adders. One, quoted by M. A. Courtney in *Cornish Feasts and Folklore* (1890) was to draw a circle on the ground round the snake as soon as it was seen, mark a cross inside the ring, and recite the first two verses of the 68th Psalm. Another was to say, softly and slowly:

> Underneath this hazelen mot,
> There's a braggaty worm with a speckled throat.
> Now nine doubles has he.
> Now from nine double, to eight double,
> From eight double, to seven double,
> From seven double, to six double
> From six double, to five double,
> From five double, to four double,
> From four double, to three double,
> From three double, to two double,
> From two double, to one double,
> Now no double hath he.

This was supposed to make the snake twist itself into nothing and so compass its own death. The words of the charm had to be muttered in a low voice, for they lost their power if said aloud.

When any one had been bitten, he could be cured by bruising the body of a dead adder on the wound, or by treating it with an ointment made of adder-fat. A seventeenth-century remedy was to hold a live pigeon to the bitten place until, having absorbed the poison, the bird died. What may have been a later variant of this was the West-country custom of thrusting the injured foot or hand into the stomach of a chicken that had just been killed, and keeping it there until the bird was cold. If its flesh turned black, all was well, but if there was no change of colour, it was a sign that the poison had already penetrated into the patient's system. In her *Folk-Lore of Hereford-shire* (1912) Mrs Leather mentions a remedy of a rather expensive nature which involved killing a sheep and wrapping the sufferer in the warm and reeking pelt. One of her informants, an old man named John Hutchinson, told her he had seen this done in his youth near Eywas Harold.

Not all the old cures were, however, as complicated as these. In the thirteenth century, the Physicians of Myddvai recommended the washing of the wound with a lotion made from pounded rosemary and betony, mixed with pure water. This, they said, would cure any venomous bite, whether of snake or beast, without further treatment. Another simple remedy, still remembered in some English country districts, was to mix the expressed juice of goosegrass with wine and give it to the patient to drink.

The cast skins of adders were supposed to have medicinal value. One worn inside the crown of the hat prevented headache, or, tied round the leg, it averted rheumatism. Powdered and swallowed, these skins cured diseases of the spleen, and when laid against any pricked part of the body, they drew out thorns and splinters. In Lincolnshire, 'hetherd-broth', or broth made from adder's flesh boiled with a chicken, was given for consumption. In some areas, a dried adder's skin hung on the roof or over the hearth was believed to protect the house from fire and bring good luck to those who lived there.

In Northumberland, the snakes which infest the banks of the River Derwent, a tributary of the Tyne, are sometimes called the Earl of Derwentwater's Adders. Legend says that once there were no reptiles of any sort there; but on the day when Lord Derwentwater was executed for his part in the 1715 rebellion, large numbers of adders suddenly appeared. Thereafter their descendants continued to haunt the banks along almost the whole length of the river. They are said to be specially numerous in those regions where the stream forms part of the boundary of the Derwentwater estates.

ADDER STONE

The name 'adder stone' is commonly applied either to a small stone with a natural perforation in it, or to a certain type of coloured, glass-like pebble which is fairly uncommon and consequently has all the virtues of the strange and unusual.

Prehistoric spindle-whorls turned up by the plough are also frequently so called by those who do not recognize them for what they really are.

Such stones were formerly prized as charms against evil and were used in cures for various human and animal diseases. According to tradition, they were generated by snakes who, at certain times of the year, congregated in large numbers, coiled themselves into a living ball and, while so united, emitted saliva which hardened into a stone. Because of their serpentine origin, they were widely used to heal adder-bites. Many stories are told of their efficacy for this purpose. One such tale, related by William Henderson in *Notes on the Folk-Lore of the Northern Counties* (1879) records how a nineteenth-century Scottish labourer near Pitlochry was badly bitten by an adder. 'Severe pains came on,' said Henderson's informant, 'and a terrible swelling, which grew worse and worse, till a wise woman was summoned with her adder's stone. On her rubbing the place with the stone, the swelling began to subside.' They also cured ague and whooping-cough, kept away nightmare if hung over the bed, and when carried about in the pocket, prevented eye-troubles.

Although their healing properties are not now much regarded, their use as luck-bringers and protective charms is not yet entirely extinct, and in some parts of Great Britain and Ireland such stones, especially those accidentally found, are still preserved and handed down as amulets.

ADDER'S TONGUE FERN

The little fern known as Adder's Tongue (or sometimes as Adder's Spear) was once thought, like most plants traditionally associated with snakes, to have strong healing powers. Because its yellowish-green spike resembles an adder's tongue, it was considered a sovereign remedy for adder-bites, since 'like cures like' in folk-belief. According to the Doctrine of Signatures, its snakish 'tongue' clearly marked it as an antidote to the evils wrought by snakes. By a simple extension of the same idea, it was also thought useful in diseases of the human tongue.

Nor were these its only virtues. If gathered when the moon was waning, its leaves could be made into a plaster to heal tumours and swellings. Their expressed juice made wound-drinks and lotions for sore eyes, and in the form of ointments or plasters, they were once widely used for the treatment of wounds and cuts, by licensed apothecaries no less than by ordinary people. It was not for nothing that the French called this fern *Herbe aux cent miracles*, and that it was carefully sought in the appropriate phases of the moon by herbalists and others who had charge of the sick.

Modern herbalists still employ it in wound salves or lotions; and in some areas, country people make a tea of the leaves and drink it, especially in Spring, to purify the blood.

AFFLICTED PERSONS

Certain types of afflicted persons were thought to be luck-bringers because they were under the special protection of God. In some cases, they were also thought to have peculiar gifts of healing or foreknowledge. Idiots, who were once far commoner in rural districts than they are now, were formerly regarded as God's chosen children, and for this reason they were almost always kindly treated, even in periods much rougher and more cruel than our own. Their disjointed utterances were sometimes taken to be Divine messages, and the presence of a 'natural' was thought to shed a blessing on the community which harboured him. In this connexion it is significant that the word 'silly' originally meant blessed or happy, and only later acquired its present-day meaning of 'foolish' or 'stupid'. Idiots were among the very few people that fishermen liked to meet when they were on their way to the boats, and one encountered on a journey was generally considered a fortunate omen.

In the Highlands of Scotland and in Ireland, a dumb man was believed to have 'the sight of both worlds', and sometimes to be able to heal others by means of his spittle. Similarly, those who were deformed or crippled from birth were often thought to be specially gifted in some way, and to en-counter them on the road was a good omen. This tradition survives even today in the case of a hunchback; to see one is lucky, and to touch his hump, openly, or surreptitiously, is even more so.

On the other hand, a cross-eyed or squinting person was almost universally feared. To meet one on the way to work is still regarded as a bad sign by miners, fishermen, Spanish bull-fighters, and others who follow dangerous trades. It is, of course, realized by everyone that such a person is afflicted, and quite blameless in his affliction; but any visible defect in the eye is readily associated by the superstitious with the Evil Eye, and a glance from such an individual may mean that the person on whom it falls has been overlooked.

AGE

In some country districts it is said to be unlucky to tell one's age. This odd superstition is probably connected with the ancient and widespread prejudice against counting and numbering.

ALBATROSS

In the days of sail, an albatross flying round a ship in mid-ocean was an omen of wind and bad weather to come. It was very unlucky to kill it because, like the sea-gull and the stormy petrel, it was thought to embody the restless soul of some dead mariner. This belief was once very widespread amongst deep-water sailors, and probably helped to preserve these magnificent birds in the southern ocean; but evidently it was not quite universal, for it was not unknown for the less superstitious to shoot an albatross occasionally in order to make tobacco pouches from its webbed feet.

Echoes of these time-honoured traditions were heard in July 1959 when the cargo liner, *Calpean Star*, docked at Liverpool with engine trouble, after a voyage from the Antarctic that had been dogged by many misfortunes. Several newspapers reported that the crew blamed these on the presence on board of an albatross destined for a German zoo. On the day after the ship docked, the bird was found dead in its cage; and later, about fifty of the crew staged a sit-down strike because they were unwilling to continue their unlucky voyage to Norway and wished to be paid off at once. In the *Daily Telegraph* of 7 July, the Master is reported as saying that it had required some courage on his part to bring the albatross on board in the first place. Why this was so, he did not explain; perhaps it was not necessary for him to do so with a tradition so well known. Probably he did not himself believe that the bird would bring bad weather or misfortune, or that it was connected with the souls of the dead, but he may have feared that some or all of his crew still believed it. If he did, the subsequent events of the voyage seem to have proved that he was right.

ALLAN APPLES

A Cornish name for the season usually known as Hallowtide was Allantide. Until towards the end of last century, it was customary then to give each member of the family a very large apple, called an Allan Apple, as a luck-bringer. Whoever ate one of these on Hallowe'en would be fortunate in the coming year. If a young unmarried girl slept with one under her pillow, she would dream of her future husband. Like many other Hallowe'en customs, this harks back to the remote period when the year began on 1 November, and Hallowe'en was therefore New Year's Eve, a proper season for divination and luck-bringing rites. Allan Apples are still occasionally given to children but the custom is no longer general, and the magical significance of the fruit has been almost entirely forgotten.

ANKOU. *See Churchyard Watcher.*

ANTS

In Cornwall ants, locally known as Meryons or Muryans, were once thought to be fairies in the last stages of their earthly existence. Legend said that these elfin creatures went through many gradual transformations, always becoming smaller and smaller, until finally, after living for some time as Meryons, they disappeared altogether from this world. This brings the ant considerably nearer to the human race than might at first appear, for according to one tradition, the Cornish fairies were once Druids who refused to accept Christianity and so were condemned to lose their human status. Another tale says unbaptized children took this form after their death, being safe from Hell because of their innocence, but unable to enter Heaven because they were not christened. In both versions of the legend, they eventually become muryans, and hence it was considered very unlucky to destroy an ants' nest. It was also said at one time that if a piece of tin was put into such a nest when the moon was new, it would turn into silver, provided that it was inserted at a certain fortunate moment which varied in different parts of the county.

Ants' eggs were formerly used in magical compounds intended to destroy love. In Topsel's *History of Four-footed Beasts and Serpents* (1607), the following cure for warts and swellings is given: 'Reckon how many warts you have, and take so many ants, and bind them up in a thin cloth with a snail, and bring all to ashes, and mingle them with vinegar. Take off the head of a small ant, and bruise the body between your fingers, and anoint with it any imposthumated tumour, and it will presently sink down.'

APPLE

The apple-tree seems to have been regarded as holy or magical from very early times, and in almost every country in which it grows. In ancient Ireland, it was one of the three things that could only be paid for by living objects, the others being a hazel-bush and a sacred grove. It grew in the Celtic Paradise, where the hills were clothed with trees that bore fruit and blossom together. The mysterious land to whic[1] King Arthur was taken for the healing of his wounds was the Vale of Avalon, the Apple Vale, which seems originally to have been Paradise, though by some later writers it was equated with Glastonbury. Even today, almost everyone refers to the fruit eaten by Eve in the Garden of Eden as an apple, though in the Authorized Version it is called simply 'the fruit of the tree'. We meet the apple-tree and its fruits in ancient Greek, Roman and Norse legends, and in many folk-tales; and traces of the veneration once paid to it still linger in some of our superstitions and customs.

Mrs Leather[1] remarks that old labourers in Herefordshire regarded the destruction of an orchard as an almost sacrilegious act. It was commonly said there that if an orchard was destroyed to plant a hop-yard in its place, the latter would never pay the cost of cultivation. She also mentions a

[1] E. M. Leather, *op. cit.*

custom whereby, if a man wanted to enclose a piece of common land, he had to plant an apple-tree on it. The lord of the manor preserved his rights over the enclosed land by exacting an annual tribute of the fruit.

Many omens and charms are, or were, associated with apples. If the sun shines through the trees on Christmas morning (or in some districts, on Easter morning) it is a sign of a good crop to come and a prosperous year for the owner of the orchard. The fruit must be blessed by rain on St Peter's or St Swithin's Day, see Rain, and in some districts it is said to be unfit to eat until after this has happened. Blossom appearing in autumn is a death-omen for someone in the owner's family, and especially so if the flowers come while there is still fruit on the branches. A well-known couplet says:

> A bloom on the tree when the apples are ripe
> Is a sure termination of somebody's life.

Similarly, if when the fruit is picked, an apple is left behind and hangs there till the Spring comes round again, a death is foretold. There was, however, a Yorkshire variant of this belief. In his *Folk-Lore of East Yorkshire* (1890) John Nicholson tells us that it was sometimes thought unlucky to strip the tree completely. An apple or two, even if only the deformed or inaccessible fruit, should be left for the birds. This was the explanation given in his time but, as he points out, the gift may originally have been intended for the fairies, or some even older spirits.

A Hallowtide game, once very popular, was for all the unmarried young people to fasten an apple apiece on a string and twirl it round before a hot fire. The one whose apple fell off first would be the first to marry; he or she whose apple remained till the end would die unwed. If an apple was peeled in one long strip, and the peeling thrown backwards over the left shoulder, the shape it made as it lay on the ground showed the initial of the future wife or husband. Another method of divination was for the inquirer to stick pips on her cheek, naming each for a possible husband. The one that stayed there longest denoted the mate-to-be. Or a pip similarly named could be placed on the bars of the fire, with the words,

> If you love me, bounce and fly,
> If you hate me, lie and die.

The lover was faithful if the pip burst noisily in the fire's heat, but not if it burnt quietly away. This was the most usual form of the charm, but in Sussex the omen worked the other way. A silent burning foretold a smooth courtship with a happy ending, a bursting pip the break-up of the affair.

A way to cure warts was to divide an apple, rub the wart with both halves, tie them together again, and bury the whole in the earth. The wart would disappear as the buried fruit mouldered away. An old remedy for rheumatism in the eye was to apply a poultice made of rotten apples, and at one time decoctions of the fruit or blossom were used in beauty culture, one being specially mentioned as good for a too red nose.

It would be curious if so magical a plant had never been used in spells as well as charms, and in fact, it was so used. Of many possible examples, here are two, both recorded as fact within the last seventy years.

In his *Folk Lore, Old Customs and Superstitions in Shakespeare Land* (1929), J. Harvey Bloom relates a story which he had from George Bailey, of Wimpstone, in Warwickshire. This man knew a certain woman carrier who was supposed to have magical powers. One snowy morning he visited her house, and she offered to prove her abilities by fetching her own sister, who lived ten miles away. She then took an apple, thrust twelve new pins into it, and put it into the fire, whilst murmuring a charm he could not hear. About noon, the sister walked in, saying that 'something she could not resist' had forced her to come.

The other spell was more deadly. In her *Shropshire Folk-Lore* (1883) C. S. Burne says that a woman was one day carrying her child in her arms as she walked along the road. The child was eating an apple. They met another woman, who took the fruit from the little boy, bit a piece from it, and returned it to him. His health, hitherto good, declined from that day on, and eventually he died.

APPLE-WASSAILING

Wassailing the Apple-trees was an ancient custom intended to ensure a plentiful crop of fruit. It was formerly observed in most apple-growing districts, and is still kept up in some parts of the West-country. Nowadays, no doubt, it is done mainly 'because it has always been done', or as a frolic; but once it was a serious luck-bringing rite, and to omit it was thought ill-omened, and likely to cause a poor yield in the following Autumn.

Apple-wassailing (sometimes called Apple-howling) was a ceremony of the Christmas season, performed usually on Twelfth Night, or Old Twelfth Night, but sometimes, as in Sussex, on New Year's Eve and the days immediately following. The men and boys of the farm, accompanied by their womenfolk, went to the orchard at dusk, carrying guns, trays, pans and kettles, and a quantity of cider. One tree was chosen to represent all. The company drank to it, threw cider over its roots, and set a piece of toast soaked in cider in a fork of its branches. Sometimes the lowest twigs were pulled down and dipped into the cider-pail; or those present bowed three times to the ground, raising themselves slowly with the motions of men burdened by a heavily laden sack. These were magical actions to ensure that what was thus imitated would later be reproduced in fact. Noise was also needed, to rouse the sleeping tree-spirit and drive away the demons of ill-luck. The armed men fired their guns through the topmost branches, the unarmed beat upon their kettles, trays and pans, as their ancestors had probably done for the same purpose long before guns were invented. In Cornwall, the people danced round the trees, and everywhere there was much cheerful shouting, blasts from a cow-horn, and the singing all together of the Wassailing Song.

The words of this vary in different districts, but in practically all versions it begins with 'Hail to thee, old Apple Tree' and goes on to adjure the tree to bear well and generously, as though it was a living creature that could hear and understand. The Sussex version runs:

> Stand fast root,
> Bear well top,
> Pray God send us a good howling crop.
> Every twig, apples big,
> Every bough, apples enow,
> Hats full, caps full,
> Full quarter sacks full,
>   Holla, boys, holla! Huzzah!

In some variants, the penultimate line runs 'And my pockets full, too', a personal note here making itself heard in what is otherwise a purely communal rite.

The orchards are still wassailed on Old Twelfth Night, 17 January, at Carhampton in Somerset, and also at Roadwater in the same county. In the latter place the wassailers return to the local inn after the ceremony. They enter by the back door, drink to the health of the house, and leave again by the front door. On no account must this proceeding be reversed, for to do so would bring bad luck to the house.

APRON

In most parts of England, it is considered ominous if a woman's apron falls off, but the nature of the portent varies in different districts. In East Anglia, it is a sign of bad luck of some sort; in Oxfordshire, it means the birth of a child within the year. Young girls in counties as far apart as Lincolnshire and Herefordshire say it shows their lovers are thinking of them. Nurses, if they twist their apron-strings when dressing, expect to begin some new work soon.

To put an apron on back to front is lucky, provided it is done accidentally and is not immediately reversed. If a housewife suffers a succession of small misfortunes in her work, she can 'change the luck' by turning her apron. To turn it when seeing the new moon for the first time ensures that the wish made then will be granted.

These beliefs do not seem to extend to the aprons sometimes worn by gardeners, butchers, and other male workers. This may be because these are always temporary garments, put on to preserve the ordinary clothes from dirt. The country woman's white apron, on the other hand, was, until about sixty or seventy years ago, a permanent part of her attire. When dirty work had to be done, a second and coarser apron was tied over the white one.

ASH

From very ancient times, the ash has been revered as a sacred and fortunate tree, connected with fire, lightning and clouds. In some pagan mythologies it appears as an ancestor of mankind. Hesiod tells us that Jove created the third, or brazen, race of men from ash-trees. In Greece, certain families were thought to be descended from them. Yggdrasil, the Scandinavian World Tree which supported the entire universe, was an ash; and when the Norse gods desired to fill the empty spaces of Midgard with a new people, they took an ash and breathed a human soul into it. Thus the first man was created and named Askr, and thereafter a woman was similarly made from an alder to be his consort. From these two all the peoples of the world were supposed to be descended.

Because of its sacred and magical character, the ash was sometimes considered a dangerous tree to destroy without good reason. In the eighteenth and early nineteenth centuries, when transportation was a common punishment for felony, Derbyshire people believed that whoever wantonly destroyed such a tree would certainly live to be transported. Unlike the oak, which is still quite often thought to protect those who stand under it from lightning, it was said to court the flash, and was therefore to be avoided during a storm. But in almost every other respect, it was a fortunate tree, and friendly to mankind.

It cured diseases; it could be used in divination and charms. Its leaves and wood protected all who kept them in the house or wore them about the person from witchcraft and evil. In Lincolnshire, the berried, female ash, locally known as Sheder, was used to defeat the spells of male witches, and the berryless variety, or Heder, to defeat those of female magicians. Snakes detested the ash and kept away from any one carrying its wood. *See Adders.* An old Devonshire legend says that the Infant Jesus was given His first bath by a fire of ash-wood, and for this reason, new-born babies in that county were, whenever possible, first washed by such a fire.

In some parts of Scotland, ash-wood sticks were preferred by herdsmen to any other because they protected the cattle from witchcraft and, if a beast was struck with one, never did it any harm. Eighty or ninety years ago, a certain disease of the limbs in horses, cattle, and sometimes human beings, was widely ascribed to shrew-mice, who were supposed to cause it by running over the victims. *See Shrew-Mouse.* A cure for this ailment was to immure a living mouse in an ash-tree, and then to rub the affected parts with its leaves or twigs. Such trees were known as Shrew-Ashes, and were much resorted to for this and other evils.

Every ash-tree, whether a Shrew-Ash or not, was once deemed to have healing properties, especially in cases of ague, rupture, rickets, whooping-cough, or warts. Mrs Leather[1] has described an old tree which, in the early years of the present century, grew in a coppice near Eyton in Herefordshire. 'Its trunk,' she said, 'is covered with hairs, small locks of human hair placed in notches made in the bark. Eyton folk believe that an offering of child's hair to this tree will cure the cough.' In Leicestershire, anyone afflicted with warts could rid himself of them by taking a corresponding number of pins and thrusting each one, separately, into an ash. He then had to withdraw it, prick one of his warts with it, and finally push it back again into the tree. By this rather painful method, the warts were transferred, one by one, to the ash, and as long as they remained embedded in it, their original owner would be troubled by them no more.

The editor of Brand's *Popular Antiquities* (1849 edition) recorded a Worcestershire charm for ague which was said to be infallible. The patient sought out a tree-grafter and asked him to cut the first branch of a maiden ash on his behalf. He then went home, and the branch was cut in his absence. The cure was effected as soon as the work was finished, always provided that no money was paid to the woodman for his services. If any such reward was given, the charm would not work.

Probably the best-known and most firmly credited of all ash-cures was that employed to heal rupture or rickets in children. A young ash-sapling was split, and the child was passed through it, three or nine times, usually from his father's hand to that of another man. He was then taken home, and the tree was tightly bound up in order that the cleft might heal. As it did so, the rupture or rickets healed also. If, however, the tree did not recover, neither did the patient, and if at any time, even many years later, it died or was felled, the disease returned immediately in a more virulent form, and the sufferer died, like the tree with whose life his own had been joined by the healing ceremony. It was therefore vitally important, not only to bind the cleft up properly at the time, but also to protect the tree afterwards from damage or destruction. Kindly landowners sometimes gave an ash to the parents of ruptured or rickety children, or promised that one which had already been used in the cure would never be felled. In her *West Sussex Superstitions* (1878) Charlotte Latham relates how, a few weeks before she wrote, a cleft ash in

[1] E. M. Leather, *op. cit.*

Fittleworth parish was bought by a man who intended to cut it down. The father of the child who had been passed through it besought him to spare it, saying that the infirmity would certainly return if the tree was destroyed. The owner agreed that this would be so, and readily promised not to fell it.

The details of the rite varied slightly in different districts. In some parts all had to be done in complete silence, in others, the father said, 'The Lord giveth' as he passed the child through the cleft, and the other man replied, 'The Lord receiveth.' Sometimes the ceremony was performed once only, sometimes on nine successive mornings, the sapling being bound up on the last day. Invariably it was done at sunrise, and the child, who had to be naked, was turned about so that his face was always towards the rising sun. The tree itself must be without blemish, a maiden ash that had never been cut or lopped. Mrs Latham tells us that in nineteenth-century Sussex nine persons went with the child on nine successive days and each in turn passed him through the split ash. In most districts, however, only two or three people were present, including one of the parents, usually the father. As a rule, he was not allowed to cut the tree himself. This work was done by two other men, who were also responsible for binding up the cleft afterwards.

ASH-KEYS

A failure of the crop of ash-keys, the winged seeds of the ash, foretells a death in the Royal Family within the year. A strong country tradition says there was such a failure in 1648, followed by the tragic death of Charles I in January 1649.

In Scotland and northern England, a bunch of ash-keys, worn or carried about, protected the bearer from being overlooked. A country remedy for persistent bed-wetting was to send the afflicted child out, alone, to choose an ash-tree and then, on another day, to gather keys from it. These had to be laid with the left hand in the hollow of the right arm, and so carried home, where they were burnt upon the hearth. If the child then made water upon their ashes, it was believed that he would be permanently cured. Charlotte Latham[1] was told by a Sussex woman in the latter half of the nineteenth century that she had tried this cure for her own little boy, with complete success.

A remedy for ulcerated ears, given in the thirteenth-century *Book of the Physicians of Myddvai*, involved boiling ash-keys briskly in the sick man's urine, making a fomentation therewith, and putting black wool soaked in the liquid into the ear. If this is done, say the pious authors, 'by God's help, it will cure it'.

[1] Charlotte Latham, *op. cit.*

ASH-LEAF

Ash-leaves, like the tree on which they grow, were formerly thought to be lucky, and were used in charms and divination. It was, however, especially the even ash-leaf, that is, one with an equal number of divisions on each side, which was most valued. Such leaves are rare, and to find one, either accidentally or after long search, was a sign of good fortune. In the West-country it was usual to say, when picking it,

> Even ash, I do thee pluck,
> Hoping thus to meet good luck.
> If no good luck I get from thee,
> I shall wish thee on the tree.

If the finder then wore it in his hat or buttonhole, or carried it in his pocket, he could expect success and happiness, or at least, safety from mishaps and the effects of ill-wishing, for some time to come.

In Northumberland, when a girl wished to know whom she would marry, she looked for an even ash-leaf, and said:

> Even, even, ash,
> I pluck thee off the tree.
> The first young man that I do meet,
> My lover he shall be.

She then put it in her left shoe and wore it thus, hidden under her foot. The first man she met thereafter would ultimately marry her. This was held to be certain, even though such a match might, for various reasons, seem highly improbable at the time of the meeting.

A Yorkshire variant of the same charm was for the girl to gather the leaf secretly, saying:

> Even-ash, even-ash, I pluck thee,
> This night my own true love to see,
> Neither in his rick nor in his rare,
> But in the clothes he does every day wear.

If she slept that night with it under her pillow, she would see her future husband in a dream.

ASHEN FAGGOT

The Ashen Faggot still makes its appearance on Christmas Eve in numerous West-country homes and inns, as it has done from time immemorial. It is a large bundle of ash-sticks, bound with nine ash or withy-bands, which in Devon and Somerset takes the place of the Yule log and, like the latter, has to be brought in with ceremony and lit from a fragment of its predecessor that has been saved throughout the year in order to ensure continuity of good fortune. Its normal size calls for a large, and preferably an open hearth, but in some modern houses, where there is no such fire-space, a miniature faggot is often made, to preserve the old tradition.

Unmarried girls in the household will often choose a band, name it for themselves, and watch to see when it breaks in the heat of the fire. She whose band breaks first will be the first to marry. In inns and public-houses, the parting of the first band is also carefully watched for, since it is usually the signal for a round of drinks, with other rounds and fresh toasts for each subsequent breakage. Brand, in his *Popular Antiquities*, quotes a poem written in 1795, in which the poet mentions the 'pondrous ashen faggot' in the farmer's hall, and says:

> . . . nine bandages it bears,
> And as they each disjoin (as custom wills)
> A mighty jug of sparkling cyder's brought,
> With brandy mixt, to elevate the guests.

Legends connected with Our Lady, or with King Alfred, are often told locally to account for these time-honoured customs; but there can be little doubt that, like those associated with the Yule Log, they sprang originally from the ancient fire and fertility rites once practised in pre-Christian times at the Winter Solstice.

ASHES

The ashes left on the hearth when the fire had died out were often used in charms and divination because they were thought to retain some of the magical properties of the fire from which they came. In Yorkshire a rite known as Ass-riddling was practised on St Mark's Eve, to discover whether any person in the household would die within the year. Before the family went to bed, the ashes were riddled on the hearth, and so left. In the morning, all looked to see if a footprint was visible in them. If there was no such mark, all was well; but if there was one, then the person whose foot it fitted would die within twelve months. Elsewhere similar divinations were tried on other significant dates, such as New Year's Eve or Hallowe'en. A Manx variant of the tradition was that if the print pointed towards the door, someone would die, but if it pointed inwards, there would be a birth in the family during the coming year.

In some districts, when a death had occurred, the chaff and straw from the dead man's bed were burned in an open space, and the resulting ashes were allowed to lie untouched through the night. Here too, a footprint was looked for in the morning, that of the person who would die next. In this case there was no time limit, and years might elapse before the omen was fulfilled.

A form of love-divination, apparently confined to men, is recorded by S. O. Addy in his *Household Tales and Traditional Remains* (1895). If a young man, as yet fancy-free, desired to know whom he would eventually marry, he scattered ashes (or in some cases, seeds) along a quiet lane on Hallowe'en. The first girl to follow the trail so laid would be his future wife.

Ashes from the sacred bonfires lit at Beltane, Midsummer, or Hallowtide, or from any kindled by Need-fire, were deemed to have fertilizing and protective powers, and were scattered over the fields for the good of the crops. In Wales, all who gathered round such fires took some of the ashes home with them to protect their houses. It was usual also to scatter some inside shoes, for this preserved the wearer from any great sorrow or misfortune.

ASPEN

A country name for the aspen is the Shivver-tree, a name which in some districts is also given to the poplar. The leaves of both trees tremble at the slightest stirring of air, so that they seem to move without ceasing when all around is still. Because of this, both trees were formerly credited with the power to cure agues and fevers. A very old magical tradition held that ailments could most efficaciously be treated by something that resembled their effects; and since ague causes the patient to shake and tremble, he was likely to be healed by the shaking tree.

In his *Folk-Lore of the Northern Counties*, William Henderson relates the story of a Lincolnshire girl who was thus cured of ague. She was advised to pin a lock of her hair to an aspen, saying as she did so, 'Aspen-tree, aspen-tree, I prithee to shake and shiver instead of me.' As was usual in such charms, her journey home had then to be made in complete silence, otherwise the magic would not work. She followed the advice given, and many years later, when she was an old woman, she told Henderson's informant that she had never been troubled with ague again. Another method was to bore a small hole in the tree-trunk, insert the patient's nail-parings, and close the hole securely. As the bark grew once more over the opening, so the disease would disappear.

Two widespread legends are told to account for the aspen's trembling. One is that it was condemned to shiver thus for evermore because it was the only tree that would not bow down to Our Lord when He passed through the forest. The other is that it shudders perpetually with horror because its wood was used to make the Cross on Calvary.

ASS. *See Donkey.*

AURORA BOREALIS

The comparatively rare appearances of the Aurora Borealis (or Northern Lights) in regions far south of the Arctic Circle have almost always been regarded as omens of war, disaster, bloodshed, and the deaths of kings and heroes. This is very easy to understand because, to people who do not know what these vivid electrical displays really are, it looks as though the skies themselves were burning, or as though fiery spears were being shaken in the heavens by an invisible spirit-hand. Hence the name of Burning Spears which is sometimes applied to them. Another and less alarming title, perhaps first given to a slight and mild display, is The Merry Dancers.

In northern England, especially in Northumberland and Durham, they are still called Lord Derwentwater's Lights because of a strong tradition that they flared all over the sky with startling brilliance on the night when that young and well-loved Earl was executed for his share in the rebellion of 1715. Nor was this the only occasion when the Aurora signified disaster for North-umberland. In his *Acts of Stephen*, Henry of Huntingdon describes how, shortly before the rebellion of 1138 in that county, he saw the whole northern sky aflame with balls of light and fiery sparks, and thought it must foretell either a great effusion of blood or the burning of towns and villages. The ill-fated rebellion that followed brought both.

H. J. Westbrook tells us in his *Stockton Heath and Immediate Neighbourhood* that when the Aurora was seen in that Cheshire township during the nineteenth century, the people were terrified by it and were convinced that the end of the world was at hand. They were eventually reassured by a sea-captain who had often seen it before when afloat. Since then, scientific knowledge has increased so greatly that it might have been expected to destroy this ancient superstition completely. It does not seem to have done so, however. When war seemed likely, but still perhaps avoidable in the early part of 1939, the fears of some were heightened by appearances of the Northern Lights as far south as London; nor did it go unnoticed, or unmen-tioned, that just before the Pearl Harbour disaster, brilliant displays were seen on three successive nights in the United States, southwards as far as Cleveland, Ohio.

B

BANNS

It was formerly considered very unlucky for an engaged couple to hear their marriage banns read in church. If they did so, their children would suffer. In some districts it was believed that the first child would be an idiot, in others that if the girl was present, all her children would be deaf and dumb. Until about the middle of last century, it was customary in a number of parishes for the clerk (or sometimes the oldest man in the congregation) to say 'God speed them well', after the last reading, to which all present replied 'Amen'. But even this communal blessing was not always thought sufficient to avert the dangers inherent in the presence of the two most nearly concerned.

A superstition found in Perthshire was that if the banns were published at the end of one quarter, and the wedding took place at the beginning of the next, the marriage would be in some way ill-fated. In *Lincolnshire Notes and Queries* (1888) it is recorded that, on one occasion in October 1887, the banns of two young people were read, and on the same day, the bell was tolled for the death of a married woman. Local people regarded this as an extremely bad omen and predicted that the girl would not live a year after her wedding. In northern England, where those whose banns were being read were said to be 'asked' or 'shouted' in church, the bells were often pealed after the third reading. This was called the Spur-peal (from *spier*, to ask) and, like wedding-bells, was intended to bring a blessing on the couple and drive away evil influences.

To refuse to go on with the marriage after the final reading was very unlucky. It was also considered to be an affront both to the community and to the Church. J. E. Vaux, in his *Church Folk Lore* (1902) says that those who thus belatedly broke their engagement were said to be 'scorning or mocking the Church'. In some dioceses they could be fined for it by the Vicar. Sixteen entries of such fines occur in the accounts of Great Yarmouth between 1811 and 1825, and there are other instances elsewhere. But it was not always only the Church which took retaliatory measures. In 1888 an engaged couple at Cold Aston in Derbyshire quarrelled after their banns had been published, and cancelled their wedding only a few days before the advertised date. This so offended the villagers that Rough Music was made for the culprits, and two straw effigies were burnt, one outside the man's door and the other outside that of the woman. *See Rough Music.*

All these beliefs and practices seem to be relics of the time when a betrothal was considered almost as binding as a marriage, and the publication of banns (first instituted in the twelfth century) constituted, as it were, a preliminary wedding whose obligations could not be flouted with impunity.

BAPTISM

Although Baptism is a purely religious rite whereby a child or adult becomes a Christian, and at the same time receives the name by which he will be known throughout life, the ceremony has always been surrounded by a variety of superstitious beliefs and practices. Of these, some may be derived from the pre-Christian naming ceremonies of our pagan forefathers, many of which included the use of purifying water and rituals of admittance; but for most there is sufficient explanation in the fact that Baptism is the first important step in a child's life and, like all first steps, was once thought to need careful observances and safeguards, both to protect the baby and to ensure the full benefits of the rite.

The modern custom of delaying the ceremony for a few weeks, or even months, was unknown in earlier times, and would have been considered extremely dangerous. The baby was believed to be in constant peril from witches, fairies, and evil spirits until he was christened. He had to be protected by charms of all sorts, such as saining with fire, incantations, and the placing of iron, salt, garlic, or his parents' clothes in the cradle. These, and many more, were common precautions, but obviously the best method was to ensure that the interval between birth and baptism was as short as possible. During this period, the chosen name had to be concealed from all but near relatives, and sometimes even from them, lest a witch seize upon it and use it in a spell. Nor could it be used in speaking to the child before it was sanctified and formally bestowed by the Church. *See Names.* The baby's first journey into the outside world had to be to his christening; to take him out of the house before this would be very unlucky, and almost certain to result in misfortune, illness, or an early death.

Another reason for hastening baptism was the widespread belief that it benefited the child physically as well as spiritually. Many mothers thought that a baby would not thrive until he was christened. In some districts, the rite was regarded as a specific remedy for fits or convulsions. Charlotte Burne remarks in her *Shropshire Folk-Lore* that if an unbaptized child suffered from these troubles, the clergyman was just as likely to be sent for as the doctor. The water used also had medicinal powers, and at one time incumbents were quite often asked for it by women who believed it would strengthen their children if used for bathing them, or given as medicine.

In Ireland it was considered fortunate for a baby to be the first baptized of several brought to the church at the same time. There was, however, a very widespread prejudice against first christenings in a new church or at a new font. It was said that a child so christened would be claimed by the Devil, or he would die young, or both. In his *Strange Survivals* (1892) Baring-Gould relates that he was once asked by a blacksmith in Dalton, Yorkshire, to baptize the latter's son (the first boy in his family after seven daughters) on the following Sunday. A new church had just been built in this parish, and Baring-Gould pointed out that if the father would consent to wait for a few more days, his baby could be the first to be christened in the new building, which would by then have been consecrated. The man refused, saying he had always heard that in such cases the Devil would claim the child. If it had been another girl, he said, it would not have mattered, 'but as it's a lad, well, Sir, I won't risk it'.

When boys and girls came together to be baptized, the boys had to have priority, otherwise they would grow up beardless, while the girls who preceded them at the font would grow beards instead of them. Probably few people believed this quite literally, but the idea that any inversion of the usual order would make boys effeminate and girls hoydenish does seem to have been entertained within comparatively recent times.

It was a bad omen if the baby sneezed during the ceremony, and a far worse one if he did not cry when he felt the water on his face. Crying was a sign that the Devil was being driven out. Its absence was very unlucky, and was sometimes taken to mean that the child would not live long. Charlotte Latham[1] records how at a Sussex christening in the late nineteenth century, the baby's grandmother was seriously worried because he had not cried, and reproached the nurse afterwards for not pinching him to make him do so. This belief still lingers in many districts as a vague idea that it is somehow unlucky if the child remains silent, though the old notion of a death omen has now mercifully vanished.

It was usually considered unwise to wipe the baptismal water from the baby's face. It should be left to evaporate naturally. In most areas it was customary for the christening cap to be left on during the night after the ceremony, and sometimes longer, and consequently clergymen who made it too wet were unpopular. In his *Church Folk Lore* J. E. Vaux mentions a custom, already declining when he wrote, whereby the tenth child of a family came to church with a sprig of myrtle in his cap, to mark him as a 'tithe child'.

Until the beginning of the present century, bread and cheese, or cake (often a piece of the Groaning Cake) was carried by some member of the christening party, usually but not always, a woman, and given to the first person of opposite sex to the child who was encountered on the way to (or in some districts, from) the ceremony. Refusal of the gift brought very bad luck to the baby, a belief which sometimes had to be explained to startled strangers upon whom the food was thrust without warning by people totally unknown to them. This custom was formerly very widespread in England, and seems to have persisted longest in the northern and western counties. In Cornwall the offering was known as *Kimbly*, or *Cheeld's Fuggan*, the former being usually bread, and the latter a cake made with saffron and currants. Hamilton Jenkin observes in a footnote to *Cornwall and the Cornish* that the custom was still kept up by certain families in St Ives when he was writing in 1932.

The curious term 'half-christened', or 'half-baptized' is still used occasionally by old people to describe a person who has been privately baptized at home, but has not afterwards been publicly received into the Church. Such private christenings are now very rare, being confined usually to cases of real

[1] Charlotte Latham, *op. cit.*

emergency, when an unbaptized child is in imminent danger of death. Formerly, however, from the time of the Commonwealth until the early years of the nineteenth century, they were far from uncommon. The usual custom was for the private ceremony to be followed by the public reception of the already baptized child in the church which his parents normally attended. This second part of the rite was sometimes delayed for a considerable time. In a letter printed in the *Church Times* on 3 March 1955, reference is made to a man born in 1815 who was christened at home in infancy, and then, at the age of two, walked with his nurse to the parish church for the completion of the ceremony. Such a child was said to be 'half-christened' until he was so received; and if, as sometimes happened, the public reception was omitted altogether, he remained 'half-christened' all his life. *See Godparents: Unbaptized Child.*

BARGUESTS. *See Dogs.*

BARNACLE GEESE

The belief that Barnacle Geese are hatched from timbers rotting in the sea, and are consequently more fish than bird, was widespread in Great Britain and Ireland during the Middle Ages. It was responsible for a companion belief that these birds could be eaten without transgression during Lent and other fasting seasons. The latter notion, though not always supported by faith in the traditional reason for it, seems to have been current in Ireland only a generation ago, and to have existed there from at least as early as the twelfth century, and perhaps earlier.

In his *Topographia Hibernicae* (1186) Giraldus Cambrensis says that in Ireland birds called *Bernacae*, resembling marsh geese, but smaller, 'are produced from fir timber tossed along the sea and are at first like gum. Afterwards they hang down by their beaks as if they were seaweed attached to the timber, and are surrounded by shells in order to grow more freely. Having thus in the process of time been clothed with a strong coat of feathers, they either fall into the water or fly freely away into the air. They derive their food and growth from the sap of the wood or from the sea, by a secret and most wonderful process of alimentation. I have frequently seen, with my own eyes, more than a thousand of these small birds, hanging down on the sea-shore from one piece of timber, enclosed in their shells and already formed. They do not breed and lay eggs like other birds, nor do they ever hatch any eggs, nor do they seem to build nests in any corner of the earth. Hence bishops and religious men in some parts of Ireland do not scruple to dine off these birds at the time of fasting, because they are not flesh nor born of flesh.'

Four hundred years later, William Turner (*Avium praecipuarium*, 1544) says that rotting planks of ships develop fungi that turn into feathered birds. He had doubted this, he says, although it was credited by 'all the coastal people of England, Ireland and Scotland', but his doubts were laid to rest by an Irishman named Octavian who claimed to have seen and handled the half-formed birds. John Gerard, in his *Herball* (1597) speaks of 'certain trees' in Scotland and the northern islands, upon which grew shells, or barnacles, containing living creatures. The latter, 'falling into the water, do become fowls, whom we call barnacles, in the North of England brant geese, and in Lancashire tree geese'. Nor, if we can believe him, were such marvels confined to Scotland and Ireland, for he tells us that he had himself found, between Dover and Romney, a rotting tree-trunk lying in the water. It was covered with long crimson bladders at the end of which were shells. These, when opened, were found to contain bird-like creatures in various stages of development, the most advanced being 'birds covered with soft down, the shell half open, and the bird ready to fall out, which no doubt were the fowls called barnacles . . .'

This curious and persistent tradition survives today in a superstition, still found occasionally amongst old sailors, that barnacles from a ship's bottom will turn in due course into geese.

BARREN GROUND

That previously fertile soil could be made sterile by a curse, or by the shedding of innocent blood or some other crime committed upon it, was once widely believed. The existence of isolated patches of barren ground is often attributed in legend to this cause. In Montgomery churchyard, the grave of William Davies has such a patch upon it. He was hanged in 1821 for a crime which it is more than probable he did not commit. Certainly, he protested his innocence to the last, and tradition says that he prophesied the grass would not cover his grave for a generation in proof of that innocence. More than one generation has passed since that day, but it is a fact that the grass has never yet completely covered the grave, on the top of which a long, cross-shaped patch of sterile ground can still be seen.

At Porth Hellick in the Scilly Isles, a bare spot surrounded by flourishing grass which never encroached upon it was long pointed out as the place where Sir Cloudesley Shovel was first hurriedly buried in 1707. His body was washed ashore and interred there after the terrible shipwreck of 22 October, in which four ships were lost and about fifteen thousand men are said to have been drowned. Scillonian legend says that the Admiral refused to listen to the advice of a seaman who knew the coast, and so wantonly threw away the lives of his men, as well as his own. In consequence, God has never allowed the grass to grow upon the place where he was laid for a short time, before his corpse was removed to Westminster Abbey.

In Bloomsbury, a field now covered by buildings was known as the Field of the Forty Footsteps because it was marked by deeply-scored footprints which could not be obliterated, even when the ground was ploughed. It is stated in the *Gentleman's Magazine* for 1778 that 'there are people now living who well remember their being ploughed up, and barley sown to deface them; but all labour in vain; for the prints returned in a short time to their original form'. They were said to be those of two brothers who killed each other in a duel during the reign of Charles II.

Barren patches are sometimes attributed to the Devil or some other evil spirit. The sterile ground on the top of the Stanner Rocks in Herefordshire is called the Devil's Garden because Satan once reserved it for his own use. A less usual explanation accounts for the grassless patch on the top of Dragon Hill, under the Berkshire White Horse. According to local tradition, St George fought the dragon on this hill, and nothing now grows on its summit because the monster's blood gushed out there and poisoned the ground.

BARRING THE WAY

The custom of barring the way to a newly-married pair as they leave the church is still occasionally observed at weddings. A rope or chain is stretched across the churchyard-gate, or across the road, and the bridegroom has to pay toll before it is lowered. The money so given is spent on ale or other drinks in which the couple are toasted. In November 1953, the *Craven Herald and Pioneer* reported a wedding at Hubberholme where the gate was chained, and the best man paid £3 0s 1d on the bridegroom's behalf for the right of free passage. In March of the same year, the *Daily Sketch* described a similar ceremony at Eyemouth. There the way was barred by fishing-creels and a rope, and the latter was cut by the bride after her husband had given money to the creel-men.

It is probable that in earlier times she would have been expected to jump over it. In many places formerly the bride, and sometimes the groom and guests also, had to leap or be lifted over some obstacle immediately after the ceremony. At Bamborough, within living memory, a Petting Stone near the churchyard gate was used for this purpose, the bride being lifted over it. On Holy Island still, every bride has to step over the Petting Stone which, in this case, is the socket or footstone of a now vanished Saxon cross in the church-yard. She is helped on to it by two of her oldest male relatives, and she must cross it in one stride, otherwise her marriage will be unfortunate. This rite was performed at a Holy Island wedding in September 1953, and was reported in the *Sunday Times* and other newspapers.

Where a fixed petting stone was lacking, other obstacles of a temporary nature were often used. At Belford in Northumberland, a stool was placed at the church door. When the bride had jumped over it, complimentary verses about her and her husband were recited. This was called Saying the Noning; the bridegroom was expected to reward the Noning Sayer with silver at the end of the performance. At Embleton in the same county, bride, groom and guests were all required to climb over a bench. At Ford, the original custom was for the bridegroom to leap over, or wade through, the water called the Gaudy Loup, or pay a fine in default. But since this water was some way from the church, a stick or rope across the road was afterwards found more convenient, and both bride and groom had to leap over it.

At Fingest in Buckinghamshire, a variant of this ancient ceremony still survives. According to the guide book now sold in the church (9th impression, 1956): 'No wedding at Fingest is supposed to be lucky unless the bridegroom lifts his bride over the Church gate when leaving after the ceremony. The gate is locked so that the newly-wedded couple cannot get through it, while all their relatives and friends gather round to watch the custom being duly observed.'

Various explanations have been given for this custom, the commonest being that in her leap the bride leaves all her pets and humours behind her. It is possible that it was originally regarded as a form of passage-rite, connected with the passing of bride and groom from one state of life to another as yet untried and new.

BAT

In the Isle of Man and along the Welsh Border, witches were said to transform themselves occasionally into bats, and to enter houses in that form. Mrs Leather[1] relates the story of a man at Weobley Marsh who saw 'something like a bat' fly into his room. He struck it with his handkerchief, but when he went to look for the corpse, there was nothing there. He said afterwards that he knew from this it was a disguised witch, one of those who then lived upon the Marsh, because a real bat would certainly have been killed by his blow. A Scottish belief recorded in the *Wilkie MS* was that when bats in their flight rose upwards and then came swiftly down to earth again, it denoted that the witches' hour had come, the hour when witches had power over all human beings not specially protected against them.

In spite of the witch-connexion, Manx people say it is extremely lucky if a bat falls on any person. Many women outside the island would doubt this, because of the very general belief that if a bat alights or falls on a woman's head, it becomes entangled in her hair and cannot get away until the hair is cut. It seems, however, that this is also a superstition, without foundation in fact. In *The Countryman* (Spring 1960) there is an account of experiments conducted in 1959 by the Earl of Cranbrook with the help of three gallant young women, who allowed him to thrust a bat into their hair.

[1] E. M. Leather, *op. cit.*

Four different kinds of bat were used, and in each case, the creature escaped quite easily without getting entangled in any way.

In Oxfordshire, it is a death omen if a bat flies three times round a house. When bats come out early in the evening and fly about as though playing, it is a sign of fine weather to come.

Children, when they see a bat, sometimes avert ill-luck by singing or saying:

> Black bat, bear away,
> Fly over here away,
> And come again another day,
> Black bat, bear away.

or

> Airy mouse, airy mouse, fly over my head,
> And you shall have a crust of bread,
> And when I brew and when I bake,
> You shall have a piece of my wedding cake.

BAY

The bay-tree, once sacred to Apollo and to Aesculapius, God of Medicine, has always been considered a fortunate plant, beneficial to mankind both as a healer and as a protection against evil. For the ancient Greeks and Romans, it symbolized victory, honour, and renown. Letters announcing victories in battle were wrapped in its leaves, and heroes, poets, and the winners at the Pythian Games were crowned with it. The Romans adorned their houses with its luck-bringing branches at their New Year festival, and centuries later, Stow mentions it in his *Survey of London* as one of the plants commonly included in Christmas decorations. It was also carried at many Christian funerals because, owing to its power to revive when seemingly quite dead, it was regarded as a symbol of the Resurrection.

A very long-lived and widespread tradition said that this tree was never struck by lightning, and consequently a man standing under it would be safe even in the worst thunderstorms. Growing near a house, it preserved those within from all kinds of infection, and particularly that of the plague. The leaves, if carried about, protected the bearer from evil spirits and the contagion of disease. Placed under the pillow at night, they were thought to induce pleasant dreams. A form of divination, not yet quite forgotten, was to throw them on the fire and note how they burnt. If they crackled noisily, it was a sign of good luck to come, but if they burnt away silently, the omen was bad.

The sudden withering of bays was held to be an exceedingly evil omen, foretelling either an outbreak of pestilence, or the death of kings. Tradition

says that all the bays died before the death of Nero, though the winter was
mild. Shakespeare refers to this ancient belief in *Richard II* (Act II Scene IV)
when he makes the Welsh captain say:

> ' Tis thought the king is dead; we will not stay.
> The bay trees in our country are all wither'd.'

By an extension of the same notion, it is sometimes thought to be a death
omen for someone in the household if such trees die in a garden.

BEANS

Beans, like many other plants with strong-smelling flowers, are traditionally associated with death and ghosts, and have been so from early pagan
times down to our own day. In ancient Rome, they were distributed and
eaten at funerals. It is recorded in the *Denham Tracts* (1895) that until about
the beginning of the nineteenth century, a similar custom was observed at
some, though not all, north-country burials. When it finally lapsed, a
memory of it was preserved in the children's couplet,

> God save your soul,
> Beans and all.

During the Roman festival of the dead, held in May, black beans were used
in ceremonies intended to placate and ward off ghosts, and in early Greek
ritual, the scapegoat who annually died for the people was chosen by means
of a black bean drawn in a lottery. In his *Remaines of Gentilisme and Judaisme*
(1686/7) Aubrey mentions a charm used in his boyhood to avert evil spirits,
which consisted in saying very quickly, three times in one breath,

> Three blew beans in a blew bladder,
> Rattle, bladder, rattle.

A very widespread country belief that persisted at least as late as the end of
last century, and perhaps later, was that the souls of the dead dwelt in the
flowers of the broad bean. These flowers are still thought to be ill-omened in
many districts. Old colliers in northern and midland England say that
accidents in the pit occur more frequently when they are in bloom than at
any other time. Cases of lunacy are also thought more likely then, for the
scent of the flowers is supposed to induce mental disorder, bad dreams, and
terrifying visions. A Leicestershire tradition says that if any one sleeps all
night in a beanfield, he will suffer from appalling nightmares, and will
probably go mad afterwards. Another very common superstition is that if in

a row of beans, one should come up white, it is a death omen for someone in the grower's family.

A well-known charm for curing warts is to rub them with the white inner lining of a bean-pod, and then throw the pod away, or bury it in a secret place. As it rots, so will the warts disappear. This charm has been tried with success in Oxfordshire within the last ten years. In Ireland, poultices made from the flowers are sometimes used to reduce hard swellings. A former use for the plant, half medical in origin and half magical, was to make women beautiful. The pods steeped in wine and vinegar, or the distilled water of the flowers, improved the complexion, and so, according to Bulleyne's *Booke of Simples* (1562) did a lotion made from bean-meal mixed with cold milk.

In Leap year, broad beans are said to grow the wrong way up. Various dates are given in different districts as the only fortunate days for setting beans (and peas) but these seem to spring less from superstition than from agricultural custom and knowledge of local weather conditions. In the northern counties gardeners should

> Sow peas and beans on David and Chad,
> Whether the weather be good or bad,

that is, on 1 and 2 March, the festival days of St David and St Chad. Farther south, beans are set 'when the elm leaves are as big as a farthing', or on certain dates in early May, often connected with local fairs. A limit to the variety of these days seems to be set by a well-known rhyme which says,

> Be it weal or be it woe,
> Beans should blow before May go.

BEARS

Superstitions about bears might be thought rather unlikely in Britain, since the only living specimens here are confined in zoos, and there must be many people, even today, who have never seen one. Formerly, however, they were quite common in this country. Bear-baiting was a favourite sport at wakes, fairs, and other festivals until it was suppressed, with difficulty, in the nineteenth century. Dancing bears, who travelled about the countryside in charge of a bearward, were a familiar sight until much later. There are old people still living today who can remember seeing them in their childhood. In the hey-day of the performing bear, it was a general belief that these animals bred only once in seven years, and when they did, they brought bad luck to all other breeding animals. If a cow lost her calf unexpectedly, or a sow her litter, it was assumed that bears were breeding somewhere in the neighbourhood.

Another belief was that if a child rode on a bear's back, he would never catch whooping-cough in the future, and if he already had it, he would be cured. Such a remedy sounds rather more alarming than the disease, but in fact, it was quite safe. Performing bears, being valuable to their owners and therefore well treated and often loved, were usually fairly docile, and unlikely to harm any one who did not frighten or injure them.

Like other animals which shared the daily life of men, bears were sometimes said to return in ghostly form after death. One such haunted the precincts of Worcester Cathedral in the seventeenth century. There is a quite well authenticated tale of a soldier who, whilst on sentry duty in the Tower of London in 1816, saw a large bear coming towards him. He struck at it with his bayonet, but the weapon went right through the creature without harming it, and stuck in the wall beyond. The man fell down in a fit and died a few days later.

BEASTINGS. *See Calves.*

BEDS

The belief that it is unlucky to turn beds or mattresses on certain days of the week is still quite common. The days vary in different districts, but the most usual are Sunday and Friday. Monday is also avoided in some places. A bed turned on a Sunday causes the sleeper to have bad dreams all the week. In Somerset, whoever turns a bed on a Friday turns ships at sea; in Oxfordshire, to do so changes the bed-maker's luck, and in Herefordshire it turns the sweetheart away. An old Lancashire belief was that, after a birth, the mother's bed should not be turned until the child was a month old.

The manner of turning it is noticed in an Oxfordshire rhyme which says,

> If one day you would be wed,
> Turn your bed from foot to head.

If three people take part in making one bed, someone will die in it within the year.

The position of the bed also has its significance. Some housewives say that it should always point east and west; if it points north and south, the sleeper will be restless and suffer from nightmares. Others keep to the opposite rule, believing that it is the east-west alignment that causes trouble. A dying person's bed, if it stands across the floor-boards, must be moved round so as to point in the same direction as the boards, otherwise death will be hard and painful. *See Death, Easing.*

It is unlucky to enter a bed at night on one side and leave it next morning by the other. A person who rises in a bad temper, and for whom everything seems to go amiss for no apparent reason, is said to have 'got out of bed the wrong side'.

BEES

Bees in antiquity were sacred as divine messengers and foretellers of the future, and in Christian tradition they were reverenced as the little winged servants of God. A Welsh legend says their origin was in Paradise. They were white when they lived in the Garden of Eden with Adam and Eve, and only turned brown after the Fall. Since then, it has been their privilege to make wax for the altar-lights and honey for the use of men, and to worship God by this service and by their hummed anthems of praise. The latter they offer at all times, but particularly on Christmas Eve when, according to a very widespread tradition, they hum the Hundredth Psalm in their hives at midnight in honour of Christ's birth.

It was long considered sacrilegious to kill a bee because of its holy character, and it is still thought to be unlucky in many districts. Bees are, or were, regarded as the wisest of insects, having knowledge of the future and many secret matters. They cannot live if there is anger or hatred in the household of their owners, or if they themselves are the subject of a quarrel. Either they will pine and die, or they will fly away. Similarly, they cannot tolerate blasphemy and swearing; if any one swears in their presence, he is likely to be unmercifully stung. They hate unchastity, and can detect it even when it is unsuspected by the family and neighbours of the guilty person. Here again, they may attack the offender. It used to be thought that if a girl could walk unharmed through a swarm of bees, it was a sure proof that she was a virgin.

If a bee comes into the house, it is a sign of good luck, or of a stranger coming shortly. It must, however, be allowed to stay or fly away of its own accord; if it is captured or driven away, the luck is destroyed. This belief applies equally to the honey-and the bumble-bee. East Anglian fishermen think it a very good omen if a bumble-bee is found on board when the vessel is at sea. A honey-bee alighting on anyone's hand predicts money to come, and one settling on a person's head and staying there for a time means that he or she will eventually rise to greatness. In Wales it is believed that a bee flying round a sleeping child foretells a happy life for the sleeper.

In some parts of England it is an omen of war if bees are idle or unfortunate in producing honey. If they nest on a house-roof, the daughters of that house will not marry. Children are often said to be safe from their stinging because they love them. Bee-stings are believed to avert rheumatism. It is a fact that bee-keepers rarely suffer from this complaint, and many attribute their immunity to the stings they receive in the course of their work. Country people say that when the disease is already present, it can be cured by allowing a bee to sting the affected part.

The idea that it is unlucky to buy or sell bees was once widespread and is not yet altogether extinct. At one time it was thought safe to do so only if payment was made in gold, but this has been largely forgotten since the disappearance of gold coins. Bought bees will not prosper, though they may be exchanged for goods of the same value, such as a small pig or a sack of meal. A swarm given or borrowed is likely to do better. A very usual method of starting a stock formerly was to borrow a swarm, on the understanding that it would be repaid if the donor's bees ever failed, or he himself came to want. In Northumberland, it was deemed unlucky for one person to be the sole owner of bees. There should be a partnership between ≈ man and a woman of different households. Joint ownership by a man and his wife was not enough, presumably because they were considered to have been made one by marriage.

The commonest belief about hive-bees is that there is a strong bond of sympathy between them and their owners, and that they should be told of every notable event in the families of the latter. At one time it was thought necessary to inform them of every birth, marriage, success, joy or grief, and of every death, especially that of the bee-master. In cases of death, this is still quite often done. Only two or three years ago, a bee-keeper living on the outskirts of Oxford was asked whether he had told his bees of a recent death in his family. He replied scornfully, 'Of course I have; did you think I wanted to lose 'em?'

The old method of notifying an owner's death was for his eldest son, or his widow, to strike the hives three times with the iron door-key and say 'The master is dead'. If this was not done, the bees would die, or fly away, and fresh misfortune would follow. The hives had then to be put into mourning by tying pieces of black crêpe upon them. In some districts, they were turned round, or moved to a new place, at the moment when the corpse was being carried out of the house. At the funeral feast, sugar, or biscuits soaked in wine, or samples from the dishes served to the mourners, were taken to the bees. In his *Yorkshire Folk-Talk* (1892) M. C. Morris relates how a farmer's widow, describing her husband's funeral to him, said the bees had been given something of everything, 'Bacca an' pipes an' all.' The pipes, which were presumably of clay, were ground to powder and mixed with the tobacco, and the bees ate it all up, 'aye, hivvry bit,' said the woman, 'ah seed it mysen'.

There seems to have been a close connexion between bees and death in folk-belief. The soul was sometimes thought to take the form of a bee for a short time immediately after death. There are also tales of bees seen issuing from the mouths of sleepers and later re-entering their bodies by the same way. If such a bee was killed, or otherwise prevented from returning, the man died. The same stories are told in some areas of soul-butterflies. *See*

Butterflies. If bees deserted a hive for no apparent reason, it was an omen of death for their owner. If they swarmed on the dead branch of a tree, or on rotten wood, it was a death-warning for someone in his family, or in that of the owner of the wood, or sometimes simply for any one unlucky enough to see them doing it. Charlotte Latham[1] records the case of a Sussex woman who saw such a swarm on a dead hedge-stake, and said to her husband, 'That is a token of death and it is sent to me.' She believed she would die in her approaching confinement, and in fact, she did die very soon after it. Her husband told the doctor he had expected her death from the time she had seen the bees on the dead wood.

In Lincolnshire, special notice used to be taken of the first swarming after a bee-keeper's death. If the swarm was easily taken it showed that the bees accepted their new master, but if they settled on dead wood, he would not live long to possess them. If they flew away altogether and were lost, it meant that the dead man had called them to himself.

The appearance of a strange swarm in a garden or yard was sometimes said to be unlucky. In Suffolk, such a swarm, if kept, and not afterwards claimed by its real owner, foretold a death within twelve months. On the other hand, Sussex people believed that to find a stray swarm was a sign of extraordinary good luck, and in Cornwall the finder could claim it for his own if he quickly threw a handkerchief over it.

The custom of 'ringing' or 'tanging' bees when they swarm, that is of making a loud clattering noise with pans, gongs, bells or fire-irons, is still observed on some farms. It is said to make the bees settle quickly and prevent them flying too far afield. At one time it was thought that if it was not done, the owner could not claim the swarm if it settled on someone else's land. To maintain his rights, he had to follow wherever the bees led, but while this noise went on, he could not be accused of trespass.

BEETLE

A black beetle running across the floor of a room, or found lurking any-where in the house, is a sign of bad luck. If it crawls over a person's shoe, or runs over any one lying down, it is a death omen, either for the individual concerned or for someone closely connected with him.

In many parts of Britain black beetles, though disliked, are sometimes spared because it is considered unlucky to kill them. The result most often prophesied is heavy rain, but it may also be misfortune for the killer. In the Isle of Man, the penalty is seven wet days and much personal bad luck.

These insects do not commonly appear in charms or cures, but one case of their use in a remedy for whooping-cough has been recorded, and there may have been others. A writer in *Notes and Queries* (Vol. IX) states that a relative

[1] C. Latham, *op. cit.*

was visiting a cottage in Lincolnshire when a child arrived with a small paper box in her hand. This she gave to the householder, asking her to put into it the first black beetle she found by chance, and without looking for it. The child explained that her sister had whooping-cough, and that her mother wanted the beetle to hang round the patient's neck. As the creature decayed inside the box, so the cough would gradually disappear. The use of a beetle for this purpose is rare, the most usual victims in such cases being spiders or small frogs. *See Death Watch Beetle.*

BELLS

The sound of church bells was once widely believed to drive away demons, both those who brought storms and pestilence, and those who constantly flitted about the world seeking to harm the souls and bodies of men. They hated bell-music because it was made by holy things, and also because it disturbed the atmosphere in which they had their incorporeal being. It is possible that the latter reason represents the older form of the belief. In pre-Christian times as well as later, ordinary bells, not connected with any sacred rite or building, were sometimes used, together with other noise-producing instruments, to defeat evil spirits. The idea that these entities dislike loud noises still survives in some crop-protecting customs of the Balkans and Central Europe and also, perhaps, in the clamour raised during the making of Rough Music.

Church bells were often pealed during thunderstorms to prevent damage by lightning and thunderbolts, and to protect those within hearing for material and spiritual peril. 'Wherever this bell sounds,' says an eighth-century form of blessing, 'let the power of enemies retire, so also the shadow of phantoms, the assault of whirlwinds, the stroke of lightnings, the harm of thunders, the injuries of tempests, and every spirit of the storm-winds'.[1] Aubrey remarks in his *Miscellanies* that 'at Paris when it begins to thunder and lighten, they do presently ring the great bell of the Abbey of St Germain, which they believe to make it cease. The like was wont to be done heretofore in Wiltshire; when it thundered and lightened, they did ring St Aldhelm's bell, at Malmesbury Abbey. The curious do say that the ringing of bells exceedingly disturbs spirits.' In the Pyrenees and some other parts of Europe, the church bells are still rung during hail or thunderstorms to protect the crops.

Since diseases were anciently thought to be the work of demons, church bells were frequently rung when epidemics were raging. In the sixteenth and seventeenth centuries, they were pealed or tolled during outbreaks of the plague. This was recommended by doctors of that period, not on religious or superstitious grounds, but because the clamour was thought to dissipate

[1] Pontifical of Egbert, Archbishop of York, A.D. 732-66, *Surtees Society*, XXVII.

those heavy and corrupt airs that were then supposed to be one of the causes of the disease. Probably, however, simple folk remembered the old beliefs of their ancestors when they heard the sound, and took comfort from it for reasons quite unconnected with the fashionable scientific notions of their own day.

A curious tradition concerning the tenor bell in the Abbey Church at Dorchester-on-Thames is that snakes cannot endure its note, and that consequently none is ever found in that township. Dorchester is now little more than a large village, but in the seventh century it was the cathedral city of St Berin (or Birinus) the Apostle of Wessex, who died and was buried there in A.D. 650. Legend says he was killed by an adder-bite, and that ever since then he has protected his people from a similar fate by the agency of his bell. The latter, which was cast about 1380, has a Latin inscription invoking his protection, though snakes are not mentioned in it. Whether this tradition runs back to Anglo-Saxon times, or if it is even as old as the bell, is uncertain; but evidently it was known in the early eighteenth century, for Cox mentions it in his *Magna Britannia* (1727). He quotes a rhyme, still remembered locally, which runs,

> Within the sound of the great bell,
> No Snake nor Adder e'er shall dwell,

and adds, 'which to confirm the oldest men of the Place say they never saw any venomous Creature within that district, and have heard their Fathers say the same'.

Many traditional stories seem to ascribe life and conscious thought to church bells. They ring of themselves in the presence of a saint, or when a crime has been committed near them. They bring down misfortune upon those who steal or destroy them. Several are said to have been lost when being moved because of a curse uttered by some workman helping with the work, or because of an ill-timed boast. Rostherne Mere in Cheshire is supposed to contain such a bell, which broke its ropes while in transit and rolled to the water's edge. One of the men swore at it, and it sank immediately, never to be recovered. Its note is heard, however, according to local tradition, once a year, on Easter Sunday. A mermaid comes up a subterranean channel from the River Mersey and rings the bell at dawn, and then she sits on it and sings very sweetly for a short time. Many people formerly used to go to the mere on that day in the hopes of hearing her, but it is not recorded that any one ever did hear her. Combermere in the same county has a similar legend, but of a more terrifying nature. After the dissolution of the monasteries, the Abbey bells were moved to Wrenbury Church, and as they were being ferried across the lake, one fell in. The man in charge, angered by the thought of the trouble involved in raising it, swore loudly, taking the

Name of God in vain. At once a strange figure rose from the water and dragged him to his death, and neither he nor the bell has ever been seen since.

Another very common tradition is that bells can be heard pealing underwater in the church-towers of towns that once existed and were overwhelmed by floods. Bomere in Shropshire has such a legend. A town, variously said to have been Roman or Saxon, stood on its site, and was drowned for its wickedness. On certain nights, the sound of bells pealing is heard there or, according to one version, the Sanctus bell's note is heard on Christmas Eve, ringing again as it rang during Midnight Mass when the waters overwhelmed the church and the town. The group of rocks known as Caer Wyddno, seven miles out to sea in Cardigan Bay, is locally supposed to mark the spot where the capital city of the lost Lowland Hundred once stood. Here, it is said, on quiet, calm days, the bells can be heard faintly pealing, as the water moves them to and fro in the depths of the sea. So too, off the coast of Lancashire, near Blackpool, a ghostly peal is occasionally audible, coming from the drowned church of Kilgrimod.

The strange booming sound sometimes emitted by a bell when no one has touched it was formerly regarded as a sure omen of death in the parish before the week was out. This is not really very surprising, for it is a heart-chilling sound to hear. It was specially ominous if it was heard during a service, when most of the parishioners were gathered together, or during a wedding. In the latter case, the early death of either the bride or the bridegroom was foretold. The ordinary wedding peal, of course, brings good fortune, and was no doubt originally intended to avert the evil spirits that were believed to be specially active always at the great moments of life and death. Mrs Leather[1] records an instance of a peal used for the opposite purpose. At Peterchurch, about the end of last century, the ringers were not rewarded for ringing at a marriage, and in revenge, they returned to the belfry and rang the bells backwards, to bring bad luck to the defaulting bridegroom. Church bells were sometimes rung also to help women in labour, *see Birth, Easing*, and at harvest, to ensure the safety of the gathered crop. Grease taken from them was believed to have curative powers if applied as an ointment. Cases have been recorded within this century of its use for ringworm, shingles, and other skin troubles.

Ordinary bells have their superstitious lore as well as those connected with churches. If one rings of itself anywhere, on land or on shipboard, the omen is bad. If two ring at the same time in a house, it is a sign of a parting. If a telephone bell tings intermittently, with no incoming call to account for it, it foretells bad news. This curious modern adaptation of an ancient belief is quite often found, even amongst people who know that the sound is due to a fault in the mechanism.

In the days of sail, the ship's bell was regarded as in some sense an embodiment of the vessel's soul. Sailors believed that it always rang when a wrecked

[1] E. M. Leather, *op. cit.*

ship went down, even if it had been securely lashed in place beforehand. Nor did the final disaster always silence it. M. A. Courtney[1] speaks of a ghostly bell that was often heard to strike four and eight bells in a churchyard near Land's End. The sound came from the grave of a sea-captain who had refused to leave his sinking ship when she was wrecked on the Cornish coast. He went down with her exactly at midnight, as he was striking the hour on the bell. To hear it in the churchyard was apparently ominous, for Miss Courtney further records how a sailor once went to the grave to find out whether the legend was true or not. He heard the ringing, and was lost at sea on his next voyage.

The seamen's belief that a bell ringing of itself is an omen of disaster is reflected in the common superstition about the ringing note sometimes emitted by a tumbler or a wine-glass. This foretells a wreck at sea or the death of a sailor, and should be stopped at once by placing a finger on the rim of the glass. If this is done quickly, the omen is averted. *See Death Bells*.

BESOM

The early household besom, or broom, was made from the broom-plant, or from birch-twigs or heather, and shared some of the traditional lore attaching to these plants. It was also regarded as an essentially feminine tool, and was sometimes used as an image or symbol of the woman of the house. If she wished to indicate that she was away from home, she set a besom outside the house-door, or thrust it up the chimney with its twigs showing above the roof.

That witches rode to the Sabbats upon broomsticks was a very common belief at one time. They were supposed to anoint their bodies with a salve given to them by the Devil, and thereafter to be able to fly through the air upon a variety of sticks or stems, including broomsticks. The choice of the latter as a likely means of transport is probably due to the fertility associations of the broom-plant, and also perhaps to the female connexion of the besom, though male witches were thought to ride in this way as well as women. In some confessions recorded at the trials, we hear of sticks being used for ritual purposes, but there is little evidence that the witches ever did much more than straddle them, or leap about with them between their legs. Dame Alice Kyteler, the Irish witch of 1323, had a greased staff on which she 'ambled and gallopped through thick and thin'; but no one seems to have suggested that she ever flew upon it. The same uncertainty exists in other instances of supposed flight, and in any case, the broomstick as such is mentioned only occasionally, ragwort-stems, straws, cornstalks, and other things being quite as often used.

The besom, or broomstick wedding is now usually associated with gypsies,

[1] M. A. Courtney, *op. cit.*

but at one time it seems to have been known in Wales amongst people who were not gypsies. A birch-besom was set aslant across the open door, either that of the bride's home or that of the cottage in which the couple were to live. The young man leapt over it into the house, and the girl then did the same. Care had to be taken not to touch the doorpost or the broom, or to move the latter accidentally, otherwise the ceremony was void. It had to be performed in the presence of witnesses, and one person, chosen for his standing and importance in the community, acted as officiant. Such a marriage was considered quite valid, however strongly the clergy might condemn it. It could, however, be broken without difficulty if, during the first twelve months, the besom was replaced in the doorway, and the dissatisfied partner jumped backwards over it from the house into the open air. The same conditions applied here as at the wedding. There had to be witnesses, and the person jumping had to avoid touching the broom or doorpost as he or she leapt. If the rite was properly performed, both parties were considered free to marry again.

The gypsy wedding was slightly different. A broom-branch was laid on the ground in the open, and the bride and groom jumped backwards and forwards over it, holding hands as they did so. A rush ring was then placed on the girl's finger, to be replaced later by a gold ring bought from the joint earnings of the couple. There was also another form in which an ordinary besom was held by the father of the bride, or of the groom, with its bushy end resting on the ground, and first the young man and then the girl leapt over it in turn.

In North Wales today it is sometimes said that someone has 'jumped over the besom', meaning that he or she has been respectably married in a church or at a registrar's office. But in some parts of Yorkshire, to say that a woman has done so means that she has had an illegitimate child, and to call a woman 'a besom' is an insult. Moreover, if a girl accidentally steps over a broom-handle, she will be a mother before she is a wife. Mischievous boys have been known to put brooms in places where girls would be likely to step over them without noticing. This, of course, was done as a joke, but it is probable that in the hey-day of the superstition evilly-disposed persons did the same in the genuine belief that they would thus bring about the downfall of the young woman concerned.

To make besoms in the month of May, or during the Twelve Days of Christmas was formerly considered unlucky. Housewives were careful to lay in good stocks beforehand in order to avoid the necessity of making or buying them in these periods. *See Sweeping.*

BETONY

Betony is said to have been named after Beronice, the woman healed by

Our Lord of an issue of blood. For many centuries, it was credited with a variety of protective and healing powers. In the *Anglo-Saxon Leech Book* it is stated that: 'Betony is good whether for the man's soul or his body, and to shield him against monstrous nocturnal visitors, and against frightful visions and dreams'. In the Middle Ages, and later, it was used in charms against witchcraft, and also to cure haemorrhage, insomnia, and fatigue.

By tradition it was at enmity with the vine, whose tendrils curled away from it. Consequently, it was used to cure or prevent drunkenness. According to Gervase Markham[1] a sure way to be safe from intoxication was to mix powdered betony and colewort and take a little – 'as much as will lie upon a sixpence' – every morning, while fasting.

BIBLE

The Bible, as the fount of truth, was often used in divination, both to foresee the future in general, and to resolve personal doubts and perplexities. In order to find out whether the coming year would be fortunate or otherwise, the inquirer opened the Bible at random on New Year's morning, while still fasting, and without looking at the page, thrust a pin into it, or laid his finger upon it. The verse thus blindly chosen foretold the good or evil nature of the following twelve months. The same rite could be performed at any time by those seeking guidance in particular difficulties; the words pricked or touched by the finger indicated what the inquirer ought to do, or what the outcome of the matter would be.

This form of divination is sometimes used today, and is often prompted by genuine religious feeling, the enquirer believing that God will thus give guidance through the sacred writings. It is also very ancient. In pagan times the works of Homer or Virgil were similarly consulted. Christians substituted their own Scriptures usually, but the *Sortes Virgilianae*, or divination by Virgil's *Aeneid*, continued in use until at least as late as the seventeenth century. There is a well-known story that Charles I, when in Oxford, was persuaded to try his fortune thus, and was confronted by an ominous verse in the fourth book, prophesying the loss of his kingdom and friends, and his own early death. Lord Falkland, who was with him, seeing the King somewhat troubled by this evil omen, tried to distract his thoughts by reading his own fortune in the same way. Here again, the omen was disastrous, foretelling death in battle. Both these prophecies were fulfilled. Charles lost his crown and died on the scaffold at the age of forty-nine, and Lord Falkland fell at the Battle of Newbury in 1643.

The Bible could also be used in love-divination and for the detection of thieves. *See Bible and Key*. Cautious young men sometimes consulted it when choosing a bride. If any one wanted to be sure that the girl to whom he was

[1] Gervase Markham, *Country Contentments*, 1611.

attracted would make a good wife, he turned to the first chapter of the *Book of Proverbs* and read the verse whose number corresponded with her age. This indicated (though not always in very clear language) either her general character or her suitability as his life-partner. It can hardly have been a popular method of divination with its subjects, for the majority of the verses read more like warnings than encouragements. The maiden of seventeen was particularly unlucky, for her verse runs: 'Surely in vain the net is spread in the sight of any bird.' If a young man was sufficiently doubtful to try the experiment at all, he was scarcely likely to disregard so definite a warning as that.

The book was also used in protective and healing charms, and for the detection of witches. A test for the last-named was to weigh the suspected person against the Church Bible. *The Gentleman's Magazine* for 1759 records how in that year Susannah Haynokes, of Wingrove, was accused of witchcraft and, on her husband's demand, was so tested. She was stripped to her shift and weighed against the heavy book, 'when, to the no small mortification of her accuser, she outweighed it and was honourably acquitted of the charge'. The same trial was undergone in 1780 by two Bexhill women, both of whom proved heavier than the book and were so cleared of suspicion.

Those who attempted the perilous task of gathering fernseed, or cutting down a hawthorn tree, sometimes protected themselves by doing the work over a Bible. Scottish women who were obliged to leave their babies alone for a time guarded them from fairies by leaving an open Bible in the cradle. One laid under the pillow at night protected the sleeper, and ambitious mothers often made their children sleep thus in the belief that it would make them learn to read quickly and well. In the *Transactions of the Devonshire Association* (1878) we read of a farmer who, having lost one or two pigs by witchcraft, bought another, and put a Bible over the sty-door to prevent the newcomer from going the same way. In Yorkshire, a leaf torn from the book and buried under the flagstone before the house-door caused any entering thief to stumble and so rouse the household by the noise he made.

A charm to cure a sick person in the Island of Colonsay was to fan his face with the leaves of the Bible. Isolated texts, written or printed, were used to heal or prevent disease in many districts. Irishmen wore the first five verses of St John's Gospel round their necks to ward off madness, nightmare and some other ills. This charm was evidently known in sixteenth-century England also, for Cranmer includes it with other superstitious practices in his Visitation Articles of 1548. In an article contributed to *Folk-Lore* (Vol. 49, 1938) Mrs Hayward relates how a Shropshire cattle-charmer, called in to treat an ailing beast, wrote a verse from the Scriptures on a piece of paper and put it in the manger, so that the animal might eat it with its hay. She also records that, during her childhood, there was an outbreak of scarlet fever near her home. To protect her from infection, her nurse wrote out passages from the Old Testament and made her wear them in a little bag round her neck.

BIBLE AND KEY

The charm known as the Bible and Key was chiefly used in love-and-marriage divination, and for the detection of thieves.

If a girl wished to know if she would marry, she took the iron door-key and inserted it in the Bible, either at the *Song of Solomon* or the *Book of Ruth*, in such a way that the key-ring protruded from the top. The book was then tightly bound with her right garter. Two persons supported it by placing a finger under the ring or, if she was alone, the girl herself put the third finger of each hand under it. While the book was thus suspended, the following verses from the *Song of Solomon* were said: 'Many waters cannot quench love, neither can the floods drown it. Love is as strong as death, but jealousy is as cruel as the grave, and burneth with a most vehement flame. If a man should give all the substance of his house for love, it would be utterly consumed.' If the enquirer was to marry, the Bible turned under the supporting fingers, or fell to the ground, during the recitation; if nothing happened, she would die unwed.

The fidelity of a lover could be similarly tested. The book would turn to the right if he was faithful, to the left if he was false.

The same charm was often used to find out the initials of the future partner. The Bible was prepared as before, with the key resting on the words 'Let him kiss her with the kisses of his mouth.' After the verses mentioned above had been said, the alphabet was slowly recited. The book turned when the initial of the Christian name was reached, and the alphabet was then repeated once more to find out the surname. A simpler method was to say 'Bible, Bible, tell me true, the name of the man I am to marry', after which the alphabet was said as before.

All these love-divinations have been employed within living memory, perhaps half seriously and half in fun. But when the rite was used to discover a thief, it was always deadly serious. Those taking part believed it to be infallible because the holy book could not lie, and bitter enmities, and sometimes slander actions, often resulted from its use. The enquiry could be made in various ways. The most usual method was for the owner of the stolen goods to gather all the possible suspects together, and to prepare the Bible in the manner already described, except that string was used for binding instead of a garter, and the key was thrust in at random, without reference to any particular chapter. He then placed his finger under one half of the protruding ring, the other being supported by one of the company, and slowly recited the names of all present. When the thief's name was spoken the Bible turned. Or, whilst holding one side of the ring himself, he might require everyone to hold the other side in turn. No names were mentioned in this form of the rite, but the book was expected to turn when the thief touched it. A third method of enquiry was for the company to sit round a table. The Bible was put in the middle of the table, and the enquirer twisted the key upon it in such a way that it turned round several times before falling on the book. The person towards whom it pointed when it fell was the guilty man.

The charm would, however, work equally well in the absence of the culprit. In *Traditions, Superstitions and Folk-Lore* (1872) Charles Hardwick refers to a slander action heard at Norwich Assizes in 1866. The defendant had accused a man of theft, saying, 'You are the thief and no other man. You have robbed the fatherless and the motherless, and got in at the window. I can prove it by the turn of the Bible.' The defence was that the accusation was true, in proof of which it was stated that a Bible had been suspended by a piece of string and allowed to turn slowly round, while various names were said. When the plaintiff's name was spoken, it swung round the other way. To make doubly sure, the ceremony was performed a second time, and the result was the same.

BIRCH

The birch in popular tradition had protective powers. Its branches in or on a house brought good luck and averted the Evil Eye, and small twigs worn in the hat or buttonhole served the same useful purpose. Throughout northern Europe it was associated with the return of Summer and was used to decorate houses on the great festivals of that season, especially May Day, Whitsuntide, and Midsummer.

Mrs Leather[1] tells us that in the mid-nineteenth century every Hereford-shire cottage had little crosses of mixed birch and rowan wood over the door on May morning, and similar crosses were put into the seed-beds and over the pigsties. They were put there for good luck and to defeat the spells of witches which were thought to be especially strong at that season. Sometimes they were to be seen on other occasions also, as for instance, when there was a known witch in the vicinity, or when there was some reason to fear over-looking by some malicious person.

Another Herefordshire custom, once general and still kept up on a few farms, was to bring in a tall birch tree on May Day, adorn it with red and white streamers, and set it against the stable door. Such a tree was locally known as a May-pole, and was left in position all through the year to protect the horses from disease or misfortune, and particularly to guard them from being hag-ridden at night by witches or fairies. That they were so ridden was once widely believed. They would be found in an exhausted state next morning, sometimes with their manes and tails so tangled that the wagoners had to spend hours in getting the knots out. The birch-maypole by the door prevented such happenings.

[1] E. M. Leather, *op. cit.*

BIRDS

Birds, which have the mysterious gift of flight denied to earthbound men, were anciently regarded as divine or semi-divine beings. For some early peoples, they were themselves gods, or the High Gods might manifest themselves in that form. Often they were thought to be agents or messengers of the heavenly powers. Priests and soothsayers of pagan antiquity studied their flight, cries and actions in order to read the future and discover whether any proposed enterprise would turn out well or ill. In Rome, the priestly College of Augurs took auspices of this kind on official occasions, and ordinary men and women everywhere believed implicitly in bird-omens, which it was considered dangerous to ignore. Long after the coming of Christianity, the art of ornithomancy, or divination by birds, was constantly practised, even though frowned upon and forbidden by the Church.

Traces of these age-old ideas are still visible in our latter-day superstitions. Certain types of bird, which will be discussed in this book under their own names, are considered lucky or unlucky, foretellers of the future, or embodiments of the souls of the dead. But birds in general also have their superstitious significance, regardless of species. Thus, many people dislike to see them in flight if they are too numerous to count, or, when starting out on a journey, they will look to see whether a flock of birds appears on the right or on the left. A single bird tapping at the window, or entering a room, or flying down the chimney, is commonly thought to be a death omen, especially if there is any one ill in the house at the time.

Night-birds seen or heard calling by day are usually thought unlucky. Those with pied feathers are often associated in legend with the Devil, and black or white ones with death and misfortune. Individuals of odd or unfamiliar appearance are occasionally disliked for superstitious reasons. In some districts they are known as 'french' birds, the word french in this instance meaning simply foreign, without any particular reference to France as the country of origin. Thus, in Cheshire, a hen blackbird, less easily recognizable than the cock because it is lighter in colour, is called a French blackbird, and a curlew, which is only rarely seen on the Cheshire Plain, is a French curlew.

There is a widespread country belief that if a young, but fully-fledged, wild bird is caught and kept in captivity, its parents will kill it by feeding it through the bars of the cage with poisonous food. Ordinary cage-birds were once believed to be in close sympathy with the family that owned them. It was necessary to tell them of a death in the house and put mourning ribbons on the cage, otherwise they would pine away and die. In Scotland, if a cage-bird belonging to the bride or the groom dies on the wedding morning, it is a very bad omen for the success of the marriage.

The notion that the dead sometimes reappear in bird-form was formerly very common, and is not yet altogether extinct. Seabirds of various kinds were thought to embody the souls of drowned sailors. In Yorkshire, children who died unbaptized turned into nightjars, and in Ireland, black or grey birds flying restlessly about at night were supposed to be souls doing penance for their sins. In his *Glimpses in the Twilight* (1884) Dr Lee says that the church at West Drayton, near Uxbridge, was haunted during the eighteenth and nineteenth centuries by a large black bird which flew about the chancel and vaults, and sometimes perched on the Communion rails. The local people said it was the spirit of a murderer who had followed his first crime by committing suicide.

Many European countries, including Britain, have legends of warning birds attached to particular families. The Oxenhams of South Tawton, Devon, were said to know for certain when any sick member of their family was about to die, because a white-breasted bird appeared in the bedroom, hovered round the patient for a time, and then vanished. The Wardours of Arundel were warned of coming death by the sight of two large white owls perched on their roof. Daniel Defoe[1] records a Sussex belief that when the Bishop of Chichester is about to die, a heron perches on the Cathedral. Similarly, the death of the Bishop of Salisbury is said to be heralded by the appearance of two large white birds, of unknown species though somewhat resembling albatrosses, which sail through the air without moving their wings. This legend seems to have been known as far back as the seventeenth century, and the omen has been twice recorded in fairly recent times, once in 1885 before the death of Bishop Moberley, and again in 1911, when Bishop Wordsworth died.

BIRTH, EASING

When maternity hospitals were practically unknown and childbirth normally occurred at home, many traditional precautions were taken to ease the pains of labour and ensure safe delivery. A competent midwife saw to it that all doors were unlocked and all knots loosened as soon as she arrived. This was at once a magical enactment of the desired unhindered passage, and a safeguard against witchcraft. It was commonly believed that malicious witches frequently attempted to prevent delivery, and one of their methods of doing so was to make or tighten knots before or during a woman's labour.

In cottages where the floor was made of beaten earth, without boards over it, the mother was often laid upon it during the last stages, so that she might draw strength from the earth whence she and all men sprang. In Norfolk, it was usual to remove the feather bed before a confinement, for fear that it might contain a few doves' or pigeons' feathers. In that case, if the woman died, her death would be hard.

Nails thrust into the wooden parts of the bed kept off demons and fairies,

---

[1] Daniel Defoe, *A Tour through the Island of Great Britain*, 1724.

and nullified the spells of witches. For the same reason, pieces of iron or other protective charm-objects were set about the room. The pealing of church bells during the critical time was thought to help delivery, but if this could not be arranged, a piece of old bell-rope might be begged from the ringers and tied round the mother's waist. Written charms hung round her neck, or placed in the bed, served the same purpose, and so also did Eagle-stones tied round the thigh, and other amulets. *See Eagle-stones.*

In the nineteenth century, a curious broadside known as Our Saviour's Letter was frequently bought by women to hang over their beds in child-birth. This was an apocryphal letter, probably of medieval origin, which was supposed to have been written by Our Lord to Agbarus of Edessa. Besides being useful in childbirth, it was also felt to be a protection against witchcraft, and was sometimes pasted on cottage walls for this reason. A copy of the broadside, as sold in Hereford during last century, is printed in Mrs Leather's book, *The Folklore of Herefordshire* (1912).

BIRTH, TIMES OF

An ancient and very widespread belief was that a child's whole life and character were influenced by the time of his birth. The day of the week and the exact hour were both important, and so too was the state of the moon, or of the time. Particular Christian festivals, like Christmas Day or Childer-mas, also had special significance. These notions had their roots in astrological doctrines concerning the influence of sun, moon, and planets upon human life, and the extreme importance to any individual of the position and conjunction of stars at the moment of his birth. But such learned conceptions, if they were ever rightly understood were easily forgotten by simple people, and in folk-tradition they have survived only in the belief that certain times of birth are fortunate or otherwise, and that those born then will have a character and destiny distinct from that of their fellows.

A very well-known rhyme tells us,

> Monday's child is fair of face,
> Tuesday's child is full of grace,
> Wednesday's child is full of woe,
> Thursday's child has far to go,
> Friday's child is loving and giving,
> Saturday's child works hard for a living,
> But the child that is born on the Sabbath Day
> Is blithe and bonny, good and gay.

There are, however, many other versions of this ditty, and the days of the week do not have the same significance everywhere. In Shropshire and parts of the East Midlands, it is Friday's child who is born to sorrow, as might be expected from the evil reputation of this day in other matters. In Cornwall, and also in the Scottish Highlands, a variant of the rhyme quoted above gives Tuesday's child as 'solemn and sad', Wednesday's as 'merry and glad', and the Thursday-born as 'inclined to thieving'. Monday's child in this version is 'full in the face', which probably means fat and healthy.

The one day about which there seems to be universal agreement is Sunday. Almost everywhere, the child born then is thought to be lucky, good and gifted. In northern England, he is free from the malice of evil spirits, and safe from the effects of overlooking and ill-wishing. In Sussex, he is safe also from death by hanging or drowning. In Germany, he will grow up strong and beautiful, and in Scandinavia, he has the power of seeing spirits. The same gifts are commonly ascribed to the child born on Christmas Day or Eve. On the other hand, birth on Childermas Day (Holy Innocents) is very ill-omened, and May-born babies, like May kittens, are usually said to be weakly and unlikely to thrive.

The most significant times of the day are twilight, midnight and the hour immediately following, and the 'chime hours'. The last-named are those at which the parish church clock chimes, or plays tunes, that is, three, six, nine, and twelve o'clock, or in some districts, four, eight and twelve o'clock. Children born at these times see ghosts and spirits, and are sometimes credited with Second Sight. The chime-hour child, like the Sunday-born, cannot be bewitched. Much the same gifts belong to those born at midnight and the hour following; they 'see more than others' and have the power to hear the Gabrel Hounds.

A baby born early in the morning is often said to have a better chance than others of reaching old age, for 'the later the hour, the shorter the life'. In Wales, birth at sunrise foretells intelligence and success, at sunset laziness and lack of ambition. A very common belief is that births are more likely to occur when the moon changes, or just before the new moon comes in, than at any other time. A Cornish child born 'in the dark of the moon' will not live long. In the same county it is said that if birth occurs when the moon is waxing, the next child will be of the same sex, but if the moon is waning, then the next child born in that family will be of opposite sex to its predecessor.

In coastal areas, births are looked for with the incoming tide, for life comes in with the flow and goes out with the ebb. If a child is born at ebb-tide, the omen is bad. A variant of this belief is that boys are born with the flow and girls with the ebb.

BIRTHMARKS

Birthmarks on a baby's face or body are often said to be caused by something seen or touched by the mother during her pregnancy. A common cure for this disfigurement was for the mother, or failing her, some other woman, to lick the mark all over every morning before she had broken her fast. The treatment had to be started as soon as possible after the birth, and continued for a period variously given as nine, twenty-one, or thirty days, or until the blemish has disappeared.

This folk-cure is still remembered in many English districts, and cases of its successful use have been recorded as late as 1950 in the Home Counties and in the Midlands. Spittle has, of course, genuine soothing qualities, and in folk-lore it has strong magical properties, especially when used fasting. Both these facts have probably contributed to the long survival of faith in the remedy. In two of the cases mentioned above, it was used by young mothers who had no knowledge of its traditional meaning, but who were simply willing to try anything suggested to them that might rid their children of the marks.

BIRTHSTONES

All precious or semi-precious stones were anciently believed to have mystical properties, and in astrological teaching, each was under the domination of one of the planets. Every month of the year was thought to have one or more particular gems, and this idea lives on today in the tradition that certain stones are specially lucky to those born in certain months. Since more than one jewel was often associated traditionally with the same month, the list of birthstones varies slightly in different times and places, but the dedications most usually accepted today are as follows:

January. The garnet, which signified truth and constancy.

February. The amethyst, which denoted sincerity and had the power of preventing drunkenness in those who wore it.

March. The bloodstone, which brought courage and presence of mind to its possessor.

April. The diamond, symbol of innocence and light.

May. The emerald, giving success in love.

June. The agate, or sometimes, the pearl. The latter stood for purity, and also for tears. The agate gave health and long life, healed fevers, drew out the venom of insect and reptile bites if laid against the bitten place, and strengthened the sight.

July. The carnelian or the ruby. Carnelians gave a contented mind and, if worn in a silver ring, ensured many friends for the wearer and preserved him from losses and harm. The ruby had even greater virtues. Like the bloodstone, it gave courage, and it also prevented impure thoughts, preserved chastity, and killed any poisonous reptile which it touched.

August. The sardonyx, which ensured married happiness.

September. The sapphire, one of Jupiter's stones, which had many magical properties; or the chrysolite, which was an antidote to melancholy.

October. The opal. This stone, though it signified hope, is still almost every-where considered unlucky, except for the October-born. Many stories are told of misfortune, or even death, following upon its wearing by those born in other months.

November. The topaz, symbol of fidelity, which protected the wearer from the effects of poison.

December. The turquoise, which brought prosperity. This stone was said to change colour when danger or illness threatened its wearer, and also to prevent quarrels between married people.

BLACK PENNY

The Black Penny was a coin or medal which formerly belonged to a family named Turnbull, living at Hume-Byers in Northumberland. It was used to cure madness in cattle, and was frequently borrowed for this purpose by Northumberland, Durham, and Yorkshire farmers. The coin had to be dipped into south-running water, and the latter was then drawn off and given to the afflicted beast to drink. A letter written by one of the Turnbulls in 1843, and quoted in the *Denham Tracts* says the Penny was 'not quite so large as a common penny, but thicker. It had a kind of raised rim or border, and seemed to be composed of copper and zinc. It had been in the family for a hundred years at least. The family lived at Hadden, near Sprouston, when they got it. It had been several times given out, and once a purse containing gold, but to what amount was not known, was left as a deposit for its safe return.'

It seems to have been lost about 1827. It was lent to a man near Morpeth who stated that he had returned it by post; but if he did so in fact, it never arrived, and has not been found since.

BLACKBERRIES

A widespread country belief, still found in many districts, is that it is unlucky to gather or eat blackberries after 11 October, Old Michaelmas Day. According to tradition, Satan cursed the fruit because, when he was cast out of Heaven on the first Michaelmas Day, he fell into a blackberry bush. Since then he has spoilt the berries on every anniversary of his fall by scorching them with his breath, or stamping or spitting upon them, throwing his cloak or his club over them, or wiping his tail upon them. Whoever gathers them afterwards will have bad luck.

In her *West Sussex Superstitions*, Charlotte Latham records how a farmer's wife near Arundel, being short of fruit for jam-making, asked her charwoman to send her children for some more. The woman refused flatly, on the grounds that the date was 11 October, and 'everybody knew that the Devil went round on the 10th of October, and spat on all the blackberries, and that if any person were to eat one on the eleventh they or someone belonging to them would die or fall into great trouble before the year was out'. Modern versions of the misfortunes attaching to a too late picking do not usually extend as far as death, but some sort of bad luck is expected to follow.

Near Ross-on-Wye, Mrs Leather[1] was told that blackberries were never eaten at all in that district until comparatively recent times because, said her informant, 'the trail of the serpent is over them'. A similar avoidance, uninfluenced by date, was noticed in Normandy some twenty years ago. *See Bramble.*

BLACKSMITHS

Blacksmiths were credited with magical powers for many centuries because of their association with fire, iron and horses. In her *Folklore of the British Isles* (1928) Eleanor Hull mentions an ancient hymn known as St Patrick's Breastplate, in which God's protection is invoked against many dark forces, including 'spells of women, smiths and druids' and 'all knowledge that is forbidden the human soul'. Such knowledge blacksmiths were deemed to possess for magic is a part of it. Many knew the mysterious Horseman's Word (q.v.), and even those who did not were often thought to have secret charms whereby they could cure the ailments of horses and draw out stones or nails that had become lodged in their feet. They could also cure human beings. In the *Hodgson MS* we read of a charm to cure a sick child in which seven smiths, all of whom had to be the sons, grandsons, and great-grandsons of smiths, took part. The child was brought to the smithy at night and laid upon the anvil. The seven smiths stood round it in a circle, and waved their hammers over its head, as though about to strike it, at the same time uttering the stroke-groan 'Heigh' with great force. If the child showed fear, it would recover, but if it took no notice, there was little hope for it. For this service, each man received sixpence and an allowance of ale, bread and cheese.

Some blacksmiths were blood-charmers. Hamilton Jenkin[2] mentions one such smith who was living in a West Cornish parish at the time he wrote. This man performed many extraordinary cures in his day. On one occasion, a workman fell from a roof and cut his head badly on a stone. The wound was hastily bound up, but it was still bleeding when the injured man came by the smithy on his way to the doctor's house. The smith, hearing what had happened, ordered the bandages to be removed, and then made some motions with his hands over the cut. The bleeding stopped immediately. The patient went home without troubling to visit the doctor, and the wound healed up very quickly afterwards.

[1] E. M. Leather, *op. cit.*   [2] A. Hamilton Jenkin, *op. cit.*

Many people still believe that when runaway couples came to Gretna Green, or other places just across the Scottish Border, they were always married by the blacksmith. This is not the case, for though smiths did often officiate at such marriages, they were not by any means the only men who did so. At Coldstream, the last recognized practitioner was a shoemaker named Willie Dickson, and his predecessor was a mole-catcher by trade. Marriages here did not take place in the smithy, but at the Bridge End Inn, the first house across the Border. Elsewhere, men of other trades performed the rite, but the notion nevertheless persists today that a smith was the only possible 'priest' on these occasions. It is probable that in this idea we have a dim memory of the former magical importance of his calling.

Blacksmiths in the nineteenth century often refused to shoe horses, or do any work with nails on Good Friday. The reason usually given was that nails must not be touched then because of the terrible use to which they had been put on Calvary. R. M. Heanley[1] tells us that he was once out driving on Good Friday in the neighbourhood of Skegness, when his horse cast a shoe. The blacksmith flatly refused to shoe the animal, saying that Old Skrat would surely get him if he put his hand to hammer or nails during any part of that day.

BLACKTHORN

In the West Midlands and along the Welsh Border, the blackthorn, which bears white blossoms on a leafless and nearly black branch, is both a holy and an ominous plant. It is said to bloom, like the Holy Thorn, at midnight on Old Christmas Eve. According to one legend, it was from this tree that the Crown of Thorns was made, though the same is said of many other varieties of thorn. In Herefordshire a plaited crown used to be made from it on New Year's morning, held in the fire till it was scorched, and then hung up with the mistletoe, to be kept as a luck-bringer. A Worcestershire variant of this custom was to make the crown very early on New Year's morning, before it was light, bake it in the oven, and carry it out to the nearest cornfield. There it was burnt, and the ashes scattered over the ridges of the first sown wheat (or on some farms, the last sown) to bring success to the crop.

In general, however, it is considered an unlucky plant to have in the house. A blossoming branch, if brought indoors, is an omen of death for someone in the family.

BLOOD

Primitive peoples in most parts of the world believed that blood was some-

[1] R. M. Heanley, 'The Vikings: Traces of Their Folklore in Marshland', *Saga-Book of the Viking Club*, 1902.

thing more than a natural fluid necessary to continued life and strength. They regarded it as the seat or vehicle of the soul, the life-essence. If a man lost any, he was spiritually as well as materially impoverished, and if too much flowed from him, he died because his soul passed out of him with the blood. Power rested in it, so that it could be used in magical or religious rites, and it was believed to have a vitality of its own which persisted even after it had been separated from the parent body.

These archaic notions coloured many long-lived superstitions and customs. When blood was shed untimely, especially innocent blood, it brought a curse with it. Where it fell, grass would not grow. *See Barren Ground.* Numerous stories are still told of indelible blood-stains that cannot be washed out, no matter how often they are scrubbed or scraped. Always they return to give silent testimony of the crime committed there. In some tales of this kind, it is not the floor or the ground which cannot be cleansed, but the actual weapon which with the deed was done. At one time, it was widely believed that a murdered corpse would bleed if touched by the murderer or even if he came near it. *See Touching the Dead.* The dead man's eyes might be closed to earthly sights and feelings, but his soul-blood recognised the slayer and gushed out to accuse him.

A very persistent belief was that a witch's power could be broken by drawing his or her blood. 'Scoring above the breath', that is, drawing blood by scratching above the nose or mouth, was a common practice in the hey-day of the witch-belief, resorted to not only by angry mobs but also, on more than one occasion, by constables and others in authority.

Faith in this charm was responsible for many assaults upon suspected persons, long after witchcraft had ceased to be a legal crime. In 1823, three women were charged at Taunton with injuring Anne Burges, of Wivelis-combe, by tearing her arms with a large iron nail, and making fifteen or sixteen serious cuts upon them. This they did in the presence of a number of people who presumably shared their ideas, since they made no effort to rescue the victim. The women's defence was that Anne Burges had bewitched one of them, and that they had been advised by a Devonshire wiseman to draw her blood in order to break the spell.

Other spell-breaking charms involved the use of the victim's own blood. If any person or animal had been bewitched, some of his blood might be boiled, with appropriate incantations and rites, on a hot fire at midnight, or thrown directly on to the glowing coals. The witch would feel the pain wherever he or she might happen to be, and so be forced to lift the spell. Magical cures were also quite often effected by human or animal blood, smeared or dripped upon the seat of the trouble. In the Middle Ages, when leprosy was still a danger in Britain, it could be cured by washing in the blood of children or maidens, or by standing under a gallows and allowing the hanged man's blood to drop upon the stricken person.

Various forms of first-aid were used to stop bleeding in the days when housewives had to depend more upon their own knowledge than upon that of doctors and chemists. A thick black cobweb might be laid upon the cut, *See Cobwebs*, or powdered bistort sprinkled upon it. Sometimes a puff ball was put into the wound, or the bruised roots of comfrey were bound upon it. In Northamptonshire, a pellucid vitrified stone called Kitkat was often applied.

If all these failed, recourse might be had to magical charms, of which there were many, handed down from mother to daughter, or preserved by the local wisewoman or cunning-man. In Susannah Avery's household book, compiled in 1688, we read that if the word *Veronica* is written in ink on the ball of the left thumb, 'it will in a very short time stop ye bleeding.'[1] Another remedy was to say over the cut,

> In the blood of Adam death was taken,
> In the blood of Christ it was all to-shaken,
> And by the same blood I do thee charge
> That thou do run no longer at large,

or

> As I was going to Jordan wood,
> There was the blood and there it stood.
> So shall thy blood stay in thy body, N . . .
> I do bless thee in the Name of the Father,
>   Son and Holy Ghost.

A Highland charm which could be used only once is recorded by Isabel Cameron in her *Highland Chapbook* (1928). It had to be said in a loud voice, with the speaker's arms outstretched, by a man to a woman, by a woman to a man, and so on alternately until the haemorrhage was checked. The words were:

> The charm of God the Great:
> The free gift of Mary:
> The free gift of God:
> The free gift of every Priest and Churchman:
> The free gift of Michael the Strong:
> That would put strength into the sun.

There were also, and still are in some districts, blood-charmers, *See Blacksmiths*, who possessed some secret knowledge whereby they could arrest the flow of blood in men and animals. Usually they were present at the scene of the accident when they did this, but some were able to heal at a distance. Mrs Leather[2] relates how, a few years before she wrote in 1912,

---

[1] *A Plain Plantain*, ed. R. G. Alexander, 1922.   [2] E. M. Leather, *op. cit.*

a Herefordshire man out hunting staked his horse badly, so that the animal was in serious danger of death from loss of blood. A bystander advised him to send for the local blood-charmer, and this was done. The charmer, who was working in the fields, went a little way off and seemed to be praying, after which he returned to the messenger and said the blood had now stopped. On his return, the man found that this was so, and that the blood-flow had ceased just about the time of the charmer's prayer.

Nose-bleeding has its own lore and omens. A sudden attack is usually said to be a sign of misfortune, although if it come on in the presence of a particular person, it may denote love for that person on the part of the sufferer. A single drop from the left nostril is a good sign according to some, but more generally one or two drops from either side foretell a death in the family, or a serious illness.

The commonest method of stopping nose-bleeding is to drop the iron door-key down the patient's back, or to put a bruised dead-nettle on the nape of his neck. A Norfolk charm to prevent the onset of the attack is to wear a skein of silk, preferably red, which has been knotted by nine maidens. In Yorkshire and Northamptonshire, the same result is achieved by wearing a dead and dried toad in a bag round the neck.

BLUE VEIN ON NOSE

A blue vein across the bridge of the nose is said to be a sure sign that the person concerned is likely to die by drowning. This belief is still current in the West of England.

BOASTING

One of mankind's most ancient and deep-seated superstitious fears is the dread of boasting, or of seeming to make too sure of any good thing, present or to come. From very early times, and almost everywhere in the world, it has been thought dangerous to speak openly of any fortunate circumstance in the speaker's life, or to anticipate future happiness by a too complete and too early preparation for it. Such 'making sure' may have disastrous consequences, either as a direct punishment for presumption, or because the attention of something usually rather vaguely envisaged but quite definitely feared has thereby been attracted to the rash individual concerned.

Similarly, to comment openly on another person's beauty or health, or any other advantage that he enjoys, may bring misfortune down upon him. In some parts of the world still, it is extremely ill-advised for a newcomer to make complimentary remarks to or about any one, and especially about children, as enthusiastic travellers have sometimes found to their cost. The speaker may be suspected of overlooking those whom he praises and he will certainly be blamed for any illness or bad luck that may subsequently befall them. In Ireland, if a stranger praises a baby too warmly, the mother will often snatch the child away, touch wood, make the sign of the Cross, or say very quickly 'God be between him and harm', in order to avert the evil omen.

Even people who are not normally superstitious usually touch wood or iron when they make a boast, or speak of some hoped-for good thing, in the half-acknowledged belief that if they do not, their luck will change for the worse. Some consider it enough to say 'touch wood' without actually doing it, but usually some handy wooden or iron object is quickly and silently touched. By rights, the wood used should come from an oak, or from some other once-sacred tree, such as an ash, hazel, hawthorn, apple, or willow, because these, being sacred, had protective powers. In the course of centuries, however, this has been largely forgotten, and today any wood is pressed into service. Children sometimes touch their own heads, or those of their companions, implying stupidity or wooden-headedness. This, of course, is a joke; but when, as occasionally happens, it is done by adults, it tends to lose its mocking character and to become a substitution-rite, as genuinely superstitious as the true wood-touching from which it originally sprang.

Touching iron is equally efficacious because of the magical properties of that metal, see Iron. In Britain, it is rather less usual than touching wood, perhaps because many people think that the origin of the wood-rite was an appeal to the protection of the Cross, and that their action has therefore a religious as well as a magical significance. But iron-touching is quite well known here, as elsewhere, and it is sometimes resorted to when anything ill-omened is encountered, or when some tabu other than that on boasting has been broken. Thus, on board ship or in mines, if a forbidden word had been spoken, the evil omen can be averted if the speaker and all who heard him touch 'cold iron' as quickly as possible.

BONES

Bones, like blood and some of the organs of the body, were once thought to be centres of psychic power, and to be the vehicle or dwelling-place of the soul. Life and consciousness remained in them after the death of the original owner, and it was therefore very dangerous to disturb them when they lay in the tomb. See Graves. Misfortune, or even death, inevitably followed such an act, which was forbidden alike by reverence for the dead and superstitious fears of their vengeance. Nevertheless, this widespread and strongly held belief did not prevent the quite frequent theft of bones from churchyards and prehistoric tumuli for use in magic and witchcraft.

Both human and animal bones could be, and were, employed in spells and healing-charms, and also in divination. In Britain, divination by the blade-bone of a sheep was formerly well known. See Sheep. In Africa still, thieves are detected, lost goods found, and problems solved by the ceremony of 'throwing the bones'. Different kinds, usually those of domestic or wild animals, are used to represent individuals, or spirits, or the forces of nature, and are thrown like dice, the answers to the enquiries being read from the manner of their fall by those versed in such matters. Among the Australian aborigines, death-spells are cast by 'singing magic' into a bone and pointing it in the direction of the victim, who then pines away and dies.

Aubrey mentions in his *Remaines* an unpleasant custom whereby the ashes of burnt human bones were mixed with ale in order to induce extreme intoxication in those who drank it. Dysentery could be cured by mixing powdered bones with red wine, and gout by making a plaster of earth or mucilage scraped from the shin-bones found in a churchyard. A charm against cramp was to carry about a knuckle-bone, or the patella of a man or a sheep. Those afflicted with headaches could find relief by driving a nail into a dead man's skull, or by drying and powdering the moss found upon it and using it as snuff.

Epileptic patients were given small quantities of a grated skull mixed with their food, or were made to drink from the skull of a man or woman who had committed suicide. In the *Stamford Mercury* of 8 October 1858, it is reported that 'a collier's wife recently applied to the sexton of Ruabon Church for ever so small a portion of a human skull for the purpose of grating it similar to ginger, to be afterwards added to some mixture which she intended giving to her daughter as a remedy against fits, to which she was subject'. This charm, or some variation of it, was well known all over Great Britain.

The prominence of the skull in bone-magic may have been due to the idea that it was more likely than any other bone to be the soul-seat. In Ireland, an oath sworn upon such a relic was specially binding, particularly if it was taken to clear a man of an accusation. To lie in such circumstances was to risk sudden death, or some other terrible consequence. The pagan Scandinavians and Germans made drinking-vessels from the skulls of their slain enemies, perhaps as a sign of victory, but quite as probably because thus, as also by drinking their blood, they gained for themselves the courage and strength of the dead men. At Llandeilo in South Wales, a skull supposed to be that of St Teilo was until comparatively recently used as a cup for sick people who came to drink the waters of the healing-well dedicated to the saint. In 1826, when alterations were being made at Higher Chilton Farm in Somerset, the workmen, by a curious atavism, drank their beer from the skull of Theophilus Brome, which was kept in the house.

His was not the only skull to be thus preserved at the wish of its owner. Several houses in different parts of Britain have such gruesome relics which, like that of Theophilus Brome, cannot be removed because they fill the place with screams and appalling disturbances whenever any one attempts to do

so. One such is at Bettiscombe Manor in Dorset, all that now remains of
Azariah Pinney's Negro servant who died there of consumption in the
seventeenth century. Legend says that this skull, like the others, has some
strange form of life, and not only screams when it is moved, but returns by
its own power, rolling back to the house-door from wherever it has been
put.

Another is at Burton Agnes Hall in Yorkshire, now bricked into the walls
to prevent its accidental removal. It is that of Ann Griffith, one of the co-
builders of the Hall, who, when dying, desired her sisters to keep it in the
house. They were forced to comply with her request because of the terrifying
noises which filled the rooms until they did so, and which, according to
tradition, have broken out again on every subsequent occasion when the
skull was taken away.

Similar stories are told of Wardley Hall, near Manchester, Tunstead Farm,
near Chapel-en-le-Frith, and several other places. Various explanations have
been given for them; but it seems clear that they sprang originally from the
archaic notion of the soul dwelling in the skull and, in these instances,
acting as guardian and protecting spirit of the place in which its earthly life
had been passed.

BRACKEN

If a stem of bracken that has grown to its full height is cut crosswise close
to its foot, certain marks will be seen upon it which resemble the Greek letter
Chi, the first letter in the Greek form of Christ's name (*Χριστος*). By some
these marks have been construed as I.H.S., or as J.C., initials which also
belong to Our Lord. Because of this, witches and evil spirits were formerly
thought to detest the bracken, and to avoid those who carried it.

Other meanings have been read into these curious markings. All ferns are
traditionally associated with thunder and lightning, and according to one
belief, the lines on the bracken-stem represent an eagle, which is a thunder-
bird. In some parts they are thought to show an oak-tree, which is also
connected with thunder, or King Charles II, who hid in an oak. The name
Oak-fern, sometimes given to bracken, springs from this idea. Occasionally
they are supposed to be of diabolical origin, the print of the Devil's foot; and
in many districts they are simply the initials of the man or woman whom the
cutter is destined to marry.

The minute spores of bracken were the originals of those famous fernseeds
which could make those who gathered them invisible, and had the still more
useful property of endowing them with powers of control over all living
things. This belief was widespread in Europe at one time, and flourished in
Britain no less than elsewhere. In his *Passages in the Life of a Radical* (1841)
Samuel Bamford relates a Lancashire story in which a youth named Bangle,

being unable to gain a certain girl's love by ordinary means, consulted a wiseman who lived at Radcliffe Bridge. He was told that his only hope lay in gathering fernseed, three grains of which would enable him to summon magically any living creature that walked, flew, or swam. Such seeds worn in the shoe made the wearer invisible, and according to another tradition, if carried in the hand, they helped him to discover hidden treasure, or the gold lying concealed below the earth's surface.

Gathering fernseed was a perilous and difficult operation which could only be performed on Midsummer Eve, when the bracken was supposed to flower and to produce its seeds immediately afterwards. These had to be collected at once, between the hours of eleven and midnight. The seeker went in silence to the chosen place and laid a white cloth or a pewter dish under the fern. In northern England a Bible was sometimes substituted for the dish, or set under it. To touch the fern with the bare hands was very dangerous; it had to be bent over with a forked hazel rod, and the seeds allowed to fall out on to the cloth, dish, or book. According to some accounts, it was permissible to shake the plant with the rod, but evidently this was not a universal belief. In his *Popular Antiquities*, Brand records that in 1793 a Middlesex man told him he had often been present at seed-gathering attempts in his youth, and that these were frequently unsuccessful because the seeds had to fall of their own accord, without the help of shaking or any other action on the gatherer's part.

That spirits sometimes tried to prevent the collection of the magical seeds, and thus made the whole experience very alarming, is evident from many stories, including that of poor Bangle, mentioned above. He achieved his end and forced the girl to come to him; but the demons he saw during the gathering so terrified him that he died three months later. Richard Bovet tells us in *Pandaemonium* (1648) of one attempt that was both frightening and unsuccessful. 'I remember,' he says, 'I was told of one who went to gether it, and the spirits whisk't by his ears like bullets, and sometimes struck his hat and other parts of his body; in fine, although he apprehended he had gotten a quantity of it, and secured it in papers, and a box besides, when he came home he found all empty.'

BRAMBLE

Because of the widespread belief that diseases could be healed if the patient crawled, or was passed through some natural aperture or arch, a bramble which had rooted at both ends, and so formed an arch, was formerly re-garded as a curative agent. In Sussex, as late as the seventies of last century, cattle were drawn through such a bush in order to cure them of the shrew-mouse evil. *See Shrew-Mouse*. Similarly, children were sometimes passed through a bramble arch instead of a split ash to cure them of rickets, or serious skin-troubles, or whooping-cough. On the Welsh Border, the whooping-cough ritual included an offering of bread-and-butter, which was laid under the arch after the child had been passed through it. The disease was thought to be left behind with the food. Mrs Leather[1] records that in one Herefordshire district it was thought necessary for the adults to recite the Lord's Prayer as they handed the child to and fro, and for the little patient to eat part of the bread-and-butter meanwhile. What was left of it was then given to some bird or other creature on the way home. The bird would die thereafter, and the cough would disappear. Rheumatism, and some minor ills, like boils, gatherings, and blackheads on the face, could be cured by crawling three times on hands and knees under the rooted arch, if possible, from east to west, the way of the sun.

In Cornwall, bramble-leaves were used to heal burns, scalds and inflammations of various kinds. Nine leaves were floated in a basin of water drawn from a Holy Well or, if that was not obtainable, pure spring-water. Each leaf was then separately passed over and away from the diseased part, the operator saying three times to each one:

> There came three angels out of the east,
> One brought fire and two brought frost.
> Out fire, and in frost,
> In the Name of the Father, Son, and Holy Ghost.

The bramble is one of several plants, of which the Crown of Thorns is said to have been made. *See Blackberries.*

BREAD

Of all the foods prepared and made by human hands, none is so surrounded by ancient beliefs and omens as bread. From time immemorial, it has had immense practical importance as the main article of diet in corn-growing countries, and besides this, or perhaps because of it, it has usually been regarded as sacred, either symbolically or in itself. For pagan peoples it was holy as the gift, and in a sense, the embodiment of the Corn Spirit, and for Christians everywhere it has a deep religious significance because of its association with the Sacrament of the Eucharist. At one time, it was considered almost sacrilegious to throw it away or burn it, and this is still considered by many to be an unlucky act. Roman Catholic children are told that it makes Our Lady cry. More generally, it is said that whoever does it will live to go hungry.

Many country housewives make a cross upon the dough when setting it to rise before the fire. Experienced breadmakers say this prevents it from 'falling'

[1] E. M. Leather, *op. cit.*

either before or after it goes into the oven, but the traditional reason is that it redeems the bread from the power of the Devil and protects it from witches. In some parts of Scotland, no woman may sing while she is baking, nor must she ever make bread while there is a corpse in the house. Along the Welsh Border, it is a sign of a funeral if the dough splits along the top when it is being shaped into loaves. Only one person must put the bread into the oven; if two people do it, they will quarrel. While the actual baking is going on, no other loaf must be cut with a knife, or the new batch will be spoilt. If it is necessary to divide bread during that time, it should be broken. In Herefordshire, if a girl who is kneading rubs her dough-covered hands on a boy's face, he will never grow whiskers.

A 'coffin,' or long hole, inside a loaf is an omen of death for someone in the house. If a loaf comes apart accidentally in a girl's hand, she will not marry that year. In some districts, such a breakage foretells a quarrel in the family. In Shropshire no woman may test bread by pricking it with a knife or a fork, nor may she use either of these instruments to pass a slice to someone else. She should use a skewer, otherwise she 'will never be happy maid or wife'. It is very unlucky to set a loaf upside down on the table by accident, and still more so to do it deliberately. The breadwinner of the household will fall ill, or a ship will be lost at sea, or the Devil will fly over the roof. It is equally ill-omened to cut it at both ends, or to take hold of it when another person is cutting it.

Bread baked on Good Friday or Christmas Day was once generally supposed to have magical and healing virtues. If such a loaf was kept in the house during the following year, it protected the house itself from fire, and those living therein from accident and misfortune. If it was put in the stable or granary, or thrust into a heap of corn, it kept away rats, mice, and weevils. Probably few people nowadays believe in these protective powers, but there are still some who consider a Good Friday or Christmas loaf to be a good remedy for dysentery, diarrhoea, and kindred ills. Like the hot cross buns used for the same purpose, *see Hot Cross Bun*, such bread is allowed to become dry and hard, and then, when the need arises, it is crumbled into powder, and given to the patient in hot water.

Ordinary bread could be used in healing charms as well as that sanctified by the day on which it was made. Brand[1] mentions a sixteenth-century remedy for a sore, or an aching tooth. The patient was required to take a piece of white bread, mark it with a cross, and say a Paternoster over it. He then laid it on the sore or the tooth, with the cross next to the afflicted part. A Suffolk cure for whooping-cough, recorded in 1877, was to wrap a slice of bread in a piece of cloth and bury it for three days. It was then dug up again and given to the patient to eat. The earthy flavour which it had acquired in the meantime was considered to help in the cure. In an article contributed to *Folk-Lore*

[1] J. Brand, *op. cit.*

(Vol. 31, 1920) E. A. Wright mentions an Oxfordshire variant of this charm. An entire loaf was rolled in a cloth and buried for twenty-four hours in a large hole. When taken up again, it was not given to the patient, but to the rest of the family, in order to prevent them from catching the disease. In some parts of the West Midlands, bread-and-butter asked from a post-humous child, or from a woman whose maiden and married names were the same, *see Names*, cured whooping-cough, but only if it was taken and eaten without thanking the giver.

It is unlucky for any person to take the last slice of bread-and-butter from a plate, unless it is offered to him. If a spinster does so, she will remain un-married all her life. On the other hand, the last slice, if offered and taken, brings good luck in terms of love or money. The children's version of this belief is that it means either 'a handsome husband or £10,000 a year'.

BREAKAGES

It is still a quite common belief that if anything is accidentally broken in the house, two more breakages will certainly follow. Therefore, to preserve more valuable possessions, two worthless objects, or the pieces of the thing already broken, should be deliberately smashed at once, so that the omen may be fulfilled without further loss.

A Suffolk superstition recorded in *The Book of Days* (1864) was that when a maid had a run of bad luck with her mistress's china and glass, she should be made to buy something as a replacement. This was not a punishment for her carelessness, or a compensation for the mistress; it was an attempt 'to change the luck'.

To break something that has been given as a love-token or pledge is very unfortunate; the love-affair will end badly. In Scotland, if a bride breaks a dish or plate during her wedding-feast, her married life will be unhappy.

For the effects of breaking a mirror, or a wedding ring, *see Mirrors*, and *Wedding Ring*.

BRIDGES

Bridges, which unite two places otherwise separated from each other, are obvious symbols of transition, and have been so regarded since their building was first attempted. From very early times they have been associated in men's minds with the passage of souls to the next world, and therefore with death. In some pagan mythologies, the dead were believed to pass hence over a bridge constructed by the gods. Bifröst, the Scandinavian Rainbow-bridge between Midgard and Asgard, was one such. Another was the Irish Bridge of the Cliff, which tilted under the unworthy and could only be crossed by the brave. In ancient Greece, Demeter in one of her aspects was called the Lady of the Bridge; in Rome, the high priest was Pontifex Maximus, the bridge-builder, whose bridges were not material, but spiritual. Our own *Lyke-Wake Carol* speaks of the Brig o' Dread, over which the dead had to pass at the end of their long journey across Whinney Moor. Aubrey tells us in his *Remaines* that this curiously pagan-sounding dirge was sung over Christian corpses in Yorkshire as late as the beginning of the seventeenth century. In the version that he gives, the Brig o' Dread is described as 'no brader than a thread' in which it resembles the Mahommedan soul-bridge, Al-Sirat, that was finer than a hair and sharper than a sword-edge. The latter spanned the midmost part of Hell, and those who were unworthy to cross it fell from its height into the fire beneath.

It was formerly thought very unlucky to be the first person to go over a new bridge. Similar fears were widely felt about the first use of other new things, but in the case of bridges, and also churches and other important new buildings, dim memories of ancient sacrifice may have helped to keep the superstition alive. The idea that a building would not stand unless something living was laid under its foundations was once very widespread. Traces of this belief can be seen in the children's singing-game, *London Bridge is Falling Down*, and also in the legends concerning the various Devil's Bridges found in different parts of Europe. In these tales the Devil builds or helps to build a bridge, demanding as his fee the first living creature to cross it after completion. He means, of course, a human being whose soul he can thus claim, but usually he is cheated by the simple device of sending an animal or a bird across first.

There is a German story that the builder of the Sachsenhäuser Bridge at Frankfort found himself unable to finish the work within the stipulated time, and so called upon Satan for help. The usual reward of something living was agreed between them, but the builder evaded the true payment by driving a cock across the bridge as soon as it was finished. A very similar tale is told about the Devil's Bridge, near Aberystwyth. The Evil One agreed to build a bridge across the Afon Mynach for an old woman whose cow was marooned on the other side. Here again, he lacked the wit to specify a human being as his fee, and the old woman, instead of hurrying across herself to find her cow as he had expected, sent her little dog over, which, since it was indeed a living creature, he was obliged to accept.

These ancient associations with death and the Devil probably account for some of the still existing superstitions about bridges. One well-known tradition says that if two people part on, or under, a bridge, they will never meet again. In some Scottish and Welsh districts, it is considered dangerous to speak when standing or walking underneath one. The most widespread modern belief is perhaps that connected with railway bridges. It is unlucky to pass under one while a train is running overhead, or to be on a road-bridge spanning a railway while the train passes below. In an article contributed to

Folk-Lore (Vol. 65, 1954) Peter Opie remarks that in some parts of Wales, this is so firmly believed that bus-drivers approaching a railway-bridge will draw their vehicles to the side of the road if they see a train coming, and wait there till it has passed.

BRIMSTONE

Farm-workers, and others whose work makes them peculiarly liable to rheumatism, often carry a piece of brimstone about with them to cure or prevent the disease. The same stone cures cramp, if the sufferer takes a piece to bed with him, and either holds it in his hand, or puts it under the mattress. In Parson Woodforde's *Diary*,[1] there is an entry on 27 November 1789, in which he says: 'I thank God had a better night of rest than I have had the 3 last Nights. Had no Cramp at all. My Brother recommending me last Night to carry a small Piece of the roll Brimstone sewed up in a piece of very thin Linnen, to bed with me and if I felt any Symptom of the Cramp to hold it in my hand or put it near the affected part, which I did, as I apprehended at one time it was coming into one of my legs, and felt no more advances of it. This I thought deserving of notice, even in so trifling a book as this.'

BRIONY

In Lincolnshire and the northern English counties, the names 'mandrake' and 'womandrake' are often applied to the male and female briony respectively. Like the true mandrake, this plant was (and to a certain extent, still is) thought to have strong aphrodisiac qualities, and to induce fertility in human beings and horses. The dried and powdered root of the male variety was used for women and mares, and that of the female plant for men and stallions. A little of the same powder given to horses improved their condition and made their coats glossy. In her *Lincolnshire Folklore* (1936) Ethel Rudkin records that the common dose for this purpose was as much as would cover a threepenny bit, administered twice a week in food. One of her informants warned her that this dose must never be exceeded, or the animal would 'go on too fast' and become very excited, and so too would human beings if they took too much.

Witches were supposed to use briony roots in their spells, either because they could not find a true mandrake root, or because, like many country people, they confused the two plants. Coles in his *Art of Simpling* (1656) remarks that they 'make thereof an ugly image, by which they represent the person on whom they intend to exercise their witchcraft'. In folk-medicine, briony was often employed in remedies for women's ills and for rheumatism, and sometimes as a purgative.

[1] *The Diary of a Country Parson, 1758-1802*, ed. J. B. Beresford, 1924-31.

BURIAL, COMPLETE

To the very natural dread of losing a limb by accident or amputation was formerly added a superstitious fear of incompleteness in burial. Among primitive peoples it was believed that a person buried without a leg or arm would be maimed in the next world as in this. The Christian version of the same belief was that he would lack the missing member when he rose on the Last Day and so be at a disadvantage through all Eternity. If, however, the separated parts could be interred with the corpse the difficulty was over-come and the dead man would rise again in his complete form. These ideas were not infrequently responsible for unnecessary deaths caused by deferring amputations until it was too late, and also for the careful preservation of the severed parts, whenever that was possible, in order that they might be placed in the coffin when the time came. Even fallen or extracted teeth were often saved, sometimes for years, and laid in the grave at last with their former owner.

The curious blend of pagan and Christian belief inherent in this custom is clearly shown in a story related by R. M. Heanley.[1] During the nineteenth century, a man living at Croft in Lincolnshire lost two fingers in a chaff-cutter. His mother put the fingers in a little coffin and asked the Vicar of the parish to bury them in the churchyard. She said she knew that Almighty God was well able to unite them with her son's body on the Last Day, wherever they might be, but she did not wish Him to have the trouble of looking for them. He would be 'strange and throng' on that great day, and it hardly became people like her to make Him 'breffet all over t' plaeace and tew Hisself' if it was possible for the fingers to be put handy in God's own acre.

BURIAL GROUND

In many areas there is, or was until recently, a strong prejudice against allowing a dead kinsman to be the first person buried in a new burial ground. In some districts, it was believed that his soul would be seized by the Devil, in others, that he would become the Churchyard Watcher until the next funeral occurred, *see Churchyard Watcher*, in all, that he would suffer a dis-advantage of one kind or another. Only when some wandering tramp, some chance-come stranger, or even an animal had been interred there would the new graveyard be safe for the loved dead.

Henderson[2] mentions two cases, one in Aberdeenshire and the other at Bovey Tracey in Devon, where the cemetery remained empty until, in Scotland, a tramp, in Devon, a visitor's servant, died and was buried therein. After these first interments, there was no more difficulty in either parish.

---

[1] R. M. Heanley, *op. cit.*   [2] W. Henderson, *op. cit.*

R. M. Heanley[1] records how, when a new piece of land was added in 1886 to the churchyard at Wainfleet All Saints, one of the churchwardens paid the sexton to bury a dead dog in one corner as soon as the ground had been consecrated. He afterwards admitted quite openly that he had done so, and probably most of the parishioners approved of his action, since he had thereby saved their own dead from the risk of being the ill-fated first.

In an article published in *Folklore*, Miss R. L. Tongue[2] remarks that in West Somerset there is often difficulty of this kind when a new cemetery is opened. On one occasion a vicar, knowing of the superstition, was agreeably surprised to see the first funeral in a new ground pass off smoothly and well. In the village, however, it was noticed that a large black dog had disappeared just before, and the general belief was that 'the sexton had known what to do'.

The closing of an old graveyard was often resented by the local people because by it the last person buried therein would be doomed to be the Churchyard Watcher for ever, since no other corpse would come to relieve him. To break up a cemetery, or put it to other uses, is quite commonly thought ill-omened. It may result in hauntings, or in very bad luck for the person responsible. Hamilton Jenkin tells us in his *Cornwall and the Cornish* that in 1925 he learnt that a certain field near Mullion had never been ploughed or broken up because it was believed to have been a burial place once. No one dared to disturb it, for whoever did so would suffer the loss of his eldest son, or meet with some other dire misfortune. *See Graves.*

BURIAL OMENS

Many signs and omens were, and some still are, read from the conduct and circumstances of a funeral.

If rain falls during the proceedings, it augurs well for the dead man's soul. The couplet which says

> Happy is the bride that the sun shines on,
> Happy is the corpse that the rain rains on.

is well known all over Britain. A ray of sunshine striking directly on the face of someone attending a funeral is unlucky; it marks him as the next to die. Mrs Rudkin[3] records a Trentside belief that if any one enters the house before the next-of-kin when the party returns from the burial, he will not live long. Similarly, if any person attempts to precede the coffin on its way to the

[1] R. M. Heanley, *op. cit.*
[2] R. L. Tongue, 'Odds and Ends of Somerset Folklore', *Folklore*, Vol. 69, 1958.
[3] E. H. Rudkin, *op. cit.*

church, serious bad luck or sudden death will be his lot. No one must do this until the clergyman comes to meet the cortège inside the churchyard.

It is unlucky if there is an odd number of people present at a burial. One among them will die soon, for the dead man is looking for a companion. In Yorkshire, if an unmarried person has been to three funerals, he (or she) must be present at a wedding service, before attending a fourth, or he will die unmarried.

When horses were used to draw the funeral carriage, they had, on arrival at the house, to be taken out of the shafts and put into the stable for a short time before leaving again for the church. If they refused to start, another death in the same family would follow soon, and so too, if the hearse had to be turned after the corpse had been placed in it. If, during the journey, one of the horses turned his head towards any house and neighed, someone in that house would die before long.

Meeting a funeral is usually considered ill-omened, especially for brides, or for any one starting on an important journey. Whoever does so should turn and follow the procession for a little way. When 'walking funerals' were common, it was customary for a man who met one to take a short turn as a bearer. That done, he bowed to the company and departed in safety, but if this precaution was neglected, he would soon need bearers himself. In Oxfordshire, where these beliefs prevail, as in other countries, there is a variant which says it is extremely unlucky to meet an empty hearse. If it already contains a corpse, all is well, for the demands of Death have been satisfied for the time being. Derbyshire people say that only the first person to meet a funeral after it has started on its way is marked for death; in Lincolnshire, it is not necessarily the individual himself or herself who will die, but someone of the same sex.

A very persistent superstition, especially in small communities where deaths are normally few and all are known, is that 'one funeral makes three'. If after a long period without a burial, one should take place, two more will follow quickly. Henderson[1] remarks that in Durham the same idea was expressed by the saying that if the Cathedral bell tolls once, it will toll thrice. A funeral on New Year's Day is very ill-omened, and foretells at least one other in the parish in every month of the coming year. A Sunday burial is also unlucky and predicts three more within the week.

To postpone a funeral for any reason whatsoever is considered dangerous in many districts. It is variously said to denote one, three, or more deaths in the family, or in the neighbourhood, within the week or, in some places, within three months. If the waiting period includes a week-end, the omen is certain, for this involves the corpse lying unburied over a Sunday. If this happens, whether through a postponement or otherwise, the dead man will do his best to take someone with him. Although the fears roused by post-

[1] Wm. Henderson, *op. cit.*

ponement are now all for the living, it is possible that they sprang originally from the idea that the soul was thus kept waiting for the rites needed to help it on its way, and so was cruelly earthbound for an unusually long period.

In Ireland, warts could be cured by a passing funeral. The person afflicted with them took a stone and threw it after the corpse in the name of the Trinity, reciting the dead man's names as he did so, and stating that he was thus forcing his warts upon him. This was never done if the funeral was that of a near relative. Another method was to rub the warts as the coffin went by and say three times, 'May these warts and this corpse pass away, and never more return.' As the dead body decayed in the ground, so would the warts wither and finally vanish. See Carrying a Corpse: Graves.

BURIAL PREPARATIONS

It is generally considered to be a bad omen if, when a corpse is being prepared for burial, the eyes are found to be still open. The dead man is looking for someone to accompany him into the grave. Until very recently, it was usual to place coins on the eyes as soon as death had occurred, a custom often explained as an attempt to prevent this ominous staring, but perhaps also connected with the old belief that the dead must be provided with money to pay their way in the next world. See Burial with Goods. Similarly, a 'limber corpse', that is, one which has not stiffened as quickly as is usual, signifies another death in the household before very long.

In some districts, it was formerly considered essential to tie the feet of the corpse with string or woollen thread as soon as laying-out was completed. Is this was not done, the spirit might return or, worse still, some other spirit might enter the body and use it for its own purposes. R. M. Heanley[1] relates a curious story concerning a death at Croft in Lincolnshire during the seventies of the last century, where this precaution was forgotten. About a fortnight after the funeral, the dead man returned to his home in the form of a large toad, which stationed itself under his favourite chair and could not be dislodged. A lady visiting the house was asked to tie its feet and put it under an old apple-tree in the garden, which no member of the family had dared to do. She was considered a suitable person to perform this office because the dead man had liked her, and it was hoped that he would listen to her if she explained that he had had his turn, that now it was the turn of the survivors, and he must not 'come awming and messing aboot no more'. She refused to tie the feet, but she did remove the creature to a hollow under the apple-tree. Apparently this satisfied the spirit, for the toad did not return.

The clothes in which the corpse was dressed for burial were often prepared many years beforehand. Although anything connected with death was commonly considered very ill-omened, a simple acceptance of the

[1] R. M. Heanley, op. cit.

inevitable caused many people in the past to make their own funeral garments long before they came to old age. The shroud, cap, and stockings needed were carefully sewn and knitted, sometimes when the maker was still quite young, and laid away in lavender in a special drawer or chest. In Northumberland, they were included as a matter of course in the wedding trousseau. In this way death, whenever it came, found its victim ready, with everything to hand for those who had to perform the last offices. There may also have been an underlying belief, or at least a hope, that what was thus fully prepared for might, by the very fact of preparation, be somehow averted or delayed.

In northern England, it was supposed to be lucky to be buried in linen, an idea probably stemming from the time when only the rich and the determined were so interred. Until 1666, linen was the usual material for shrouds, but in that year an Act of Parliament forbade the use of anything but wool for burial clothes, or for the quilling inside the coffin. This Act, which was not repealed until 1814, was greatly resented, and so often evaded that it had to be strengthened by amendments in 1678 and again in 1680. Many families who were rich enough to do so preferred to use linen for their dead relatives, and then pay the fine of £5 levied for each offence. Numerous churchwardens' accounts show entries of such payments during the years when the Act was in force. Those who could not afford to defy the law thus sometimes evaded it by not using a winding-sheet at all, and simply covering the corpse with sweet-smelling flowers, or hay.

Shrouds were, of course, the most usual grave-garments, but sometimes other clothes were used instead. These were very often white; in the case of a woman, a white nightdress was, and still is, a common choice. Brides who died soon after the wedding were frequently buried in their bridal dress. Similarly, a baby who died within a month of his baptism was wrapped in the white Chrism-cloth which denoted that he was a Christian, and was thereafter referred to as a Chrism-child. Those who customarily wear a distinctive dress are still very often interred in it instead of a shroud. Monks and nuns wear their habits, soldiers and naval men are buried in their uniform. Gypsies normally wear their best clothes, and this practice is sometimes followed by others who dislike the melancholy associations of the shroud. In 1938, when a little girl died in an Oxford hospital, her mother brought her best clothes to the Sister of the ward, together with a new woollen coat which she had just bought. She asked that the child should be dressed in these for her funeral, and most particularly that she should wear the coat, 'to keep her warm'.

When the corpse was fully clothed, it was laid in the coffin with its feet towards the rising sun, following the line along which graves were customarily made. See Graves. Before the coffin was finally nailed down, every fastening in the shroud had to be carefully loosened. Knots were untied, strings cut (including usually, but not invariably, the string binding the feet), and all pins removed. If this was not done, it was believed that the dead man would be hampered when he rose from the grave on the Last Day.

BURIAL WITH GOODS

The custom of burying goods of various kinds with the dead is still sometimes observed as an act of piety and affection. In primitive times, such grave-goods were deemed essential to the welfare of the soul in the next world. The weapons, clothes, food, and other possessions that he needed here were equally necessary beyond the grave, where life was thought to be very much as it is on Earth. If the dead man was denied them, he would be inadequately equipped, and would be at a disadvantage amongst his fellow-shades. Not only did affection dictate that he must have all he required, but fear also played its part, for the deprived and angry ghost might return to haunt the neglectful living.

Traces of this primitive conception can be seen today in the burial of toys in children's coffins, and of jewellery, books, or other favourite articles with adults. Married women are commonly buried with their wedding rings, but this is not universal. In some districts it is, or was, considered impious, and dangerous to the soul, to include any jewellery whatsoever. Baring-Gould was once told by a Yorkshireman that when the latter's mother died, he wished her wedding-ring to be left on her hand. The woman who laid her out was shocked by the suggestion, and said, 'You mun no send her to God wi' her trinkets about her.' In Sweden formerly, mirrors were laid in the coffins of young girls so that they might tidy their hair on Judgement Day. Married women did not require them, for they wore their hair braided and were buried with it thus.

In Ireland, clay pipes filled with tobacco were sometimes laid on new graves for the use of the dead. R. M. Heanley[1] records how he once saw a broken jug and mug on a grave in Wainfleet. The dead man's widow told him that she had put them there because her husband had valued them highly and would certainly want them in the next world. Grief and confusion had made her forget to put them in the coffin, and so she did the next best thing. 'I deads 'em both,' she said (that is, she killed them by breaking them, and so released their spiritual essence), and having done this, she left them on the grave for the soul to find.

The same woman said she had put a groat in her husband's mouth 'to pay his footing'. This is a very ancient idea, reminiscent of the coin buried with the dead in pagan Greece to pay Charon's fee for ferrying the soul across the Styx. About fifty years ago in Oxfordshire, a penny was sometimes laid in

[1] R. M. Heanley, *op. cit.*

the dead man's mouth, or in his hand, though those who put it there were usually vague as to why it should be done. That the provision of money for the soul's use was once very common in this country is shown by the many silver or copper coins of different periods that have been found in graves all over England.

J. E. Vaux[1] tells us that when he was a curate in London about the middle of last century, a young girl died in his parish, and certain favourite possessions were buried with her. Among these was her workbox, and also a photograph of Mr Vaux. The burial of the latter was obviously dictated in this case by affection for its original, but it might have had a very different significance. The interment of the image, picture, or clothes of a living person in a grave was once supposed to be a sure way of causing that person's death, and was occasionally done deliberately as an expression of hatred, or as a secret method of murder.

A country custom found in many sheep-rearing districts was to bury a tuft of wool with a shepherd. This was done so that he might produce it on Judgement Day to show he had been a shepherd in this life, and therefore unable to attend church regularly, owing to the demand of his flock. In Yorkshire, a Bible or hymn-book and the dead person's Sunday School class ticket were sometimes laid in the coffin as a proof of his former piety. A somewhat similar practice in Russia was to put a parchment certificate of good conduct in the corpse's hand.

In some districts, candles used to be included among the grave-goods, to light the soul on its perilous journey. Irish corpses were occasionally provided with a hammer so that they might knock on the gates of Purgatory, and in Scotland, a bell was often put under the dead man's head, perhaps to announce his arrival, or more probably, because the sound of bells has always been thought a powerful protection against demons.

The sword laid on the coffin at military funerals is a relic of the time when the dead warrior's weapons were buried with him. Similarly, the presence of favourite dogs or horses in a funeral procession reminds us that these animals would once have been slaughtered so that they could accompany their master to the Underworld. At a gypsy funeral at Garsington in 1953, the dead woman's two horses were killed in spite of an attempt made by the R.S.P.C.A. inspector to save them. Her sons said it was essential for her welfare hereafter that all the proper rites should be observed, and these included the death of the horses. Her caravan was burnt to ashes at the same time, and all her crockery was smashed and buried.

It was formerly customary to lay a portion of the food eaten at the funeral feast upon the grave, so that the dead man might share in his own last celebrations. In South Northamptonshire during the last century, the finest flowers obtainable were placed inside the coffin, in addition to the more usual

[1] J. E. Vaux, op. cit.

wreaths left on the grave. If the dead person was old, small sprigs of yew or box were added.

BUTTERFLIES

Butterflies have from early times been widely associated with human souls. In ancient Egypt, the soul at death was thought of as leaving the body as the butterfly leaves the chrysalis. In Burma the *win-laik-pya*, or soul-butterfly, is believed to fly abroad when its owner sleeps, meeting the soul-butterflies of other persons and animals and returning when the sleeper wakes. Burmese children are still taught never to awaken any one too suddenly, for fear the *win-laik-pya* cannot get back in time, in which case the man dies.

In Gaelic tradition, the newly-dead were thought to be sometimes visible in the form of a butterfly hovering over the corpse. In Ireland, this was a sign of everlasting happiness for the soul. In Scotland, a golden butterfly flying over a dying man was a very good omen for his future welfare. A legend not unlike the Burmese one mentioned above is recorded by Alexander Carmichael in *Carmina Gaedelica*. It tells how a soul wandered through time and space, and returned at last to the body in butterfly (or in some versions, in bee) form. It was about to enter the sleeping man's mouth when a neighbour killed it. In one form of the story, the man died at once; but in another, and more horrible version, the body lived on and went about its daily affairs, carrying the substance of the dead soul in its left hand, and the shadow of its withered heart in the right.

A further extension of this idea is that all butterflies are souls who linger on Earth, either permanently, or while they are waiting to enter Purgatory. Thus one chance-met might be the spirit of a relative or friend, and for that reason should never be harmed or killed. Eleanor Hull[1] records how an Armagh girl in 1810 was reproved by her companions for chasing a butterfly because it might be the soul of her grandfather. In Nidderdale and Devonshire, they are supposed to be dead children who died unbaptized, and so cannot enter Heaven.

This death-and-soul connexion, which protects the insect in some areas, causes it to be feared and persecuted in others. To see three together is unlucky, to see one flying at night is a death omen. In many parts of Britain, it is believed that the first seen in any one year should be killed, otherwise misfortune will follow. A writer in *Notes and Queries*, Vol. VII, says that once, when visiting a Lincolnshire house, he mentioned that he had just seen his first butterfly. He was at once asked if he had crushed it with his foot, and on inquiring why he should do such a thing, was told that had he done so he would have been able to crush all his enemies throughout the year.

In Gloucestershire, it used to be said that if the first butterfly seen in sum-

[1] E. Hull, *op. cit.*

mer was a white one, the observer would eat white bread all the year. In other words, he would be prosperous and able to eat fine food. If it was brown, he would only be able to afford the humbler brown bread. In Westmorland formerly, the white variety were called Papishes, and were hunted by gangs of boys on Oak Apple Day; the variegated kind were King George's Butterflies and were (technically at least, though not always actually) safe from destruction on that day. Along the Scottish Border, red butterflies were formerly hunted because they were supposed to be witches.

BUTTER-MAKING

Butter-making by means of ordinary rotary churns turned by hand is always a somewhat uncertain task, often made unduly hard by the apparently inexplicable refusal of the butter 'to come'. Hence it is not surprising that it was once thought subject to the spells of witches and fairies. Witches were believed to be able to enchant the cream from a distance and to draw away the 'soul' or essence of the butter by magic, thereby making the dairymaid's task practically impossible. To prevent this, many charms were used. Some took the form of rhymes or couplets recited as the churn-handle was turned. The dairymaid might say

> Churn butter, dash,
> Cow's gone to t' marsh.
> Peter stands at the toll-gate,
> Begging butter for his cake,
> Come, butter, come,

or if she was from the south Midlands, she might say,

> Come, butter, churn,
> Come, butter come.
> The great Bull of Banbury
> Shan't have none,

or any of the many similar charms in which the powers of good were invoked and those of evil defied.

In some English districts it was believed that salt should be thrown on the fire before beginning the work. In Ireland a smouldering turf was often kept under the churn throughout the proceedings. If the churn was made of rowan-wood, or there was a ring of rowan round the handle, the witch's power was nullified. A silver coin thrown into the cream, or three white hairs from a black cat's tail, served the same purpose. A very common practice was to plunge a red-hot poker into the cream when the butter would not 'come'. This was supposed to burn the witch, and as it also altered the temperature, it was often effective.

Along the coasts, the state of the tide affected both the making and the quality of the butter. *See Tides.* In Scotland, butter made from the milk of cows which had grazed in the churchyard was thought to cure consumption, a disease once generally believed to be the result of witchcraft. A somewhat startling Irish method of making the butter specially rich and creamy was to dip the left hand of a dead man into the cream. Fortunately for the reputation of Irish butter, we must suppose that this magical practice was always extremely rare, if only because of the difficulties involved in obtaining such a hand. *See Dead Hand.*

C

CAESARIAN OPERATION

A child born by Caesarian operation is commonly expected to have unusual bodily strength throughout his life, and also the power to see spirits and to find hidden treasure.

CALF

The risks and uncertainties of calving, no less than its importance to any dairy or cattle farmer, have given rise to many curious beliefs, some of which are still remembered by the older workers.

A stable lantern must never be put down on a table; it may cause a cow to slip her calf. The connexion between the two events is never clearly explained, but the belief still exists in a good many districts.

The first cow to calve in the year is said to set the fashion in timing. If she calves by day, so will all the others, and similarly, if she calves by night, so will they. To prevent the worry and loss of sleep involved in night-calving, cows were dried off, whenever possible, on a Sunday.

An old cure for contagious abortion was to nail the aborted calf on the wall of the byre where all the cows could see it. This acted as a warning to the rest of the herd. Another method was to bury the slipped calf under the byre-threshold, where every cow must pass over it as she went in and out. As the carcase rotted in the earth, so would the disease disappear. The danger of milk-fever was averted by hanging the afterbirth on a whitethorn or a crabtree and leaving it there to decay, or by wrapping a holed stone in white paper and hiding it in the rafters.

In Herefordshire it was thought unlucky for a cow to bear twins. In the Cleveland district of Yorkshire, the first-born of twins was expected to be fruitful and the other barren, unless the latter was mated with another born in the same manner. This belief applied to calves of either sex.

It is, or was until recently, a country custom to present neighbours with small quantities of Beastings, the first milk of the cow after calving, with which to make beastings-pudding. To send such gifts brought good luck to the herd, but the recipient had to be careful to return the bottle *unwashed*, otherwise the new-born calf would die, or the cow's milk would fail.

If a calf has a white streak down its back, it will not thrive, and in some areas it is thought unlikely to do so if it is weaned when the moon is waning. To put one's hand on a calf's back is still thought very unlucky on many farms. The animal will become ill, or will meet with an accident. To step over a calf as it lies on the ground causes its death. Henderson[1] mentions a charm used on a farm in Co. Durham where great difficulty has been experienced in rearing the young stock. After the deaths of several, the leg and thigh of one dead beast was attached by ropes to the chimney and left hanging there. The farmer's wife told Henderson's informant that when this had been done the trouble stopped, and she had no more losses.

The dried tip of a calf's tongue was often called the Lucky Tip or the Lucky Bit, and was used as a charm against poverty. If it was carried about in the pocket, that pocket would never be empty of ready money. In addition, the Tip protected its owner against assault and battery.

CANDLES

Candles, which were once the chief source of household light, have collected many superstitions during their long history of service to mankind. If one gutters as it burns, so that the grease collects unevenly and gradually lengthens into a 'winding-sheet', it is an omen of death for the person sitting opposite to it or, if not for him, then for someone else in the family. If it burns with a dim blue flame, a spirit is passing, and in most places this too is a death omen.

A bright spark in the wick is sometimes said to indicate the coming of strangers, but more generally it means a letter for the individual nearest to it. If he wishes to know when it will arrive, he must take the candlestick and knock with it on the table while repeating the names of the following weekdays. Should the spark fall out with the first knock, the letter is already in the post, otherwise it will fall when the destined day of arrival is mentioned.

A wavering flame where there is no draught to cause it means windy

[1] Wm. Henderson, *op. cit.*

weather to come. If the candle will not light easily, rain is foretold, and in some districts, a bluish flame indicates frost.

It is unlucky to light a candle from the fire on the hearth. In Lincolnshire, it is said that whoever does so will come to want and die in the workhouse. To snuff one accidentally is a sign of a wedding. No candle should ever be allowed to gutter to extinction in the socket of the candlestick. It should be blown out before it reaches that stage, otherwise misfortune will come to someone in the house or, according to a coastal tradition, a sailor will be drowned at sea.

It is very ill-omened to leave a candle burning in an empty room, and if it is left there for any length of time, a death will follow. An exception to this rule is the Christmas candle, which should be left burning all through the night of Christmas Eve in order to ensure light, warmth and plenty in the coming year. At one time, specially large candles were made for this purpose, and these were a customary gift from grocers to their regular customers. It was usual for such a candle to be lit by the head of the household, or by the oldest member of the family, and extinguished by him in the morning. It was often considered unlucky to touch it after it had been lit, and if it went out prematurely, or was accidentally blown out, the omen was very bad.

Although the large Christmas candle is rarely seen now, many people still set lights in their windows, sometimes in sets of three, on Christmas Eve. Legend says this was done to guide the Christ Child through the darkness. In medieval times, no stranger attracted to the house by this light was ever turned away, lest it should be Our Lord Himself who thus sought hospitality.

Candles are burnt by the dead to protect them from evil spirits, *see Death, Immediately after*, and for much the same reason they are lit at a birth or a marriage, and on other ceremonial occasions. If one of those surrounding a corpse falls from its stick, it is a sign of another death in the house within twelve months. There is a Welsh tradition that if a lighted candle on the altar of a church is blown out by the wind, or otherwise accidentally extinguished, the death of the clergyman is foretold.

It was formerly thought very unlucky to light three candles with a single taper, a belief which still survives in the widespread dislike of lighting three cigarettes with one match. *See Cigarettes*. In Cornwall, Berkshire, Lincolnshire, and some other parts of England, three candles burning together in a room are a sign of a wedding. In general, however, three lights at once are considered ill-omened, whether they are candles, lamps, or rushlights. One, two, or four are permissible, or as many more as may be desired, but never three. One of the trio must be put out at once, otherwise misfortune of some sort will follow very soon.

Actors usually dislike three candles on the stage or in a dressing-room. In Worcestershire, it is said that those who sit in a room so lit will quarrel.

Barry O'Brien tells a story in his *Life of Parnell* which shows that the Irish leader was acquainted with the superstition. A friend once visited him when he was ill and found him lying in a bedroom lighted by four candles. During his visit, one of these went out, whereupon Parnell immediately blew out another, remarking that it was extremely unlucky to have three lights together.

Candles were sometimes used in charms of various kinds. A girl could call her lover to her by thrusting two pins into a lighted candle and reciting a well-known verse over it. *See Pins.* In Lancashire, a ceremony known as Lating the Witches was sometimes performed on Hallowe'en. A lighted candle was carried about on the hills from eleven o'clock until midnight. If it burnt steadily during that time, the person carrying it would be free from witch-craft throughout the following twelve months, but if it went out, it was an omen of evil. In Hone's *Year Book* (1829), there is a letter from a woman describing how, as a child in 1818, she went Lating the Witches over Longridge Fell with a party of thirty people, each one carrying a large lighted candle.

In 1490, Johanna Benet was accused of attempting to murder a man by naming a wax candle after him and using sorcery upon it, so that as it was consumed, so he wasted away. Nearly four hundred years later, in 1843, the Norwich magistrates heard a somewhat similar tale. During a prosecution for assault, a Mr and Mrs Curtis declared that Mrs Bell had bewitched the man by candle-magic. Mrs Curtis had seen her light a candle, stick it full of pins, and repeat a form of words over an oyster-shell full of dragonsblood and water. As soon as she had done this, Mr Curtis's arms and legs were-magically 'set fast'. It does not seem to have been suggested that Mrs Bell was actually a witch, or that she used anything but an ordinary candle, but rather that she was simply a spiteful woman employing a form of magic which, in the opinion of the two Curtises at least, was available to any one who had the wherewithal to buy a pound of candles and an ounce of dragonsblood.

CARROTS

Carrots are commonly said to improve the eyesight, and to enable those who eat them constantly to see in the dark. In folk-medicine, they are used to cure asthma, rheumatism, and the stone. These remedies have some basis in fact, for carrots do contain salts of medicinal value, and modern herbalists now prescribe their juice for cataract, night-blindness, and other eye-troubles. Formerly, they were used in love-philtres and aphrodisiacs also. John Gerard mentions them in his *Herbal* (1597) as 'serving for love-matters', and recommends the use of the wild variety rather than the garden plant for this purpose.

CARRYING A CORPSE

Tradition demands that when a dead man is carried to his burial, he must leave the house feet foremost, and by the front door. If for any reason, this door cannot be used, then he must be passed through a front window, even if this means taking out the window frame or enlarging the hole in the wall. On no account must he ever leave by the back door, for this would imperil his soul's welfare.

It is also essential that he should travel sunwise on his journey, or at least, start out in that direction. When walking funerals were usual, it was customary in some districts for the procession to halt by any wayside cross, and for the coffin to be either bumped upon it, or carried right-handed round it. In Ireland, if a church was passed, it was similarly circuited. When the church was reached, the corpse was often taken two or three times round the churchyard wall, or round the cross inside it, going the way of the sun. J. E. Vaux[1] relates that at Holne in Devonshire, the cross was always so encircled, to the great distress of one rector, who regarded the practice as 'popish'. He would have been nearer the mark if he had described it as pagan. Eventually, when all his remonstrances proved fruitless, he destroyed the cross and hid the fragments. At Whitchurch in Pembrokeshire, the funeral procession used to go round a stone called *Maen Dewi* (St David's Stone). Mrs Leather records[2] that at Peterchurch, where there are two chancels and a terminal apse, the coffin was always carried round both chancels and set down in the most westerly one before the service.

At one time, it was considered dangerous to carry a corpse twice over the same bridge. If one was so placed that the procession would normally cross it when going from the house to the church, and then again from the church to the cemetery, one or other of the journeys had to be made along another route, even if it meant going a very long way round. If this precaution was neglected, the twice-crossed bridge would fall at some time in the near future.

A very widespread belief, still far from extinct, is that if a corpse is carried over private land, its passage establishes a right of way for ever.

In most old parishes, the customary road or path taken by funerals is known as the Church Road, or sometimes as the Corpse Way, or Corpse Gate. In the centre of the parish, this might be the ordinary, hard road, but funerals from outlying farms or hamlets might have to travel over a path running for at least part of the way over moors or fields. Such a path was never ploughed over, but stood out clearly, hard and dry, and wide enough to allow the bearers to carry the coffin without difficulty. It was formerly considered very unlucky to use any other route, and likely to prevent the dead man from resting in his grave. Great efforts were sometimes necessary

[1] J. E. Vaux, *op. cit.*   [2] E. M. Leather, *op. cit.*

to adhere to the Church Road in bad weather if it led over wild country, but usually these were willingly made. Atkinson describes in his *Glossary of the Cleveland District* (1868) how on one occasion the bearers had to struggle through almost impassable masses of snow in order to follow the traditional road over the high moors; and in Scatcherd's *History of Morley* (1874) we are told that the people of Walton, near Wakefield, resolutely refused to use a much more convenient route to Sandal Church because a certain path over a field was the established Corpse Gate.

There were, however, times when floods or snowdrifts, or some other accident, forced a funeral procession to go another way, usually over private land. In such cases, it was firmly believed that a right of way was automatically created, not by mere tradition but by the law of the land. This belief has been responsible for fierce fights between mourners and the servants of landowners trying to protect their master's property. In a letter published in *The Times Literary Supplement* on 18 July 1918, a Westmorland correspondent stated that only twelve months before, he had been obliged to interfere when his mother's servants tried, with the best intentions, to stop a funeral passing over her property. In some counties, there are also stories, which may well be founded upon fact, of corpses being deliberately carried over private land for the express purpose of creating a right of way.

Usually, however, when it was absolutely necessary for a funeral to cross such land, those concerned tried, in one way or another, to protect the owner from the effects of the supposed law. In one Oxfordshire parish, during the early years of the present century, a coffin had to be taken down a private gated road. Every gate was carefully locked beforehand, and the keys were deposited in the owner's house. When the procession reached the first gate, one of the undertaker's men was sent up to the house for the keys. The gate was unlocked to allow the coffin and the mourners to pass through, and then locked again, the keys being returned to the house. By going through this lengthy procedure at each gate in turn, it was believed by all that the landowner's rights were preserved.

Another traditional method was for the undertaker to stick pins into every gate or stile on the way. In two West-country parishes, it was stated that the owners took a small fee from burial parties crossing their property. This was apparently thought sufficient to prevent a right of way there, but it does not seem to have been a common practice elsewhere.

In 1948, a man was drowned in Iffley Lock, near Oxford, and the police wished to carry the body over the privately-owned toll-bridge which connects the Lock with the village. Although they offered to pay for their passage, the bridge-keeper refused them permission, saying that if the corpse was carried over, the bridge would automatically be freed, and the owners, his employers, would not be able to charge a toll thereafter. In this parish it has long been customary, when anyone dies in the two or three houses on the other side of the river, to ferry the corpse over the water and land it a little below the church, so as to avoid going over the bridge. This custom still prevails, the latest funeral of this type being one in 1949.

The origin of this curious and widespread belief is very uncertain. It has no actual foundation in English law, as is often supposed, and in fact, no right of way is created by the passage of a corpse. Various explanations touching upon Roman and Hebrew usage have been suggested for it, together with the rather more likely theory that it comes from a confused memory of the old Corpse Roads. These by necessity often ran over private lands, but the dead were, by immemorial custom, allowed to pass over them to burial. From this, an idea might have arisen that their passage in itself created the right of way, and that such a right applied to any road they took, not only to the accepted Corpse Ways or Church Roads. Although these roads are not mentioned in Halsbury's *Laws of England*, it is stated there that the members of a funeral party could not be made to pay toll on a turnpike road when on their way to or from the funeral, a provision which presumably included the corpse as well as the mourners. This may have given rise to, or at least strengthened, the notion that the dead man destroyed the toll, as in the case of the Iffley Bridge.

Sailors commonly dislike carrying a corpse on board ship. It brings bad luck to the vessel and, when a death occurs at sea, it can usually be avoided by the ceremony of committing the body to the waters, with the appropriate service. If, however, it is absolutely necessary to bring the corpse home, then it must always lie athwart the vessel, and never 'end on'; and when the home port is reached, it must leave the ship before any member of the crew does so.

CAT

The cat has always had a very special place in folk-belief. At various times, and in different places, it has been regarded as a holy or a diabolical beast as a bringer of good fortune or as an omen of evil. In antiquity it was sacred to more than one divinity. The Egyptian Bast, or Pasht, was cat-headed and attended by cats, and consequently every member of the tribe was loved and venerated in ancient Egypt. To kill one was sacrilege. When a household pet died, its owner shaved off his eyebrows in token of mourning and performed funeral rites for it. The followers of Diana revered cats because they were under her special protection, and because she once assumed that form. So too, in pagan Scandinavia, Freya, the goddess of love and fertility, was associated with them, and her chariot was drawn by them. In almost every country where they were known, cats were believed to have mystical powers for good or evil and, among other gifts, to be able to see spirits, foretell the future by their actions, and control the weather.

In later times, they were connected in popular belief with witchcraft. It is usually supposed today that the witch's animal-familiar was always a cat, but in fact, the records of the trials show that this was not invariably the case. 'The witches have their spirits,' wrote George Giffard[1] in 1587, 'some hath one, some hath more, as two, three, four or five, some in one likeness and some in another, as like cats, weasels, toads or mice.' Any small creature that could be kept in a house was likely to be suspected, and at various times accused witches have confessed to having spirits in the form of cats, dogs, ferrets, rats, and even insects.

That they sometimes took cat-shape themselves was firmly believed and, again, sometimes confessed. Even as late as 1718, when the witchcraft-terror was dying out, William Montgomery of Caithness, declared that he was nightly harassed by hordes of these creatures, who gathered round his house and could be heard talking in human language. One night, he rushed out with a hatchet, killed two, and wounded several others. Next day, he was confirmed in his delusion by the news that two old women had been found dead in their beds, and another had a bad cut in her leg for which she could not, or would not, give any explanation.

In Britain, the black cat is generally considered lucky, and in some parts, the white cat is correspondingly unlucky. In the United States of America, as in Belgium, Spain, and some other European countries, a directly opposite belief prevails, a fact which has sometimes caused confusion and alarm to our American visitors who see us coaxing and cherishing a creature which to them is definitely ill-omened.

It is a very good sign if a black cat comes into a house or on board a ship, especially if it does so uninvited. It must never be chased away, or it will take the luck of the house or ship away with it. One of its functions is mentioned in the old saying that 'whenever the cat of the house is black, the lasses of lovers will have no lack'.

To meet a black cat is usually thought to be fortunate, especially if it runs across the path in front of the observer. There are, however, some variants of this belief. In East Yorkshire, while it is lucky to own a black cat, it is unlucky to meet one. In some districts, the good fortune will only come if the animal is stroked three times, or is politely greeted. Some say that the omen is bad if it crosses the path from left to right, or turns back on its tracks, or runs away from the person seeing it. To meet a white cat is ill-omened in any circumstances, except, of course, in America or the other countries where it is the traditional luck-bringer.

Tortoiseshells are lucky to their owners in Britain, as blues are in Russia. In Sussex and some other counties, a kitten born just after Michaelmas, when the blackberry season has ended, is called a blackberry-cat and is expected to be extremely mischievous in its youth. The same tradition applies to other

[1] George Giffard, *A Discourse on the subtile Practises of Deuilles by Witches and Sorcerers*, 1587.

young animals born at this time, and seems to be connected with the legend of the Devil's fall to Earth at Michaelmas and his spoiling of the blackberries then and ever since. *See Blackberries.* May-born kittens are sometimes said to be unlucky. *See May Kittens.*

If a cat leaves a house when there is illness within, and will not be coaxed back, the sick person will die, and so will he if he dreams of cats, or sees two fighting. It is often said that cats will temporarily desert a house while there is an unburied corpse in it, returning only after the funeral. If one jumps over the coffin, it is a bad omen for the dead man's soul unless the poor creature is killed at once.

If the household pet sneezes near the bride on her wedding-morning, she will have a happy married life. At other times, a cat's sneeze means rain, and if there are three sneezes, all the family will have colds before long. An old and cruel superstition said that when a cat fell ill, it should be put outside at once because its sickness, even if not infectious, would run right through the house. So too, a dying cat was often thrust outside for fear that Death, when it came for the animal, would stay for some member of the family also. In some northern districts, it is, or was, thought unlucky to 'flit a cat', that is, to take it along when moving from one house to another. Many a poor creature has been abandoned and left to fend for itself because of this idea.

Miners will not pronounce the word 'cat' when down the mine, and in Cornwall formerly, if one was found there, the men would not work on that level until it had been killed. Seamen also avoid the name when at sea, but to have a cat on board is lucky, especially if it is a black one without any white hairs on it. On the Yorkshire coast, if a fisherman's wife keeps a black cat in the house, her man will return safely from sea. Baker remarks in his *History of Scarborough* (1882) that in that town, 'this gave black cats such a value that no one else could keep them; they were always stolen'. To throw a cat overboard raises an immediate storm at sea; but few sailors would ever dream of doing such a thing to their luck-bringer, and it is extremely rare to hear of any shipwreck in which the cats are not among the first to be saved.

Actors say it is very ill-omened to kick a cat. It is lucky to have one about the theatre, but if one runs across the stage during a performance, some misfortune will follow.

When cats run about wildly, or claw at carpets and cushions, wind is coming. When they wash over their ears, rain is foretold, when they sit with their backs to the fire, frost, or in some districts, a storm.

A well-known cure for a stye in the eye is to stroke it with a black cat's tail (a tom cat for a woman, a queen for a man) and say,

I poke thee, I don't poke thee,
I poke the queff that's under the 'ee,
O qualyway, O qualyway!

drawing the tail downwards over the stye on each line of the verse. A dried catskin held to the face is a remedy for toothache, three drops of cat's blood smeared over it will cure a wart. Stroking with a tortoiseshell cat's tail also cures warts, but only in the month of May. In the seventeenth century, a cat's body, fur and all, if boiled in olive oil was considered an excellent dressing for wounds. A magical method of transferring any disease was to throw the water in which the patient had been washed over a cat, and then drive the creature from the house. *See Washing*.

CATTLE

In the days of Celtic heathendom, cattle were venerated as sacred animals in the British Isles, as they were in many other parts of the world. They were also believed to live in close sympathy with their owners, sharing their joys and sorrows. These ideas are reflected in many legends and superstitions which survived into Christian times and, in some cases, down to our own day.

One well-known and very widespread tradition says that cattle turn to the east as midnight strikes on Christmas Eve and kneel in adoration of the Christ Child, at whose birth their forefathers were present long ago. In some English districts, they are said to do so on Old Christmas Eve, 5 January, and this, like the blooming of the Holy Thorn on the same night, was formerly considered proof that the old date was the right one. Mrs Leather[1] mentions a Herefordshire farmer who saw his cattle kneeling then, with the tears streaming down their faces. She also tells us that at Weobley, only the three-year-old oxen were thought to kneel, but elsewhere in the county it was those aged seven who did so, because that was the age of the oxen in the stable at Bethlehem.

In some parts of Europe, cattle were believed to acquire the gift of speech on Christmas Eve. It was, however, dangerous for any human being to listen to their talk. Whoever did so would meet with misfortune, or perhaps, like the man in a French legend, he would hear them speaking of his own early death. If so, he would certainly die on the day named, however young and healthy he might be, for at that holy season the animals had foreknowledge, and knew what would occur on the farm during the coming year.

Along the Welsh Border, farmers and their families used to go to the byre on Twelfth Night and toast each ox by name in cider or strong ale. A cake with a hole in the centre was then hung on the horn of the first ox, and omens were read from the manner in which he tossed it. If he threw it off at once, it was a sign of general good luck. If he did not, he was tickled or pricked to make him do so, and according, as he tossed it behind or before him, the

[1] E. M. Leather, *op. cit.*

cake was claimed by the mistress or the bailiff, and with it the good fortune which it signified.

Many tales are told in England, Wales and Ireland of fairy cattle, and of magical cows which gave unlimited supplies of milk until their generosity was abused by some avaricious person. At Grimsargh in Lancashire, there was a legend that once, long ago, during a period of drought and famine, a gigantic dun cow appeared and saved the people from starvation by an unending flow of milk. But when a witch tried to get more than her share by milking her through a sieve, the cow died, either from grief at the trick or from exhaustion. The White Cow of Mitchel's Fold in Shropshire was of the same divine or fairy lineage, and so was the famous Dun Cow of Warwick who appears in tradition in various forms, as a magical milk-giver, as a monster slain by Guy of Warwick, and to this day, as a ghostly portent of death in the Earl of Warwick's family.

Although fairy cattle were sometimes dun, or red, or even, in one Irish case, sea-green, they were usually said to be white, with red ears. It may be that this belief is reflected in the ominous tradition of the Chartley cattle, which are almost white, with red ears, black muzzles, and black-tipped horns. The birth of a black calf from white parents in this herd was formerly said to be an omen of death in the Ferrers family, which owned it, and to have been so as far back as the reign of Henry III. Such births were recorded in 1827, 1835, and 1842, and in each case as many family deaths followed as there were black calves. The omen has now lost much of its force because the strain has become more mixed, and the appearance of black animals is less unusual than it once was.

Until well into the present century, it was considered very ill-omened to make an offer for any beast which was not for sale. The animal would fall ill immediately and would probably die. In some districts, it was thought unlucky to strike cattle with the human hand, 'the flesh of a sinner'. A stick should always be used, preferably one of ash-wood, or 'of no value', and when employed to drive cattle to summer pastures on the hills, it should be thrown after them when the journey is ended.

If straying cattle break into a garden or private enclosure, it is a death omen for someone in the garden-owner's family. As many animals as break in, so many deaths will there be within the year. In some parts of England it is thought that cattle, as well as bees and rooks, should be told of a death in the household. If this is not done, ill-luck will befall them, and one or more will die. A writer in Notes and Queries (4th series, Vol. IV) relates the story of a Yorkshire man in the North Riding who lost his wife and forgot to tell the one cow he owned. The creature died soon afterwards, and by common consent, her death was attributed to the fact that she had not been told of her master's loss.

Country people say that when cattle feed hard all together, or when they lie down in low pastures, rain is coming. If they stand or rest on high ground, the weather will be fine. *See Calf: Cow.*

CATTLE DISEASE

Cattle diseases, like those of human beings, were often attributed in the past to witchcraft, or the invisible wounds made by elfshots, and consequently many of the remedies employed were magical, or semi-magical, in character. Charms of all sorts were freely used to ward off any evil influences that might cause disease. Holed stones or horseshoes were hung over the byre-door for this purpose, or a written charm obtained from the local wisewoman or cunning-man might be concealed in the roof or under the floor. 'Wicken' (rowan-wood) crosses were fixed over the individual stalls and when need arose, charm-stones, such as the Clach Dearg, were sent for, sometimes from a considerable distance, and dipped in water which the animals subsequently drank.

These, and many similar protective devices, including the use of magical herbs, cold iron, holy water, incantations, or leaves from the Bible, were well known in farming circles from Anglo-Saxon times down to the late nineteenth century. Reginald Scot, in his *Discoverie of Witchcraft* (1584), describes a rite used in his day. Wax had to be taken from the Paschal Candle at Easter and moulded into a little candle, from which hot wax was dropped between the ears and horns of the beast. This had to be done early on a Sunday morning, the charmer invoking the Trinity as the drops fell. What was left of the wax was then set crosswise on the threshold or over the main door, so that all the animals had to pass over or under it as they went in and out. If this was done, says Scot, 'for all that year your cattle shall never be bewitched'.

A Yorkshire cure for diarrhoea, mentioned by F. K. Robinson in 1876[1] was to grind clay pipes and the lower jawbone of a pig to powder, and make a gruel from it which the sick animal ate. A quite common 'remedy' for blood-streaked milk was to milk the cow straight on to the floor. When troubles developed in the leg or foot of any beast, the first sod on which it trod in the morning was carefully dug up and turned over. This was said in Lincolnshire to be a certain cure.

In the Pendle district of Lancashire, when a beast died from hydrocephalus, its head was cut off and carried over the county boundary into Yorkshire and there buried, in the belief that the disease would thus be transferred from its place of origin to the next county. Other ailments were sometimes treated in the same way, the head or some other part being secretly buried on a neighbouring farm. When witchcraft was suspected, a little blood would be drawn from the sick animal and boiled. This was supposed to cause the witch intense agony, and force him or her to lift the

[1] F. K. Robinson, *A Glossary of Words used in the Neighbourhood of Whitby*, 1876.

spell. Or the blood, hair or urine of the beast might be mixed with salt or meal, and burnt with elaborate rites at midnight, care being taken to see that every window, door, and cranny of the house was closely sealed. In his *Forty Years in a Moorland Parish* (1892), J. C. Atkinson mentions a charm used by the celebrated Wiseman of Stokesley, John Wrightson, who practised his arts during the late eighteenth and early nineteenth century. A sheep's heart into which nine new pins, nine new needles and nine small nails had been thrust had to be burnt on a fire of coals and ash-wood, with some of the sick beast's hair and blood. While it burnt, certain psalms were read three times. The whole operation had to be performed at midnight behind closed doors, and to be finished by one o'clock in the morning. In most of these burning rites, it was believed that the witch would be drawn by an irresistible fascination to the house, but on no account must he or she be admitted, or the charm would not work.

In districts where ritual bonfires were customarily lit at Beltane or Midsummer, it was usual to drive the cattle over the embers to guard them from the dreadful cattle plague. Sometimes such fires were specially kindled to protect a particular parish or farm against an epidemic already raging in the neighbourhood. *See Needfire.* But when the disease came too near, or had actually invaded the farm, more drastic remedies were considered necessary. To save the rest of the herd, one animal not yet infected was sacrificed, sometimes in circumstances of shocking barbarity. To whom or to what this sacrifice was offered was rarely stated, and probably those who offered it were not very clear in their own minds on this point; but that the custom was a relic of straightforward paganism surviving well into the nineteenth century can hardly be doubted.

Heanley[1] tells us that in 1866, during an outbreak of cattle plague in the Lincolnshire marshes, a certain farmer killed one of his calves and buried it under the byre-threshold with its feet pointing upwards. Nevertheless, the plague came to his farm, as to all the others. Heanley's own cowman said this was only to be expected because the farmer had been too mean, and had killed a weakly animal which would probably have died in any case. He should have chosen his best. 'T'ain't in reason,' said the cowman, 'that old Skraat 'ud be hanselled wi' wankling draffle,' and evidently he was not, for the offering was obviously refused. But who Old Scrat was, whether Satan, or Odin, or Loki, or some even remoter spirit, was not explained.

In this instance, there was no suggestion of cruelty in the method of killing, but unfortunately, this was not always the case. Calves or oxen were sometimes burnt or buried alive to avert the plague or other diseases, or to save the herd from witchcraft. At Troutbeck about 1866 a butter-making farmer, whose cows had produced too many bull-calves, burnt a young bull alive in his barnyard. Twenty years earlier, an ox had been similarly sacrificed

[1] R. M. Heanley, *op. cit.*

at Haltwhistle in Northumberland to stop the spread of murrain. Similar atrocities have been recorded in Scotland, Wales, Cornwall, Northampton-shire, and the Isle of Man; and as late as 1876, the *West Cumberland Times* reported that a local farmer had buried a living calf in the sight of its mother in order to cure contagious abortion on his farm.

CAUFF-RIDDLING

Cauff-riddling was the Yorkshire name for a form of divination involving the use of chaff. The inquirer went at midnight on St Mark's Eve, New Year's Eve, or some other significant date, to a barn, leaving the doors wide open, and there riddled some chaff. If nothing was seen while he did so, the omen was good. If, however, he was destined to die that year, a coffin carried by two bearers would be seen passing the doors.

William Henderson[1] records an instance of the use of this divination some years before he wrote. A woman and two men went to a barn near Malton on St Mark's Eve and there performed the rite. The two men riddled the chaff in turn without result, but as soon as the woman began, the coffin and its bearers appeared. The men rushed out at once, but nothing was visible. The woman died within the year. Henderson adds that the story was related to his informant by someone who knew all the people concerned, and spoke of them by name.

CAUL

If a child is born with his head covered by the thin membrane commonly known as a caul, or a mask, he will be lucky in life and will never be drowned, provided the caul is kept. If he travels by sea and takes it with him, the ship that carries him will not be wrecked. If he becomes a lawyer, he will be eloquent and successful in his cases. In Holland, a person so born can see ghosts; in Scotland, and also in Iceland, he will have Second Sight and be free from the power of sorcerers and fairies. The general English belief in the fortunate properties of the caul is reflected in its north-country name, *Sillyhow*, which means blessed or happy hood.

It is not, however, enough merely to be born with a caul. It must be carefully preserved, for if it is lost or thrown away, its life-saving and luck-bringing powers are lost with it. If it is sold, they pass to the buyer. Cauls were, and still are, quite frequently sold to sailors, who thus seek to purchase immunity from drowning. Modern instances are known of as much as £20 being given for one, and even in 1813, when the value of money was greater, *The Times* published an advertisement stating that a caul was available for twelve guineas. Another advertisement in the same newspaper, dated 8 May

[1] Wm. Henderson, *op. cit.*

1848, asked six guineas, and added that the caul 'for which fifteen pounds was originally paid, was afloat with its late owner thirty years in all the perils of a seaman's life, and the owner died at last at the place of his birth'. In 1944 an Oxfordshire woman was offered £10 for her child's caul by the midwife, who wanted it for a sailor friend. The mother refused, preferring to keep the luck and safety for her own little boy.

It is, of course, considered very unlucky to throw away or destroy a caul deliberately. An article in *Folk-Lore* (Vol. 68, 1957) mentions a Somerset woman in the early years of this century who kept her child's caul until he was two years old. She was then persuaded by some friends to throw it away, and very soon afterwards the child was drowned in a shallow pond. No doubt this was simply a tragic coincidence; but almost everyone in the village where it happened was convinced that the accident would not have occurred had the caul been kept. In some parts of England, it is said that if anyone parts with, or loses, the caul with which he was born, he will lose the power of staying quietly at home, and will be forced to wander in later life, whether he wants to do so or not.

Henderson[1] records a case that came to his notice in the 'sixties of last century, where the caul seems to have been used as a warning agent. A girl who had been born with one kept it stretched out in paper in her chest of drawers, and regularly consulted it in times of doubt or difficulty. If all was going well, it remained smooth and unchanged, but whenever danger threatened, it was found to have shrivelled. If she was about to fall ill, it became damp, and if anyone was traducing her, it rustled. When she cut her hair, it changed colour and seemed uneasy. She believed it would disappear when she died. This last was not a usual belief. In many districts, it was thought that a caul must be buried with its owner, otherwise the dead person could not rest in his grave. His ghost would return to search for it, an idea reminiscent of the numerous stories of beheaded persons searching for their heads, and perhaps an extension of the widely held notion that a corpse must be complete on burial. *See Burial, Complete.*

CELANDINE

Celandine was sometimes called Swallow-wort because of the old belief, mentioned by Pliny, that swallows used this plant to cure dim sight in their young. John Gerard denies this in his *Herbal*, but he says the herb is good for the eyes of human beings, and also for those of hawks, an important matter in the days when hawking was a favourite pastime.

In folk-medicine, celandine was used to heal jaundice because its flowers, like the disease, are yellow. The bruised leaves laid upon the affected part were thought to cure ringworm, and the expressed juice, taken when fasting,

[1] Wm. Henderson, *op. cit.*

to avert infection. A remedy for warts, recorded in Oxfordshire as still in use in 1931, was to rub them with the juice.

CHAIR

In East Anglia, it is considered unlucky for a visitor, on leaving the house, to put the chair on which he has been sitting back against the wall of the room. If he does so, he will never come to that house again.

If a nurse accidentally overturns a chair in the ward, a new patient will arrive very shortly.

CHALICE

The chalice used in the Sacrament of Holy Communion was formerly believed to have the power of healing those who approached it reverently, and also of bringing a curse upon anyone who misused it. The latter belief was very strong amongst thieves at one time. It was usually considered unlucky to steal anything from a church, but nothing was so dangerous as a stolen chalice. Although these vessels are commonly made of precious metals and are easily portable, cases of their theft were once very rare, since only the most hardened and sceptical robbers dared to take the risks involved.

A cure for whooping-cough recorded in Yorkshire about the middle of last century was to take the afflicted children to a Roman Catholic convent or presbytery and allow them to drink holy water out of a chalice. They were strictly forbidden to touch the vessel, which was held to their lips by the priest. An interesting detail about this remedy was that, although it was resorted to by Protestants as well as Catholics, only a chalice used in Roman Catholic services was considered efficacious. The same cure is said to have been tried in Coventry during the early years of the present century.

Anything that had been in contact with a chalice was also thought to have healing power. In her *Rustic Speech and Folklore* (1913), Elisabeth Wright mentions the case of a Liverpool woman who burnt her hand badly in 1910. Her landlady, who was a church cleaner, cured the burn by binding it with an old chalice veil.

CHARM WANDS

Glass wands, shaped like a walking-stick with a curved handle and having hair lines in the glass, or rods filled with a multitude of small coloured seeds, are now sometimes seen in houses where they are kept as curios or ornaments. Formerly, however, they were hung up as a protection against witchcraft and evil spirits. It was believed that any entering demon or witch would be forced to count the lines or seeds during the hours of darkness, and would be prevented, while doing so, from enchanting or injuring any person or thing in the house. Disease and infections were similarly supposed to fly to the wand and to be held there. In the morning, the evil influences could be harmlessly wiped away with a cloth.

If such a charm-wand was accidentally broken, the omen was bad, and illness or misfortune of some kind was expected to follow.

CHICORY

Chicory was believed to have the power of making its possessor invisible. It also shared with moonwort and springwort the perhaps more useful gift of opening locked doors or boxes if it was held against the locks. These charms, however, would only work if the plant was gathered at noon or at midnight on St James's Day (July 25th). It had to be cut with gold, and in perfect silence; if the gatherer spoke during the operation, he would die, either at once or shortly afterwards. Another odd property of the herb is mentioned in Dyett's *Dry Dinner* (1599), where it is stated that 'it hath bene and yet is a thing which superstition hath beleeved, that the body anoynted with the juyce of chicory is very availeable to obtaine the favour of great persons'.

Chicory perhaps owes its magical reputation to the lovely blue of its flower, which may have caused it to be identified or confused with the famous Luck-Flower of German folklore. That also was blue and, usually, of unstated species. Whoever carried it could make rocks open before him, and so gain entry into the subterranean regions beyond. Several legends relate how some bold adventurer came thus to an unknown cavern, and there found gold and jewels which he was allowed to take for himself. In most versions of this tale, the ending is tragic because the man, excited by so much sudden wealth, forgets the all-important flower when he leaves. The rocks close upon him as he passes through them to the outer world, and either injure him seriously, so that he is a cripple for the rest of his life, or kill him outright.

CHILD, CRAWLING

A widespread country tradition says it is very unlucky to step over a young child as it crawls about the floor. To do so stunts its growth.

CHILD'S FIRST DAYS

Many precautions and luck-bringing customs were formerly observed during the first days of a new-born baby's life, both to protect him from immediate evil during the perilous period between birth and baptism, and to ensure his good fortune in later life. Most of these have died out now, perhaps because so many children are born in hospitals, where there is neither time nor inclination for magical rites. Many were, however, kept up until the beginning of the present century, and a few are still observed occasionally in households where childbirth normally occurs at home.

The perils of witchcraft and of fairies were averted in Scotland and some parts of northern England by 'saining' mother and child. This was done by carrying lighted candles round the bed in which they lay or, in some more devout households, by carrying an open Bible round it. In almost all districts, charm-objects of various kinds were put into the cradle, see Cradle, especially before baptism. In Yorkshire, a new-born baby was laid in the arms of a maiden before anyone else had touched him. In Cumberland, immediately after birth, the top of his head was washed with rum to bring him good luck, and if he happened to be born on a Friday, he was then laid upon a Bible. In Suffolk, his head was washed with gin, to ensure a good complexion. His first real bath in the West of England was given, whenever possible, before an ash-wood fire. See Ash.

In most districts, it was considered very unlucky if the first covering put upon him was new. He had first to be wrapped in something old, and only after that could the fine new clothes prepared for him by his mother during her pregnancy be used. For this reason, the midwife usually brought an old petticoat or some similar garment, with her when she was summoned to a confinement.

In many parts of England, a baby was given Cinder Tea as soon as possible after birth, that is, water into which a red-hot cinder had been dropped. Along the Welsh Border, the first food given was often honey (or if that could not be obtained, moist sugar) mixed with butter. Both these were said to be good for the child's health, but they also had magical significance, the cinder being a symbol of life-giving fire, and the honey deriving strengthening and sweetening properties from the bees who made it. See Bees. Among the pagan Norsemen, and also in Ireland, honey was given to a boy-baby on the tip of his father's sword, so that he might grow up a strong and brave fighter. In the Scottish Highlands formerly, the nurse took a green ash-stick and held one end in the fire until the sap oozed out from the other. This sap she collected in a spoon and gave it, alone or mixed with honey, to the child as his first food, both to strengthen him physically and to protect him from fairies. In some English districts, when a new-born baby seemed restless and made sucking movements with his lips, he was given a little jelly made from the brains of hares.

A very common belief was that the child must always be carried upstairs before he was taken down. His first journey in this world must be upwards, otherwise he would not rise in life or, according to another and probably later version, he would be unable to reach Heaven after death. If the birth-chamber was at the top of the house, so that it was impossible to go higher, the nurse could overcome the difficulty by mounting on a box or a low stool with the child in her arms. In some districts, it was considered that his first descent, his first journey into the outside world, and his mother's first appearance after her confinement should take place on a Sunday.

The first gift made to a newly-born child is often a silver sixpence. In Oxfordshire, it is still quite usual to give such a coin to any baby seen for the first time, whether the giver knows his parents or not. It has to be put into his right hand, and at one time, omens were read from the manner in which he grasped it. If he held it tightly, it was a sign he would save money when he was older, and perhaps be a miser. If he held it loosely, he would be generous, and if he dropped it, he would be a spendthrift.

In northern England, salt, an egg, bread, and a box of matches were often given as well as the sixpence. The matches, which symbolized fire, and the salt were safeguards against evil, and the food and money were charms to ensure that the new-born child would never come to want. These gifts were sometimes brought by people who came to visit his mother, but more usually, they were given when he was first taken to another house. Hence, he did not receive them until after he was baptized, because to take a child out of doors before he went to his christening was widely considered to be extremely unlucky.

In East Anglia, the first kiss received from anyone except the baby's mother was thought to influence the child in later life, according to the character of the person who gave it. Great care had therefore to be taken to see that it was bestowed by someone known to be good-tempered and kind, so that the baby might grow up with the same good qualities. That this might sometimes be difficult to accomplish is obvious, and evidently it was not always possible, for Mark Taylor[1] records one case when he was told by a lady that 'her old nurse was much disturbed because the wrong person had kissed and so "tempered" the baby'.

CHILDERMAS

Childermas is the old name for Holy Innocents Day (28 December), when the slaughter of the children by King Herod's orders is commemorated. For many centuries, it was considered to be the unluckiest day of the year, when nothing of importance was attempted, and as little work as possible was done. Edward IV's coronation was postponed because the Sunday originally chosen was found to coincide with Childermas. Aubrey tells us in his *Miscellanies* that Louis XI of France would never attend to any business

[1] Mark Taylor, 'Norfolk Folklore', *Folk-Lore*, Vol. 40, 1929.

on that anniversary. He 'used not to debate any matter, but counted it a sign of great misfortune towards him, if any man communed with him of his affairs; and would be very angry with those about him, if they troubled him with any matter whatsoever on that day'.

This belief still lingered in some parts of Britain at the beginning of the present century. No new work or enterprise begun on Childermas was thought likely to prosper. New clothes should not be put on for the first time, fingernails should not be pared, and no household washing, scrubbing, or scouring should be done. In Ireland, thread was never warped on what was locally called 'the cross day of the year'. It was, of course, unlucky for births and marriages, and for the start of journeys, especially by sea. The weekday on which it fell was also unlucky throughout the following year.

An exception to this widespread tradition of misfortune is recorded by William Henderson,[1] who says that in Lancashire, Childermas was considered an appropriate day for children's parties. In the Middle Ages, it was the last day of the Boy Bishop's reign, which began on St Nicholas's Day (6 December). For him and his followers, it was therefore part of a high festival season; but Gregory in his account of the Boy Bishop ceremonies[2] remarks that other children were ceremonially beaten then, 'that the memorie of this murther might stick the closer; and, in a moderate proportion, to act over the crueltie again in kind'.

CHIMNEYSWEEP

The chimneysweep, by virtue of his blackened face and his connexion with fire and the hearth, is a very lucky person to meet by chance. He should be bowed to, or otherwise greeted; in some districts, it is customary to spit and wish on seeing him, and those who do so confidently believe that the wish will be granted. If he meets a bridal procession on its way to or from the church, it is a very good omen for the married pair, and doubly so if he offers good wishes, or walks a little way beside the bride. From time to time, Press photographs of such fortunate wedding encounters appear in the newspapers. This is a sure sign that the tradition is still very much alive, since no editor is likely to waste his space upon pictures that have no interest or meaning for his readers.

In all such luck-bringing meetings, however, whether at weddings or elsewhere, it is essential that when first seen, the chimneysweep should be coming towards the observer. If he is walking away, so that only his back is visible, the omen is bad. He must also be 'in his blacks', that is, he must be returning from his work with soot-begrimed face and clothes. There is no magical virtue in a sweep with a clean face.

[1] Wm. Henderson, *op. cit.*   [2] *Episcopus Puerorum in Die Innocentium*, 1684.

CHOUGH

In Cornwall Arthur is said to live on in the form of a chough, and for this reason it was formerly considered very unlucky indeed almost sacrilegious, to kill it. A similar belief was held about the raven.

CHRISTMAS GREENERY

The decoration of houses at Christmas with evergreens, the symbols of enduring and renewed life, is a direct descendant of a very ancient, pre-Christian, luck-bringing custom. Long before the Christian era, men brought in green branches at the Winter Solstice as a magical rite to ensure the return of vegetation. In the hey-day of the Roman Empire, every house was hung with laurel and bay at the Kalends of January, the New Year festival. So also, Christian people in their turn adorned their homes for their own mid-winter feast, and from very early times used for this purpose not only the holly, ivy and mistletoe that we know, but also rosemary, bay, laurel, and, as Stow says, 'whatsoever the season affordeth to be greene'.

So ancient and magical a custom naturally has its surviving superstitions. By long tradition it is unlucky to bring evergreens in before Christmas Eve, for that would be to anticipate the festival, or to take them down before Twelfth Night. To throw them away too soon is to throw away life and prosperity, and may cause a death in the family. Of late years a belief has grown up that it is unlucky to leave them hanging after Epiphany Eve (5 January), but this seems to be a modern notion, perhaps springing from the general shortening of the festive season, and a desire to be rid of branches that have become dry and dusty. The older tradition was that they must come down by Candlemas, the day on which the wider ecclesiastical Christmas season ends. To leave them after that was very unlucky, but until then there was no danger, and it was quite usual at one time to keep them until the later date. It was of Candlemas, not of Twelfth Night, that Herrick sang three hundred years ago:

> Down with Rosemary and Bayes,
> Down with Mistleto . . .

Ideas about the disposal of Christmas evergreens once they are down vary in different districts. In some, they must be ceremonially burnt. In others, it is unlucky to burn them; they must be thrown away and left to wither. Nowhere is it permissible to burn any such branches, and particularly the holly, while they are still green, though after hanging in hot rooms for twelve days or longer, there is little danger that they will be. But if by some chance a sprig or bough has retained its freshness and is burnt, a death in the family is likely to follow.

Very often, when the rest have been removed, a bunch is kept back, to bring good luck to the house throughout the year, and preserve it from lightning. *See Holly: Ivy: Mistletoe: Yew*.

CHURCHING OF WOMEN

A belief that it is unlucky for a woman after childbirth to leave her house for any purpose before she goes to be churched is still very much alive in many parts of Britain. If she does so, she will meet with misfortune, and she will also bring bad luck to any person she meets, or house that she enters. At one time, access to any home was often denied to her, forcibly, if necessary, and even today, she is frequently an unwelcome visitor. Henderson[1] states that in northern England during the nineteenth century, it was firmly believed that if she ventured out before going to be churched, she had no remedy at law if anyone insulted or attacked her.

In 1952, the vicar of an Oxfordshire parish stated that none of his parishioners ever dreamt of breaking this rule, and that women who never normally went to church quite frequently asked him to perform the ceremony as quickly as possible, so that they might be free to go out and do their household shopping. Many other clergymen, in both town and country parishes, have had similar requests made to them. Edward Peacock[2] records that in Lincolnshire during last century, it was considered not only unlucky but downright sinful for any mother to go out before being churched. When the ceremony had been performed, she was spoken of as being 'clean'.

In some districts still, there is a tradition that if an unchurched woman visits a house, the woman of that house will have a child within the year.

Along the Welsh border, it was formerly considered ill-omened, or at least, incorrect, for the husband to be present at his wife's churching. If he insisted on coming, he must not sit in the same pew with her.

The Christian service of Churching is a form of thanksgiving for safe delivery, and no suggestion of ritual uncleanness after childbirth attaches to it. In pagan and Biblical times, however, a woman was deemed to be 'unclean' after a birth, and therefore dangerous to herself and others, until she had been purified, and long after the advent of Christianity, she was thought specially liable to the attacks of demons, fairies, and all the forces of evil. The modern superstitions mentioned above represent the last stages of these archaic and half-forgotten ideas.

[1] Wm. Henderson, *op. cit.*
[2] E. Peacock, *A Glossary of Words used in the Wapentakes of Manley & Corringham, Lincolnshire*, 1877.

CHURCHYARD WATCHER

In many parts of Britain, and also in Brittany, it was believed that when a man was buried, he became the Watcher of the Churchyard until such time as he was relieved of his task by the interment of another corpse. A variant of this tradition was that he who was first buried in any year became the Watcher, and served in that capacity for twelve months after his funeral. Until that time had passed, or until he was released by the next burial, he could not go to his rest, and was compelled to guard the graves in the churchyard and to summon all those in the parish who were about to die.

This belief was once very firmly held in Ireland and the Scottish Highlands, and lingered on in both countries until a comparatively late date. It sometimes led to unseemly incidents when two funerals were timed to take place close together. If the two processions approaching the graveyard came within sight of each other, it was not unknown for the horses to be whipped into a gallop, or for the bearers to break into a run, as both parties raced to be first in at the gates. Occasionally, quite fierce fights broke out, each set of mourners striving desperately to hold back the other while their dead kinsman was rushed to the holy ground and so saved from the consequences of being the last buried. Nevertheless, one corpse or the other had to be the last, and upon him fell the weary task of watching, and of calling those who were destined to join him in the churchyard during his term of office.

When the Watcher summoned the dying, he travelled by night through the countryside in a cart, the sound of which was a sure omen of death. It was never seen, but it could be heard trundling and creaking along the lanes and roads, halting outside some house for a while, and then going on again. When that happened, a death in the house was held to be certain before long. If someone within was already ill, he died while the cart stood outside, and his soul went away with it when it started once more.

A somewhat similar vehicle was the Death Coach, of which many tales are still told in the English West-country and in Wales. This, however, unlike the Watcher's cart, was visible, all black, and driven usually by a headless coachman. Occasionally, the Devil drove it, or it might have as passenger some named ghost, such as that of Lady Howard who was supposed to fetch the souls of the dying in the neighbourhood of Okehampton. Stories of notorious sinners whose spirits were carried away in black coaches driven by a mysterious being, probably the Devil, are common all over England.

In Brittany, the summoner of the dead was called the Ankou. He too went about in a cart, sometimes visiting houses, sometimes stopping to touch with an invisible hand any belated traveller he might meet on the roads. Such a man saw nothing, but he felt a strong shudder go through his body, and knew that he was doomed. If the encounter occurred late at night, he had still a few months, or even as much as two years, to live, but if it happened early, he would die within a few days or weeks. In any case, death could not be long delayed, for the Ankou's touch was fatal.

Although the Ankou was often said to be the last man buried, and therefore a Christian soul, other and more terrifying explanations were sometimes given for his existence. Some said he was a spirit specially created by God to summon the dying, and therefore, though dreaded, he was a friend rather than an enemy of mankind. Others said he was Adam's eldest son, condemned by his father's sin to lead men to the grave, or the soul of a man who blasphemously denied God while he lived, and was henceforth compelled to serve Death for evermore. It seems probable that originally it was Death himself who thus drove about the Breton lanes, usually invisible, but sometimes manifesting himself in the form of a skeleton, or of an old man with white hair, tall and very thin, and wearing a flat broad-brimmed hat.

This seems the more likely because, according to some accounts, he was not, like his British counterpart, concerned only with those whose death was already certain. He himself caused their deaths. He took whom he would, going about with a scythe which he swept continually to right and left, mowing down all who were unlucky enough to come within its orbit. This freedom of choice appears again in a legend concerning a pit in the Bois de Huëlgoat, which was said to be one of the mouths of Hell. Here the Ankou had a palace which was always brilliantly lit by thousands of candles. Each candle was a human life. When he was tired of roaming the countryside, the Ankou spent his leisure hours going round and round the palace, blowing out the flames at random, sometimes two or three or more together, as his fancy dictated.

CIGARETTES

A common modern superstition, which seems to have flourished first among soldiers and to have spread from them to civilians, is that it is unlucky to light three cigarettes from a single match, the consequent misfortune falling chiefly upon the person whose cigarette is the last to be lit. Even those who do not believe it often acknowledge its existence by inquiring of a friend to whom the last light is offered whether he or she 'minds being the third'. In one notable instance, however, it was not the last but the first of the trio who suffered. According to a story published in the *Weekly Despatch* of 31 October, 1920, when King Alexander of Greece dined aboard H.M.S. *Ramillies*, one match was used to light his cigar and those of his aide-de-camp and the Captain. The King remarked, 'Before the year is out, one of us three is doomed to die.' This, of course, was a joke; but a few days later, he was bitten by a monkey and died from the effects of the bites.

Various explanations are given for this widespread belief which, in its present form, is obviously not very old, since cigarettes were not fashionable until towards the end of the nineteenth century. One is that during the trench warfare of 1914–18, the passage of a lighted match attracted the attention of a sniper in the opposite trench, and just gave him enough time to shoot the third man. Another puts its origin back to the sharpshooters of the Boer War, and it is a fact, recorded by veterans of that war, that the superstition was rife in the Army then. But the tradition that it is ill-omened to light three candles or lamps with one taper existed long before either of these wars were fought. *See Candles.* It is mentioned at least as far back as the seventeenth century, and is probably much older. It would seem, therefore, that the cigarette superstition is simply a modern variant of an ancient conception, providing yet another example of the well-known power of folk-belief to change in detail while remaining the same in essence.

CLACH DEARG

The Clach Dearg, or Stone of Ardvorlich, belonging to the ancient Scottish family of Stewart of Ardvorlich, was long famous for its healing powers, particularly in diseases of cattle. It is a ball of clear rock crystal, set in four silver bands, and is supposed to have been brought to Scotland from the East.

Like several other charms of this kind, it was used in conjunction with water. The latter acquired curative powers after the Stone had been dipped into it, and was then given to the afflicted person or animal to drink. The seeker had to draw the water himself and bring it into the house where the Stone was. When the dipping ceremony had been performed, the water was bottled and carried away. If it was taken into any other house on the way home, its virtue was lost, and it was therefore essential to leave the bottle outside, should any visit have to be paid on the return journey.

CLERGYMEN AND NUNS

As long ago as the twelfth century, Bartholomew Iscanus, Bishop of Exeter, ordained penalties in his *Poenitentiale* for those who believed that good or evil could come to them from hearing jackdaws and ravens croak, or from 'meeting a priest'. He might have been discouraged, if not very surprised, could he have known that this old belief would still be alive six hundred years later. Old-fashioned fishermen in many areas think it unlucky to meet a clergyman of any denomination when they are on their way to the boats, or to see one standing near their vessels. Many will turn back at once, and either start out again later or remain ashore for the rest of that day.

The word 'minister' must not be spoken at sea, nor should the church, chapel, or manse be mentioned. Clergymen are often unpopular passengers on board ship, and bad weather or, if it is a fishing-boat, poor hauls, are sometimes ascribed to their presence. In 1920, when a liner bound for Canada developed a heavy rolling motion, with consequent general sea-sickness among the passengers, the inconvenience was put down to the fact that there were several Trappist monks on board.[1] In the Faroes, where whale-hunting is of great importance, if a boat containing a minister gets between the whales and the shore, the hunt will not be successful.

Hamilton Jenkins records in his *Cornwall and the Cornish* (1932) that at a Methodist conference held in West Cornwall not long before he wrote, a strong protest was made concerning the disrespectful behaviour of the local children. It was said that they 'touched cold iron' as soon as they saw any of the ministers assembled for the conference, thereby implying that they were unlucky and dangerous people to meet. Probably they did it as a joke; but there may also have been a lurking half-belief in their minds, surviving from earlier times. Certainly the method of protection used was in accordance with very ancient tradition.

Nuns are sometimes said to be ill-omened passengers in aeroplanes, but usually to meet or see them is a lucky sign rather than the reverse. The writer of an article in *Folk-Lore*[2] was told in 1926 by her South London char-woman that the latter's son, who had been unemployed for seven weeks, had just found work after seeing two nuns walking up the road. She was with him when he saw them, and told him good luck would follow, only he must come indoors at once so as to avoid seeing their backs after they had passed. Elsewhere three walking together have been recorded as fortunate, but not if they are walking away from the observer. In some districts, it is usual to spit on seeing a nun, but whether to avert evil or to increase the good luck (as in the case of a piebald horse seen on the road) is not clear.

These beliefs have nothing to do with anti-clerical feeling or its opposite, and those who hold them are sometimes religiously inclined and sometimes not. They seem to spring from a time when whatever was holy and con-secrated was thought to be a centre of mystical power, beneficent or otherwise as the case might be, but certainly beyond the control of ordinary men. In the case of the seamen's superstitions, there may also be traces of Christianity's early days, when many had a foot in both camps, acknow-ledging Christ on shore, but still putting the old gods first when out on the perilous sea.

CLOCK

Clocks which mark the passage of time from the cradle to the grave and are so intimately associated with the lives of men, are sometimes thought to

[1] Personal communication from one of the passengers to the Editor.

[2] Mrs E. Wright, 'Scraps of English Folklore, XV. London'. *Folk-Lore*, Vol 37, 1926,

have knowledge of what has happened, or is about to happen, in a house or parish.

A sudden change in the rhythm of the ticking is usually considered a death omen, especially if the ticking becomes faster. If a clock strikes thirteen or, having been left unwound, suddenly chimes or strikes of itself, a death is certainly foretold. Numerous stories are related of clocks stopping for no apparent reason when the owner dies. In some areas, they are artificially stopped as soon as death has occurred, for the dead man has nothing more to do with time.

The striking of a church clock during the sermon, or during the last hymn, predicts a death in the parish within the week. Similarly, if it strikes while the bell is being tolled for a funeral, another funeral will follow shortly. It is a bad omen if it strikes during a marriage ceremony; if there is any danger of this, the bride should wait outside until the chimes have sounded. In Wales, if the town clock strikes while the church bells are ringing, there will be a fire soon afterwards.

At St Mary's Church, Reading, the old clock, now replaced, was said to have been cursed by a man unjustly condemned for a crime he did not commit, and consequently it never went well. The present clock, its successor, evidently did not inherit the curse, for it is quite dependable.

CLOTHES

Clothes, both ceremonial and everyday, are so very closely connected with their wearer that it is hardly surprising to find them surrounded by a variety of superstitions, many of which are still vigorously alive. It is lucky to put a garment on inside out when dressing, if it is done accidentally, but it must be left as it is and worn inside out, otherwise the luck will be changed. On the other hand, to do up buttons or hooks wrongly is unlucky, and in this case, the garment must be taken right off and put on anew, to avert the evil omen.

To mend clothes whilst wearing them is always unfortunate. In some districts it is said to be a death omen, in others, a sign that the mender will make enemies, or come to want. In mending, as in dressmaking, the use of black or dark thread on light-coloured materials is very unlucky.

When putting on new clothes for the first time, it is usual to make a wish. If there is a pocket, a coin should be put into it at once, to ensure plenty of money whilst wearing the coat or dress in the future. Children appearing in new clothes are often pinched by their companions, while some sort of rhyming formula is recited, like

> Health to wear it,
> Strength to tear it,
> And money to buy another.

New clothes should be (and usually are) worn at Easter, otherwise the crows will befoul the old ones, and more serious bad luck will follow. A whole new outfit is, of course, the ideal to be aimed at but if this cannot be afforded, then a hat, a pair of gloves, a scarf, or even a pair of new shoe-laces will serve. In some districts, this custom is observed at Whitsun, or at Christmas. In an article contributed to *Folklore* (1958)[1] Alan Smith says that in East London it is quite usual for children to take a day's holiday from school before Easter, and again before Christmas, in order to buy the necessary new clothes for these festivals.

The clothes of the dead are commonly said to wear badly when given away, or worn by the heirs. They fret for their former owner and have no staying power, even when they are comparatively new. In his *English Folklore* (1928) A. R. Wright records the case of a man who disappeared from Heywood in Lancashire, and was presumed by his family to be dead because his clothes began to rot. He returned, however, some five years later, and was fined for desertion. The detail about his clothes came out in evidence during the court case.

When tramps and beggars were more numerous than they are now, many otherwise charitable people thought it unlucky to give them old clothes unless they knew them well. This reluctance to give clothes to a stranger almost certainly sprang from a half-forgotten fear of witchcraft, one of the principles of which was that anything that had once been in contact with an individual could afterwards be used to affect him for good or evil, even from a distance and when the physical contact had been completely broken. Rags from a dress or coat, an old glove, anything once worn and now discarded could be used in malicious spells, or to strengthen the power for harm of a wax or clay image. *See Images*. Similarly, the clothes of a living person, if secretly buried in a grave, would cause him to pine away and die of some wasting disease as the garments mouldered in the earth. When Agnes Sampson,[2] of North Berwick, was tried for witchcraft in 1590, she confessed amongst other things, that she had asked one, John Ker, to obtain for her some part of James VI's clothing. With this and the venom of a toad, she intended to injure the King magically. Ker refused; but in her confession she averred that if she had been able to get even a piece of linen which the King had worn and soiled, 'she had bewitched him to death, and put him to such extraordinarie paines, as if he had been lying upon sharp thornes and ends of needles'.

CLOVER

Clover was one of the anti-witch plants which protected human beings

[1] Alan Smith, 'Notes on the Folk-Life of the East London Child', *Folklore*, Vol. 69. 1958.
[2] *Newes from Scotland* . . . London. 1591.

and animals from the spells of magicians and the wiles of fairies, and brought good luck to those who kept it in the house, or wore it in their buttonholes or hats. It could be used in love-divination; and to dream of it was very fortunate for young people, since such a dream foretold a happy and prosperous marriage.

Although all clover had these magical properties, it was the rare four-leaved kind that was especially powerful. Such a plant, when found, enabled the finder to see fairies, detect witches, and recognize evil spirits. Anyone wearing the four-branched leaf was safe from malicious enchantments, and one hidden in the cow-byre or dairy prevented witches from harming the milk-supply or the butter. If a girl wore such a leaf in her right shoe, the first man she met on her first journey with it would be her future husband, or if not he, then another man of the same name.

There is a story in the *Denham Tracts* of a Northumberland girl who, when returning from milking, saw fairies dancing in the field. No one else could see them, though she pointed them out. She was not normally second-sighted, and it was afterwards discovered that the source of her vision lay in the circular pad she wore on her head to support the milk-pail. Amongst the grasses with which it was stuffed was a four-leaved clover.

COAL

Coal, which is a symbol of fire and therefore both fortunate and protective, is one of the luck-bringing gifts which the First Foot carries with him when he enters the house as the first visitor of the New Year. If there is no First Foot available to perform this office, the householder himself should bring in a little coal before doing anything else on New Year's morning. It must be carried through the front door and come from outside; it is not sufficient to bring it up from an indoor cellar to the kitchen or living-room. For this reason, a supply is often stacked in readiness just by the door on the previous night. The proper observance of this ritual ensures prosperity for the family throughout the year.

In Lincolnshire, a lump of coal is sometimes put among the other gifts in the Christmas stocking. If the recipient spits on it, throws it on the fire, and makes a wish while it burns, that wish will be granted.

It is usually thought lucky to find a piece of coal lying on the road, but only if it is picked up. In some districts it is considered necessary to spit on it, throw it over the left shoulder and then walk on without looking back. Here too, a wish formed while this is being done will be fulfilled, soon or eventually. Elsewhere it is enough to take the piece home, but on no account must it be left where it lies without some notice being taken of it. To do this is to leave one's luck behind.

Pieces of coal, chance-found or given, are still very often carried about as amulets. In their *Lore and Language of School-children* (1959), Iona and Peter Opie state that children frequently take a piece with them when sitting for an examination. Soldiers have been known to carry small lumps into battle, in order to ensure survival, and burglars also are said to do the same when they are 'working', as a charm against detection and arrest. Along the southern and western coasts of England, a sure way to bring luck to a sailor is to give him a piece of coal that has come from the sea, that is, one found lying on the sands where the tides have washed over it or, better still, a piece dropped from some ship and brought ashore by the tide. *For omens connected with coal when burning, see Hearth.*

COBWEB

A thick cobweb applied to a cut is commonly said to be the quickest way to stop the bleeding. Many people still resort to this rough-and-ready method of first aid, which is in fact quite often effective, provided the cut is not too deep, and the user can bring himself to disregard the dust that probably hangs about the web. Housewives have even been known to leave a few cobwebs in some corner of an otherwise spotless house, in order to have one ready in time of need.

Cobwebs were also used occasionally to cure other ills besides cuts. When ague was very prevalent, they were rolled into pills and swallowed by the patient to obtain relief during an attack. Within this century, similar pills have been used to relieve asthma and to prevent sleeplessness. In his *History of Four-Footed Beasts and Serpents*, Topsel mentions a magical remedy for warts. 'Some chirurgeons there be,' he says, 'that cure warts in this manner; they take a spider's web, rolling the same up on a round heap like a ball, and laying it upon the wart; they then set fire on it, and so burn it to ashes, and by this way and order the warts are eradicated, that they never after grow again.'

While the cobweb's traditional power to allay bleeding is based to some extent upon fact, it is probable that belief in its curative value for other ailments is due to its connexion with the spider, an insect which appears in a variety of healing charms, and is the centre of many old legends, Christian, Mahommedan, and pagan. *See Spider.*

COCK

The cock is a bird of many legends. Almost everywhere, it is a sun-bird because it crows to herald the dawn and bears a flaming red comb which signifies the sun. It is the enemy of ghosts and evil spirits and protects mankind from them, and because it often crows at night as well as by day, it is an emblem of watchfulness. In several mythologies, it is sacred to the war-god, a dedication very suitable to its bold and pugnacious character, and it is also widely connected with the Corn Spirit and the harvest. From this last belief came the bristling corn-cocks that used to stand so proudly at the gable-ends of ricks, and the custom, found in many areas, of twisting the last strands of corn into the form of a cock at harvest-end.

A Christian tradition says it was the first living creature to proclaim Our Lord's birth at Bethlehem, by crying *Christus natus est*, and since that time, cocks have crowed throughout the night of 24 December. So too, at the Last Day, all the real cocks of the world, as well as the metal ones on church towers, will crow to warn the living and to awaken the dead in their graves. The pagan Norsemen also believed that the dawn of Ragnnarok, the day on which all things would perish, would be signalled by the crowing of a gold-crested cock.

Many omens are associated with this bird. When one crows at midnight, or near it, a spirit is passing. In numerous districts, this spirit is identified as the Angel of Death, and the sound is interpreted as a death omen for those who hear it, or for someone connected with them. In the English northern counties, it is a death omen if one crows three times between sunset and midnight.

Its crowing at other times is often a warning. Aubrey tells us in his *Remaines* how 'at the same instant, that Mr Ashton was goeing out of the house, when he was goeing to France, the Cock happened to crow; at which his wife was much troubled, and her mind gave her, that it boded ill luck. He was taken at sea & after tryed, and executed'. Mrs Leather[1] records a story, told to her by a woman at Weobley, that when the latter's husband lay ill, her tame cock crowed under his window every morning. She took this to be a sign of his death, which did in fact follow, and she killed the bird so that 'it shouldn't put him in mind of it, like'.

A cock crowing near the house-door, or coming indoors, foretells the arrival of strangers or unexpected visitors. If it perches on a gate to crow, or calls at nightfall, the next day will be wet, and so too, if it roosts in the poultry-house later than usual in the morning. In Lincolnshire formerly, the first pancake made on Shrove Tuesday was given to the cock in the barn-yard. No second cake could be made until he had received it. As many hens as came to help him eat it, so many years (or more hopefully, months) would the daughter of the house have to wait before she married.

An old method of detecting a thief was to place a cock under some vessel, and make all the suspected persons touch the latter in turn. The cock would crow when the thief touched it. In his *Popular Romances of the West of England*, Hunt relates that a farmer at Towednack in Cornwall, having missed some of his property, invited all his neighbours to touch a brandice under which a

[1] E. M. Leather, *op. cit.*

cock had been put, saying as they did so, 'In the Name of the Father, Son and Holy Ghost, speak.' Nothing happened until one woman, who had already shown signs of great uneasiness, touched the brandice. Before she had time to utter the required words, the cock crowed. She afterwards confessed that she had stolen the goods.

A somewhat similar story is told of Cunning Murrell, the celebrated Essex wiseman who lived at Manningtree in the nineteenth century. He made all the suspected individuals pass separately through a darkened room and touch an earthenware pot under which the bird was concealed. This pot he had previously smeared with a mixture of oil and blacking. When all had passed through the room without a sound from the cock, he examined their hands, and found only one man with clean fingers. The cock had not crowed because the thief had not dared to touch the vessel.

A white cock is often said to be lucky, and to protect the farm on which it lives. To kill or harm such a bird is very ill-omened. In *Notes and Queries* (Vol. X, 1908), there is a story concerning some sailors who, from a ship lying off the coast of Fife, twice saw a meteor falling towards a farmer's stacks. On each occasion, a white cock crowed just before it struck, and the meteor changed course and swept harmlessly away. The sailors persuaded the farmer to sell them the wonder-working bird, and on the following night, the meteor fell into the stackyard, with the result that all the ricks were burnt. This tale is told in other parts of Scotland also, though the colour of the cock concerned is not always recorded.

Black cocks usually have a more ominous significance. They figure frequently in tales of witchcraft and pagan sacrifice. A French method of raising the Devil was to carry such a bird at midnight to a cross-roads where four ways met, and cry three times 'Poule noire a vendre!' The Devil would then appear and take the cock, giving a handful of money in exchange. In Scotland, and also in Cornwall, epilepsy could be cured by burying a black cock, without a single white feather on it, on the spot where the patient fell in his fit. A more elaborate Highland remedy, recorded by Isobel Cameron in her *Highland Chapbook*, was to take nail-parings from the sufferer's fingers and toes, bind them with hemp, and wrap them, with a silver sixpence, in a paper inscribed with the Names of the Trinity. The parcel so made had then to be tied under the wing of a black cock, and the unfortunate bird was then buried in a hole in the ground. Perhaps as a kind of Christian strengthening of this essentially pagan rite, the most God-fearing man in the neighbourhood was required to sit up and pray all night by the fire, which must on no account be let out.

A contributor to *The Countryman* (Winter 1949) records a curious modern survival of cock sacrifice, with an odd Christian bias. A nurse was looking after a dying man in Cornwall, and just before the end, she saw his wife go to the window and wring the neck of a black cock. She explained that she did this to help her husband. When his soul came to the gates of Heaven, St Peter would see the cock with him, and being thus reminded of his own denial of Our Lord, would be moved to mercy and more likely to let the dead man into Heaven. She added that the cock must be a black one.

CONFETTI

The modern custom of throwing confetti, or rice, for luck over a newly-married pair is all that now remains of an ancient fertility rite intended to ensure both prosperity and the fruitfulness of the marriage. In earlier times, corn was used for the same purpose. In his *Health's Improvement* (1665), Thomas Muffet tells us how in the seventeenth century 'the English, when the bride comes from church, are wont to cast wheat upon her head; and when the bride and bridegroom return home, one presents them with a pot of butter, as presaging plenty and abundance of all good things'. J. E. Vaux[1] says that wheat was still thrown in Sussex and north Nottinghamshire when he wrote at the end of last century, although by that time rice had become more usual in most other places.

Because corn and rice are both staple foods, the one of Europe and the other of the East, they had a natural meaning in a fertility rite. Confetti, being merely paper, is quite meaningless in itself. Nevertheless, it is the modern substitute for the life-giving grains, and when thrown at a wedding, has exactly the same significance as they had, though this fact is not always recognized by those who throw it today.

CONFIRMATION

Confirmation, like Baptism, was once thought to have curative powers, especially for rheumatism and kindred ills. Cases have been known of candidates presenting themselves a second, and even a third, time for this reason. Mrs Leather[2] mentions one old woman who, at some period in the nineteenth century, was confirmed three times, in three different churches, as a cure for rheumatism. It is not clear whether the choice of the different churches was for superstitious reasons, or to avoid recognition. Probably it was the latter, since this detail is not recorded elsewhere.

It was, however, widely supposed that the charm would not work unless the candidate was touched by the Bishop's right hand. In northern England, and also in East Anglia, confirmation with the left hand was not only useless for curative purposes, but also definitely unlucky. The person so confirmed would never marry.

[1] J. E. Vaux, *op. cit.*   [2] E. M. Leather, *op. cit.*

CORAL

From antiquity down to our own times, red coral has been used in amulets and charms of many kinds. It is said to avert the Evil Eye, and in southern Europe it is still very often worn for this reason. In England formerly, it protected its owner against epilepsy and the spells of witches, and preserved any house or ship that contained it from damage by lightning, storms and whirlwinds. When worn on the person, it served as an indication of its wearer's state of health, turning pale when he was ill and regaining its true colour as he recovered.

It was also valuable in that it preserved and strengthened teeth and, if rubbed on their gums, enabled babies to cut their first teeth quickly and easily. The coral-and-bells, which is still a quite usual christening gift, was primarily intended as an aid to teething, but it had the additional virtue of protecting the child from the effects of magic. 'The Coral,' observes Reginald Scot,[1] 'preserveth such as bear it from fascination or bewitching and in this respect they are hanged about children's necks.' A necklace of the beads was often given for the same reason, and also to prevent bad dreams and night-terrors.

CORK

A very common charm for the prevention of cramp is to wear a garter of corks round the leg. Another way of averting attacks is to put corks between the springs of the bed and the mattress, or to sleep with a piece of cork held in the hand. These remedies are all well known today, and many people who have tried them are prepared to vouch for their efficacy.

CORNSPRINGS. *See Prophetic Waters*

CORPSE-LIGHTS

An old and widespread tradition says that when the soul leaves the body at death, it does so in the form of a small flame which is sometimes, though rarely, visible in the death-chamber, but is more often seen afterwards in the churchyard where the body lies or, if the soul cannot rest, as a strange light in some house or other haunted place. The Icelandic sagas refer more than once to wavering fires seen on the tops of burial mounds wherein warriors had been laid with their treasures about them. These were the souls of the warriors guarding their buried wealth. Baring-Gould tells us in his *Book of Folk-Lore* how he was once told that a flame had been seen at hay-harvest, dancing over the fields and running up the ricks in a parish adjoining his

[1] Reginald Scot, *op. cit.*

own. The local people believed it was the soul of a young man who had helped in the previous hay-harvest and had since died of consumption. When Irene Munro was murdered at the Crumbles in 1920 and hastily buried in the sands, a rumour spread that strange lights had been seen near the place where her body was found. It is probable that this tale was not heard until after the discovery of the corpse, but even so, it is interesting that it should have taken so ancient a form at so late a date.

In many parts of Britain, and especially in Wales, belief in the Corpse-Candle was once very common. This was a small flame, or ball of fire, which was seen floating from the churchyard towards the house of a dying person, or one who, though still in health, was destined to die shortly. It travelled always by the same route as the funeral would subsequently take. A small blue flame denoted the death of a child, a larger and yellowish one, that of an adult. If several were seen together, as many deaths might be expected in the near future. If two coming down different paths met, two funerals would meet at that spot, and if any such light stopped or turned aside, some accident would cause the funeral procession to stop or turn aside at exactly the same place.

Corpse-Candles were commonly said to be the souls of the dying man's kinsmen in the churchyard who came to summon him to join them there. In the West-country, it was believed that only those who had relatives buried in the parish would be so warned. In Wales, there was a legend that St David had promised his people that no one in his territories should die without time for preparation, because a light would be sent beforehand to warn him.

Many stories are told of the appearance of Corpse-Candles. Baxter in his *Certainty of the World of Spirits* (1691) relates that Bishop Rudd's house-keeper at Llangatten in Carmarthenshire saw five lights together in the room where the maidservants slept. Shortly afterwards, the room was newly plastered. Before the plaster was dry, a coal-fire was lighted in the grate, and next morning five girls were found suffocated by the mingled fumes of coal and lime.

Mrs Crowe tells two other stories in her *Night Side of Nature* (1848), one from Wales and the other from Scotland. The first concerns a lady who was riding to visit friends and expected to be met at a certain point by their manservant. He was not there when she arrived, and while she waited, she saw a light moving towards her about three feet above the ground. She turned her horse aside to allow it to pass, but it halted in front of her and remained there, flickering, for about half an hour. Eventually, she heard the sound of the servant's horse coming, and the light then vanished. Some days later, this servant died and, owing to a mishap, his funeral procession was forced to halt for thirty minutes on the spot where the light had stopped.

The other tale, which Mrs Crowe heard from one of her own relatives, was of a newly inducted Scottish minister who saw a light in his churchyard. He went in to see what it was, whereupon it moved away from him, though there was no one there to carry it. He followed it through a wood and up a hill to a farmhouse into which it disappeared, returning very shortly with another and similar light. Both floated together over the same road and vanished into a grave. Next day, the minister learnt that the grave belonged to the family in the farmhouse, and that a child of that house had died of scarlet fever on the previous evening.

It was not dangerous to meet a Corpse-Candle, provided that the observer did not attempt to touch it, for if it passed him, its errand was not to him. Sometimes, however, its presence at any particular spot foretold a death there which might or might not be that of the person who saw it. In a letter written in 1656 to Richard Baxter and quoted by him in the book already mentioned, John Davis of Gleneurglyn stated that a light had been seen hovering over a ford in the River Istwyth, and a few weeks later, a girl was drowned there. So too, in the same letter he says that his sexton's wife saw a blue flame on the end of her table. Soon afterwards, returning from an expedition, she found a dead child lying on the opposite end. It had been newly christened and being ill, was brought to the sexton's house and laid on the table, where it died.

COUVADE

It is still quite commonly believed that a man suffers pains of various kinds during his wife's pregnancy, and that this is due to the existence of close sympathy between the married pair. If he does not, it is a sign that the marriage is not happy. 'A good husband always has toothache at such times,' said an Oxfordshire woman in 1936. About the same time, and in the same county, a young man, father of three children, said he always knew when his wife was pregnant because he began to feel unwell for no apparent reason, and to suffer from violent toothache. The latter seems to be the most usual ailment, but cases of men suffering from other pains, general malaise, and even morning sickness have been recorded within this century. This idea of shared pain is so well known that men with toothache are often asked by their friends if their wives are pregnant, and dentists are not infrequently told by their male patients that this is the cause of their teeth troubles.

It is usually thought that the husband suffers at the beginning of the pregnancy, and that his pains vanish towards the end. Mrs Leather[1] relates how an old Herefordshire woman told her the Almighty had arranged it thus so that the woman might reserve her strength for the final ordeal. Occasionally, however, the man's troubles continue through the period. In his *Natural History of Oxfordshire* (1677) Dr Plot mentions the case of a man

[1] E. M. Leather, *op. cit.*

personally known to him, who suffered violent stomach pangs which ceased only when his wife's labour began. G. L. Gomme says in *Ethnology in Folklore* (1892) that in Yorkshire formerly, if a girl had an illegitimate child and would not name the father, her parents searched through the parish until they found a man ill in bed. This illness coinciding with the birth was considered proof of paternity.

These curious beliefs are the last traces of a very ancient and widespread custom, found almost everywhere amongst primitive peoples, which is known to folklorists as the Couvade. When a child was born, the husband took to his bed, taking the baby with him, and was treated as though it were he who had just been confined. He was given foods appropriate to a lying-in woman, and such medicines or treatment as were customary in the district. The woman rose as soon as possible after the birth and went about her work, while everyone's attention was concentrated on her husband. This custom existed in India, Borneo, South America and elsewhere, as well as in many parts of Europe. Amongst the Basques formerly, and in Corsica, it was the father who received the congratulations of his neighbours as he lay in bed with the baby beside him, while the mother did her ordinary work and only came in to feed the child from time to time.

In Guiana, it is still usual for the woman to work until the last possible moment, and then to rise when the baby is only a few hours old, while the man lies in bed and is fed only on weak gruel and cassava meal. In the Balkans during the First World War, the husband often lay by his wife during the confinement, groaning when she groaned, and afterwards staying in bed for a stated time. Professor Vukanović records a case in 1921 when an Arbanian Moslem, several of whose children had already died, lay Couvade for forty days in the hope of saving his last-born son. He ate only sour milk during this period, and various protective charms were placed by his bed, including garlic, scissors, a cartridge, and a comb.[1]

The object of the Couvade seems to have been primarily the protection of the child against evil spirits, although originally it may have had something to do with the assertion of paternity. Birth, like all beginnings, was a period of great peril, with which the woman was not competent to deal because, according to primitive ideas, she was unclean after confinement until certain rites had been performed. The father, being both ritually clean and altogether stronger, took her place, himself protected by various charms, and so guarded the child and the household against the onslaughts of demons.

In its primitive form, Couvade appears to have been a rite of simulation. The father did not really suffer; he merely pretended to do so in order to deceive the evil spirits, and as a means of establishing his claim to the child.

[1] T. P. Vukanović, 'Traces of Couvade among Balkan Peoples', *Folklore*, Vol. 70, 1959.

In the present, fragmentary form of the belief, his pains have become genuine, arising from sympathy, and as has already been said, his sufferings are usually thought to occur at the beginning of the pregnancy instead of, as formerly, at the time of confinement and immediately afterwards.

COW

According to a French legend, cows always have a sweet breath because, when Our Lord was born in the stable at Bethlehem, a cow, seeing Him shivering in the cold, warmed Him with her breath and drew the hay over Him with her lips. As a reward for this act of kindness, she was promised that her breath, and that of all her descendants, should ever afterwards be sweet, and in addition, she was given the privilege of carrying her calf for nine months, like a Christian woman with a soul to be saved.

Red cows appear in some pagan creeds as personifications of the dawn, or clouds, or lightning. It is possible that they had some special significance for the ancient Hebrews also, since it is definitely stated in *Numbers*, 19.1, that the victim offered for the purification of the people must be 'a red heifer without spot, wherein is no blemish, and upon which never came yoke'. In England the milk of a red cow was formerly supposed to be superior to that of any other, and to have healing properties. Such milk is often specially mentioned in seventeenth- and eighteenth-century medical books as an essential part of remedies for various ills, particularly for consumption and chest ailments. Red is, of course, a life-giving colour in mythology and folk-tradition alike because it is associated with fire and with blood, and red objects of various kinds figure constantly in healing charms and folk-cures.

Old farmers say that every herd has a 'master cow' which leads the others into mischief. If a cow lows after midnight, it is a death omen for someone in the neighbourhood, and similarly, if a cow lows three times in a man's face, he has not long to live. In Lancashire folk-speech, the name 'cow's lane' was sometimes given to the Milky Way, the traditional path of souls, as it was also in some parts of Germany. This may be connected with the old north European belief that whoever gave a cow to the poor during his life would be guided by that cow along the perilous soul-road after his death, and so would be sure of reaching Heaven in safety.

Witches were supposed to be able to steal the milk of cows from a distance by means of a magical tedder, the strands of which were plaited the wrong way. They could do the same by going through the motions of milking with a rope, or a pot-hook, or the legs of a stool, and sometimes they came in the form of hares and sucked the udders of cows lying out in the fields. When the true milking-time came round, such bewitched animals would give only a poor supply, or none at all.

Various charms were used to counteract these thefts, one of which was to make the rope used to tether the animals' feet out of horsehair, and to thrust a stick of rowan, or some other magical wood, through it. In an article in *Folk-Lore* (1895) R. C. Maclagan[1] relates the story of a Bernera farmer whose cows gave so little milk that he was sure they were bewitched. He used such a rope, with excellent results; but as soon as the cows were released, they all rushed to a certain woman's house and began tossing at the walls. This was regarded by the local people as clear proof that the woman had previously bewitched them, and so strong was the feeling against her on this account that she had to leave the district.

In his *Discourse on Sympathy* (1658), Sir Kenelm Digby records a country belief that if milk boiled over and fell on the fire, salt must immediately be thrown on the place where it fell. If this was not done, the cow which gave it would suffer from an ulcerated udder. *See Calf: Cattle.*

COWDUNG

The use of cowdung as a poultice was once very common in rural districts. This is sometimes listed among superstitions, but in fact, it is simply another example of the country habit of using the materials nearest to hand and easiest to obtain. Because it is soft and heat-engendering, cowdung makes an excellent poultice, however strange its employment for such a purpose may seem to modern eyes. Not so very long ago, sufferers from tumours, ulcers, cancer of the breast, boils, whitlows, and swellings of various kinds would look for a fresh cowpat in the fields and apply it to the afflicted part, laying it on while it was still soft and warm, and renewing it from time to time as it became necessary. Severe chills, pneumonia, and kindred ills were often similarly treated.

One Oxfordshire woman said in 1933 that she regularly used this remedy for cancer of the breast, and found great relief from it. It was quite clean, she said, because cows, unlike other animals, are very clean feeders. In the same county in 1948, a man attempted to cure baldness in much the same way. He put a cowpat in a handkerchief and slept with it tied to the top of his head. In this case, however, the treatment was not successful.

COWSLIPS

Cowslips are variously said to derive their name from the fact that they spring up wherever there is cowdung, or from their scent, which resembles that of a cow's breath. Another name for them is Herb Peter, given because the flowers resemble a bunch of keys, and St Peter has the keys of Heaven in

[1] R. C. Maclagan, 'Notes on Folklore Objects Collected in Argyllshire', *Folk-Lore*, Vol. 65.98,1

his charge. They are also known as Palsywort because they were, and sometimes are still, used in remedies for that disease.

A curious and quite widespread tradition says that if cowslips are planted upside down, the flowers will be red instead of yellow. An alternative theory is that they will turn into primroses.

Along the Welsh Border, when a girl desired to know the name of her future husband, she made a cowslip ball and tossed it, saying, 'Tisty, tosty, tell me true, who shall I be married to?' She then recited the names of all the likely young men in the neighbourhood, and the ball fell to the ground when the right one was mentioned.

In the seventeenth century, careful housewives made conserves or cordials of the flowers, and used them to cure loss of memory, vertigo, pains in the head, insomnia, and a variety of nervous ills. They were also made into lotions to increase the beauty of women, or restore it if it had been lost. Country people still recommend cowslip wine, taken just before going to bed, as a remedy for sleeplessness, and other preparations of the flowers for failing memory, paralysis, and the relief of pain.

CRADLES

When cradles were in common use, it was considered very unlucky to bring a new one into the house before the birth of the baby. This belief, based on the universal fear of making sure of anything too soon, has now been transferred to the more modern perambulator. In Yorkshire, when a family bought a cradle for the first time, it was thought essential for it to be fully paid for before it was brought over the threshold, otherwise bad luck would befall the child.

To rock an empty cradle usually meant another birth before long. There was a very common saying that 'if you rock an empty cradle, it will very soon be filled'. But in Scotland and the Border counties, as also in Cornwall and some European lands, it had a more ominous meaning. The baby who normally lay in it, or who had only recently outgrown it, would fall ill and would most probably die. In Sweden it is said to make the child fractious and noisy.

During the dangerous period between birth and baptism, protective objects were often put into the cradle to guard its occupant from fairies, witches, and evil spirits. A pinch of salt, garlic, or a piece of iron served this purpose. A knife might be stuck into the woodwork for the same reason, or a rowan-wood cross fixed on the cradle-head. In Scotland, the mother's petticoat laid over a boy, or the father's coat over a girl, was a strong protection. In some areas, it was considered unlucky for any person to pass between the fire and a cradle containing an unbaptized child.

In northern England the cradle was customarily left when goods were distrained for debt. The underlying notion was simple kindliness, but it was also generally supposed that ill-luck would come to any person who broke this rule.

If a woman desired to have no more children, she was careful to keep the cradle in the house, and also some of the baby-clothes. If these were sold or given away, another birth would follow, however unlikely this might seem at the time.

CRAMP RINGS

A very old remedy for cramp, as well as for rheumatism and kindred ills, was to wear a ring made from the handles or hinges of coffins, or from the screws and nails used in their construction. At one time, such rings were often made of silver, taken from the coffins of the wealthy, but when fashions changed and baser metals were more commonly used for handles and hinges, they were deemed equally efficacious. Sextons and others were frequently applied to for pieces of old coffin-metal found in the church-yard, and from these the cramp rings were made.

Their curative powers were undoubtedly enhanced in popular belief by their contact with the dead, but it seems to have been the metal itself from which their efficacy was chiefly drawn. Galvanic rings made of silver, with a piece of copper let into the inside, were sometimes used instead of coffin-rings, and are still to be seen occasionally today. Another form consisted of two hoops soldered together, one hoop being of zinc and the other of copper. Edward Peacock[1] records a cure effected by an old copper wedding ring. A man working in the fields at Yaddlethorpe in Lincolnshire found it caught on a harrow-tooth. He gave it to his wife, who suffered greatly from cramp, and she later assured Mr Peacock that it had completely cured her.

From the time of Edward the Confessor until the Reformation, English monarchs were believed to have the power of endowing cramp rings with healing properties by blessing them on Good Friday. They were made from the King's own offering to the Cross on that day, and were hallowed by him at a special ceremony. Andrew Boorde mentions the custom in his *Brevyary of Helth* (1547) and says that the rings, when blessed, were distributed 'without money or petition'. The last English ruler to perform this rite was Queen Mary I, who hallowed the rings by taking them in her hands, passing them from one hand to the other, and repeating an ancient form of prayer or blessing over them.

CRICKETS

Beliefs about crickets vary considerably. As a rule, these friendly little

[1] Edward Peacock, *A Glossary of Words used in the Wapentakes of Manley and Corring-ham, Lincolnshire*, 1877.

insects, which love to make their home with human beings, are thought to be fortunate. If they leave a house suddenly, after long dwelling therein, it is an omen of death, and to kill one brings sure misfortune.

On the other hand, their chirping is sometimes regarded as a death omen, or the sign of a coming storm. If they suddenly invade a house where none was before, bad luck is expected in some districts; and the appearance of a white cricket on the hearth is almost everywhere considered an extremely bad omen, foretelling a death in the family soon.

CROW

The crow shares some of the darker traditions of the raven, and is usually, but not always, considered a bird of evil omen. In Celtic folklore, it was connected with certain terrible beings who were once goddesses, and who lived on after the coming of Christianity as hags or monsters.

To meet a single crow is generally thought unlucky. To hear one croaking on the left side in the morning is a very bad sign. If a single bird flies three times over a roof, or perches on it, or flutters round a window, it is a death omen for someone living in the house. So too, if one croaks three times near a dwelling, or if four fly together over it, sorrow is coming. If several flutter round a man's head, he is marked for death. If all the crows in a wood suddenly forsake it, famine or some other disaster will follow. In East Yorkshire, it is said that if a crow perches anywhere in a churchyard, there will be a funeral there within the week.

Yet to see three together in a row is lucky in some places. Two seen at once foretell a wedding or, if they are flying over a house, a birth in the family.

Pliny says that the constant chattering of crows foretells misfortune. In country belief today, persistent croaking of one or more birds foretells rain. At one time, the first bird heard in the morning predicted good weather if its cries came to an even number, and rain or storms if the number was odd. As with rooks, if these birds tumble about in the air, high winds and bad weather are expected.

CUCKOO

The cuckoo, like the swallow, is a sure herald of Spring, and therefore it is usually, though not invariably, a lucky bird. Its stay in Britain is shorter than that of the swallow, and is celebrated in many country rhymes. In Shropshire, people say,

> The Cuckoo sings in April,
> The Cuckoo sings in May,
> The Cuckoo sings at Midsummer,
> But not upon the day.

An East Anglian version runs,

> In April, come he will,
> In May, he sings all day,
> In June, he changes his tune,
> In July, he prepares to fly,
> In August, go he must,

to which Sussex adds a further two lines,

> If he stays until September,
> 'Tis as much as the oldest man can remember.

In Wales, it is unlucky to hear the cuckoo call before 6 April, and very lucky to hear it first on 28 April. Both there and in Somerset, it is a sign of misfortune to hear it after Old Midsummer Day, and may be a death omen.

Ancient legends about the cuckoo suggest that it was once thought to be an embodiment of Spring, the bringer rather than the herald of warm days and bursting vegetation. At Towednack, the Cuckoo Feast held on the Sunday nearest 28 April was supposed to commemorate the day on which the bird brought Spring to Cornwall. During a cold and wintry April, a farmer invited his friends to sit by his fire, and threw a hollow log upon it. A cuckoo flew out of the log, and at once the weather changed and became warm and springlike. In Sussex, the Old Woman who has charge of all cuckoos lets them out at Heathfield Fair on 14 April, but who this season-controlling Old Woman may be is not clear. If she is in a good temper, she releases many, but if she is cross, she allows only one or two to take flight, with good or bad effects upon the weather.

Elsewhere too, the bird's first appearance, and sometimes its departure, is regulated by the dates of local fairs. Hertfordshire people look for it after the Spring Fair at Sawbridgeworth. In Worcestershire, it comes in time for Tenbury Fair in April and leaves after Pershore Fair on 26 June. In Herefordshire, it is said to go to Orleton Fair to buy a horse when it first arrives, and to Brampton Bryan Fair to sell the animal before it flies away.

All over Britain and Europe omens were, and sometimes still are, read from the circumstances in which the first cuckoo-call of the year is heard. If it comes from the right, or from in front, it is a sign of good luck, if from the left or from behind, of evil fortune. In whatever direction the hearer is looking at the precise moment when he hears it, there will he be a year from that day. If he is looking downwards on to the ground, he will be dead and buried before twelve months are past. In Germany, a call from the north is a death omen. One from the south foretells a good butter year, and from the east or the west prosperity and good fortune.

In Wales, children born on the day when the first cuckoo is heard will be lucky throughout life. In Scotland, it is fortunate to be out walking when the first notes are heard, and here too, particular notice should be taken of the number of calls, for as many as there are, so many years of life has the hearer still before him. In Northumberland, if anyone is standing or walking on a hard road then, or on barren ground, the omen is bad, but to be on soft ground, or on grass, is a good sign. Almost everywhere it is thought lucky to have money in the pocket; it should be turned over at once, and if a wish is made at the same time, it will be granted. To lack it (even though there may be plenty at home or in the bank) foretells poverty in the coming year. It is equally ill-omened to hear the first cuckoo when fasting, for that denotes real hunger in the future, or when lying in bed, which foretells illness. Whatever the hearer is doing at the time, or whatever his condition, so will he be for most of the next twelve months.

A charm to ensure good fortune is to roll on the grass as soon as the first note is heard. To do this also cures lumbago and kindred ills, and should the bird call a second time while the rolling is in progress, the cure is certain. If an unmarried person turns round three times and then removes the left stocking (or in Ireland, the right one), a hair of the same colour as that of the future wife or husband will be found on the sole of the foot. If there is no hair, there will be no marriage that year. A girl can find out how many years she must wait for her wedding by counting the first cuckoo-notes; or, either on the first day or later in the cuckoo-season, she can go to a cherry-tree, shake it, and say 'Cuckoo, cuckoo, cherry-tree, how many years before I marry?' The bird will duly reply, sometimes at greater length than she desires. The same cuckoo-and-cherry charm can be used, by those bold enough to do so, to discover how long the inquirer has to live.

In East Anglia, it is said that a cuckoo perching on a rotten branch is a death omen, and so also if it flies directly over a man's head. On the remote island of St. Kilda, where it is a rare visitor, its appearance was thought to be an omen of some remarkable happening, such as the death of the landowner or the coming of a notable stranger. On Rona formerly, it was said that the bird was only seen or heard there after the death of the reigning Earl of Seaforth.

Cuckoos are rain-birds as well as bringers of warm weather, and in some parts of England, their persistent calling is held to be a sure sign of rain. In the northern counties and in Scotland, where the bird is called the Gowk, the term 'gowk-storm' is often applied to rough weather round about the time of its arrival. In Cheshire, the cuckoo is called the Welsh Ambassador, and in some parts of the Midlands it goes by the far less high-sounding name of Suck-egg, a title explained by the well-known country rhyme:

> The Cuckoo is a bonny bird, he sings as he flies;
> He brings us good tidings, he tells us no lies.
> He sucks little birds' eggs to make his voice clear,
> And never sings cuckoo till summer is near.

A very long-lived belief was that cuckoos turned into hawks in winter. Aristotle knew of this tradition two thousand years ago and firmly rejected it, a fact which did not prevent its persistence in this and other countries until very recently. Only about thirty years ago, the Cheshire ornithologist, A. W. Boyd, was shown a field at Great Budworth where the change was supposed to have occurred.[1] Another theory was that the birds roosted in holes in the ground or in hollow trees (which has some bearing on the Towednack story already mentioned). In the Scottish Highlands, where the cuckoo was associated with the fairies, it was sometimes supposed to enter fairy hills and barrows and pass the winter there.

CUCKOO FLOWER

The Cuckoo Flower, or Lady's Smock, is traditionally a fairies' plant, and for this reason it was, and sometimes still is, considered unlucky to bring it into the house. Its presence in a May-garland was also forbidden, and in most places where such things are made, it is commonly omitted even now. At one time, this rule was so strictly enforced that if a few sprigs were woven in by mistake, the whole garland had to be taken to pieces and remade. In Oxfordshire, many people still refuse house-room to this pretty flower but, oddly enough, the crossed hoops and floral crosses carried about on May morning in Oxford itself contain it more often than not.

Cuckoo flowers were formerly used medicinally to purify the blood, strengthen the heart, and prevent scurvy. They were frequently eaten in salads, or as a cress.

CURLEW

The plaintive and human-sounding cry of the curlew is usually thought to be an evil omen, especially when it is heard at night. In northern England, it foretells a death; in many coastal areas, it is a sign of a coming storm, or a fatality. Buckland records in his *Curiosities of Natural History* (1866) that an old man told him there was always an accident when these birds were heard, and that once, just after a flock had passed over, a boat was overturned and seven men were drowned.

Many people think that the Seven Whistlers are curlews, although many other birds have had this doubtful honour ascribed to them. *See Seven*

[1] Communicated to the Editor by A. W. Boyd.

Whistlers. In Scotland they are called whaups which, as E. A. Armstrong points out in his *Folklore of Birds* (1958), is also the name of a long-beaked goblin that haunts the eaves of houses by night. In Devonshire, they are sometimes known as Wisht Hounds, and in parts of Yorkshire as Gabrel Hounds, both of which names connect them with the ghostly and ominous Wild Hunt.

CYCLAMEN

Long before it became popular as an indoor and greenhouse plant, cyclamen was valued as a medicinal root. It was used as a purgative and an emetic, and as an antidote to poison. Because its leaves are shaped rather like the human ear, it was considered efficacious in diseases of that organ. According to the *Herbarium* of Apuleius, if a man's hair began to fall out, he could avoid further loss by putting the herb up his nostrils. Its most valued medicinal property was that it helped to make childbirth easy. Its powers in this direction were thought to be so great that in the sixteenth century pregnant women, not yet come to their time, were warned to avoid the places where it grew lest, by treading on it accidentally, they might bring on a miscarriage.

Cyclamen was used in love-charms and aphrodisiacs. Gerard tells us it was sometimes incorporated in little cakes which, if eaten, made 'a good amorous medicine to make one in love'. It was also a drinkers' herb because, by tradition, it loved the vine and hated all such sobering plants as betony and colewort. A little put into a cup of wine so increased the potency of the latter that whoever drank it quickly became intoxicated even if the amount taken was only moderate.

At one time, it bore the unromantic name of Sowbread, because swine were thought to feed upon it.

D

DEAD HAND

The hand of a man who had died on the gallows, or who had committed suicide, was formerly believed to have strong curative powers. It healed those who were touched by it of many diseases, and especially those which affected the neck and throat. When executions were public, sufferers from goitre, king's evil, wens, cancer, tumours, and sores of various kinds often went to a hanging, and persuaded or bribed the hangman to let them stroke the affected part with the criminal's hand, as soon as possible after the breath had left his body. Wayside gibbets where malefactors hung in chains were also visited by people afflicted with the ailments mentioned above, and by childless women who believed that the touch of the dead hand would remove the curse of barrenness. The seeker went secretly and by night to the gibbet, and there climbed a ladder to reach the swinging corpse, or was lifted up by friends standing in a cart. He or she drew the hand three, or seven, or nine times across the seat of the trouble and then went home in the sure faith that the evil had been left behind with the corpse.

Although executed felons or suicides were commonly supposed to have the strongest powers, the hands of the ordinary dead were sometimes used to heal the same and other ills. John Aubrey[1] mentions a man at Stowell in Somerset who cured a wen in his cheek by stroking it with a dead kinswoman's hand. Acting on the advice of one who had already tried the remedy, he first said the Lord's Prayer and asked a blessing, and then stroked the wen with the hand. 'He was,' we are told, 'perfectly cured in a few weeks.' Aubrey adds that in the case of a female patient, a man's hand would be required. In Cornwall, it was believed that there was no virtue in the hand of a near relative, but that of any unrelated person could heal. The touch of a dead child's hand cured the king's evil. A writer in *Notes and Queries* (1859) records that round Penzance at that period it was supposed that if a sore was stroked by any dead hand, and the bandage formerly used on it was dropped upon the coffin during the burial service, the sore would disappear for ever.

Henderson[2] relates a gruesome story about an attempted cure of this type which did not succeed. About the year 1853 a man hanged himself at Hesilden-dene, near Hartlepool. His body was placed in an open shed to await the inquest. A miner's wife went alone to the shed and lay all night beside the corpse, with its hand resting on a wen in her neck. She had been assured that this would heal her, but it did not; instead, she suffered badly from the effects of her terrifying vigil, and eventually she died from the wen. Charlotte Latham[3] tells us that at Storrington, 'Mrs. Charles Standen . . . who has for some years had an enlarged throat, on hearing that a boy was drowned at Waltham Lock, set off immediately and had the part affected stroked with the dead hand nine times from east to west, and the same number of times from west to east.' The result, if any, in this case is not recorded.

Things which had been in contact with such a hand were also deemed to have curative powers. A stye on the eye could be healed by stroking it nine times with a gold wedding ring taken from a dead woman's hand, or a silver ring taken from that of a drowned sailor. Mrs Leather[4] says that at Orcop a

[1] *Royal Soc. MS.* fol. 361-2.   [2] Wm. Henderson, *op. cit.*
[3] Charlotte Latham, *op. cit.*   [4] E. M. Leather, *op. cit.*

cure for whooping-cough was to make the ailing child eat a slice of bread-and-butter that had previously been placed in the hand of a corpse.

The effect of the dead hand upon butter is described under *Butter-making*, and its use by thieves under *Hand of Glory*.

DEATH, EASING

The idea that death is difficult, and that the dying need help to enable them to go easily, was once very common. To save them from the pains of 'dying hard', it was necessary for certain rites to be performed as soon as it became obvious that death was inevitable. The way was cleared for the departing soul by opening all the locks in the house, withdrawing bolts, and loosening knots. If the bed lay crosswise to the floorboards or the ceiling beams, it was turned so as to stand parallel with them. Since death, like birth, comes easier in contact with the earth, the dying man was sometimes lifted out of bed and laid upon the floor. This practice began at a time when most cottages had earthen floors, but it was quite often followed in houses with wooden floors also. In either case, the shock of being transferred, while in a state of extreme weakness, from a warm bed to the cold floor would probably be enough to hasten death and secure the desired quick passing.

Any pillow or mattress likely to contain pigeons', doves', or game-fowls' feathers had to be withdrawn. Death was held to be impossible while the patient lay on such feathers. This belief was the origin of the widespread custom known as Drawing the Pillow. The latter was pulled from behind the dying man's head, often in such a way as to hasten his end by making him fall backwards with a jerk. If, however, it was desired to prolong his life for a few more hours, perhaps because some beloved child or relative was known to be hurrying towards the house but had not yet arrived, the pillow was left in place, and sometimes a small bag or bunch of the death-delaying feathers was put into the bed as an extra precaution.

All these were semi-magical rites which, though sometimes fatal in their effects, were intended simply to ease a passing which was in any case certain to occur very soon. Occasionally, however, more direct methods were used. In her *Shropshire Folk-lore*, Charlotte Burne remarks that 'within the memory of credible witnesses, affectionate relatives have been known, from motives of pure kindness', to act in a manner which would seem quite horrifying to us now. She says that about the middle of last century, one Ruyton doctor found it necessary to warn relations in attendance on the sick that he expected to find his patient alive when he next called. At Baschurch in the same period, a curate visited an old man who was very ill, but not apparently in any immediate danger of death. On his next visit, he was astonished to find him dead. The widow explained that her husband had tried hard to die, but he could not, so to help him, she had taken a piece of tape and 'put it round his neck and drawed it tight, and he went off like a lamb'.

In an article contributed to *Folklore*, Enid Porter[1] records a curious custom observed until 1902 in an Isle of Ely village. When a sick person's recovery was despaired of, but death was unduly delayed, the village nurse might be asked to bring a certain pillow, covered with black lace, which was said to have been made originally by a nun at Ely and handed down through the years from one nurse to the next. This was placed behind the dying man's head, after he had been made unconscious by a dose of crushed opium pills mixed with gin. It was then quickly pulled away, so that the patient fell backwards with a jerk, which was usually his last movement in this world. This custom came to an unlamented end in 1902, when the last woman to own the pillow died, and her son burnt it.

That this, and some of the other customary methods of easing death, came very near to and sometimes reached the point of murder apparently never occurred to the simple folk who employed them. Like the woman at Baschurch, they only wanted to help; and having accepted the fact that death could not be averted, they did what they could to ease the dying man's passing.

DEATH, IMMEDIATELY AFTER

Just as the dying were believed to need help in their passing, so the newly-dead were believed to need the active aid and protection of the living during that uncertain period between the moment of death and the funeral. The ancient notion that the soul had to be helped on its perilous journey to the next world, and especially so at the beginning of that journey, survived in a variety of customs that were once very general, and even now are not altogether forgotten in many districts. Certain actions, if performed at once or as soon as possible by the relations, were deemed to provide that help and to ensure the soul's welfare, both by defeating the attacks of demons who sought to bear it away to Hell, and by clearing its path of every sort of hindrance. Love and kindliness dictated the careful performance of such actions without delay, and so also did fear, for if they were omitted it was probable that the ghost would haunt the house thereafter.

As soon as death had occurred, any window or door that had not already been opened to let the man die was flung wide, and every remaining knot untied. The mirror in the death-chamber was veiled or turned to the wall, lest the spirit become entangled in the reflection and so be unable to pass on. Another reason for doing this was to prevent any living person looking into it and perhaps seeing the dead man looking back at him from the glass. This was a sure sign of another death in the family very soon, for it showed that the soul was waiting to take someone else with it, usually, but not always, the person who saw it there.

[1] E. M. Porter, 'Some Folk Beliefs of the Fens', *Folklore*, Vol. 69, 1958.

Animals were commonly ejected from the room and not allowed to return until the corpse had been removed. If any cat or dog jumped over or on to the body, the omen was so bad that in some districts it was considered essential to kill the poor beast at once. Clocks were sometimes artificially stopped, and household fires let out. Perishable foods, especially butter, milk, meat and onions, were thrown away, otherwise the spirit might enter and corrupt them. In some parts of Scotland, this was prevented by thrusting a nail, or some other iron object, into them. Whisky was similarly protected, to prevent the loss of its essence and colour. In Brittany, on the other hand, when a death was caused by cancer, butter was often deliberately placed near the corpse, in the belief that the disease would enter into it and could thus be thrown away with it.

A green turf wrapped in paper, or a heap of salt, sometimes with a lighted candle in the centre, was put on the dead man's breast, or else a bucket containing earth, or salt and water, was set under the bed. The usual explanation given for this was that it prevented swelling, but originally it seems to have been done as a charm against demons and other forms of evil. In the *Wilkie MS.*, there is an account of a salt-rite known as *Dishaloof*, which was formerly practised in the Scottish Lowlands. When the body had been laid out, the oldest woman present waved a lighted candle three times round it, and laid three handfuls of salt upon the breast. Three empty dishes, with a sieve between them, were set as near the fire as possible, the underlying idea here being that the soul hovers round the hearth for a certain period after death. All present then left the room and came in again, backwards, repeating a verse known as the Rhyme of Saining. With their backs still turned, they tried to put their hands into the sieve. The first person who succeeded in doing so was held to do most to help the soul; but if no one managed it, the omen was very bad.

There was a variant of this rite in which the dishes were put on a table near the bed, and the company, after putting their hands into them, danced round the table in a hand-joined ring, singing the curious words, 'A dis, a dis, a dis, a green griss, a dis, a dis, a dis.' Bread, cheese and spirits were then set upon the table and eaten by all. When the mourners had thus shared a feast with the dead man, they went home, satisfied that they had done all in their power to aid and protect him.

These customs, with the beliefs from which they sprang, have mostly ceased now, although some at least are still observed occasionally. One ancient notion, however, is still quite common, namely, that between the death and the burial, the corpse must not be left alone. 'You may leave the sick,' said an Oxfordshire woman only recently, 'you must never leave the dead.' As late as 1951 great indignation, culminating in a sharp quarrel between neighbours, was felt and freely expressed on a modern housing estate near Oxford because a dead woman, who had been devotedly cared for by a relative until the moment of death, was left alone in an empty house until the day of the funeral. The offence in this case was aggravated by the fact that the door of the house had been locked. The dead must never be locked in, nor must they be left in the dark. It is usual in many families to keep candles burning in the death-chamber, by night always and often by day also, both to avert darkness and because fire drives away evil spirits.

Formerly, neighbours and friends used to 'wake' or watch by the corpse, both as a mark of respect for the dead man, and to relieve his relatives, who would otherwise have to watch continuously themselves. Such gatherings were known as 'wakes' or 'lykewakes' when they took place at night, and 'sittings' when they were by day. In Scotland and Ireland, they were often attended by large numbers of people, many of whom came from a considerable distance. They were frequently very cheerful, even hilarious. The watchers sat in the death-chamber with the corpse and whiled away the hours with singing, drinking, story-telling, and games. Henderson[1] says that in the Border counties cards were sometimes played, the coffin serving as a table because it was considered unlucky to use the ordinary round table on which the lighted candles stood. Even practical jokes were not unknown yet no irreverence was intended. The company was there to help and protect the dead man, an end to which the noise, the laughter and the burning lights and fire all contributed, and in many parts it was felt that the livelier and more crowded the wake, the greater was the honour paid to him.

In Wales, similar customs were once observed but, with the spread of Methodism in that country, the wakes became more sober, and prayers and hymn-singing replaced the earlier revelry. Towards the end of the nineteenth century these gatherings died out, and sitting-up at night, if it was done at all, was done only by kinsfolk and very close friends. Mrs Leather[2] records that in the parts of Herefordshire nearest to the Welsh Border, families sometimes watched through the night after a death, not in the death-chamber but in some other room. They believed that the spirit was in and about the house, and so it was not necessary to be with the corpse in order to maintain the watch.

A last trace of the former communal wakes seems to have survived in the Welsh *gwylnos*, which lingered on until the first few years of the present century. On the night before the funeral, the neighbours gathered at the house for a short service of prayers and hymns conducted by some layman. The minister did not attend. In the morning, a similar service was held just before the coffin was carried out for the burial. *See Death Bells.*

DEATH, TIMES OF

Among coastal dwellers it is commonly said that death is most likely to

[1] Wm. Henderson, *op. cit.*   [2] E. M. Leather, *op. cit.*

occur with the ebb-tide. As life comes in with the flow, *see Birth, Times of,* so it goes with the ebb, and in some places it is thought that no one can die until the tide begins to run out. If a sick man lingers through one ebb-tide, he will survive until the next. Dickens refers to this belief in *David Copperfield* when he makes Peggoty say: 'People can't die along the coast except when the tide's pretty near out. They can't be born unless it's pretty nigh in.' The most probable moment is usually said to be at dead low water.

In some parish registers formerly, the state of the tide was recorded along with the date and other details of the death. R. M. Heanley[1] says that, according to his own observations, death along the Lincolnshire coasts did in fact occur most frequently at the ebb, a phenomenon for which he could not account except by the possibility that a change of temperature was involved which affected the dying person.

Sailors believe that a sick man on board ship will not die until land has been sighted.

In Ireland, those who die at midnight on Christmas Eve are considered fortunate, for the gates of Heaven stand wide open then, and the soul passes straight through them, without any waiting period in Purgatory.

DEATH BELLS

Bells have always been closely associated with death and with funerals. As they were once thought to avert many perils during life, so at the supreme moment of death they were rung to drive away the demons that beset a death-bed, and afterwards to protect the soul as it set out on its long journey to the next world. In Christian tradition, of course, the Passing Bell is rung when someone is dying, to ask the living to pray for the departing spirit, as the Nine Tailors are rung to announce a death that has already occurred, and the great bell is tolled at a funeral in token of mourning. 'We call them soul-bells,' wrote Bishop Hall of the Passing Bell three hundred years ago, 'for that they signify the departure of the soul, not for that they help the passage of the soul.' Nevertheless, many, even among the devout, continued to believe that their music did protect the dying and the yet unburied dead, and traces of this idea lingered to a late date. To omit or delay any of the customary ringings was until quite recently considered not only disrespectful to the dead man and his kin, but also unkind, because it was likely to hamper the spirit in its passing.

In *Notes and Queries* (1852) Cuthbert Bede mentions the case of a Huntingdonshire child who died upbaptized and was buried shortly before he wrote. No bells were rung for him, and for this omission, a neighbour expressed deep sympathy for the mother, 'because when any one died, the soul never left the body until the church bell was rung'. Henderson[2] was told by a

[1] R. M. Heanley, *op. cit.*   [2] Wm. Henderson, *op. cit.*

Buckinghamshire friend how, on the death of a farmer, the bells began tolling at five o'clock in the morning, and were immediately stopped for two hours by the clergyman's orders. The dead man's widow bitterly resented this, saying that it was a cruel act 'to keep the poor soul those hours a-waiting'. At one time, it was usual to ring for the dying or the dead at any hour, but this custom seems to have died out during the nineteenth century, and in most places the bells were tolled only between sunrise and sunset. In some parishes, if an inquest was necessary, they were not rung until after the inquest was over.

The Passing Bell and the Nine Tailors are sometimes confused in accounts of parish customs. They are, in fact, quite separate, the one rung, as the name denotes, for a dying man, and the other only after death has occurred. The word 'tailors' is a corruption of 'tellers', the full title meaning the nine tellers or strokes which indicate the death of a man. Hence the saying, 'Nine Tailors make a man.' The living are notified that someone had died, first by the tolling of the bell, then by nine strokes for a man, six for a woman, and three for a child, and finally by a single note for every year of the dead person's age. In a few of the parishes where this custom is kept up, the number of strokes indicating sex varies a little, but nine, six and three are the most usual. At Ayot St Peter in Hertfordshire, the Nine Tailors are rung for Our Lord on Good Friday. At Dewsbury it is, or was, the custom to ring the Devil's Passing Bell on Christmas Eve, followed by the age of the year, because the Devil died when Christ was born.

It was formerly usual in several counties, including Lancashire, Shropshire and Devonshire, to peal the bells, either when the coffin reached the lychgate and was received into the churchyard, or after the funeral, as the mourners were returning home. This custom, which has died out now, was far more Christian in its underlying idea than the melancholy tolling, for the bells were pealed as a sign of rejoicing that the dead man had gone home.

DEATH COACH. *See Churchyard Watcher.*

DEATH CROSSES

When a death occurred outside the home, either as a result of accident or murder, a rough cross was often cut in the turf, or scratched on a stone, as near as possible to the death-site. The reason for this custom is uncertain, but it seems probable that it was an attempt to pacify, or drive away the ghost, and keep him from haunting the spot. This appears the more likely because in many places it was usual to renew such crosses by re-cutting them from time to time, either on the anniversary of the death, or when it became necessary to save them from obliteration. It made no difference whether the dead man was a neighbour or a passing stranger, and the renewal rite was often continued long after his name, and everything else about him except the place and manner of his end, had been forgotten.

At Iffley, near Oxford, some crosses in the grass verge of a lane were thus renewed within living memory, though they have disappeared now. One scratched low down on a gate-post is, however, still visible, and commemorates a man who was thrown from his horse and killed just opposite the gate.

Another form of this custom is recorded by Mrs Aitken in *Folk-Lore* (Vol. 37, 1926). A gardener at Pyrford in Surrey told her in 1901 that he had been in many parishes, and had always found that crosses were kicked in the dust in cases of accidental death or murder out of doors. He added that 'if a man's been killed in an accident on the road, the policeman'll always kick a cross; and some people keep on kicking a cross in the same place year after year'. He gave no reason for this custom, and perhaps knew none; but the probability that it sprang, at least originally, from a fear of haunting seems even stronger in this case than in those mentioned above, since the completely impermanent nature of a dust-cross rules out any idea of a memorial to the dead.

DEATH WATCH BEETLE

The tapping sound made by the Death Watch Beetle foretells a death in the house. This belief is still quite common amongst nervous people, and is easily understandable in view of the eerie sound thus made by an invisible agent, and the fact that any unexplained knocking has always been regarded as an omen of death or misfortune.

DEISEIL. *See Sunwise Turn.*

DEPARTURE

When a man leaves his house to go on a journey, he must never look back, nor must he retrace his steps for any reason whatsoever. To do either of these things imperils his journey at its beginning, and will certainly bring him bad luck or danger during its course.

This belief is very ancient, and exists in many parts of the world. When Lot fled from the destruction of Sodom, an angel warned him not to look back, and evidently he refrained from doing so, since he came in safely to the city of Zoar. But his wife was less strong-minded and, because she took a last backward glance at her old home, she was turned into a pillar of salt.[1] Along the coasts of Britain it was, until very recently, considered extremely

[1] *Genesis* XIX, 17–26.

unlucky to call after a fisherman once he had started out for the boats. To do so might cause him to look back and so put him in peril whilst at sea. If he had forgotten anything he needed for the voyage, some member of his family would run after him with it and thrust it into his hand as he went along. On no account must he be called and so made to turn round, however urgent the reason for doing so might be. In India and some other parts of the East, the same superstition applied to all travellers, whether by sea or on land.

It is still commonly believed in many areas that if, after starting out, any person finds himself absolutely obliged to return home, he can nullify the bad omen by sitting down as soon as he reaches the house and counting nine, or ten, or twenty. Only after he has done this is it safe for him to attend to whatever it was that brought him back, and then to set out on what has now become a completely new journey, unshadowed by the evil omens of the first. In some districts, however, sitting down and counting are not thought enough; he must stop to eat and drink in his home before leaving for the second time.

A kindred belief is that it is unlucky to watch a departing person completely out of sight. When two friends part, the one left behind should not stand waving till the last moment, but should turn away while the other is still visible, otherwise the two may never meet again. Similarly, when seeing someone off by train or car, the vehicle should not be watched until it disappears from view, or bad luck will follow. In coastal areas, to look at a departing ship until it is out of sight brings misfortune to the vessel itself, whether it contains any one known to the watcher or not.

Another still surviving superstition concerning departure is that a guest-chamber should not be swept until the guest who recently occupied it has been out of the house for an hour or more. To do the work too soon may bring him bad luck on his journey or, according to another version, will prevent him from returning to the house on any future occasion.

DEW

Dew, which seems to fall mysteriously from Heaven out of a clear night-sky, and vanishes so quickly in the early morning, has always had magical significance in folk-tradition. In classical mythology, it was the moon's daughter, the child of Selene and Zeus, and in later times it came to symbolize virginity, precious and soon gone.

It could be used in charms and spells, and was quite commonly prescribed in seventeenth-century medicine as a lotion for sore eyes, skin-troubles, and the itch. Snuffed up the nostrils, it cured vertigo, and when gathered from the leaves of fennel or the greater celandine, it strengthened the sight. Aubrey tells us in his *Natural History of Wiltshire* how one, William Gore of Clapton healed his own gout by walking through the dewy grass 'with his shoes pounced'. Long after his time, weakly children in nineteenth-century Derbyshire were anointed with dew to give them strength.

May dew, that is, dew gathered very early on May-day morning was the most potent, both for good and evil. Henderson[1] mentions two Scottish witches who were seen brushing it from the grass of a field with a hair-tether. The tether was taken from them and hung in the cowbyre. Thereafter the cows gave so much milk that there were not enough vessels on the farm to contain it, but when the tether was burnt, the yield returned to normal. Yet, if dew could be used by witches, it also protected those who washed in it from their spells, and brought good luck. In south-east Europe, cattle were anointed with it on May-day morning to free them from the perils of witch-craft throughout the year.

If a sufferer from goitre gathered May dew before sunrise from a young man's grave, passing his hand three times from the grave's head to its foot, and then laid the liquid so gathered on the goitre, he would be cured; but in this charm, it is probable that the magical power came as much from the dead man as from the dew.

The most famous use of May dew was as a cosmetic. If a girl gathered it very early in the morning, preferably from under an oak, and bathed her face in it, she would be beautiful all the year. It was long the pleasant custom for women of all ranks to go to the fields for that purpose on 1 May, as Pepys's wife did in 1667, and many others before and after her. In Edinburgh until fairly recently, young people went up to Arthur's Seat before sunrise to 'meet the dew' and bathe their faces in it, a charm that not only beautified their complexions but also ensured twelve months of good luck.

The shining liquid which the Sun-dew plant excretes in order to catch flies was once thought to be a special kind of dew, which had the virtue, unshared by the ordinary sort, of not drying away in the sunshine.

DISHALOOF. *See Death, Immediately after.*

DOCK

A common country belief is that wherever stinging-nettles are found, there also will be found the dock, whose leaves heal the nettle's sting. Children lay the cool leaves on the stung place, saying

> Out nettle, in dock,
> Dock shall have a new smock,
> But nettle shan't have nothing.

Workers in ironstone quarries who develop a peculiar sore on the forearm

[1] Wm. Henderson, *op. cit.*

as a result of their work sometimes cut a dock-root across and rub the fresh-cut surface on the sore. This is done every third day until the cure is complete.

DOCTORS

Before the introduction of the National Health Service, it was sometimes considered unlucky to pay a doctor's bill in full. To do so implied a dangerous confidence in restored and continuing health that could only bring misfortune, and would probably result in his services being needed again very soon. Some patients, therefore, made it a rule to hold back a token sum, perhaps a shilling, from the total amount due. On the other hand, gypsies always paid their bills punctually and in full, because they believed that unpaid-for medicine would not work.

To call in a doctor for the first time on Friday is unlucky, and should only be done in cases of real and immediate emergency. In some districts, it is held to be a certain omen of death for the patient.

The common dread of being the first to enter or use a new building does not, apparently, apply to doctors' surgeries. On the contrary, the first patient to be treated there is certain to be cured. In 1943 a well-known Oxford specialist notified her patients that she was moving to a new surgery, and received a number of letters asking that the writer might be the first person seen by her in it.

If the seventh child of a seventh child becomes a doctor, he or she will be extremely successful and achieve many striking cures.

DOGS

The dog, man's first friend and servant, has almost always and everywhere been credited with the power of seeing ghosts and spirits, gods and fairies, and the Angel of Death in all his various forms. In Wales, the death-bringing hounds of Annwn were visible to earthly dogs, though not to human beings, as Hel, the death-goddess, was in pagan Scandinavia. In Ancient Greece, when Hecate hovered at the crossroads, foretelling death for someone, the dogs were aware of her and gave warning by a great clamour of barking. Like cats and horses, dogs are commonly believed to see ghosts and evil spirits. Usually, though not always, they fear them greatly, and in numerous recorded instances, their terror has been the first indication of the presence of some supernatural visitant. There are also many legends of dogs who have themselves appeared as ghosts, in some cases acting as a death warning for members of particular families.

The howling of dogs is still widely considered an ominous sound. If one howls in the night, it is a death omen or, at least, a herald of coming misfortune. If a dog howls persistently in front of a house where someone lies ill, that person will die, especially if the animal concerned belongs to him, or to some other inmate of the house. If it is driven away and then returns to howl again, the omen is certain. So too, if any dog howls suddenly, once or three times, and then falls silent, it is a sign that a death has occurred somewhere nearby, either at that precise moment or very recently. In Poland and some parts of Germany, if many dogs howl, it foretells an outbreak of plague before long.

If a favourite dog whines continuously for no apparent reason, some misfortune will overtake the family very shortly. In Lancashire, it used to be said that a dog's life was bound up with that of its owner, and that if the latter died, so would the dog. This belief may well have been strengthened by known cases of dogs which pined and died after the loss of a loved master or mistress.

A strange dog coming to the house means a new friendship in the Scottish Highlands, but one passing between a bridal couple on their wedding day is, or was, a bad omen. To meet a spotted or black-and-white dog on the way to a business appointment is lucky in England, but in India it foretells a disappointment. In Lincolnshire, after meeting a white dog, it is necessary to maintain silence until a white horse is seen, or bad luck will follow. In some places, three white dogs seen together are fortunate. Black dogs are sometimes thought unlucky, especially if they cross in front of the observer, and in Lancashire, if a strange one follows any individual and will not be driven away, it is a death omen. Irish people consider it unlucky to meet a barking dog early in the morning. Among fishermen, the word 'dog' is one of those which must not be spoken at sea, and in some coastal areas the *tabu* is extended to the animal itself, which must not be taken out in the boat.

Normandy peasants say that all dogs should be treated with respect, for who knows what they really are? The dead sometimes appeared in the form of dogs, and witches' familiars occasionally took that shape. When young Thomas Darling, of Burton-on-Trent, was foolish enough to offend Alse Gooderidge in 1596, she, being a witch, sent her familiar in the form of 'a little parti-coloured dog, red and white', to afflict him with fits. Elisabeth Device, one of the Lancaster witches tried in 1612, also had a dog-familiar, a brown animal called Ball, by whose aid she killed John Robinson, of Barley, and his brother James. This was stated in evidence given by her daughter Jennet at the trial.

Ghostly black dogs, sometimes strange-seeming and enormous, sometimes indistinguishable from living dogs, are very common in English tradition. They haunted lonely stretches of road, bridges, fords and boundary-lines, and sometimes churchyards, ancient burial-mounds, and the sites of gibbets. Occasionally they were associated with particular houses or families. Their appearance was usually ominous of death or disaster, although in Lincolnshire they were not feared as they were elsewhere, and were sometimes kindly, even protecting women travelling alone. There were also other strange creatures, known in different districts as Padfoot, Shuck, Trash, or Skriker, which sometimes appeared in dog-form and sometimes in other animal-shapes. The Barguest of northern England could be a calf, a pig, a goat, or a dog at will, but no one could ever mistake it for an ordinary beast because of its great size, its saucer eyes, its feet which left no marks, and its dreadful howling. If these death-predicting monsters were ever the ghosts of once-living dogs, they seem to have suffered terrifying changes in the spirit world, and to have retained only a slight connexion with the dogs of Earth.

When rabies was still known and dreaded in England, a dog that howled on Christmas Eve was often killed immediately because of a belief that it would certainly go mad before the year was out. Healthy dogs were some-times killed if they had once bitten anybody, because it was thought that if they subsequently developed hydrophobia, even years afterwards, the bitten person would be afflicted with the same terrible disease. Many curious remedies for a mad dog's bite were recommended before Pasteur's time. One which was purely magical but nevertheless well known was to make the patient eat some of the dog's hairs, or a piece of its cooked liver. In 1866, it was stated at an inquest in northern England that after a child had been bitten, the dog was killed and thrown into the river, but was fished out again so that its liver might be extracted and given to the child. In spite of this remedy, which many deemed infallible, she died.

A piece of dog's tongue, dried and hung round the neck, was formerly used in Yorkshire to cure the King's Evil. The melted-down fat of dogs was until quite recently valued as a cure for rheumatism. One of the many methods of healing diseases by transferring them to something else was to take some of the patient's hairs, place them between slices of bread-and-butter, and give them thus to a dog. The animal took the disease with the food, and the original sufferer was thus healed. This remedy was once quite often used by old-fashioned nurses to cure children's ailments, such as whooping-cough, measles, and similar complaints.

DONKEY

Tradition says that the donkey's back was originally unmarked, and that the dark cross now visible upon it appeared as a badge of honour after Our Lord had ridden upon an ass into Jerusalem on the first Palm Sunday. A French story says they sprang into being during the Flight into Egypt, when Our Lady rode on a donkey carrying the Infant Jesus. Yet another legend associates them with Balaam's ass. In this, they are supposed to be the marks of the blow which that animal received from its master, reproduced in every donkey since as a silent memento and reproof of his fault.

The hairs from the cross were widely believed to have strong curative powers until quite recent times. If worn in a bag round the neck, they prevented toothache, eased teething troubles in babies, and cured fits and convulsions. They were also efficacious in cases of whooping-cough, either worn as above, or finely chopped and given to the patient to eat in bread-and-butter. In Brand's *Popular Antiquities* there is a quotation from the *Athenaeum* in which it is stated that such hairs, usually three in number, must be plucked from a donkey of opposite sex to the sufferer, and also that they were not very easily obtained (at least, not with the owner's knowledge) because, once they had been taken, the animal was afterwards of little worth. These two beliefs were not, however, universally held, and in most places the hairs were pulled from any available donkey, without consideration of sex or expectation of injury to the beast.

Riding on a donkey also cured many ills, particularly if the rider sat with his face to the tail. In Essex, it was said that if a child's first ride in this world was on an ass, he would never afterwards suffer from toothache. Charlotte Latham[1] records a Sussex cure for whooping-cough which consisted of hanging hairs in a bag round the patient's neck, setting him backwards on the donkey from which they were taken, and leading the animal 'to a certain spot fixed on in your own mind, three times running, for three succeeding days'. Mrs Latham's informant said she and her brother had both been cured in this way, and that the necessary bags for the hairs were made, and the donkey lent, by the wife of the clergyman of the parish.

In his *Yorkshire Folk-Talk* (1892) M. C. Morris relates how, during a severe epidemic of measles in a village near Whitby, a farmer and his wife took their two children to the seashore, four miles from their home, and there made each child in turn ride on a donkey, facing its tail, nine times up and down a certain stretch of the sands. Three hairs were drawn from the animal's tail (not from the cross, as was more usual), and these were hung round the child's neck during the proceedings. A thistle was also held over the children's heads during their rides, but whether this was part of the rite, or merely an encouragement to the ass, is not clear. Finally, the whole party returned home and, Morris remarks that, 'by a singular coincidence', this family, unlike most others in the village, escaped the infection.

Whooping-cough and ague could also be cured by passing the patient, three or nine times, under a donkey's belly and over its back. Sometimes this had to be done on nine successive mornings. Scarlet fever and other infectious ailments could be healed by cutting off some of the patient's hair and giving it to a donkey in its food, or thrusting it down its throat. The disease was thus transferred to the animal. A curious Highland charm to cure the effects of a scorpion's bite, mentioned by Isabel Cameron,[2] was to whisper into the ear of the first ass met upon the highway, 'I am bitten with a scor-

[1] Charlotte Latham, *op. cit.*   [2] Isabel Cameron, *A Highland Chapbook*, 1928.

pion.' Presumably the evil was thus passed to the beast, for nothing more was needed. A very well-known method of preventing contagious abortion among mares was to let a black donkey run with them in the field.

In Devonshire, it is unlucky to step on ground where a donkey has recently been rolling. A very general saying is that no one ever sees a dead donkey. If, however, anyone does so, it is a sign of great good fortune. C. F. Tebbutt records an instance of this belief in his *Huntingdonshire Folklore* (1951). A donkey's carcase having been brought to a local slaughterer's yard one day in 1937, all the men working there leapt over it three times for luck, and declared that now they could be sure of winning something in that week's football pools.

DOVES AND PIGEONS

Doves were sacred in many ancient religions. In Syria, they were Astarte's birds, as in Greece, they were those of Aphrodite, whose chariot they drew. In Rome, they were associated with Venus. Among the Hebrews, they were symbols of purity, a common offering at purification ceremonies in the Temple, as they were also, though for very different reasons, in the temples of the goddess Ishtar. In Mecca still, Moslems regard them with respect and never kill them. In Christian tradition, they are emblems of the Holy Ghost. An old legend says that although the Devil and his servants, the witches, could transform themselves at will into almost any bird- or animal-shape they wished, they could never assume that of the dove, or of the lamb.

Doves were also connected with the three *Parcae*, or Fates, those grim beings who spun the life-threads of men and brought death at last by cutting them. It is perhaps because of this that doves and pigeons often have an ominous significance in latter-day superstition. A dove flying round a pithead is a sure sign for miners of a disaster in the pit. In 1902, when one was seen at Glyncarrwg in Glamorganshire, three hundred colliers stopped work. A white pigeon settling on the chimney, or one of any colour entering a house, foretells a death, and so too, if one flutters near or knocks upon the window of a sick-room.

In her *Shropshire Folk-Lore*, Charlotte Burne quotes a very curious story concerning two brown-and-white pigeons who acted as a certain death-warning to the inhabitants of Cayhowell Farm. Richard Gough,[1] whose sister was married to the farmer, Andrew Bradocke, says that whenever a member of the family was mortally ill, these birds came about a fortnight before the sick person died, and flew away after the death. This he saw happen on three separate occasions, once when the farmer's mother died, then when his own father, who was staying there, did so, and lastly, when Andrew Bradocke himself perished of a fever.

[1] Richard Gough, *Antiquityes & Memoryes of the Parish of Myddle*, 1700, quoted C. S. Burne, *op. cit.*

The pigeons flew about the gardens and yards, pecked at seeds, and behaved like others of their kind. At night, they roosted under the shelter of the eaves. They never appeared except before a death. When, after the loss of her husband, young Mrs Bradocke was ill, her anxious brother called every day to see if the pigeons would come. They did not, and she recovered, but later on, when the farm was let and the tenant fell ill, they came as before and the man died.

The heart of a pigeon stuck with pins was sometimes used by lovesick or revengeful girls in charms to summon their straying lovers, and occasionally it was burnt over a hot fire in spell-breaking rites. A common remedy for fevers in the seventeenth century was to apply half a pigeon to the soles of the patient's feet in order to draw away the disease. The choice of a pigeon does not seem to have had any superstitious meaning here, for other things, such as bullock's milts, sheep's lungs, or split tench were used for the same purpose. The first two have certainly been so used within this century, and it is quite likely that the others have also.

The most widespread superstition concerning these birds is that no one can die when lying on a pillow or mattress stuffed with their feathers. *See Death, Easing.* A reason sometimes given for this belief is that the dove is the emblem of the Holy Ghost and that Death cannot come where the Holy Ghost is.

DRAKE'S DRUM

The drum which Drake is believed to have taken with him on his voyage round the world now hangs on the walls of Buckland Abbey, near Plymouth, and is said to roll of itself before a war. Tradition has it that when he was dying, the great Admiral directed that it should be taken back to Devon, and promised that if any one beat upon it when England was in danger, he would come again and fight for her. It used to be said in Devonshire that he had twice done so, returning not in his own form but reincarnated in the bodies of other famous seamen, first as Blake in the seventeenth century, and afterwards as Lord Nelson.

In the course of time, the drum legend altered, and emphasis shifted from the man to the object. Now the drum sounds without the help of human hands when a war is coming. It is said to have been heard in 1914, and again at the end of the war that started in that year. In his *Drake* (1935) Douglas Bell mentions a curious incident that occurred when the German High Seas Fleet surrendered at Scapa Flow in 1918. As the British Grand Fleet closed round the enemy vessels, a drum began to roll in the flag ship and continued to do so at intervals until the fleet dropped anchor. Although messengers were twice sent to find out who was beating it, and the commander himself finally made a personal investigation, every man was found at his battle station, and no drummer was ever discovered. Among the sailors a belief sprang up that it was Drake's drum that rolled then.

Another odd story, recorded by R. L. Hadfield in *The Phantom Ship* (1937) concerns a silver replica of the Drum which was presented to H.M.S. *Devonshire* in 1929. Although anything connected with Drake might be expected to be lucky to sailors, this was not. Misfortune followed the ship from the moment she was launched, including an explosion in a gun-turret in which seventeen lives were lost. Officers and ratings alike came to the conclusion that the Drum was to blame; and so firmly did this idea take root that when the *Devonshire* went to sea in 1936, the silver replica was left behind, safely hanging in St Nicholas' Church in Devonport, where it could do no more harm.

DROWNING

Primitive peoples believed that when a man drowned, he did so because he had been taken by the indwelling spirits of the water, who could not be deprived of their victim without great peril. To rescue such a man was highly dangerous, for the sea, or pool, or river would not be cheated of its due, and if it lost one victim, it would take another. It is this once universal and now half-forgotten idea which lies at the root of a curious reluctance to save a drowning person which has sometimes been shown, not only in ancient times but within living memory. Cases have been recorded, in Britain and many other parts of the world, of men drowning in the presence of strong swimmers and competent boatmen who did not raise a finger to help them. It was not lack of physical courage which held back the onlookers, but the far older and more deep-seated fear that if one man was saved, the water would claim another in his stead, probably the rescuer himself.

In the *Observer* (21 November 1926) St John Ervine, commenting on the fact that in *Hamlet* the witnesses of Ophelia's death apparently made no effort to save her, remarked that 'even to this day' people in the west of Ireland 'will watch a man drowning, not because they are cruel, but because they firmly believe that the sea or river will have its victim, and that it will revenge itself on the rescuer by drowning him in place of the rescued'. Nor was this belief confined to Ireland, then or at any other time. On the contrary, it was found almost everywhere. G. F. Black,[1] writing in 1901, says that within the previous forty years he had found traces of it more than once in the Orkney and Shetland Islands. One Orkney man flatly refused to take his boat out to a drowning man, and removed the oars so as to make certain that no one else could do so. Another boatman was known to have passed a drowning woman without paying any attention to her; and in a third case of

[1] G. F. Black, *Orkney and Shetland Folk-Lore*, 1901.

this kind, three men stood and watched a neighbour drown, and then walked calmly home.

Similar instances have been recorded elsewhere, though happily not within very recent years. A lingering trace of the ancient terror is sometimes found in the vague idea that to rescue the drowning is somehow unlucky, and that consequently, an attempt to do so requires rather more courage than other forms of rescue, as for instance, from a burning house or from wild animals.

In Cheshire formerly, it was believed that whoever found a drowned body washed up on the shore must give it Christian burial, otherwise he would be haunted by the angry ghost for the rest of his life. This, however, was far from being a universal belief. More usually, it was thought dangerous to deprive the sea of its lawful prey in this manner, and likely to result in some living person being drowned in its place. Eleanor Hull[1] quotes a Hebridean saying to the effect that 'the sea will search the four russet divisions of the universe to find the graves of her children', and clearly it was better that her search should be made as easy as possible. Thus, the drowned dead washed ashore were often buried hastily and with little ceremony within the tide-marks, that is, within the limits of the sea's kingdom. Christian burial was not given to them as of right until 1808, when Davies Gilbert, then Member of Parliament for Bodmin, introduced a Bill providing for their burial at the expense of the parish. This made legal and general what had formerly been done only occasionally through the piety and charity of individual rectors.

Before a drowned man can be buried, his corpse must first be recovered. It is commonly believed that it will rise to the surface on the seventh, eighth, or ninth day after death. When search was made for such a corpse, a hollowed-out loaf filled with mercury was often floated on the water, in the belief that it would stand still over the spot where the dead person lay. In 1953 this ancient method was tried, though without success, at Sale in Cheshire, when a child was drowned in the Bridgewater Canal.[2] Another well-known practice was to fire a gun over the water. It was thought that, if the body was any-where near, the concussion would break the gall-bladder and so cause the corpse to float. Cornishmen believed that boats used in such a search would come to a sudden standstill over the drowned person. An old Cheshire tradition said that if any Christian was lost in the River Dee – once known as the Holy Dee – a light would appear over the spot where he lay because this river, unlike most others, never held back a christened corpse, but guided the seekers to it by means of lights.

Fishermen and deep-water sailors have many superstitions about drowning, as might be expected. The word must never be spoken at sea, lest it evoke the peril which it names. The seamen of an older generation often refused to learn to swim, on the grounds that if the sea got them, it was useless to

---

[1] E. M. Hull, *op. cit.*   [2] *Sale and Stratford Guardian*, 27 March 1953.

struggle and only prolonged the pains of death. Many believed that the souls of the drowned lived on the form of sea-birds, and that it was their voices, warning the living, that were heard in the cries of the Seven Whistlers. It is the dead also who occasionally display mysterious lights, unaccounted for by any human activity. Towards the end of the 1914–18 war, strange lights seen along the Cornish coast were said to be flashed by drowned Cornishmen who had perished as a result of German submarine action. These souls had returned to their native coves and rocks and there, like the wreckers of old, they lured ships to destruction. But, said this modern version of a very old legend, it was only German ships or submarines which saw them. The craft of other nations passed safely by, and the lights never flashed for them.

In many parts of Europe, the drowned dead are thought to wail in storms. In Norfolk, they can be heard crying their own names in the noise of the wind. Cornish fishermen dislike going anywhere near the scene of a former shipwreck, for the dead crew sometimes call to the living there, especially before a storm. If they call to any individual by name, that man's fate is sealed. Numerous stories testify to the belief that the drowned can appear to the living, however far distant they may be, to announce their own deaths. In most of these tales it is to some fairly remote kinsman that they come, rather than to someone nearer and more deeply loved; and when the vision has vanished, a pool of water on the floor proves to the horrified seer that it was no delusion.

Yorkshire fishermen consider it unlucky to see a drowned animal, such as a dog or cat, when on their way to the boats. Many will turn back in such circumstances, and stay ashore for that day. *See Life-demanding Rivers.*

DUMB CAKE

Making a Dumb Cake was a well-known charm to induce a vision or a dream of the maker's future wife or husband. There were several different versions of this rite, but in all complete silence had to be maintained throughout the proceedings, hence the name.

A cake was made of flour, water, eggs and salt, sometimes by several young people together, sometimes by one person alone. In an Oxfordshire ritual described by Angelina Parker in *Folk-Lore* (Vol. 24, 1913) a single girl made it whilst fasting on Christmas Eve, pricked her initials on it, and then left it on the hearthstone. At midnight, the husband's fetch, or double, would come into the room, prick his initials beside those of the girl, and walk out again. Care had to be taken that the house-door was left open for him from the moment the charm was started until after he had left, for if he came and found it shut against him, something dreadful would happen.

In some parts of northern England, two or more girls met to make the cake and, having done so, they divided it equally and then walked backwards upstairs to their bedrooms, where they ate their portions before getting into bed. During the night, they would dream of their future mates, always provided that no word was been spoken from first to last. In the Midlands, a similar ritual was carried out by three girls, but here the cake was shared and eaten downstairs, exactly at midnight. They then walked backwards to bed, but before they did so, every pin had to be removed from their dress, and every fastening loosened. If the charm had been correctly performed, the apparitions of their husbands would then appear, pursuing the girls upstairs and snatching at their clothes. Since these had already been loosened, their wearers could slip safely out of them without being grasped by ghostly hands, and once they were in bed, the visions would vanish. What exactly would happen if the phantoms did succeed in seizing them is not clear, but almost certainly, the consequences would have been extremely ominous.

The dates on which this form of divination should be attempted varied from place to place. Aubrey in his *Remaines of Gentilisme and Judaisme* seems to imply that any Friday night would be suitable, but usually the practice was confined to St Mark's Eve, Christmas Eve, Hallowe'en, or St Agnes's Eve (20 January). In north-east England, if the rite was performed on the last-named night, it had to be preceded by a rigid fast lasting the whole day, during which no food, drink, or speech was permitted. This was known as St Agnes's Fast. In the *Denham Tracts* it is related that one woman tried this form of the charm and saw not one but three apparitions, the last of which seemed to have a wooden leg. The prophecy was fulfilled to the letter. She was three times married, and her last husband was a man with a wooden leg who had been married to someone else at the time of her vision.

A Northumberland variant of the St Agnes's Eve ceremony omitted the cake altogether, and substituted an egg which had been boiled hard by the performer, emptied of its meat, and the shell filled with salt. The girl had to eat this, shell and all, and then go to bed backwards, saying,

> Sweet St Agnes, work thy fast.
> If ever I be to marry man,
> Or even man to marry me,
> I hope him this night to see.

An entry in the *Tyneside Naturalists' Field Club Transactions* (Vol. 95) says that men sometimes tried to induce a vision of a future bride on St Agnes's Eve by eating a raw red herring, bones and all.

E

EAGLE

From very early times, the eagle has been venerated, admired and feared in nearly every country where it exists. It had an honoured place in the mythologies of India, Persia, Assyria, and the empire of the Hittites. In ancient Greece, it was closely associated with Zeus, the Sky-Father; in Rome, it was the sacred bird of the Legions, who bore its image on their standards. It was the king of the heavens, the bringer of storms and thunderbolts, the sun-bird who could stare into the sun's light without being dazzled. Pliny tells us that its power to look open-eyed into the solar glory was so important to it that if one of the young birds was unable to do so, the mother threw it out of the nest and left it to perish.

According to one tradition, it never grew old because it was able to renew its youth periodically. It first flew so near the sun that its feathers burst into flames, and then dived straight downwards into the sea and quenched the fire. Afterwards it brooded on its nest until new feathers had grown, and with them, new youth. Another story said it could not die of old age or sickness like other birds, but only of hunger, because in the course of time its beak grew inwards, and became so crooked that it could not open it to feed.

Eagles have vanished now from English skies, though they still survive in Scotland. In Wales, where they were once plentiful, especially in the Snowdon district, their cries were said to predict calamity, or some great event, like the birth of a hero, or the rise or fall of a dynasty. When they flew low over the plains, disease, death, or defeat in war were threatened, but when they soared high over the mountains, circling continually in the upper air, the omen was good. A solitary bird perched like a sentry on a crag denoted the approach of an enemy, but if many were seen together, it was a sign of peace. In stormy weather, it was often said that the eagles were breeding whirlwinds on Snowdon, which they were supposed to do by flapping their wings. In one Welsh legend about Arthur, where the hero sleeps in a mountain cave, he is guarded by eagles, though he himself, when he appears in bird form, is always a raven, a chough, or a puffin, never an eagle.

It is said to be very unlucky to rob an eagle's nest. Whoever does so will never know peace or rest again. It is likely also to be a dangerous enterprise, but perhaps it was once thought worth while to attempt it for the sake of the eagle-stone that might be found in it, *see Eagle-stones*, and because the eggs themselves had magical value. One such egg, shared and eaten by two persons, was supposed to protect them both henceforth from evil of various kinds, and especially the spells of witches.

Because these birds have marvellously keen eyesight, their gall, mixed with honey, was considered a good remedy for failing sight in human beings. They themselves were said to keep their eyes clear and strong by eating hawkweed, which is in fact good for the sight and was formerly often recommended in the form of lotions or infusions to cure eye-diseases.

EAGLE-STONES

The name eagle-stone was given to small aetites (*lapis acquilaris*) of a light brown colour which women wore as amulets during pregnancy and child-birth to prevent miscarriages and secure easy delivery. They were usually imported from the East and, being rare, exotic, and credited with magical powers, were greatly prized by those lucky enough to possess them. In the seventeenth and early eighteenth centuries, it was customary in England for the owners of such stones to lend them to their friends and neighbours as occasion required. Women wore them in little bags round their necks during most of their pregnancy, and tied them round the thigh during labour.

Lupton, in his *Notable Things* (1660) says they bring love between man and wife, 'and if a woman have a painfull travail in the birth of her child, this stone tyed to her thigh brings an easy and light birth'. In the *Master Papers*, there is a letter from Sir Streynsham Master to his married daughter, dated 4 February 1716, in which he tells her he has sent an eagle-stone in an Indian silk bag, together with a paper belonging to it on which is written: 'Eagle stones, good to prevent Miscarriages of Woman with Child, to be worne about the Neck and left off two or three weeks before the reckoning is out.' In a later letter, Sir Streynsham says, 'I am told by my Lady Dawes that in the time of Labour one should be tyed to the thigh to cause an easy delivery.' On 11 February, his son-in-law acknowledged the arrival of the stone, 'to our great Sattisfaction', and promised that it should 'thankfully be returned so soon as it has done its office'.

Belief in the magical powers of these stones, as well as their name, sprang from a very ancient tradition that they could only be found in the nests of eagles. These birds were said to have great difficulty in laying their eggs, and to be unable to do so without the help of the stone. It also had the power of preserving the nest from poison.

EAR-RINGS

Ear-rings worn in pierced ears are commonly believed to be good for the sight. For this purpose, a pair obtained by any ordinary means, such as gift or purchase, is usually deemed sufficient, but in a case recorded by the

Exeter and Plymouth Gazette on 15 March 1877, a further magical element was introduced. A woman at Braunston went round from house to house, collecting pennies to the value of four-and-sixpence, with which she proposed to buy a pair of ear-rings to cure her bad eyesight. She said the charm would not work unless the money was received only from men, that is, from those of opposite sex to her own, and if, while collecting it, she carefully refrained from saying either 'please' or 'thank you'.

Plain gold ear-rings were formerly worn by most seamen, in the belief that they would protect their wearers from drowning.

It should perhaps be mentioned that only the type of ring which requires pierced ears is considered efficacious either as a cure for bad sight or as an amulet against drowning. Those which are merely screwed on have no power.

EARTH

Earth, the fruitful dust from which men and all things spring, was anciently believed to have mystical powers, both for healing and for magic. Death and birth came more easily if the dying man or the mother was laid directly upon it, *see Death, Easing and Birth, Easing*, and at other crises of life, it was resorted to for help in both good and evil. All earth had these properties, but the most efficacious was that taken from holy ground, such as a churchyard, or from a place where three lands met.

An easy cure for whitlows was to thrust the afflicted finger into the ground. If a man struck by lightning could be buried up to his neck in earth without delay, he would be, or at least, might be, saved. The *Leicester and Nottingham Journal* for 13 May 1775, reports the case of a young man, sorely troubled with rheumatism, who allowed himself to be buried, naked, with only his face showing, for two hours at a stretch. He said he already felt much better for the treatment, and was prepared to repeat it for a further three hours on the morrow.

Aubrey[1] tells us that in 1642 a West-country woman suffering from cancer of the breast was advised to make a plaster of mud drawn from a boggy place where cattle had stood, and apply it to the affected part. An Irish remedy for influenza was to make a similar plaster of clay scraped off the threshold of the house and lay it on the chest. This had peculiar power for the double reason that the threshold is always sacred, and because of the many blessings pronounced there by visitors who followed the Irish custom of saying 'God save all here' before entering.

In the Shetland Isles, when anyone suffered from the stitch, churchyard mould was brought from a grave in the churchyard, heated, and laid on. This cured the malady, always provided that the mould was returned to the

[1] J. Aubrey, *Royal Soc. MS.* fols. 56, 57.

grave before sunset. Henderson[1] mentions a cunning man at Stamfordham in Northumberland who healed ringworm by rubbing earth from his garden on to it at sunrise, while repeating certain words. The charm, like many others, could only be used by one person at a time, and had to be passed from a man to a woman, from a woman to a man, but never to any person of the same sex as the one who possessed it at the time.

A turf, which combined the magical powers of earth and grass, served in Gloucestershire as a charm against ill-wishing and witchcraft. It had to be worn under the hat, so that the wearer was both 'over the sod and under the sod', and was consequently beyond the reach of any living person's malice. In Cornwall, warts could be healed by digging up a turf, and then laying it face downwards, saying, 'Wart, wart, dry away.' As the grass withered on the reversed clod, so would the wart. A seventeenth-century remedy for colic, mentioned in *The Queen's Closet Opened* (1655), was to put a turf, grass downwards on the stomach and 'let it lie till you find Ease'.

A Berkshire form of divination practised by girls in the nineteenth century was to place a turf, a bowl of water, and a green bough in a row in a hayfield, and crawl towards them blindfolded. To touch the water predicted motherhood, to touch the bough foretold that the girl would live to be a widow, but to touch the turf meant an early death.

In Wales, the soil from the top of the Holy Mountain used to be sprinkled over the fields after the Spring sowing to ensure good crops. Until the late years of the nineteenth century it was also placed in coffins in the belief that it would help the soul of the dead man on his way to the next world.

EEL

A well-known country method of preventing cramp was to wear an eelskin garter round the leg, next to the skin. Swimmers sometimes wore such garters to avoid the dangers of cramp in the water. So too, when the Stamp-Stainer was called in to heal a sprain by stamping on it, the limb had to be bound up with an eelskin afterwards, to complete the cure. *See Stamp-Stainer.*

Warts also could be caused to vanish by rubbing them with eel's blood. This remedy, which was still current in the nineteenth century, was perhaps a simpler version of a charm mentioned by Schröder in his *History of Animals as they are used in Physick and Chirurgery* (1659). In this, it was necessary to cut off the creature's head, rub it while still bleeding on the warts, and then bury it. As it rotted in the ground, so the warts would go.

A live eel placed in his drink was supposed to cure a man of the vice of drinking too much. It may well have done so, at least temporarily, as a kind of shock-treatment.

[1] Wm. Henderson, *op. cit.*

Along the Scottish border, any river-pool which contained a ramper-eel (or lamprey) was avoided by swimmers, because of a belief that the creature would seize them and suck their blood away.

For the supposed origin of eels, *see Horse-hairs.*

EGGS

Eggs are very obvious symbols of resurrection and continuing life, and they were so regarded by many ancient peoples. Coloured eggs were exchanged in antiquity at the Spring Festival by the Greeks and Romans, Persians and Chinese, as we today exchange Easter eggs at the Feast of the Resurrection. In some parts of Europe, scarlet Easter eggs are planted in the fields and vineyards to protect the crops from thunder and hail, and not so long ago, in England, one of the more beautifully decorated Pace-eggs was put aside at Easter and kept in the house throughout the year for luck.

Children are still told that such eggs have a mysterious origin. They are fetched from Rome by the church bells, *see Bells*, or are laid by the Easter Hare. *See Hare*. A charming Polish legend relating to the *pisanki*, or coloured eggs which always appear in large numbers on the Easter Table, is that they were first prepared by Our Lady herself at Nazareth. To amuse the Infant Jesus, she took hard-boiled eggs and painted them red and green and yellow. Polish countrywomen say that since that day, all good housewives have done the same, but because eggs are emblems of resurrection, they do it now at Eastertide.

Ordinary eggs have their folklore also. It is commonly said to be unlucky to bring them into the house, or take them out of it after sunset. They must not be sold then, or carried on board ship. Sailors never refer to them by name when at sea, the term 'roundabout' being often used instead. It is unlucky to dream of eggs, especially those which have been spoiled. To do so foretells a death in the owner's family. Small, yokeless eggs are ill-omened also, if brought into the house. At one time, these were thought to be laid by cocks, and they are still occasionally called cock's eggs or, in Lincolnshire, wind-eggs.

Numerous rules surround the setting of eggs under the hen. There must be an uneven number, usually thirteen. If an even number is set, the eggs will not hatch out, or if they do, all the birds will be cockerels. Nor will they hatch if they have previously been carried over running water. It is unlucky to set them on a Sunday, and in the *Denham Tracts*, it is stated that housewives in Scottish Border counties avoid the month of May also. Setting after sundown is sometimes recommended, particularly for those who want hen-birds; if it is done earlier, only cocks will hatch out. Henderson[1] mentions a Border belief that if all the eggs in a sitting turn out to be hens, it is an omen

[1] Wm. Henderson, *op. cit.*

of a death in the farmer's family, and so too, if double-yoked eggs are laid.

The last egg laid by an old hen is kept on some farms as a charm to protect the poultry, or one laid on Good Friday may serve the same purpose. A small black cross marked on the eggs before setting guards them against witchcraft and weasels.

A well-known form of marriage divination is for the enquirer to prick the small end of a new-laid egg on New Year's Eve, Hallowe'en, or some other significant date, and let three drops of the white fall into a basin of water. From the shapes these assume, details about the future husband or wife, the number of children of the marriage, and so on, can be read by those versed in such matters. The same charm is often performed with melted lead and water.

Eggs could be used in malevolent magic also. An entry in the parish registers of Wells-next-the-Sea, Norfolk, records how in 1583 fourteen men, whose names are given, were drowned 'by the detestable working of an execrable witche of Kings Lynn, whose name was Mother Gabley'. She accomplished her end 'by the boiling or rather labouring of certayn Eggs in a payle full of colde water, afterward proved sufficiently at ye arraingment of ye said Witche'.

Nearly four hundred years later, an echo of Mother Gabley's magic was heard in a Scarborough court during an inquest on a seventeen-month-old child. The *Lindsey & Lincolnshire Star* for 1 October 1904, reported that, according to the medical evidence, death was caused by convulsions due to rickets, but that the mother believed it was the result of witchcraft. She told the Coroner that thirteen months before, her next-door neighbour had been turned out of her house in consequence of something that she, the witness, had said to the landlord. Before she left, she threatened to bewitch the child by boiling eggs and mashing them. She never saw the baby, but after she had gone, the house was haunted intermittently by strange shadows and noises. Eventually the child died, and in view of what had been said, the mother was convinced that it had been bewitched in revenge.

EGG-SHELLS

Many people not otherwise superstitious will carefully break the empty shell of an egg just eaten because they were taught in childhood that not to do so was unlucky. Witches might use unbroken shells, either to work evil upon the individual concerned, or as means of transport. The idea that they could travel magically overland or by sea in shells was once quite common. In 1673, during the trial of Anne Baites of Morpeth for witchcraft, one of the witnesses stated that he had often seen her riding thus, both indoors and in a field. In coastal areas, a shell left intact is said to turn ships at sea, or cause a shipwreck.

Among poultry-breeders, it is very unlucky to burn an empty shell. All the birds, and especially the one who laid the egg, will at once cease laying.

The strings of blown shells so beloved by schoolboys are disliked in many districts. They bring misfortune if they are kept in the house, and should always be hung in some empty shed or outhouse where they can do no harm.

A Lincolnshire folk-cure for bed-wetting is to give the child egg-shells ground up in milk or water.

ELDER

The elder is a tree with a very mixed reputation in folk-belief. It was formerly considered unlucky to bring its wood into the house, and extremely unlucky to burn it. Hedgers who were allowed to take home faggots for their own use always sorted out the elder and left it behind. In his *Notes upon Certain Superstitions Prevalent in the Vale of Gloucester*, John Jones relates how on one occasion, when an old hedgerow was being removed, the wood was bound into faggots with the exception of the elder which was, as usual, left on one side. On being asked what was to be done with the latter, the employer said it was to be burnt with the rest, whereupon one man declared he had 'never heard of such a thing as burning ellan-wood', and flatly refused to help in tying it up for so ill-omened a purpose. Lincolnshire people say that to burn it brings the Devil into the house. In Shropshire, as late as 1938, some of the older people still believed that to do so would cause a death in the family within twelve months.

Some farmers do not like to use elder-sticks when driving cattle to market, nor will their wives use the wood to make skewers for dressed poultry. To beat a growing child with such a stick stunts its growth, and when cradles were fitted with rockers, it was dangerous to mend the latter with elder-wood. If this was done, witches could rock the cradle violently from a distance, or injure the baby in some other way. The same witches sometimes transformed themselves into elder-trees, and if such trees were cut, they bled. The legend of the Rollright Stones says a King and his army were turned into stones by a witch, and that she then became an elder growing near them. There is a tradition that on Midsummer Eve formerly, the local people used to go to the King-stone and hold a feast there, and that afterwards the witch-tree was ceremonially cut. Blood ran from it, and as it did so, the King-stone nodded its head.

Another story of a bleeding tree which, though not definitely stated to be an elder, almost certainly was one, comes from Syresham in Northampton-shire. A man cut a stick for his little boy and was horrified to see blood spouting from the cut. Some time later, a woman suspected of witchcraft was seen with her arm bound up, and this coincidence was regarded as clear proof that she was in fact a witch.

An explanation often given for the ill-omened character of the elder is that Judas Iscariot hanged himself upon such a tree, or that the Cross was made from its wood. The latter tradition is shared by the aspen, the poplar, and several other trees. In Yorkshire, to crown a man with elder-twigs was considered a mark of extreme degradation and infamy because of the legendary associated with Judas's death. But the true root of the various elder superstitions seems to be pre-Christian and connected with ancient animistic beliefs. In Scandinavia and Germany, it was the abode of the Elder Mother, whose permission must be asked before it was lopped or cut down. Danish woodmen said 'Hyldemoer, Hyldemoer, permit me to cut thy branches', before doing so. A Lincolnshire version of the same request was

> Owd gal, gi' me of thi wood,
> An' I will gi' thee some of mine
> When I grow into a tree.

It was widely considered very unlucky to proceed with the work without some such formula. Heanley[1] tells us that he once visited a woman whose baby had recently suffered from convulsions. She complained that her husband had foolishly cut some elder-wood to mend a cradle-rocker 'without axing the Old Lady's leave', and consequently the offended tree-spirit had pinched the child until he was almost black in the face. When the rocker was wrenched off and replaced by one of ash-wood, he recovered.

Heanley goes on to say that, being interested in this curious tale, he put a knot of elder-wood before his servant and asked him if he was afraid to cut it. The man replied that he was not because this was dead wood, but had it been alive, he would not have dared to do so without asking permission. He added that many years before, when working on Wainfleet Flats, he had cut an elder without doing so, and on his way home the 'Old Gal' smote him so violently that he was in bed for a month, and was always lame afterwards. The doctor said it was rheumatic fever, but he knew better.

Nevertheless, if the elder was sometimes dangerous to men, it could also be helpful. It was commonly supposed to avert lightning, and to preserve any house near which it grew from being struck. In *The Book of Days* (1864), it is related that when some Suffolk children were warned not to shelter under an elder-tree in a storm, they replied that they would be quite safe there because the Cross was made of elder-wood, and therefore the tree is never struck by lightning.

Although witches used it, as has been seen, parts of it were sometimes employed in charms against witchcraft. In Herefordshire, the dried and powdered pith was given to people supposed to be bewitched. Henderson[2]

[1] R. M. Heanley, *op. cit.*   [2] Wm. Henderson, *op. cit.*

mentions a belief that the juice of the inner bark, if applied to the eyes of a christened person, enabled him or her to know what witches were doing anywhere. The Durham wiseman, William Dawson, who flourished in the nineteenth century, was once consulted by a farmer who had suffered heavy losses with his stock. In order to find out if this was due to witchcraft, Dawson advised him to take six knots of bottree (elder) wood and arrange them neatly under a new ashen dish or bowl. If, without being touched by human hands, they were subsequently found disarranged, it would show that the trouble was due to a spell. The farmer did as he was told, and found the knots in utter confusion; after which, on Dawson's instructions, he broke the spell by driving nails into the heart of one of the dead beasts and burning it, with appropriate ceremonies and words, on a hot fire at midnight.

Elder was once used in remedies for a variety of ills, including quinsies, sore throats, warts, fits, erysipelas, rheumatism, and the bites of adders and mad dogs. In Sussex, a stick with three, five or seven knots in it prevented rheumatism, if carried about in the pocket. A piece of elder-wood on which the sun had never shone, cut between two knots and worn round the neck, averted erysipelas, and a necklace of nine sticks was a charm against epilepsy, provided that it was never allowed to fall to the ground. If it did so, its efficacy was lost, and a new one had to be made. In Gloucestershire, such a necklace also cured convulsions in children, but here the preparations were somewhat complicated. The twigs could only be gathered by the father of the child concerned. He had first to seek for an elder that had been seeded by birds on the pollard top of a willow, and then to cut the twigs on the night of the full moon. If these conditions were not observed, the charm would not work.

Warts could be driven away in Northamptonshire by crossing them with an elder-stick. Elsewhere other methods were used. The wart could be pricked so that the blood fell into an elder-leaf which was then buried, or a stick could be notched with as many notches as there were warts, and then secretly buried after each wart had been touched with the notch that represented it.

Elder-leaves gathered on May Eve healed wounds, if laid upon them. A well-known country remedy for jaundice was to boil the inner bark of the tree in milk and give the decoction to the patient to drink, the yellow bark being considered efficacious for the yellow disease. The same bark boiled in water was given for the falling sickness, or epilepsy. An Oxfordshire treatment for burns and scalds, used within living memory, was to mix the inner rind with fresh butter, bandage it on securely, and then plunge the burnt or scalded part into cold water.

Seventeenth-century horsemen cured a horse that could not stale by striking it gently with an elder-stick and binding elder-leaves on its stomach. They also saved themselves from the discomfort of galling by carrying two little elder-sticks (or one with two notches in it) in their pockets when riding. The latter charm is not entirely unknown amongst horsemen even today.

ENGAGEMENT RINGS

It is very unlucky to lose or break an engagement ring. As the betrothal was sealed by the giving of the ring, so the loss of the latter foretells its ending, either because of quarrels between the pair, the death or desertion of one of them, or some other unforeseen happening.

The choice of stones is also important, though this can only be a fairly modern extension of the ancient lore of precious stones. In earlier times, gemmed betrothal rings were not usual. One of gold or silver was commonly used, sometimes made in the form of a true lovers' knot, or a gimmal-ring consisting of two hoops which could be separated, one part being given to the man at the betrothal ceremony and the other to the woman. On the marriage day, they were united to form the wedding ring.

The modern preference is for diamonds, sapphires, emeralds or rubies, all of which, besides being beautiful and valuable, have fortunate properties of one kind or another. The birthstone of the fiancée is a luck-bringer, although those belonging to some months, being only semi-precious, are not always considered good enough for an engagement ring. *See Birthstones*. Few young women today would choose a turquoise, but at one time, it was a favourite stone because it was thought to prevent dissension between husband and wife, and also to give warning, by changing its colour, of any danger or illness threatening its owner.

Pearls are still quite often disliked in spite of their beauty. They signify tears, and are therefore not good omens of a happy marriage. Opals are almost always thought unlucky, partly because they are changeable and inconstant, and partly because they are widely believed to be ill-omened jewels for all except those who are born in October.

EYEBROWS

Eyebrows meeting across the nose are often considered a bad sign, perhaps because of the dark and frowning look they give to the face. They are said to denote a brooding or violent temper. In some parts of England, those who possess them will not 'live to wear wedding clothes', which may mean either an early death or misfortune in love. In Scotland, a 'close-broot' man was thought to be immoral, or destined to die by hanging. He was exceedingly unlucky as a First Foot, and equally so if he was the first person encountered outside the house in the New Year. In Greece, he was suspected of being a vampire, and in Iceland, Denmark, and Germany, of being a werewolf. An old Icelandic name for such a man was *hamrammr*, meaning one who is able to change his shape.

An exception to this widespread dislike of meeting eyebrows is recorded by Henderson,[1] who says that in northern England they were a sign that their owner would be lucky in life.

EYES

Eyes, which reveal their owner's thoughts and feelings more clearly than any other part of the body, have always been considered vehicles of strong spiritual power. As a glance can convey a message of love or hate, scorn or encouragement to the person looked at, so it was from time immemorial believed to be capable of conveying an actual blessing or curse. An angry or envious look, even from some quite ordinary individual, might have ill-effects, and this was still more likely in the case of anyone whose eyes were oddly set or coloured, since that peculiarity might mark him as the possessor of the dreaded Evil Eye.

Faith in the Evil Eye is almost universal and very ancient. 'Some persons' eies are very offensive . . .' says Aubrey in his *Remaines*, 'there is *aliquid Divinum* in it, more than every one understands.' This idea existed in ancient Assyria, Greece, Rome and Egypt, and still does in many parts of Europe today. The basic conception is that certain persons can bring misfortune or illness to human beings and animals, and destroy or damage inanimate objects, simply by looking at them. Hence the term 'overlooked', which was often applied to those who were thought to have fallen under some enchantment.

An interesting point about this age-old tradition is that the possession and operation of this power was not always voluntary. Many who had no leanings towards evil were thought to be afflicted with it, and in some cases, the glance did its work against the will of the person concerned. Aubrey speaks of a man who bewitched his own cattle without meaning to do so. In *About Yorkshire* (1883), Thomas and Katharine Macquoid mention a man at Fyling Thorpe who 'always walked about with his eyes fixed on the ground, and never looked at any one to whom he spoke; his glance was cursed, and he dare not speak to one of the rosy children, lest some blight should fall upon it'. In Carr's *Craven Glossary*, we read of another Yorkshireman who always directed the first glance of the morning, which was commonly believed to be the most deadly, upon a pear-tree outside his house, so that the full venom might be expended upon it instead of upon some innocent passer-by. The tree slowly withered and eventually died.

People with eyes of differing colours, or set deep in the head, or too close together, were often suspected of having the Evil Eye. So were those who

[1] Wm. Henderson, *op. cit.*

squinted or were 'trough-eyed', having one eye lower than the other. Even today, the last two are considered unlucky to meet, and fingers are often quietly crossed until they have passed, or the ground is spat upon as soon as their backs are turned.

If anyone who was evil-eyed chose to use his powers, the effect upon his victim was assured unless some strong charm was immediately used to nullify the curse. It was best to keep away from such people as far as possible, and at all times to avoid incurring their displeasure. Gypsies are often said to have 'the power of the eye', and there are people today who are careful to give them alms which they would deny to any ordinary beggar. In one Somerset village within this century, the midwife had it, and great care was taken not to offend her, lest she should overlook the mother or the child. It is not recorded that she ever did so. Nevertheless, most women preferred her services to those of the district nurse when they were confined, since to do otherwise might have incurred her anger, and she continued to practise until she retired through old age.

Charms against the Evil Eye were, and are, innumerable. Spittle, fire, and the sign of the Cross gave protection, as in most other cases of threatened evil. Blue beads are worn in many countries, as they were in ancient Egypt, or little amulets in the shape of a horned hand, *see Hands*, the crescent moon, wheel, or serpent, or the Italian *cimaruta*, which is a sprig of rue fashioned in silver, and having other protective emblems attached to its tips. A Manx way of curing an overlooked cow was to sweep the road outside the gate and throw the gathered dust over her, while invoking the Trinity. In the West-country, salt was sometimes strewn on the stricken beast, from head to tail on one side and from tail to head on the other, the operator saying meanwhile: 'As Thy servant Elisha healed the waters of Jericho by casting salt therein, so I hope to heal this my beast in the Name of God the Father, God the Son, and God the Holy Ghost.'

Red thread, especially if it has been knotted by someone 'having knowledge', with an incantation pronounced over each knot, is a Scottish antidote. Another is to drink in the Name of the Trinity water which has been drawn in a wooden ladle from a running stream, and into which gold and silver coins have been dropped. A more elaborate variant of this charm is to take a clay or wooden vessel to a ford or bridge over which the living and the dead have passed. The healer, who must not speak to anyone on his way to or from the stream, kneels down, cups his hands, and so lifts water into the vessel, three times below the bridge or ford, and three times above it. The Trinity is invoked, a silver coin is put into the water, and the vessel is taken back to the house, where it is carried three times round the fire or chimney-chain, going the way of the sun. The water is then either sprinkled over the Eye-smitten person, or given to him to drink. What is left is sometimes poured out on a rock, or thrown behind the hearthstone.

F

FAIRY RINGS

Fairy Rings are those green, sour ringlets which sometimes appear on pasture land. The name is also given occasionally to circles of small white or yellow flowers growing in fields. They are traditionally said to spring up where fairies customarily dance, or to grow above a subterranean fairy village. It was formerly believed that if anyone ran nine times round such a ring on the night of the Full Moon, he would hear the fairies laughing and talking below. This could only be done with safety if the runner went the way of the sun, for to go widdershins round would put him in the power of the ring's owners. In Northumberland, it was also considered dangerous to make more than nine circuits. If this magical number was exceeded, some evil would befall the runner.

In general, as with most things connected with fairies, it was held wiser to avoid such places altogether. To sit inside a ring on certain nights, such as May Eve or Hallowe'en, was an extremely foolhardy act which opened the way to enchantment, or the spiriting away to Fairyland of the rash person concerned. May-dew gathered from the grass or flowers of a ring was unlucky. Cattle and sheep were believed to recognize the peril of such circles, and to refuse to graze inside one. Above all, it was dangerous to attempt to destroy a fairy ring since this, naturally, gave offence to its owners who had their own very efficient methods of revenge. In any case, it was commonly held to be labour in vain because, no matter how often such a ring was ploughed or dug up, it would always reappear in the same place within a very short time afterwards.

FEET

Omens of the future and indications of character are sometimes read from the shape and appearance of a person's feet, and especially from anything unusual about them. A child born with an extra toe on one or both of his feet is generally expected to be lucky in life. In Scotland, 'lucken toes', that is, those with a thin web of skin between them, are often thought a fortunate sign, although in some coastal areas, and in the Western Isles, this is said to denote that seal-blood runs in the veins of the person concerned. Another Scottish belief is that a man whose second toe is longer than the first, or great toe, will be a harsh and cruel husband.

Flat-footed people are ill-omened in some parts of Britain. If the first visitor on New Year's Day is flat-footed, the omen is bad for all in the house. Conversely, anyone having a high arched instep is an extremely lucky First Foot. To meet a flat-footed individual on a Monday was formerly very unlucky in northern England, especially when beginning a journey. Whoever did so was likely to suffer some misfortune on the way unless he at once turned back, ate and drank in his own house, and then started out afresh.

For all beginnings, and new enterprises, the right foot should be used before the left. To enter a house with the left foot foremost is widely held to be unlucky, and particularly so if it is done by a bride coming to her home for the first time after the wedding. Similarly, any journey begun with the left foot is likely to be unfortunate. When dressing, the right foot should always be shod before the left. If the latter is accidentally thrust into the opposite shoe, bad luck is certain to follow during the day.

If a child is born feet first, he will have magical or healing powers in later life. *See Footlings.*

FERNS

Ferns of all kinds were associated with thunder and lightning, and consequently they protected any house that contained them from damage by storms. They were also connected with snakes. Some, like the Adder's Tongue, cured the bites of adders, but according to a Welsh superstition, it was dangerous to carry a fern-leaf about because it attracted adders and caused them to follow the bearer. In Ireland, they are said to be flowerless because St Patrick cursed them, and in some parts of England, they are considered Devil's plants, and are known as Devil's Brushes. On the other hand, the Bracken is supposed to be marked with Christ's initials, and therefore feared by witches and evil spirits. In some areas, it is believed that pulling up a fern brings on a storm, and to tread on one unawares makes a man confused in his wits and liable to lose his way.

There was formerly a widespread belief that to cut or burn fern brought down rain. In 1636, when Charles I was about to visit Staffordshire, his Chamberlain, Lord Pembroke, wrote to the High Sheriff of that county, asking that no fern should be burnt during the King's stay, in order to ensure fine weather. An equally widespread superstition was that the spores of Bracken, known as Fernseed, conferred invisibility on their possessor, and had other magical properties.

Decoctions and plasters made from various kinds of ferns were once used for numerous ills, including wounds, snake-bites, bile, coughs, inflammation, and sore eyes. Of the fern called Polypody, Gerard says in his *Herbal*, 'That which groweth on the bodies of olde Okes is preferred before the rest', perhaps because it carried the magical virtues of the tree as well as its own. The country belief that 'fern growing on a tree' is good for stomach-ache may be connected with this idea. A West-country antidote to toothache mentioned by Thistleton Dyer[1] as current when he wrote in 1889, was to bite the first fern seen in Spring. *See Adders Tongue Fern: Bracken: Male Fern.*

FIDDLE-FISH

Fishermen consider it very fortunate to catch fiddle-fish which, though themselves inedible, bring good luck to the boat in whose nets they are caught. By custom, they are attached to the vessel and towed astern on every subsequent voyage until they fall to pieces or disappear. As long as they remain there, good hauls may be expected.

On 5 August 1949, *The Times* reported that, for the first time in ten years, fiddle-fish were brought into Fleetwood by the trawler *Jamaica*, and were at once slung over the stern by the crew, for towing in the traditional way.

FIGUREHEADS

Sailors formerly believed that a sailing ship could not sink without her figurehead. This notion suggests that the figure was somehow connected in the minds of seamen with the life and soul of the vessel, and certainly, it was usually respected, and regarded as something more than mere ornament. R. L. Hadfield[2] relates an odd incident illustrating this belief which occurred in 1928. A film company was making a film about the Q-ships of the 1914–18 war, and bought the schooner *Amy* for the purpose of sinking her during one of the scenes. Charges were fired within her, but on three separate occasions she refused to go down. An old sailor pointed out that her figurehead had been removed, and that consequently she could not do so. It was therefore replaced, and at the next attempt the ship sank easily.

FINGERS

In England, long fingers are said to be a sign that their owner is improvident and will never be able to save money. In parts of Scotland, the omen is worse; he is likely to be a thief. Similarly, if the forefinger is as long as the second, or longer, dishonesty is indicated. Crooked fingers are sometimes said to show a crabbed disposition, but a crooked little finger is a sign that the person having it will die rich. If a child is born with an extra finger (or toe) he will be lucky in life.

The forefinger of the right hand is often called the Poison Finger. It is thought to be venomous, and should not be used to apply ointments to a cut or sore. The middle, or longest finger is used for this purpose. An exception

---

[1] T. Thistleton Dyer, *The Folk-Lore of Plants*, 1889.   [2] R. L. Hadfield, *op. cit.*

to this quite common rule was recorded a few years ago in Oxfordshire, where an enquirer was told that a good remedy for ringworm was to rub spittle on the diseased part with the Poison Finger.

The third finger of the left hand, or ring finger, is sometimes credited with healing powers. If a wound or sore place is stroked with it, it will soon be cured. A very generally held belief is that a vein or nerve runs directly to this finger from the heart, which is why the wedding ring is worn on it in many countries, though not in all.

When a person does anything likely to bring bad luck, such as walking under a ladder or passing someone going the opposite way on the stairs, he can avert the threatened misfortune by crossing his fingers. The same charm can be used when anything ill-omened is seen, like a magpie or raven, or the new moon through glass.

If two people say the same words at the same moment, they should lock their little fingers together, right hand to right hand or left to left, and wish silently. The wish will come true provided that nothing more is said until the fingers are released.

FINGER-NAILS

Omens are often read from the shape and growth of finger-nails, and also from the little specks which sometimes appear on them. If a man's nails grow crookedly, or are long and claw-like, it is a sign of an evil, or an avaricious disposition. If they project in the middle, it is an omen of early death, and so too if the 'half-moons' at their base are small. If the 'half-moons' are large, long life and prosperity is to be expected.

White specks on the nails have varying significance, according to the finger on which they appear. Thus, one on the thumb-nail usually means a present, on the forefinger, the coming of a friend, on the second finger, that of a foe. In parts of Scotland, however, it is the forefinger-spot which means an enemy, one on the thumb a friend, and on the second finger, a gift. If one appears on the fourth finger, it foretells a journey. A black or yellow spot on any finger-nail is a very bad sign, and usually means a death.

Nail-paring has its lore also, and is generally supposed to be safe only on certain days. Monday and Tuesday are lucky in most districts, Wednesday and Thursday moderately so. To do it on Saturday is variously said to bring about losses, or to foretell a visit from a lover. Friday is uniformly ill-omened in this as in so many other respects, and whoever cuts his nails on a Sunday will have the Devil with him all the week. At best, he must expect some misfortune or grief before the following Saturday. Old sailors believe that to cut nails at sea during a calm will provoke a storm. In northern England, it is said that if a young married woman cuts her right-hand nails with her left hand, she will rule her husband.

A child's nails should never be cut before he is twelve months old, or he will grow up 'light-fingered'. If they become too long, the mother should bite them off. In Somerset, it is thought safe to cut them only if it is done over the Bible. This belief in the danger of premature cutting is very widespread, and is found in both European and non-European countries.

In Wales, and in the English counties bordering on it, a child's first nail-parings were sometimes buried under an ash-tree, in the belief that this would make him grow up to be a 'top-singer'. Henderson[1] records the same tradition in Northumberland also. Since the ash is a protective tree, it is possible that the rite had the additional merit of being a safe way of disposing of the parings, which might otherwise fall into the hands of witches, or other evilly-disposed persons, and be used by them in spells to harm the original owner. It is still very often considered unlucky (as well as untidy) to leave nail-parings about, though nowadays it is not definite witchcraft that is feared, but some vague conception of ill-luck.

A curiously simple method of becoming a witch is recorded by Sternberg in his *Dialect and Folk-Lore of Northamptonshire* (1851). All that the person concerned had to do was to sit on the hob of the hearth, trimming and cleaning his or her nails, and saying at the same time: 'I wish I was as far from God as my nails are far from dirt.' This sinister wish constituted an offered transfer of allegiance, which the Dark Powers would be only too likely to accept.

FIRST FOOT

The ceremony of admitting the First Foot in the early hours of New Year's morning is still widely observed in Scotland and northern England.

The First Foot is, as his name denotes, the first visitor of the New Year to enter a house. His function is to bring good luck and prosperity for the ensuing twelve months to those he visits. He comes as soon as possible after midnight, bringing gifts which symbolize plentiful food, warmth, and wealth. These now usually take the form of a piece of bread, a piece of coal, and a little money, or salt. Sometimes he also carries an evergreen branch as a symbol of continuing life, but this part of the rite is less common now than formerly.

Certain strict rules govern the choice of the First Foot. He must always be a man, since he represents the New Year itself, and a woman in that role would be exceedingly unlucky. He must never be flat-footed or cross-eyed, nor should he have eyebrows that meet across his nose. Usually he must be dark-haired, though in East Yorkshire and some districts in Northumberland, this rule is reversed, and he must be fair. Red hair is disliked almost everywhere. The luckiest of all First Foots in most areas is a dark-haired stranger who,

[1] Wm. Henderson, *op. cit.*

more than any acquaintance, might seem to personify the new-born year and its still hidden mysteries.

Since, however, dark-haired strangers are not always available in the middle of a winter night, it is customary for a friend of the right colour to act as luck-bringer to the family; or one man may go round to all the houses in a given street or village. In default of any outsider, a male member of the household is often sent outside just before midnight, and is re-admitted, with the appropriate gifts in his hand, as soon as the clock has struck.

In his *English Festivals* (1947) Lawrence Whistler described another, and possibly older, form of the ceremony. Here the First Foot enters in silence and is greeted by none. He goes straight to the hearth and there lays an evergreen branch on the fire and a sprig of mistletoe on the mantelpiece above. No one speaks while this is being done, and not until he turns and wishes all present good luck is the general silence broken. In most modern houses, however, these preliminaries, with their faintly apprehensive undertones, are omitted, and the First Foot is noisily welcomed as soon as he arrives.

In Wales, First-footing was not formerly as clearly marked as in other parts of Britain, though considerable importance was attached to the person first seen on New Year's Day. If the first caller at the house was red-haired, or a woman, the omen was bad. A correspondent in *Bygones* (17 January 1900) says that in Montgomeryshire, if a woman unfortunately arrived before any-one else, little boys were afterwards marched through the house 'to break the witch'. In the southern parts of the Principality, good luck was formerly brought by boys carrying evergreen branches and a vessel full of 'New Year's Water'. They came about three or four o'clock in the morning, and sprinkled the room and its inmates (or the house-door, if they found it shut) with the water, singing as they did so:

> Here we bring new water, from the well so clear,
> For to worship God with, this Happy New Year;
> Sing levy dew, sing levy dew, the water and the wine,
> With seven bright gold wires, the bugles that do shine;
> Sing reign of fair maid, with gold upon her toe,
> Open you the west door, and turn the old year go;
> Sing reign of fair maid, with gold upon her chin,
> Open you the east door, and let the new year in.

The meaning of these words is obscure, but the object of the visit and the water-sprinkling was clearly to bring good luck in the coming year.

In some parts of northern and midland England, as also along the Welsh Border, the First Foot sometimes came on Christmas Day instead of at New Year. In Yorkshire he was then known as the Lucky Bird. The same strict rules applied to the Christmas as to the New Year visitor and, as with the latter, careful arrangements were often made beforehand to ensure that a man of the right colour and type should be the first caller at the house.

FISH

Fish were anciently believed to have knowledge and wisdom. Those which lived in healing or wishing wells were often thought to be embodiments of the spirit of the water. Such fish were, of course, sacred, and it was sacrilegious to disturb or harm them.

Fishermen almost everywhere believe, or did until recently, that the fish upon which they depend for their living are aware of what happens on the coast, and are affected by it. If blood is shed in anger there, or if someone kills himself, they will desert that coast, perhaps for a number of years, perhaps for ever. Eleanor Hull relates in her *Folklore of the British Isles* how the herring forsook Loch Carron for several years after two men had drowned themselves, until the fishermen lit two great bonfires on the spot where the bodies were found, to appease the fish. Along the coast of Normandy, it is said that the fishing has declined because the fish followed Napoleon into exile or, according to another version, because they left when the French monarchy fell, and will not return until it is restored. A Celtic legend says that the herring shoals are ruled by a leader, a fish of more than usual size, known as the Royal Herring. It is very unlucky to destroy or harm this creature, and in some places where the shoals have deserted the coast, their disappearance is put down to someone having done so.

At the beginning of the season, the first fish caught shows by its sex what that season will bring. If it is a female, there will be good hauls, but if it is a male, the fishing will be poor. Very often, this first fish is nailed to the mast as a thank-offering, and to ensure that others will follow where it led. If by some accident, it is lost overboard, the whole trip will be unlucky. In Yorkshire formerly, it was sometimes kept until the men returned to the shore, and was then burnt as a sacrifice.

In Northumberland, it is unlucky to burn fish-bones, which must always be disposed of in some other way. Similarly, in most fishing districts, it is necessary to eat a herring, a pilchard, or a mackerel from the tail to the head, never the other way. To eat it from head to tail would turn the heads of the shoal away from the shore so that there would be no more catches. In Cornwall it is a good omen if pilchards when bulked (that is, placed in large regular heaps, alternately heads and tails) make a squeaking noise. They are calling to their companions, and another shoal may be expected shortly.

It is unlucky to count the fish caught in most places. This applies both to sea and inland fishing, to professionals and those fishing for pleasure. If the latter count their fish, they will catch no more that day, and at sea, it may result in the disappearance of the shoal. In Cornwall, however, until fairly recently, an old counting chant was used as the nets were drawn aboard. As each netted fish appeared, one man carried a number, beginning 'a mackerel', then 'a fellow', then 'a third' and so on as required. The interesting point about this custom is that the chant was not spoken in English, but in Cornish, long after the language had ceased to be used anywhere in the Duchy.

Fish could be used in cures of various kinds. The tench, the doctor-fish, healed other fish by the oils in its skin, and human beings of jaundice, *see Tench*, and eels were formerly used to cure warts, sprains, and drunkenness. *See Eels*. In Suffolk, a remedy for whooping-cough was to catch a flat fish (a small dab would do) and put it on the bare chest of the patient, keeping it there until it died. An even more alarming Northumberland cure for the same ailment was to put a trout's head into the child's mouth and 'let it breathe into the mouth'. *See Fiddle-Fish*.

FLEAS

To keep fleas out of a house, the country housewife used at one time to rise very early on 1 March, close all the windows, and carefully sweep the lintel of the door, the hinges, and every crack and crevice. This procedure, which was still followed in many places at the end of last century, was thought to prevent the insect from entering, and ensured that the house would be free of them all through the year.

Fleas (and other parasites) are said to desert the body of any person who is near death. Their sudden disappearance from anyone normally harbouring them is therefore a death omen. In cases of oncoming illness, not yet suspected by the victim, this might have a natural explanation.

FLOWERS

Flowers in general, as well as those of particular kinds, are the subject of numerous superstitions. A very common belief is that if any tree or plant blossoms out of season, it is a sign of ill-luck, often a death omen. Certain types of flowers are said to foretell death if they are brought into the house, particularly white flowers of any variety, those with drooping heads, like the snowdrop, and heavy-scented blooms, in some of which the souls of the dead were once thought to dwell. To dream of white flowers is a death omen, and so is the 'freak' appearance of white petals in a coloured flower, such as a red rose. A kindred belief is that dead flowers seen on the road should never be picked up, for they carry the contagion of death.

Actors say that real flowers on the stage are unlucky. Only artificial ones may be safely worn or used in decorating the scene. This, of course, does not apply to bouquets presented to actresses at the end of the performance, for these have no part in the play.

All flowers with yellow corollas were once thought to protect against witchcraft, and many were used in charms for this purpose. Red blossoms of any sort are generally considered fortunate because red, being the colour of blood, symbolizes life. There is, however, a strong and widespread superstition, found all over England, which forbids the taking of red and white flowers, mixed in a single bunch, into a hospital. To do so means a death in the ward, not necessarily that of the patient to whom they are given. This belief does not appear to be very old in its present form, though its roots may run far back into colour symbolism and magic; but it is now so firmly entrenched that florists often decline to sell such mixed bunches if they know they are intended for a hospital patient, and sisters in charge of wards frequently refuse to admit them. Even nurses who do not personally believe in the omen sometimes do this, on the grounds that the presence of these ominous flowers would 'upset the patients'.

FOOTLING

A child born feet first is sometimes called a Footling. Like most others whose entry into this world was in any way unusual, such a child was formerly believed to have peculiar gifts, particularly those of healing. In north-east Scotland and in Cornwall, sufferers from rheumatism, lumbago, backache, and all kinds of sprains, would send for a person so born and beg him either to trample upon them, or to press or rub his feet against the affected part. In Cornwall, by an extension of the belief, the mother of the footling acquired the same gifts after his or her birth, and was almost as frequently sent for to heal and bless as her child.

In some districts, it was believed that a footling was more likely than others to meet with an accident in later life that would make him lame. To prevent this, old-fashioned midwives rubbed laurel leaves on his feet and legs as soon as possible after the birth.

FOX

Country people have always admired foxes for their cleverness and courage even though they disliked them for their raids upon the poultry-yard. The folk-tales of every country where they are found testify to this fact, from remote times down to our own. In some parts of Europe, a fox's tongue was worn as an amulet to make the wearer bold; in others, the same effect was achieved by cooking and eating it.

The fox was one of several creatures into which it was once believed that witches could, and did, turn themselves at will. In England, the witch-animal was more usually the hare, but there are a number of fox-stories also. As late as the end of the nineteenth century, the people of Kirtlington in Oxfordshire spoke of a local woman who transformed herself thus. A fine fox was often seen near her house and was frequently hunted, though never with success. On one occasion, the hounds were so close behind it that escape seemed impossible, but the hunted beast made a sudden turn and rushed into the witch's house. When, a few seconds later, the huntsmen followed it, there was nothing to be seen but a woman sitting quietly by her fireside.

Certain families in Ireland were traditionally said to be descended from foxes, as others there, and in Scotland, were supposed to be descended from wolves or seals. Such fox-families were warned of a coming death by the appearance of many foxes round their house. It is perhaps because of this legend that in other parts of Britain a fox entering or coming close to a house is thought to be a death omen.

Welsh people think it lucky to meet a single fox, but unlucky to see several together. A Lincolnshire belief recorded in *Folk-Lore concerning Lincolnshire* (1908) is that if anyone is bitten by a fox, he is marked for death within seven years.

An old method of drawing out an obstinate thorn embedded in any part of the human body was to lay a fox's tongue on it. This had to be done at night, just before going to bed. In the morning, the thorn would have come out, even though it had previously resisted every attempt to extract it by the use of poultices or other remedies. A cure for whooping-cough was to put down a dish of milk where a fox could drink it, and then to let the patient drink what was left when the fox had finished. The same charm worked equally well with milk given to ferrets.

In many parts of England, it is still firmly believed that foxes dispose of their fleas periodically by taking a piece of sheep's wool in their mouths and wading with it into a pond or stream until only their noses are above water. The fleas, to escape drowning, take refuge on the wool, and the fox then lets it fall into the water, thus ridding himself of these pests.

This curious piece of natural history is found in numerous districts, and many countrymen assert that it is quite true. In Oxfordshire recently, one man said that, because there are no sheep in this part of the country, the local foxes use bunches of dry grass instead of wool. He had, he said, 'seen 'em at it, scores of times'. What exactly he, and other eye-witnesses have seen is not clear, but faith in this vulpine manoeuvre is still very common.

FOXGLOVE

The wild foxglove is a fairy plant in folk-tradition, and has several other names suggesting its rather ominous character, such as Fairy Weed, Dead Men's Bellows, Bloody Man's Fingers, and Witches' Thimble. In Scotland, it is considered an unlucky flower which should never be brought into a house or taken on board a ship.

Foxglove tea was an old wives' remedy for dropsy long before the plant's real medicinal value in that direction was known. Dr Withering, who first discovered its usefulness in ailments of the heart, is said to have had his attention attracted to it by noticing the effects of foxglove tea prepared by Shropshire wisewomen.

FOX'S WEDDING

When sudden spatters of raindrops fall while the sun is shining, country people say that somewhere a fox is being married. Why this event should cause such showers is not clear, but the tradition seems to exist in many parts of the world, although the animal concerned is not always the same. In Japan and Palestine, it is the fox which celebrates then, as in England, but in southern India it is the jackal, and in Canada poultry or monkeys. Occasionally English children speak of a monkey's birthday instead of a fox's wedding, but this may be due to some relative who had lived in countries where monkeys are better known than foxes, rather than to native belief.

A correspondent in *The Times* of 19 August 1953 says that when he was a child in the West Indies, he was told that these sudden showers meant that the Devil was beating his wife.

FROG

Frogs, like toads (see p. 341), were once thought to have peculiar properties, and were frequently used in healing-charms, and in others of a slightly less innocent nature. A well-known country cure for thrush was to hold a live frog with its head in the patient's mouth. As it breathed, so it drew the disease away and into itself. Warts could also be cured by rubbing a frog across them and then impaling it on a thorn tree to die.

The dried body of a frog worn in a silk bag round the neck averted epilepsy and other fits. Young frogs swallowed alive were a Yorkshire remedy for general weakness, and also for consumption. In some other districts, the same rather drastic treatment was recommended for cancer. A seventeenth-century method of stopping bleeding, mentioned in *Arcana Fairfaxiana Manuscripta*, was to bind the cut with linen cloths that had been dipped in 'ye green fome where frogges have their spawne 3 days before the new-moon'.

Like other small creatures, frogs were sometimes used in those horrible charms in which an animal-victim was tortured in order to produce corresponding pains in some human being. Addy[1] records two instances of their employment in love-magic. In one, a Derbyshire girl whose lover was untrue to her stuck pins all over a living frog and then buried it. The young man suffered extreme pain in all his limbs, and eventually returned to her. She dug up the frog and removed the pins, after which the pains ceased and the man, perhaps rather unwisely, married her. Addy's informant told him the affair had caused a great stir in the neighbourhood, and that she, who knew all the people concerned, was convinced of the tale's truth.

[1] S. O. Addy, *op. cit.*

In the other case, an East Yorkshire girl resorted to a variant of the well-known frog-bone charm. She put a pin-stuck frog into a box and left it there until it was dead and withered. Then she removed a small key-shaped bone from the carcase, and secretly fastened it to the coat of the man she wished to marry, saying,

> I do not want to hurt this frog,
> But my true lover's heart to turn,
> Wishing that he no rest may find,
> Till he come to me and speak his mind.

Thereafter the unfortunate man suffered the same agony as the frog had endured, and at the end of a week, he came to her and said he would marry her, though he knew they would not be happy together. He did so, and they were not, which is hardly surprising in the circumstances.

The better-known form of the bone-charm is not concerned with love but with power. The charmer was required to put a frog, alive, or killed in some special way which varied in different parts of the country, into a perforated box, and to bury the box in a black ants' nest. When the ants had picked all the flesh off the bones, the latter had to be thrown at midnight into a running stream. All but one would be swept away by the current, but that one would float upstream. If it was then secured and kept, it would endow its owner with all the powers enjoyed by the Toadmen, *see Toads*, and particularly that of controlling horses. It was also said to enable him to cure warts.

Belief in this charm was widespread among horsemen until quite recently, but there seems to have been some difference of opinion as to whether it was straightforward natural magic, or whether the resulting powers were derived from the Devil. As with the similar charm involving a toad's bone, it was thought by some to put the charmer in league with Satan. In several recorded cases, men who had acquired the bone by the method described above have warned others against attempting to do the same, saying that it meant selling one's soul to the Devil and knowing no rest thereafter, though whether such statements were the fruit of genuine belief or a desire to increase their importance in the eyes of their fellows, cannot always be decided.

A frog coming into a house is usually considered a bad omen, though not in all districts. In Brecon and Herefordshire, however, a frogstone, that is, one of those rough yellowish stones rather like a frog in shape which are sometimes found near lakes, is considered a very lucky thing to find.

FRONT DOOR

The front door, as the main or ceremonial entrance to a house, has its own traditions. A bride must always leave by it, both on her way to the church and later, when she is leaving for her honeymoon. When she goes to her new home, she must enter by the main door, or her life in that house will be unlucky.

After a death, the front door must be left unlocked for as long as the corpse remains in the house, or the free passage of the dead man's soul will be impeded. On the funeral day the coffin must be carried through it, and it must then stand wide open until the mourners return. If it is closed, a second death will occur in the house very soon. Another reason sometimes given for leaving it open is that otherwise the soul will be shut in and will haunt the house. In Lincolnshire it is said that the spirit may wish to return to his old home and must not find the door shut against him. It is possible that this idea springs not so much from kindly feeling towards the dead as from fear that the ghost will wail round the house seeking for entry. Whatever the reason locally given, it is, or was, generally considered extremely unlucky for all concerned to break this rule, even if it was done in ignorance.

The everyday use of the front door for all purposes is so common in towns that any superstitions about it may seem strange. In rural districts, however, it is still quite usual to keep it locked on all but ceremonial occasions, ordinary comings and goings being through the back or side door. Where this is the rule, its ritual opening for marriage, death, or first homecoming acquires a special significance.

G

GARTERS

One of the many ways of inducing dreams of a future husband was for the enquiring girl to pin her garters to her bedroom wall, arrange her shoes in the form of a T, and say, just before getting into bed,

> I pin my garters to the wall,
> And put by shoes in the shape of a T,
> In hopes my true love for to see,
> Not in his apparel nor in his array,
> But in the clothes he wears every day.
> If I am his bride to be,
> If I am his clothes to wear,
> If I am his children to bear,
> I hope he'll turn his face to me,
> But if I am not his bride to be,
> If I am not his clothes to wear,
> If I am not his children to bear,
> I hope he'll turn his back to me.

She had then to get into bed quickly, without speaking again.

In Aubrey's *Miscellanies*, there is another version of this charm which could be used for either wife or husband, but apparently only if the enquirer was away from home. 'You must lie in another county,' says Aubrey, 'and knit the left garter about the right legged stocking (let the other garter and stocking alone) and as you rehearse these following verses, at every comma, knit a knot.

> This knot I knit,
> To know the thing, I know not yet,
> That I may see,
> The man (woman) that shall my husband (wife) be,
> How he goes, and what he wears,
> And what he does, all days, and years.'

The garters worn by a bride on her wedding-day were formerly believed to bring good luck. Misson[1] describes how, at a seventeenth-century wedding the bridesmen pulled off the bride's garters just before her maids led her to the bedroom, and wore them in their hats for luck. In northern England, this garter-snatching custom was kept up in simple circles until at least as late as the first half of the nineteenth century and, in some districts, even later. They were pulled off as soon as the ceremony was ended, and the young men of the party raced for them on horseback. The winner, like the seventeenth-century gallants, wore them in his hat. To make removal easier and less embarrassing for the bride, ribbon streamers were often attached to them, and in later times, long white ribbons replaced the actual bands in some areas, and were known as garters. These were also raced for, and were supposed to bring good luck.

Red garters were believed at one time to be good for rheumatism, as those made of corks or eelskin were for cramp. In a Yorkshire witchcraft case in 1654,[2] it was stated in evidence that John Tatterson, of Gargreave, went to a wisewoman named Ann Greene to be cured of pains in his ear. She took off her garter and crossed his left ear with it three times. She also took some hair from his neck which, he said, was done without his consent. On the way home, the pain came on more strongly than before, so he went back to her, and she crossed the ear again. After that, he was cured, but instead of being grateful to her, he turned against her and became her chief accuser. *See Straw Garter.*

GERMAN BANDS

An odd weather superstition, still remembered by old people, is that the

[1] H. Misson de Valbourg, *Memoirs & Observations of M. Misson in his Travels over England*, trans. J. Ozell, 1719.

[2] *Depositions from the Castle of York relating to Offences committed in the Northern Counties in the Seventeenth Century*, ed. J. Raine, Surtees Society, 1861.

playing of a German band, in the street or anywhere in the open, brought down rain. Until the outbreak of war in 1914, many such bands came over annually from Germany at the beginning of the summer, and travelled about England, playing at village wakes, club-day celebrations, and other rural festivals, until the autumn, when they went home. Many people old enough to remember assert that their playing out-of-doors did cause rain, though why this should have been so, they cannot explain.

GLOVES

Gloves, like scissors, should never be picked up by the person who drops them, or bad luck will follow. If somebody else picks them up and returns them to the owner, the latter may expect a pleasant surprise.

Another very common superstition is that if a visitor forgets his (or her) gloves when leaving a house, he must, on returning for them, sit down before picking them up, and then put them on while standing. If this rite is omitted, he will never return again to that house.

A tradition recorded in Oxfordshire within the last few years is that gloves make an unlucky gift between friends, foretelling a parting of the ways for the two people concerned. This idea cuts across the generally accepted notion that gloves are appropriate offerings from a lover. Mrs Bray remarks in her *Borders of the Tamar and the Tavy* (1879) that on St Valentine's Day, Devonshire girls said to the young men of their choice,

> Good-morrow, Valentine, I go today
> To wear for you, what you must pay,
> A pair of gloves next Easter-day.

The youths were then expected to send them a pair of new gloves on Easter Eve. In other districts too, gloves were sometimes presented at Easter, even without the open encouragement of the Valentine rhyme, and if the young woman wore them to church on Easter Sunday, it was a good sign for the courtship. A north-country tradition mentioned by Sir Walter Scott in *The Fair Maid of Perth* was that if a woman found a man asleep in his chair and woke him with a kiss, she could claim a pair of gloves as forfeit.

Like anything else that had once been in contact with a person, gloves could be used to work magic upon him. In 1619, Joan Flower and her two daughters were charged with murdering young Lord Rosse, the Earl of Rutland's heir, by means of one of his gloves. Margaret Flower, who worked at Belvoir Castle, stole it and brought it to her mother, who rubbed it against her familiar, a cat called Rutterkin, dipped it in boiling water, pricked it, and finally buried it. The boy fell ill and eventually died. For this crime the two younger women were hanged at Lincoln, their mother escaping execution only because she had choked and died on the way to the prison.

A white glove signifies a clean hand, and is a symbol of innocence. Such a glove, real or cut out in paper, was often hung in the centre of the garland carried at the funeral of a virgin. *See Maiden's Garland.* The custom of presenting an Assize Judge with a pair of white gloves when there are no criminal cases to bring before him has the same underlying significance.

GODPARENTS

'If you stand together, you'll not walk together' is a Yorkshire saying, meaning that if an engaged couple act as godparents to the same child, something will happen to prevent their marriage. This belief is found in other counties also, and may perhaps spring from a dim memory of the pre-Reformation ban on the marriage of joint godparents, who were held to be too closely joined by spiritual affinity for subsequent marriage to be possible.

It was commonly thought at one time to be very unlucky for a pregnant woman to act as a godmother, and usually, such a woman, if asked, would refuse to do so. *See Pregnancy.* In Wales, it is a fortunate sign if the sponsors at a christening come from three different parishes. The child will live to a good old age. C. S. Burne[1] tells us that in Shropshire it was believed that if a godparent of either sex looked into the font during the ceremony, the baby would grow up to resemble him or her, even if there was no blood relationship.

GOLDEN PLOVER

The strange whistling cry of the golden plover has given rise to a variety of legends concerning its meaning and the origin of the bird that makes it. An Icelandic tale recorded by Arnason says that when Our Lord was a little boy, He and some other children once amused themselves by making clay birds on the Sabbath. A passing Sadduccee rebuked them for thus profaning the holy day, and in his anger, broke the birds. Thereupon Our Lord blessed those that He had fashioned, and at once they turned into golden plover, which flew away, praising God and declaring His glory. This they have done ever since, continually crying 'Glory! Glory!' as they fly.

Another legend, found in Lancashire and elsewhere, gives them a more melancholy origin. They are the souls of Jews who took an active part in the Crucifixion, and are now doomed to wander for ever, lamenting their crime.

In Cheshire, they are considered friendly birds, and are called the Sheep's Guide because they are supposed to warn sheep of danger by their cries. But in North Wales, where they are known as Whistlers, their note is a death omen for anyone who hears it. In some areas, the Seven Whistlers are said to be golden plover.

[1] C. S. Burne, *Shropshire Folk-Lore*, 1883.

GRAVES

Graves are customarily made with their length running east and west, so that the corpse lies with his feet to the east and his head to the west. It used to be supposed that the summons to the Last Judgement would come from the east, and that it would be better for the dead man if he could rise on the Resurrection morning with his face towards the dawn. An old Welsh name for the east wind is 'the wind of the dead men's feet'. To dig a grave north and south was extremely unlucky, and indicated either a lack of respect or definite malice towards the man who would lie in it. In some country churchyards there are a few old graves so made, and these are usually said to contain the bodies of strangers, suicides or, in some cases, dissenters.

It is unlucky to walk or tread upon a grave. To do so is disrespectful not only to whoever lies below, but also to all the dead buried nearby. If the grave trodden on happens to be that of a stillborn or an unbaptized child, the offender runs the risk of contracting the fatal disease known as Grave-merelles. See Unbaptized Child.

To leave a grave open over Sunday is still quite often thought to be ill-omened. It yawns for another corpse, and a second death in the parish will follow shortly. If an early funeral on a Monday makes it necessary to dig a grave on the previous Saturday, the sexton should not leave the hole gaping, but should cover it with planks or turf. If the earth on a new grave sinks more rapidly than is usual, it is a sign of another death in the same family within a few days or weeks.

It has always been considered dangerous to disturb a grave, and still more so to rob it. The dead man, roused prematurely from his rest, may haunt the neighbourhood, or take direct revenge upon the offender. This belief is, of course, strongest in the case of Christian tombs, but it also extends to pre-historic burial-places, as the many stories told of misfortunes that have overtaken excavating archaeologists bear witness. If an ancient grave is accidentally disturbed, the bones should be reburied as quickly as possible, otherwise the disturber may be haunted by the ghost, suffer from bad dreams or insomnia, or experience other forms of ill-luck.

Harry Price relates a remarkable story bearing on this belief in his *Poltergeist Over England* (1945). He says that in 1944 he was asked to investigate some odd disturbances at Great Leighs in Essex, which had apparently begun after a large stone at a crossroads had been displaced during road-widening operations. This stone was traditionally said to mark the unhallowed grave of a seventeenth-century witch. From the moment of its removal, very strange events had occurred in the village. Ricks had been overturned and corn-stooks removed from one field to another. The tenor bell in the church had rung by itself, and portable property of various kinds had been scattered about. Animals had strayed from unbroken enclosures, cows had calved prematurely, hens had stopped laying, and a number of chickens had been drowned. A more serious misfortune was the unexplained death of thirty sheep and two horses in one field. That all this might have been due to human mischief is obvious, but no culprit had been detected, or even suspected, and the villagers were inclined to blame the disturbance of the grave. Mr Price therefore suggested that the stone should be ceremonially replaced, and this was accordingly done. The troubles then ceased.

In some districts, it is thought most unwise to use materials from any grave, Christian or otherwise, for building or other purposes. A house containing stone from a tomb will not prosper and may even collapse, because death has been built into it. In Oxfordshire recently, a series of accidents on a particular stretch of road was locally accounted for by a rumour that stones from a pagan burial-ground had been incorporated in its surface. To plough up land in which corpses were once interred is also considered unlucky. Crops sown on such land will not do well, and there is likely to be a death soon after the ploughing in the family of the man who did the work, or ordered it to be done.

These beliefs have never been quite strong enough to restrain really hardened robbers, or even to protect every prehistoric burial-chamber from the depredations of farmers seeking stone for gateposts or culverts. They exist, nevertheless, and have played a useful part in preserving ancient monuments or old cemeteries now disused. The widespread prejudice against exhumation springs from the same root. It is true that an exhumation-order issued by the authorities is usually connected with suspicions of murder, and is therefore in itself an indication of serious trouble, but it is not only removals of this kind which are considered ill-omened. To take a dead body out of its grave for any reason whatsoever, even to place it in a more honourable tomb, is, or was, thought very unlucky, especially to the surviving members of the corpse's family. Some disaster will befall them soon afterwards, or one, or more, among them will die.

The sanctity of graves did not, however, always protect them against damage of another sort. Scrapings or chips from a stone or alabaster tomb, bits of headstones, or the moss growing upon them, were once deemed to have medicinal powers, especially for the ailment of animals. Some find old monuments have suffered very considerably from the effects of this belief in the past. One such is the alabaster tomb of Sir Hugh de Calveley in Bunbury Church, Cheshire, from which generations of shepherds have chipped off small pieces of stone, in order to grind them to powder and use them to cure diseases in sheep.

GROANING CAKE OR CHEESE

Until about the beginning of the present century, it was customary in many households to prepare a Groaning Cake, or a Groaning Cheese, or sometimes both, against the birth of a child, and to distribute pieces to all in the house as soon as the new life had begun. This brought good luck to the baby and also to those who shared the food.

The method of cutting the cake or cheese varied. If a doctor was present at the confinement, he was sometimes asked to do this, but more usually, it was the father who performed the rite. He had to be careful not to cut his finger in the process, for if he did so, the child would die within the year. In Oxford-shire, it was usual at one time to begin cutting in the centre, and so gradually to form a ring through which the baby was passed for luck at the christening-feast. Elsewhere, it was cut from the edge, one slice for each person present and no more, for there was no luck in a second portion.

What was not eaten on the actual day of the birth was kept for any visitors who might come to the house between then and the baptism. One portion was often used as the gift presented by the nurse to the first person of opposite sex to the child encountered on the way to or from the christening. *See Baptism.* It was very unlucky for anyone to refuse an offered slice, for this meant that the child would grow up without personal charm, or be otherwise unfortunate. Unmarried girls sometimes ate part of their share, and put the rest under their pillows, in the hope of seeing their future husbands that night in a dream.

The cheese used in these ceremonies was generally a very large Cheshire, the cake often a thick gingerbread, a plum cake, or a spiced rye-loaf. The name given to these foods is derived from the fact that in many parts of England a woman's confinement is called 'a groaning'.

GROWING STONES

The idea that the small stones often found in fields have grown there, and that consequently it is useless to attempt to clear the ground by picking them off, was once very common. Zincke remarks in his *Materials for the History of Wherstead* (1887) that several Suffolk farmers of his acquaintance had assured him that this was so. One, an educated man, explained the presence of the pebbles by the theory that the land itself produced them. He insisted that this was quite natural, since everything must be produced by something. Furthermore, his own experience had shown him it was practically impossible to clear a stone-infested field permanently. He had had one field on his farm picked over several times, but the pebbles always returned in as great a pro-fusion as before.

This belief was not confined to Suffolk, then or later. It has been found in several parts of England, even in this century. Its persistence may be partly due to the fact that clearing a pebbly field is exceedingly difficult, and usually the work needs to be done many times. The thinnest covering of soil is enough to conceal small stones from the pickers, and if this is blown or washed away later, it does seem at first sight as though the stones had grown again.

Another theory was that pebbles grew from conglomerates, or Pudding-stones. For this reason, conglomerates were often called Mother-stones, or Breeding-stones, or Quick-rock. The conjoined pebbles of which they consist were regarded as seeds, from which loose stones would grow. If such stones were left undisturbed, they would slowly increase in size until, in the course of centuries and under favourable conditions, they developed into large boulders.

HAIR

Superstitious beliefs concerning hair are numerous and varied, which is perhaps not very surprising when we consider that it draws its life and vigour from the person on whom it grows, and is one of the most indestructible parts of the human body.

A free and luxuriant growth is commonly said to denote vigour and vitality. Until the fashions changed in the present century, long, flowing hair was esteemed as a great beauty in women, especially if it was curly or wavy. Too much is sometimes said to show a lack of wit, perhaps because it is thought to draw away strength which should feed the brain, or perhaps merely from the slightly startled expression which a springing and unmanageable bush of hair sometimes imparts to the face. A good beard on a man, or a hairy chest, indicates virility and physical strength, and hairy arms are a sign of riches to come. The sudden loss of head-hair, unaccounted for by any illness, is a very bad omen, foretelling loss of health or property, or the death of one or more of the owner's children.

If a woman has a widow's peak, that is, if her hair grows into a point low down on her forehead, she will live to be a widow. In Devonshire, such a peak indicates long life, which might easily include widowhood. Similarly, if a married woman whose hair is normally straight suddenly develops two curls on her temples, one on each side, her husband has not long to live.

Straight, lank hair is sometimes said to show a sly and cunning nature, as curly hair is said to denote pride or, in some districts, a serene and cheerful temperament. However that may be, most women would like to have curly hair, and children are often told they can obtain it by eating the 'kiss crusts', or rough crusts on newly-made loaves. A test of pride is to draw a hair sharply between the nails of the forefinger and thumb to see whether it curls up or not after it is released. If it does, pride is proved or, in some places, a lack of steadfastness in love. Addy[1] says that in the north Midlands the same charm could be used to find out whether the charmer would ever become rich. A writer in *Lincolnshire Notes and Queries* (Vol. III) records how, when she was a child, other children used to mock her by crying, 'Curly locks, my word, isn't she proud!'

A dark-haired person is lucky as a First Foot except in a few areas, where a fair-haired individual is preferred. One with red hair is invariably unlucky. *See First Foot*. A curious prejudice against red hair is found in many parts of Britain, and was once far stronger than it is now. A reason often given for it is that Judas Iscariot was red-haired. There is no evidence for this tradition, but Shakespeare refers to it in *As You Like It* (Act III, Scene 4) when he makes Rosalind say of Orlando that 'his very hair is of the dissembling colour', to which Celia replies that it is 'something browner than Judas's'. Another theory is that the Danes, those dreaded invaders of the ninth and tenth centuries, were often red of hair and beard. It is quite likely that the prejudice springs from latent racial memories of fair or auburn invaders, though probably these were much farther back in time than the Danes.

Red hair, whether 'ginger', auburn, or copper-hued, is supposed to be a sign of a fiery and ungovernable temper, or of a passionate disposition in love. On the other hand, 'ginger for pluck' is a well-known saying. In Cornwall, people with red hair cannot make good butter. Dumbartonshire people say that a red-headed man will be an unfaithful husband. A red beard was formerly supposed to denote a cruel nature, an accusation which was sometimes extended to the yellow-bearded, of whom Cain was traditionally the first.

Hair should be cut with the waxing or waning moon, according to whether it is desired that it should grow again quickly or be kept short. It is unlucky to cut it on Good Friday, and in some parts of the English Midlands, it should not be cut on Thursday, Friday or Saturday, otherwise the cutter will never grow rich. This leaves only Monday, Tuesday and Wednesday on which the work can safely be done, for Sunday is also an unlucky day for it. 'Best never be born than Sunday shorn' is a well-known country saying. If sailors cut their hair (or pare their nails) during a calm at sea, they will cause a storm to arise.

When cutting is complete, the clippings must be destroyed by fire, and never on any account left about where an evilly disposed person or a bird can find them. The latter may weave them into their nests, in which case the person from whose head they came will suffer excruciating headaches. If it is a magpie which takes them, he will die within a year and a day. A witch may use them in spells, especially image-magic. (*See* p. 201.) The dread of witchcraft is probably responsible for the Derbyshire belief that parents should not keep locks of their children's hair if they wish them to live and prosper.

[1] S. O. Addy, *op. cit.*

When the cuttings are thrown on to the fire, it is a sign of long life if they burn up brightly, but if they shrivel or smoulder, the omen is very bad. A variant of this is that if they singe, their owner has yet another year to live. A charm to force any person to come to the charmer is to secure a lock of his hair and boil it.

If a witch, when pronouncing a curse or casting a spell, shakes her hair loose, the effect of the curse or spell will be doubled. In the Highlands, erysipelas could be caused by taking a lock of hair, red for preference, cutting it into small snippets, and casting them, with curses, in the direction of the victim. Each separate snippet would produce a sore on his body.

A Suffolk charm to cure whooping-cough when several children of the same family had it was to take hair from the eldest girl's head, cut it up and put it in milk, which the other children then drank, beginning with the youngest and working upwards through the family. The same, and other complaints could be healed by burying some of the patient's hair in the earth, or thrusting it into an incision in the bark of a rowan tree, or embedding it in bread-and-butter and giving it to a dog to eat. The disease would thus be transferred to the animal or the tree, or moulder away in the ground. Similarly, in Scotland, almost any ailment could be transferred by taking hair from the crown of the patient's head, one of his eyelashes and some of his nail-parings, and sewing them all, together with a small coin, into a piece of cloth or a bag. The package was then put out on the highway, or in some other place where someone would be likely to find and pick it up. Whoever did so would take the disease.

HAND

The hand, man's first tool and weapon, signifies power, both physical and spiritual. A blessing is conveyed by the raised hand. Healing virtue was often thought to be transmitted by touch. The King's Evil, or scrofula, was cured by the touch of the monarch's hand, and other cures were similarly effected by gifted healers of various kinds, who touched or stroked the patient.

To grasp a man's hand is a sign of friendship, to shake hands after making a promise or contract is to seal it. Allegiance was shown by placing a man's two hands between those of the king or lord to whom he pledged his faith. In Anglo-Saxon times, a handfast wedding was one in which the two concerned joined hands and vowed fidelity to each other for a year, after which the marriage could be either dissolved or made permanent by a true marriage in church. Sweethearts are still said to be 'handfasted' in some districts.

The open hand, with fingers widely stretched, is a charm against the Evil Eye. Small hand-shaped amulets of metal, wood, or ivory have been worn for the same purpose from remote antiquity. In Italy today, when the Evil Eye is suspected, its power can be averted by pointing the hand with the two middle fingers and thumb inwards, and the first and last fingers extended like horns, or by wearing an amulet made in this form.

The shape and texture of hands and fingers is supposed to denote the character, and therefore the probable future, of the owner. Gaule in his *Mag-Astromancer* (1652) says that a hard, brawny hand denotes a dull and rude man, one little and slender, a weak and timorous man, a long hand, an individual 'not only apt for mechanical artifice, but liberally ingenious'. He also says that to be ambidexterous is to be 'ireful, crafty, injurious', and that those who constantly fold their hands are covetous, and those with short hands are fools and fit for nothing.

In Co. Durham formerly, it was thought lucky to meet a left-handed (or skir-handed) man on any day except Tuesday, but to do so then was ill-omened. A possible explanation of this odd tradition, confined as it is to a part of England which was once in the Danelagh, is that Tuesday is named after Tiw, the Scandinavian god who was left-handed because he sacrificed his right hand for the good of the world. The gods of Asgard were not strong enough to bind the evil Fenris-Wolf with their own power alone. They were forced to bargain with him, and he consented to be bound until Ragnarok, the time of the world's end, only if Tiw would sacrifice his right hand. Thus Tiw became skir-handed; and it may be that the superstition has its roots in a lurking fear that a left-handed man met on a Tuesday may be the god himself, abroad in human form on his own day. *See Dead Hand: Fingers: Fingernails: Hand of Glory: Itching and Tingling.*

HAND OF GLORY

The Hand of Glory was a charm used in many parts of Europe by burglars, and also by sorcerers. It consisted of the hand of a hanged felon, cut from the body as it hung on the gibbet, pickled with various salts, and dried in strong sunlight or in an oven until it was quite hard. It was then used as a holder for a candle made of a hanged man's fat, virgin wax, and Lapland sesame.

Thus prepared, it had the power of stupefying those to whom it was displayed, and rendering them motionless, 'in such a way that they can no more stir than if they were dead.'[1] Thieves believed that if the Hand was brought into a house at night, and the candle lighted, none of the sleeping inmates would awaken while it burnt. In the *Observer* of 16 January 1831 there was an account of an attempted robbery on 3 January at Loughcrew, Co. Meath. The burglars 'entered the house armed with a dead man's hand, with a lighted candle in it, believing in the superstitious notion that a candle placed in a dead man's hand will not be seen by any but those by whom it is used; and also, that if a candle in a dead hand be introduced into a house, it will

---

[1] *Secrets merveilleux de la magie naturelle et cabalistique de Petit Albert, 1722.*

prevent those who may be asleep from awaking. The inmates, however, were alarmed, and the robbers fled, leaving the hand behind them.'

William Henderson[1] relates a story which was originally collected by Charles Wastell from Bella Parkin, the daughter of the maidservant concerned. In the last decade of the eighteenth century, a traveller dressed as a woman came to the Old Spital Inn, near Stainmore. She wished to stay the night, but refused a separate room, saying that she had to leave very early in the morning, and preferred to doze by the living-room fire. This was allowed, but the landlord told his maidservant to sit up also until the stranger had gone.

After the family had gone to bed, the girl lay down on the settle and, looking across at the supposed woman on the other side of the hearth, she saw a trouser-leg showing below the latter's skirt. With her suspicions now thoroughly aroused, she pretended to fall asleep, and saw the traveller take a Dead Hand out of his pocket. He fixed a candle on it, lighted it, and passed the whole thing several times before her face, saying, 'Let those who are asleep be asleep, and let those who are awake be awake.' He then put the Hand of Glory on the table, and went to the house-door to whistle up his accomplices. The girl jumped up immediately, pushed him through the door, locked it behind him, and rushed upstairs to awaken her master. This, however, proved to be impossible. No amount of shouting, shaking or pulling roused him, or any other member of the family. Finally, as the thieves could still be heard outside the house and might break in at any moment, she ran downstairs again, seized a bowl of skim milk, and emptied it over the Hand. The flame went out, and thereafter she had no difficulty in waking the family.

Another story in the same book suggests that milk is the only fluid that puts out such flames. In this case, there was no candle. The cook saw the thief set light to the fingers of the Hand itself, but the thumb would not burn because someone in the house (the cook) was awake. Here too, she could not rouse the sleepers, but while the thief was in another room, she tried to blow out the flames of the burning fingers. She could not do so, so she threw some beer-dregs over them. This had no effect either, and it was not until she threw milk over them that she was able to put them out. Her employers were then easily awakened, and the thief was eventually caught and hanged.

In *Secrets . . . du Petit Albert*, already mentioned, the author describes a method of protecting a house against the Hand of Glory. The householder must rub the threshold, or any other part of the house by which thieves could enter, with an ointment made of the gall of a black cat, a white hen's fat, and the blood of a screech-owl. This ointment had to be prepared during the Dog-days. If it was properly made, and smeared in the right places, no Hand of Glory brought into the house would be effective.

[1] Wm. Henderson, *op. cit.*

HANGMAN'S ROPE

As the hand of a man who had been hanged was once thought to cure various ills if the affected part was stroked with it, *see Dead Hand*, so the rope that caused his death was also supposed to have healing powers. This belief was often a source of profit to the hangman, who was able to sell the rope, or pieces of it, for quite respectable sums. A fairly widespread remedy for headaches was to tie such a rope round the head, or wear a strand from it inside the hat. Aubrey[1] mentions it as a cure for the quartan ague. In Russia formerly small pieces carried in the pocket brought good luck to gamblers.

A Lincolnshire cure for fits, apparently still known, or at least remembered in 1936,[2] was to wear constantly round the neck a strand from the rope with which a suicide had hanged himself.

HARE

To meet a hare is generally considered to be unlucky. If one crosses a man's path when he is setting out on a journey, that journey will be unfortunate for him. He must return home at once and start out afresh. Fishermen have been known to turn back after seeing a hare on their way to the boats, and to remain ashore all day. When at sea, the creature's name must never be mentioned, a substitute word being used instead if it is necessary to speak of it. In some districts, this name-tabu prevails, or did, among miners also. For a hare to cross the road in front of a wedding procession is a very bad omen, and if a pregnant woman sees one, her child is likely to be born with a hare-lip. *See Pre-natal Influence.*

A hare running down the main street of a village is said to foretell a fire. In northern England, it is unlucky to see one jumping on a wall, and to dream of one is a sign that the dreamer has enemies, or that death or misfortune is coming to someone in his family.

These omens, though widespread, are not universal. In some parts of England, it is lucky to meet a hare, and a wish should be made as soon as it has passed. In others, it is only the white hare which is unlucky. To see a black one is a sign of good fortune. A Cornish tradition says that girls who die of grief after being deserted by a lover turn into white hares and haunt their betrayers.

Witches were formerly believed to turn themselves into hares. They took other animal-shapes also, but in Great Britain and Ireland, that of the hare was the most usual. In 1662, Isobel Gowdie, of Auldearne,[3] confessed that she and other members of her coven transformed themselves at will by saying three times,

[1] J. Aubrey, *Remaines of Gentilisme and Judaisme*, 1686/7.
[2] Ethel Rudkin, *Lincolnshire Folklore*, 1936.
[3] Robert Pitcairn, *Criminal Trials in Scotland*, 1833.

I shall go intill a hare,
With sorrow and sych and meikle care;
And I shall go in the Devil's name
Ay while I come home again.

When they wanted to return to human form they said,

Hare, hare, God send thee care.
I am in a hare's likeness just now,
But I shall be in a woman's likeness even now.

Belief in the possibility of this change was very long-lived. Giraldus Cambrensis mentions it as already old when he wrote in the twelfth century, and it was still alive in the nineteenth. Witch-hares were supposed to steal the milk of cows and sheep lying out in the fields, and to do much other damage. They were frequently hunted, but they always escaped, and they could only be shot with a silver bullet. If one was wounded in the chase, a corresponding injury was expected to appear in the body of some local witch.

Stories of hare-hunts which resulted in tell-tale human injuries are told all over Britain. Atkinson in his *Forty Years in a Moorland Parish* relates how a Cleveland farmer, whose young saplings were being destroyed by a hare, waited up one night with a gun charged with pieces of old silver buttons. He saw 'a great, foul, au'd ram-cat of a heear' approaching, and fired at it. Had his bullets been ordinary lead ones, he could not have hit it, but as they were silver he succeeded in wounding the animal, which shrieked and rushed away. Next day, a certain old woman already suspected of witchcraft was found in bed, badly cut about in several places. She said her injuries were due to a broken glass bottle upon which she had fallen; but the farmer and all his neighbours were quite sure they were caused by the silver shot.

In pre-Christian times, the hare was reverenced as a holy creature, associated with fertility and the returning Spring. Divinations were made from its movements, and its flesh was not eaten by ordinary men. In northern Europe, it was sacred to the Spring Goddess, who was known to our Anglo-Saxon ancestors as Eastre, and it still has a ritual connexion with the great Christian festival that bears her name. It is the Easter Hare which lays the Easter eggs. Children in many European countries, including England, are often told to look about the house or garden, stables or outhouses, for the nest in which the Easter Hare has laid the brightly coloured eggs. The Hare-Pie Scramble which takes place every year at Hallaton on Easter Monday, and the hare-hunts that were once held on that day at Leicester and Coleshill, although connected with land-tenures and civic customs, probably have their roots in the same far-off conception of the hare as the sacred Spring beast.

A hare's right foot carried about in the pocket keeps away rheumatism, and also cramp. Samuel Pepys used one to cure his colic. He mentions it several times in his *Diary*, and evidently he found it efficacious, even though he hesitated to admit it, for on 25 March 1665, he writes: 'Now I am at a losse to know whether it be my hare's foot which is my preservative against wind, for I never had a fit of the collique since I wore it.'

HAWTHORN

The hawthorn was a holy tree in pagan and Christian legend alike, and many conflicting traditions have gathered round it. The Crown of Thorns is said to have been made from it. It has healing powers and, being connected with lightning, protects any house near which it grows from the flash. It is also associated with fairies, and therefore it is dangerous to sit under it on those special days when these intermediate spirits are most powerful, such as May Day, Midsummer Eve, or Hallowe'en. Whoever does so runs the risk of being enchanted or carried away by them.

It is very unlucky to cut down a hawthorn. In Somerset, it is only safe to do so if a prayer is first offered. In Ireland, the fairies' permission has to be asked beforehand. Eleanor Hull[1] relates a story of a farmer who, in the early years of last century, felled such a tree in the townland of Garryglass. Thereafter, his children and his cattle died, he lost his money, and finally he was evicted from his farm. Moreover, the evil results of his act lingered about the place during the tenancy of the man who followed him, and of his successor also. Neither prospered. In an article published in *Folk-Lore* (Vol. 15, 1904), A. H. Singleton states that about 1877 'a protestant man' living in Co. Meath cut down a whitethorn, though he was warned not to do so. His hand was pierced by one of its thorns, and he died of blood-poisoning shortly afterwards.

A quite common superstition today is that it is unlucky to bring white may, the flower of the hawthorn, into the house. A death will follow, or some other serious misfortune. Children are often forbidden to bring it home because if they do, their mother will die, and this notion sometimes lingers into later life, so that the by now adult children hesitate to decorate their homes with may-blossom, even though the mother does not live in the same house with them. Yet this seems to be a mainly modern superstition, which was not general in earlier times. It probably has more to do with the heavy scent of the flowers, and the fact that they are white, than with the mystical properties of the tree on which they grow.

Before the calendar-change of 1752, when May Day fell eleven days later than it does now, the hawthorn was usually in bloom for the festival. Sprigs and bunches of blossom were then quite cheerfully brought home, and used to decorate the house and weave into May-garlands. The May-Singers on

[1] Eleanor Hull, *op. cit.*

their rounds left branches outside the houses for luck, and the servant who was the first to bring in a blossoming bough was commonly rewarded with a bowl of cream. In Norfolk, young girls went out very early on May morning to gather bunches of the flowers, red or white. These had to be brought home in silence, for if a girl spoke to anyone while returning with them, she would not marry that year.

A form of marriage-divination practised in Huntingdonshire and the neighbouring counties was for a girl to hang a flowering hawthorn branch on a signpost at four lane-ends on May Eve, and leave it there all night. In the morning, she looked to see which way the wind had blown it. From that direction, her future husband would come. If the branch had blown away altogether, she would not marry.

A Lincolnshire variant of this rite was for the first blossoming branch seen to be broken in such a way that it still hung on the tree, left all night as in the other form of the charm, and brought home in the morning. The girl who did this would either see her lover in a dream, or meet him on the road as she came back with the branch.

Anyone sheltering under a thorn tree during a storm will be quite safe, however bad the storm may be. In Staffordshire, hawthorn gathered on Palm Sunday or on Ascension Day and kept in a house protected that house from lightning. In one Staffordshire parish, Miss Burne[1] was told that Ascension Day hawthorn, to be efficacious, must be brought from outside by someone else; it is not enough to gather some from trees growing on one's own ground. In Cheshire, the presence of a bough gathered at any time not only gave protection against storms, but also prevented the entry of witches, ghosts, and evil spirits.

The hawthorn globe which once hung in many Herefordshire farm-kitchens was probably a fire-charm also. It was made very early on New Year's Day and left hanging up until next New Year came round. Then, about five o'clock in the morning, it was taken down for the ceremony known as Burning the Bush. While the womenfolk made another to replace it, the farm-men took the old globe to the wheat field, set it alight, and carried it, flaming, over the ridges. On some farms, it was burnt in a bonfire of straw and furze, and some of the latter was carried on a pitchfork, while still burning, a little being dropped upon each ridge. The local belief was that the globe represented the Crown of Thorns, and that by this ceremony, the Devil was driven from the fields, the disease known as smut was prevented, and the wheat enabled to prosper.

Although the tradition of the Holy Thorn of Glastonbury lies more in the realm of religious legend than in that of pure superstition, no account of the hawthorn in folk-belief would be complete without some mention of it. The original tree is said to have come into being when St Joseph of Arimathea

[1] C. S. Burne, *Folk-Lore*, Vol. 7, 1896.

came to Glastonbury and thrust his staff into the ground on Wearyall Hill. It took root and grew, and every year it blossomed at midnight on Christmas Eve. This tree was wantonly destroyed by a Puritan soldier in the seventeenth century, but not before many cuttings had been taken from it and planted elsewhere. The daughter-trees, including one now in the precincts of Glastonbury Abbey, continued to bloom at Christmas, as their ancestor had done before them, and they still do so, although now their flowering is more usually upon Old Christmas Eve (5 January) than on the December festival date.

These thorns have always been thought of as holy trees, and at one time, people came from miles round to see them blossom. One at Orcop in Herefordshire is still regularly visited by those who hope to see the buds break at the traditional hour on 5 January. They quite frequently do so, for these thorns belong to a winter-flowering variety which blooms twice in the year, once in very early January, round about Epiphany, and then again in Spring.

It need hardly be said that to cut down such a tree is, or was, considered even more ill-omened than to fell an ordinary hawthorn. The Puritan who destroyed the original Holy Thorn paid for it with the sight of one eye. While he was hacking at it, a thorn flew up and so injured his eye that he could never see with it afterwards. There is a Worcestershire story of a nineteenth-century farmer at Acton Beauchamp who, annoyed because people trespassed on his land to see a thorn bloom at Christmas-time, took an axe and hewed it down. Soon afterwards, he broke first a leg and then an arm, and suffered the loss of his house by fire. In a similar case at Clehonger in Herefordshire, when a man began cutting the tree, he saw blood flowing from its trunk, which so terrified him that he stopped the work and left the thorn standing.

HAY-CART

To meet a loaded hay-cart is lucky, and if a wish is made on seeing it, that wish will come true. The cart must, however, be coming towards the observer. If it is going away from him, so that he sees its back first, the omen is bad, and especially so if, while he watches it, it disappears round a corner. He should be careful to look away before that happens. In some districts, it is considered unlucky to see a hay-cart that is immediately followed, without any intervening vehicle, by a straw-cart.

HAZEL

The hazel was a holy tree in the days of Celtic paganism, associated with poetry and knowledge, fire and fertility. Its nuts are still connected in country belief with love and child-birth, and are used in divination on Hallowe'en night. *See Nuts*. Rods made from its wood were formerly employed to detect hidden veins of metal in the earth, and water-diviners today often use forked hazel-twigs for their work, though they sometimes prefer other woods, such as rowan, apple, or hawthorn.

There is a Highland tradition that hazel was one of the nine sacred woods used to kindle Need-fire at Beltane and other great festivals. In England, small branches gathered on Palm Sunday, and kept alive in water, are said to protect the house that contains them from thunder and lightning. At lambing-time, if the catkins are brought indoors and set about the rooms, it is helpful to the sheep. The leaves and twigs, woven into a cap or chaplet and worn on the head, bring good fortune in Wales and the granting of wishes, and if worn at sea, they protect the vessel from shipwreck. Those who sought fernseed for its magical virtues commonly used a forked hazel-twig to shake the fern, thereby protecting themselves to some extent from the hazards of this dangerous enterprise. *See Bracken*.

Scottish children born in autumn were sometimes given the 'milk' of the hazel-nut as their first food, for that brought good luck and health. If, later on, they did not thrive as they should, they were strengthened with doses of the 'milk' mixed with honey.

HEARTH

The sacred character of the hearth is a very ancient conception. Before the introduction of side-hearths, the household fire burnt in the middle of the main living-room, and was both the literal and the symbolic centre of the homestead. There, in pagan times, dwelt the household gods, and there burnt the holy and fertilizing fire which represented life, and was never allowed to go out. Round the central hearth the family lived, worked, ate, and sometimes slept. To it the bride was led when she first came to her new home, and there the fire-irons were ceremonially put into her hands, as a token that henceforth she was mistress and guardian of the home. Inheritance also was once connected with it. In medieval Wales, when a man died, his son's inheritance of the property was shown by his right to uncover his father's hearth. The phrase, 'a desolate hearth', meant not only an empty house, but a family scattered or dead, and kinship lost.

In Ireland, and in the Highlands and Islands of Scotland, the open peat fires were ritually 'smoored' or 'raked' at night. The embers were evenly spread to form a circle, which was then divided into three equal parts, with a small heap in the middle. In each part a peat was laid, touching the centre heap, and the whole was then covered with enough ashes to subdue, but not to put out the fire. This ceremony had a religious as well as a practical meaning. It had to be performed by the woman of the house, who, as she raked the embers and put each peat into position, and again when all was finished, recited traditional prayers and invocations for the protection of the house and those within it against the perils of the night.

Such rites and beliefs belong to the open or central hearth and not to the small side-hearth of today. Yet traces of the old ideas linger on in many districts. A very interesting letter published in *The Countryman* (Summer, 1955) records how the writer's maid, when a child in Oxfordshire, was taught by her mother that the fireplace must always be kept spotlessly clean because it is 'the altar of the House'. As the altar in a church is always kept clean, so must the hearth be in a home.

It is still quite often said to be unlucky, as well as presumptuous, to poke another man's fire. Even friends hesitate to do so without permission unless they have known the householder for at least seven years. As recently as sixty or seventy years ago, no one in Scotland or northern England ever gave fire or light out of the house on New Year's Day. If this was done, a death would occur in the giver's family within twelve months. There might be times when the refusal of a live coal or a burning taper meant real inconvenience, yet even the most charitable would usually decline to give either on that one day of the year. In his *Traditions, Superstitions, and Folk-Lore* (1872), Charles Hardwick relates how a friend of his once called at a cottage near Manchester and asked for a light for his cigar. The woman of the house curtly refused, saying that she knew better than to do that on New Year's Day. She did, however, allow him to help himself from the hearth although, as Mr Hardwick points out, this was just as unlucky as if she had given him a light herself.

Many omens were, and indeed, still are, read from the behaviour of the fire in the grate. If it will not start in the morning, or if it roars fiercely up the chimney, it is a sign of quarrels to come. A spluttering piece of coal has the same meaning; it should be stirred or broken up immediately to avert the bad omen. When the fire burns all on one side, or falls into two distinct parts, it foretells a parting; when it burns hollow it is a death omen, the hollow indicating a grave. A coffin-shaped cinder flying into the room is also a death omen, and an oval one, resembling a cradle, means a birth. If a live coal falls out near anyone's feet, it denotes a coming wedding, either his or her own, or that of someone else in the house. On the other hand, such a coal exploding outwards in the direction of any one person shows that he or she has an active enemy.

A cluster of sparks on the chimney-back means news, good if the sparks are bright and bad if they are dull. A black film on the bars of the grate foretells the arrival of a stranger. If the flames are blue, or unusually bright, frosty weather is coming.

When Need-fire was kindled, all household fires had to be put out beforehand, or the spark would not come. This was often the only time when they were allowed to go out during the whole year, and as soon as the Need-fire was kindled, they were relit from its new, life-giving flames. *See Need-fire.*

HEDGEHOG

The hedgehog, which country people often call the urchin, was once widely accused of sucking the milk of cows lying out in the fields at night. This naturally diminished the supply available for the farmer, and in some districts, it was supposed to account for the appearance of milk streaked with blood. In fact, this trouble is due to chills, but the unfortunate hedgehog was usually blamed for it, and in consequence, it was quite often killed on sight. A vague tradition of general ill-luck also clung to it in some areas, and one entering a house was considered a bad·omen.

An old cure for fits was to give the patient a cooked hedgehog to eat. This was one of the pleasanter remedies for the complaint, for the flesh makes a very palatable dish, and is quite often eaten by gypsies and countrymen as a delicacy. The 'pil' from the left eye of the beast was believed to strengthen weak eyes, if dropped into them with a quill. In Lincolnshire, the jaw of a female hedgehog was used in cures for rheumatism. The skin nailed to gateposts was, before the invention of barbed wire, a common method of preventing cows from rubbing against them.

As a weather-prophet, the hedgehog was supposed to know when storms were coming, and also the direction of the winds. In *Poor Robin's Almanack* for 1733, this foreknowledge is mentioned in the lines,

> Observe which way the hedge-hog builds her nest,
> To front the north or south, or east or west;
> For if 'tis true that common people say,
> The wind will blow the quite contrary way.
> If by some secret art the hedge-hogs know
> So long before, which way the winds will blow,
> She has an art which many a person lacks,
> That thinks himself fit to make almanacks.

HEMLOCK

Hemlock, like some other poisonous plants, was traditionally associated with the Devil and his servants, the witches. The latter were said to use it in spells to evoke demons and evil spirits, and to destroy love, cause madness or paralysis, and blast fertility in men and animals. It was also one of the ingredients of those flying ointments with which they were believed to anoint their bodies before they flew to the Sabbat. In the northern counties of England, it is called Bad Man's or Devil's, Oatmeal, and children are warned not to touch it, because if they do, the Devil may seize and fly away with them.

It had, however, healing and soothing properties, and was used in folk-medicine for several painful ills. A poultice of water-hemlock (or cowbane) cured rheumatism. Hemlock-roots roasted until they were soft eased the pains of gout in the hand. A sixteenth-century sleeping-apple contained hemlock juice mixed with opium, mandrake, henbane-seeds and musk, which was rolled into a ball and held to the patient's nose until he fell asleep. A remedy for 'a Pynn and Webb in the Eye' is included in that collection of cures and household lore compiled by the Fairfax family in Yorkshire, and now known as *Arcana Fairfaxiana Manuscripta*. In this hemlock was mixed with white of egg and a little baysalt, and the whole laid to 'ye pulce of ye arme on ye contrary side', that is, the right arm for the left eye, and *vice versa*. If the affliction was 'nere the sight of ye eye', juice extracted from the roots and leaves of daisies was added, to be dropped into the eye 'and so use it, till it be whole'.

HEMPSEED

If a girl desired to see her future husband, she went at midnight to the churchyard and threw hempseed over her left shoulder, saying,

> Hempseed I sow, Hempseed, grow.
> He that is to marry me,
> Come after me and mow.

The ghostly form of the future husband would appear behind her, mowing with a scythe. If nothing happened, it meant that she would not marry that year, or perhaps not at all; but if she was destined to die young and unwed, a spectral coffin would be seen following her instead of the man.

This rather terrifying form of divination was once well known, and instances of its use within living memory have been recorded in Oxfordshire and along the Welsh Border. The details varied slightly in different districts. The churchyard was the most usual place for its performance, but in some areas it was enough to go into the garden. In Herefordshire it was necessary to walk round the church twelve times without stopping, but this requirement, if it was ever general, seems to have been forgotten elsewhere. Like many charms of this sort, it would only work on one night of the year, variously given in different localities as St Mark's Eve, Midsummer Eve, All Hallows, or Christmas Eve.

HENBANE

Henbane is an extremely poisonous plant which sometimes causes convulsions or temporary insanity, and consequently it is not surprising to find it listed among the herbs which witches employed in harmful spells. It was supposed to assist clairvoyance and, if it was burnt on a fire, its fumes enabled those versed in the art to evoke spirits, not usually of the good variety. It could be used in more or less innocent love-charms also, and in magical remedies to heal the mysterious sores caused by witchcraft.

To eat any part of it, and particularly the root, is in fact very dangerous, and was once believed to induce sterility, madness, or a deep trance from which a man could only be roused with difficulty. It is perhaps this last item which accounts for the latter-day Welsh superstition that if a child falls asleep near the growing plant, he will not waken again.

In folk-medicine, henbane was widely used as a pain-killer, especially in cases of toothache. In many country districts, the seeds and capsules were smoked like tobacco for this purpose, a practice which sometimes had very unfortunate results. Another and probably safer method was for the sufferer to drop the seeds on to hot coals and to catch the resulting vapour into his mouth as it rose. In Gerard's *Herbal*, the use of the hot root is recommended, boiled in vinegar and held in the mouth (but not, of course, eaten). Gerard adds that the quack dentists of his day often resorted to the hot coals method mentioned above, afterwards showing their patients little pieces of lute-string which they said were the pain-causing worms, thus drawn from the aching tooth by the fumes.

A cure for insomnia was to bathe the feet in a warm decoction of henbane just before going to bed.

HENS

A hen which crows, or one with feathers like those of a cock, is usually considered to be very unlucky. In some areas, the appearance of such a bird in the poultry-yard is said to be a death omen for someone in the farmer's family, and almost everywhere, it is a sign of evil of some sort. On most farms formerly, such a bird was killed at once.

If hens go to roost at an unusual time, particularly during the forenoon, it foretells a death in the household, often that of the farmer himself. Along the Welsh Border, they are said to hide themselves between a death and the funeral. If either hens or cocks come into the house, a visitor will follow soon.

In Wales, at one time, it was customary to give the hens a share of all the fruit in the house on New Year's Day. This was supposed to make them lay well during the coming twelve months. A somewhat similar notion obtained in Silesia. The peasants there took corn to church on Christmas Day and kept it by them during the service. Although no special blessing was pronounced over it, it was deemed to be sanctified by the words of the service, and was afterwards given to the poultry to eat in order to preserve them from evil throughout the year.

HOLED STONES

Stones with natural holes in them were formerly believed to have magical powers of various kinds. This applied both to large perforated rocks and standing stones, and to small holed pebbles found in the earth and used as amulets. In some areas, the belief extended to ancient spindle-whorls turned up by the plough, the original purpose of which was not remembered because such things were no longer in general use.

The Crick, or Creeping Stone, at Madron in Cornwall healed lumbago and other pains in the back if the patient crawled through it nine times on all fours, going widdershins, or against the sun. The Mên-an-Tol in the same parish was often resorted to by mothers who passed their ailing children through a large aperture in the central stone of the group. Farther north, at Fyvie in Aberdeenshire, the Shargar Stone strengthened weakly children who were pushed through the space beneath it. On Coll, in the Hebrides, sufferers from consumption crawled through a certain holed stone and left an offering of food upon it.

Sometimes such stones were frequented for other purposes than healing. In the Orkneys a menhir called the Woden Stone could marry those who clasped hands through a hole in it and vowed fidelity to each other. If they later desired to end the marriage, they could do so by going together to a Christian church, attending a service there, and then leaving by different doors. The Swearing Stone in Castledermot churchyard was so called because vows made while clasping hands through its perforated face were considered specially binding.

These, and many similar traditions in Britain and elsewhere, depended upon stones in particular localities, but small holed pebbles could be found almost anywhere. They were known as hag-stones, or witch-stones, sometimes as holy stones or, in Scotland, as mare-stones. Carried about in the pocket, or hung over the bed-head, they protected the owner against witchcraft and a variety of ills. If one was tied behind the house-door, it prevented the entry of witches and evil spirits. If it was attached to the door-key, or to the nail on which the key normally hung, the combined iron and stone acted as a powerful amulet against ill-luck. Whoever slept with one over his bed was safe from nightmares and night-sweats. Heanley[1] relates that he once found such a stone in the earth under a blown-down tree, and was told by a neighbour that this was a very lucky find, for if he kept it over his bed, he would never suffer from rheumatism.

Farmers used hagstones to protect their stock from spells and disease, and to prevent horses from sweating. In his *Remaines of Gentilisme and Judaisme* Aubrey remarks that 'in the West of England (& I beleeve, almost everywhere in this nation), the Carters, & Groomes, & Hostlers doe hang a flint

[1] R. M. Heanley, *op. cit.*

(that has a hole in it) over horses that are hagge-ridden for a Preservative against it'. Such stones were also used to help mares at foaling-time, and to protect milch-cows from having their milk magically stolen by witches, from the effect of elf-shots, and from other troubles, natural or witch-induced.

The Village Museum at Ashwell in Hertfordshire contains a perforated flint which came from a nearby farm. In an article published in *Folk-Lore* (Vol. 66. 1955), T. W. Bagshawe says that this amulet formerly hung in the stables, but when these were burnt down in 1850 and new ones built, it was not immediately restored to its old place in the rafters. Some years later, three horses died of the ailment known as Glanders, and a horse-doctor, on being consulted, suggested a charm. The flint was therefore hung up in the stables as before, and from that time forward there was no more disease. About thirty years ago, when the place was being whitewashed, the owner suggested that the flint should be taken down and cleaned. The horseman refused, saying that it must never be taken down by anyone connected with the farm. In 1952, the farm being by then mechanized and without horses, it was lent to the museum, but only on condition that someone unconnected with the farmstead removed it, and that it should be returned at once if any ill effects followed its removal.

HOLLY

Holly, being evergreen and having red berries, is a symbol of enduring life, and consequently it is considered a lucky plant almost everywhere. Christmas decorations in the home would hardly be complete without it, *see Christmas Greenery,* and unlike mistletoe, it appears in those of churches as well as ordinary houses. In some districts, when the rest of the decorations are burnt or thrown away at the end of the holiday, a holly-sprig is kept, to protect the house from lightning during the coming year. A tree growing nearby is also thought to guard against thunder and lightning, and inside or out, the dark green leaves and scarlet berries are, or were formerly, con- sidered a strong protection against witches, demons, and the Evil Eye.

Male, or prickly, holly is lucky to men, as the smooth variegated type, known as she-holly, is to women. If the First Foot on his rounds brings ever- greens with him, it is usually holly that he chooses, but in this case, it must be the male kind, for the other variety, being female, would be very ill-omened.

Holly branches must never be burnt when green. To do this is extremely unlucky, and may cause a death in the family. It is also unlucky in some places to stamp on a holly-berry, or to bring the plant indoors when it is flowering.

A north-country charm to induce dreams of a future mate required the seeker to go out in silence at midnight on a Friday, and gather nine she-holly leaves. These had to be tied with nine knots in a three-cornered handkerchief, and laid under the pillow before going to bed. The husband or wife would then appear in a dream, but only if complete silence had been preserved from the moment of setting out to gather the leaves until dawn next day.

A well-known country remedy for chilblains is to thrash them with a holly bush 'to let the chilled blood out'. This probably does some good by restoring the arrested circulation, but the choice of holly rather than anything else as a thrashing agent is made for magical reasons.

HORSE

The great importance of the horse until quite recently in battle and in agriculture is probably sufficient to account for its pre-eminence in pagan religious belief and in later superstition. Certainly, it has been sacred from very early times. The Celtic goddess, Epona, presided over ponies and horses, and sometimes appeared in their form. Odin rode through the heavens on an eight-footed horse which was white or dappled grey, a tradition that may perhaps explain the English belief that earthly horses of that colour are unlucky, or in some districts lucky, to meet. Sacrifices of horses were made at certain seasons by many ancient peoples, including the Norsemen and the Romans. In northern Europe formerly, their skulls were often set on the gables of houses as a protection, and horse-bones, probably placed there for the same reason, have been found embedded in the walls of old English houses only recently demolished.

The horse is a symbol of fertility, and is connected with the harvest and the Corn Spirit. The hobby-horses that still appear in some May-day ceremonies and ritual dances denote this, as does the appearance of the Mari Lwyd and the Hodening Horse at Christmas or Hallowtide. In Cheshire, the Wild Horse is one of the characters in the Soul-Caking Play acted on All Souls' Day, a date which falls fairly close to the end of the late northern harvest. At Higher Whitley in that county, it was formerly the custom, after the acting of the Play, for rival gangs to fight for the skull used, and afterwards to give it a ritual funeral.

Superstitions about white horses vary. Sometimes they are fortunate to meet, sometimes the reverse. Devonshire people say that a horse with four white feet is unlucky, but one with a single white stocking is lucky. Elsewhere, the luck-bringer may be an animal with one fore leg and one hind leg white-stockinged. On seeing a white horse, it is customary to spit and wish, or to make a cross on the ground with the foot, or to cross the fingers and keep them thus until a dog is seen. The same ritual is often observed on seeing a piebald, which is lucky, though a skewbald quite frequently is not.

A cure for whooping-cough is to hold the child where a piebald horse can breathe on him, or to let him ride on its back. Another curious remedy is to ask a man riding such an animal for his advice, and then do whatever he recommends, however unlikely it may seem at first hearing. In some districts, it is, or was, thought that consumption and chest complaints could be healed if the sufferer went to the stables and inhaled the breath of any of the horses, without consideration of colour or markings.

It is lucky in some areas to lead a horse through the house. In Lincolnshire at one time, it was believed that if a diseased horse was slaughtered, another would die soon, an unfortunate belief which prevented many kindly persons from putting a doomed animal out of its misery and pain. A mare in foal must not be used to draw a corpse to the grave, or either she and her foal, or a member of the owner's family, will die within the year. To find out whether a mare was in foal or not, horsemen used to spit a mouthful of water violently into her ear. If she was in foal, she would shake her head only, if not, her whole body. Along the Welsh Border, it was considered very unlucky to harness or use a horse on New Year's Day or on Good Friday. People wishing to hire a horse and trap on either of these days usually found it impossible to do so.

Horses were believed to be very susceptible to the influence of witches and fairies, and holed stones, magical plants, and many other charm-objects were hung about the stable to protect them. They were also supposed to be able to see ghosts and spirits, and to know when a place was haunted, even though their human companions did not. In his *Highland Folklore Heritage* (1926) Alexander Polson relates how on one occasion he saw a carter's horse refuse to go by a gate, although there was apparently nothing alarming there. The carter had to lead it past, while it showed every sign of fear and, once beyond the opening, could only be restrained with difficulty from bolting. A few days later, a corpse was carried through the gate on the way to the funeral.

In Wesley's *Primitive Physick* (1755), it is stated that cancer could be cured by horse-spurs, the callosities that sometimes form on the inner side of a horse's leg. They had to be dried, powdered, infused in ale, and given to the patient to drink with new, warm milk at six-hourly intervals. Parings of the spurs, or of the hoof, were also said to have the power of attracting dogs, and of enabling the bearer to charm them.

HORSE-BRASSES

The beautiful horse-brasses which were once the pride of many carters before mechanization drove the horses from the farms were originally more than mere ornaments. They were intended to protect the horse that wore them against the Evil Eye and witchcraft. For this reason, they were cast, as the modern, lighter replicas still are, in traditional life-symbolizing shapes, such as crescent moons, rayed suns, wheels, swastikas, winged globes, hearts, hands, or lotus-flowers.

The full set, which might consist of nineteen or twenty pieces of cast brass, was too heavy for daily wear, and usually appeared only on gala occasions. On ordinary days, one or two pieces were thought enough to protect the horse. Complete sets can still be seen occasionally at such gatherings as the Cart Horse Parades held in London, Manchester, and other towns on May Day or Whit Monday. They belonged normally to the carter on a farm, not to the farmer, and were handed down in his family from father to son. A really old set is now quite valuable, and much prized by collectors.

HORSE-HAIRS

It was once commonly supposed that if horse-hairs were left in water they would turn into eels. A writer in *The Book of Days* (1864) remarks that only a few months before he wrote, a Suffolk man stated that he had proved this to be true by experiment. He had, he said, put a number of horse-hairs into a spring near his home to see what would happen. A very short time afterwards, he found the water full of young eels.

The fact that some worms are not unlike hairs from a horse's mane or tail was probably responsible for a well-known folk-cure for worms in children. Acting on the magical principle that ailments can be cured by something that resembles them, careful parents chopped horse-hairs very finely, pressed them into bread-and-butter, and gave it to the child to eat.

A remedy for goitre, recorded in Oxfordshire during the present century, was to ask a horseman for a few hairs from a stallion's tail, without telling him why they were needed. If these hairs were then constantly worn round the sufferer's neck, the swelling would diminish and eventually disappear.

A strong tradition amongst schoolboys is that a horse-hair concealed in the hand during a caning will split the cane, so that it cannot be used, or alternatively, that it will prevent the victim from feeling the pain of the beating.

HORSEMAN'S WORD

The Horseman's Word was a secret charm which was widely believed in many parts of Great Britain and Ireland to give those who knew it absolute control over horses. It was known only to certain horsemen, carters, grooms, ploughmen, and blacksmiths, who were frequently, but not always, members of a local horsemen's society or brotherhood. Such initiates could tame the most savage stallion simply by whispering to it, stop galloping horses in mid-flight, make any horse follow them for miles, calm or excite it, and generally render it unmanageable or completely tractable at will.

There were, of course, other spoken charms by which witches and cunning-men were believed to be able to control animals. Almost every district in the British Isles has its stories of the use of such spells. Heanley[1] relates a tale told to him at the end of last century by the Lincolnshire carter concerned. This man lodged with a wisewoman named Mary Atkin. One morning he quarrelled with her just before going to his work, and she told him he would be sorry for it when his team reached a certain place on the road. No sooner had they arrived there than his horses stopped dead, and could not be induced to move on by any cajoling or beating. He was forced to return to the house and beg the wisewoman to remove the spell. This she consented to do after much persuasion, and at once the horses went on, none the worse for their magical experience.

The carter told Heanley that he could have freed his animals without further trouble if only he had had the presence of mind to take off the leading horse's collar and look through it backwards. In his agitation, he had forgotten this simple counter-charm, but, he said, thereafter he had been careful never to go out without a sprig of rowan-wood about him as an antidote to further witchcraft.

This is only one of many tales of the same kind. At Withypool in Somerset, a certain Anne Blackmore, who lived in the early years of the present century, was supposed to have the power of stopping horses. Her house was near the bridge over the Danesbrook, and on this bridge she frequently halted the teams of those who had offended her, making the unhappy animals plunge and sweat until their drivers were forced to take them out of the shafts and lead them home. It will be noticed that in this, as in many other recorded cases, the charmer did not approach or touch the horses. It was sufficient for her (or him) to murmur some inaudible word or phrase, both to bewitch and subsequently to release them.

Such spells were well known and, at one time, widely believed in, but they were not quite in the same category as the Horseman's Word. That belonged only to horsemen, and could be learnt and used by simple folk who were not in any other way connected with witchcraft. In Scotland, carters, plough-men, blacksmiths, and grooms who knew it formed a kind of aristocracy of their profession, and were banded together in a society known as the Brotherhood of the Horseman's Word.

The charm itself could only be learned at secret and awe-inspiring meet-ings of the Brotherhood, held at night in a smithy. The neophyte was required to take a solemn oath of secrecy, and was then initiated with curious ceremonies by the older members, of whom the blacksmith was often the chief. It is said that at 'term time' in Scotland, when farm servants changed their employment, the outgoing horseman was always very anxious to know the name of his successor.

If the latter was already a member of the Brotherhood, all was well, but

[1] R. M. Heanley, *op. cit.*

if he was not, every horse in the stable became unmanageable as soon as he arrived, and remained so either until his predecessor relented, or until he too became a member of the band.

In East Anglia and the surrounding counties, such societies seem to have existed until the end of the nineteenth century. They must have been small, for only a few horsemen were ever credited with super normal powers of control, and of these, some were believed to have gained such powers through possession of the frog's or toad's bone that floats upstream. *See Frog: Toad.* In such cases, membership of a Brotherhood was not necessarily involved, nor does a spoken word or phrase always seem to have been used.

About 1908, a certain farmer at Bourn in Cambridgeshire offended the workers at a smithy by implying that one of them had appropriated the money given to him in payment of a bill. Among these workers was a man who had already proved himself capable of controlling horses in a striking manner. This man undertook to punish the farmer. One day, when the latter drove up to the smithy in a pony-trap, he looked towards the road, passed a handkerchief over his face, and put it back in his pocket. He did nothing more, but when the farmer was ready to go, his pony would not move. It stood quite quietly from nine o'clock in the morning till five in the afternoon, and then the charmer released it by patting its neck. When asked by his admiring companions how he did it, the man said he possessed a frog's bone, and described to them in detail how he had obtained it. He seriously warned them not to attempt this charm themselves, for the Devil was concerned in it and 'you will never rest if you do'.[1]

The famous American horse-tamer, John S. Rarey, may have known the Horseman's Word, or something very like it. He came to England in 1858 and tamed a number of savage stallions in the ensuing two years. His extraordinary powers in this direction are well attested, and they have never been satisfactorily explained. He never claimed to have any secret or occult gift, but on several occasions he was seen by reliable witnesses to calm a vicious horse merely by speaking to it.

His most celebrated exploit was the taming, in 1858, of Cruiser, a savage and quite ungovernable stallion belonging to Lord Dorchester. This horse had already killed three men, and could not be approached in safety by any one but his keeper. Even he never went near it without a heavy stick in his hand. Rarey entered the enclosed yard outside the stable alone and unarmed. The beast at once charged him, but when he was only a few feet away, the tamer spoke. Cruiser stopped at once, trembling, but otherwise calm, and then let Rarey caress and gentle him, a thing no one had ever been able to do before.

How this was done is unknown. What Rarey said to the horse was not heard by Lord Dorchester and the stud-groom who were watching from the

[1] *Folk-Lore*, Vol. 46. 1955.

safety of a ladder set against the outer wall of the enclosure, but that the horse was calmed immediately was undeniable. In other cases also, Rarey seems to have used a single word or phrase which somehow established sympathy between him and the animal. Although he never at any time, either in speech or in his two books on horse-management, claimed to know the Horseman's Word or use a charm, it has been suggested that he did so. In her *Happy Days* (1936) Dr Somerville states that the father of her friend, Fanny Curry, bought a charm from him for thirty guineas, and this, to Dr Somerville's own knowledge, was successfully used by Miss Curry to calm an excited and infuriated horse on at least two occasions.

What lay at the root of faith in the Horseman's Word and other control-charms is hardly likely to be discovered now, when the horse has disappeared from so many spheres, and the art of controlling it is much less important than it once was. It has been suggested that its efficacy sprang, not from magic, but from a peculiar vibration of the voice, from an advanced degree of that special gift for horse-management which some people undoubtedly possess, or from secret and quite unmagical 'tricks of the trade' known only to professional horsemen. What is certain, however, is that within the last sixty or seventy years, many people firmly believed that such a charm existed, and that it could be, and was, used with success by ordinary farm-workers who had gained the necessary knowledge by initiation, or some other secret means.

HORSESHOES

The horseshoe has been regarded for centuries as a luck-bringing and protective amulet in every country where the shod horse is known. This is partly because it is made of iron and forged by a blacksmith, and partly because it is a lunar symbol, roughly resembling in its shape the horned new moon.

To find one lying in the road is very fortunate, and doubly so if it has been cast from the near hind leg of a grey mare. It need hardly be said that such a chance-found luck-bringer must never be passed by without attention. In some districts, it is said that the correct procedure, as in the case of nails or coal similarly happened upon, is to pick it up, spit on it, make a wish, throw it over the left shoulder, and walk on without looking back at it. The more usual practice, however, is to take it home and nail it over the house-door or on the threshold.

The belief that its presence there averts evil and brings good fortune is very old, and it is evidently far from extinct yet, if the number of real or imitation horseshoes still to be seen on town and country houses is any guide. Aubrey remarks in his *Remaines* that 'it should be a Horse-shoe that is found in the highway accidentally; it is used for a Preservative against the mischiefe or power of Witches; and it is an old use derived from the

Astrological principle, that Mars is an enemie to Saturne, under whom the witches are; and no where so much used as (to this day) in the west part of London, especially the New-buildings'. Farmers formerly hung one, three, or seven shoes over their cowbyres and stables, to guard their stock from witchcraft and, in the case of horses, from 'hag-riding' at night by fairies or demons. Sailors also nailed them to the masts of ships to avert storms and shipwreck. Nelson is said to have had one on the mainmast of *Victory*.

Ideas as to the manner in which the guardian horseshoe should be hung vary slightly. Some people say it should be with the horns downwards. Others, perhaps the majority, say this spills the luck, and that the points must be upwards, to keep it in. Both theories have ardent supporters but, in England at least, the upwards notion now seems to be the more popular of the two. In his *Horns of Honour* (1900), F. T. Elworthy records how a Somerset farmer, thinking his ailing cattle had been overlooked, hung up a horseshoe, with the points downwards. His beasts continued to suffer, and a neighbour told him that this was because the shoe was 'wrong side up'. No good results could be expected unless the horns were upwards. The man took his friend's advice, reversed the shoe and, according to Elworthy's informant, had no more trouble with his cattle.

R. M. Heanley[1] mentions two interesting Lincolnshire charms involving the use of horseshoes. One was intended to ward off delirium tremens, and consisted simply of nailing three horseshoes to the head of the charmer's bed. If this was done, he could drink as much as he liked without any fear of 'talking-over or seeing things'.

The other was more elaborate and obviously pagan in origin. Heanley tells us that in 1858 or 1859 there was an ague epidemic where he lived, and during the course of it, he took some quinine to a sick boy. The child's grandmother refused the gift, saying she knew of something much better than 'yon mucky bitter stuff'. She then took Mr Heanley into the room where the patient lay, and showed him three horseshoes nailed to the bedfoot, with a hammer fixed across them. These, she said, would keep the shaking fits away. She had fixed them in position with the proper rites, tapping each shoe with the hammer held in her left hand, and saying as she did so,

> Father, Son and Holy Ghost,
> Nail the devil to this post,
> Thrice I smites with Holy Crook,
> With this mell I thrice do knock,
> One for God,
> And one for Wod,
> And one for Lok.

[1] R. M. Heanley, *op. cit.*

In this charm the ancient Norse deities, Woden and Loki, are invoked as well as the Holy Trinity, and the 'Holy Crook' used represents the Hammer of Thor. But that the boy's grandmother realized this is highly improbable. All she knew was that the rhyme was a powerful charm, and that it, the three horseshoes, and the hammer all together would, as she believed, effect a quicker and more lasting cure than any chemist's medicine. *See Taxi-cab Numbers.*

HOT CROSS BUNS

Hot cross buns, those pleasant Christian descendants of the small wheaten cakes once eaten at pagan Spring Festivals, were long supposed to have magical and medicinal properties. For this reason, it was customary in many households to keep one or two throughout the year, both as a protection against fire and other evils, and for use as a remedy for various ailments. They were hung up in the kitchen and allowed to go dry and hard. When needed for healing purposes, they were finely grated or powdered, mixed with milk or water, and given to the patient as medicine. In some rural areas, they have been so used within living memory, especially for diarrhoea, dysentery, whooping-cough, and the affliction known as 'summer sickness'.

Tradition says they never go mouldy, and in fact, they do not seem to do so readily, as those preserved at the Widow's Son Inn at Bromley, London, clearly show. The presence of these buns, some of which are well over a hundred years old, is not due to superstition, but to a pathetic story concerning a widow who was the licensee in the early nineteenth century. This woman had a sailor son, and every year, if he was at sea on Good Friday, she laid aside a hot cross bun against his return. The time came when he did not return, but she continued to keep the buns for him, hanging one up in the bar-parlour till next Good Friday came round, and then putting it in a basket with its predecessors. After her death, later tenants did the same, and now a clause in the lease enforces the custom. Each year a sailor is called in to hang up the new bun and put the old one in the basket, and is given free beer as his reward. Of the very large number now collected, nearly all are still in good condition, only those made of inferior flour during the war years showing signs of mouldering away.

Sailors formerly took a hot cross bun on their voyages to prevent shipwreck, and farmers kept one or two in their granaries as a protection against rats. The same protective and healing powers were ascribed to bread baked on Good Friday or on Christmas Day. *See Bread.*

It must be said, however, that the beneficent properties of these buns are derived from the holy day itself, and the charms will not work unless they are actually made on Good Friday morning. Our modern custom of buying buns which have been baked on the previous day therefore renders them quite useless for these good purposes.

HOUSELEEK

Houseleek, which country people call Syngreen, is traditionally connected with fire and valued as a protection against it. If it grows on the roof of a house, that house will never be burnt down or struck by lightning. It must not, however, be uprooted or cut down, otherwise trouble of some sort (not necessarily a fire) will inevitably follow.

The plant has genuine healing properties and, according to Culpeper, was once considered 'good for all inward heats as well as outward'. Its principal use in ordinary homes was to cure burns and scalds. The soft creamy juice expressed from the leaves was laid on the burn, either by itself, or mixed with the juice of plantain, another herb with magical properties. If there was no time to press out the juice, the cool leaves were bound directly on the injured part without further preparation. The merits of this treatment were twofold, as was often the case in folk-medicine. It was both magical and practical. The plant which protected against fire was, by a natural association of ideas, thought able to heal the effects of fire; and at the same time, its 'cream' is in fact soothing and, although perhaps not an altogether ideal remedy for a really bad burn, would be likely to allay the pain, at least temporarily.

First aid remedies of a more modern kind are now usually employed for burns, but the juice of houseleek is still quite often used as a lotion for ulcers, sores, corns on the feet, and warts, and also for ringworm and kindred ills.

I

IMAGES

The making of images is one of the most ancient forms of magic, known almost everywhere in the world, and practised in all ages, from remote antiquity down to the present century. The underlying idea is that whatever resembles a man, or has been in close contact with him, can be mystically identified with him in such a way that whatever is done to the thing that represents him will be repeated, with heightened effect, in his body or mind. Thus, an image of any individual is deemed to be a magical agent through which he can be directly affected, either for good or for evil.

Images have been made at various times to cure or cause disease, to obtain or destroy love, to waste or increase wealth, and to bring success or failure in any enterprise. In the same way, they have been used to prevent childbirth or to make barren women fertile, to unite estranged lovers, or to cause poverty, madness, and a quick or a lingering death. In some cases, an existing portrait was substituted for the more usual wax or clay figure, or some other object was used symbolically, such as a wheatsheaf twisted into human shape, or a metal tablet with the victim's name scratched upon it. These were regarded as equally efficacious, provided that the appropriate rites were observed in their preparation. Faith in image-magic was once extremely strong and, in the hey-day of the European witch-belief, its use as a means of secret revenge or malice was almost universally dreaded.

The usual method was to make a figure roughly resembling the victim out of wax, clay, wood, or metal, incorporating, if possible, a strand of his hair, his nail-parings, or shreds of his clothing to make the spell still stronger. It was named after him, and incantations were pronounced over it. If it was desired to afflict him in any part of his body, pins or thorns were thrust into the corresponding part of the image. The stabbing of its head sent him mad; a pin or thorn driven into the eye or leg blinded or crippled him, and one thrust through the heart killed him outright. Or the whole figure might be slowly melted before a fire, if it was of wax, or buried in earth or placed in running water, if it was made of other materials. As it melted or mouldered away, so the victim fell ill and finally died of some wasting disease.

A person against whom such an image had been made could only be saved by the speedy discovery of the deadly object and its immediate destruction by fire. Even this was not always enough. Stow tells us in his *Annales* that when the Earl of Derby lay ill in 1594, a wax figure was found hidden in his room. It was burnt at once, but the Earl died nevertheless. Stow evidently thought his disease was due to natural causes, but Lord Derby himself was convinced that it was the result of witchcraft and, says Stow, he 'cried out that the Doctors laboured in vain because he was certainly bewitched'.

The records of the witch-trials throughout Europe show that witches were frequently accused of murder by image-magic and many confessed to it. There is no doubt that some at least of those who confessed had made such figures with intent to murder, whatever may have been the actual result of their work. It was not, however, only acknowledged witches who practised this simple and deadly form of magic. Cases of malicious image-making by quite ordinary people have been recorded at various times in Britain, as elsewhere, and doubtless there were many other instances which have never come to light.

In January 1960, a small figure of a woman, wearing a cap or bonnet and a full dress of patterned material, was discovered, during renovations to the building, in the cellar of the Hereford Rural District Council's offices. Tucked into the folds of the skirt was a paper, worn and dirty with age, on which was written the name Mary Ann Wand, and the words:

'I act this spell upon you from my whole heart, wishing you to never rest nor eat nor sleep the restern part of your life. I hope your flesh will waste away and I hope you will never spend another penny I ought to have. Wishing this from my whole heart.'

The story behind this image is unknown, but it seems probable that its maker was not a witch in the ordinary sense, but some simple individual driven to the practice of evil magic by a real or fancied injury. It would be interesting to know what effect, if any, it had upon Mary Ann Wand, or whether she deserved such bitter hatred, but it is not very likely that either of these questions will be answered now.

In the Scottish Highlands during the nineteenth century, a form of image known as the *Corps Creadh* was sometimes made from motives of revenge or hatred. The *Corps Creadh* was a rough clay figure, tightly moulded so as to render it as hard as possible, into which pins were thrust in the manner outlined above. As each pin went in, a malediction was pronounced. Then, if a lingering death was desired, the image was laid in a running stream where, slowly but surely, it crumbled away under the pressure of the moving water. In an article contributed to *Folk-Lore* in 1895,[1] R. C. Maclagan relates the story of two girls in the Western Isles, both of whom were in love with the same man. The prettier one being preferred by him, the other made a *Corps Creadh* for her rival and hid it in running water. Her victim fell ill immediately and grew steadily worse in spite of all that the doctor and devoted nursing could do for her. One day, however, a shepherd caught sight of the figure hidden in the stream and, recognizing it for the evil thing it was, destroyed it. The girl began to recover from that hour.

Instances of the survival in the present century of this ancient superstition are not unknown, even in civilized countries. The use of a photograph for spell-breaking purposes in 1922 is recorded elsewhere in this book. *See Photograph.* On 14 December 1900, the *New York Times* reported the burning of a pin-studded effigy of the President on the steps of the American Embassy in London. In his *Witchcraft* (1941) W. B. Seabrook mentions an attempt made in France to injure a pianist by making wax models of his hands, and so depriving him of the power to play. The Witchcraft Museum at Bourton-on-the-Water contains an unpleasant-looking doll dressed as an A.T.S. sergeant. It has a dagger thrust through one of its eyes, and is said to have been constructed by an aggrieved girl during the 1939 War.

IRISH STONES

In northern England, as late as the latter half of the nineteenth century, stones brought from Ireland were regarded as powerful healing charms. Henderson[2] tells us that three such stones existed in the neighbourhood of Stamfordham, and that people came from miles round to be touched by them. They healed by their own power, but the charm was considered to be

[1] R. C. Maclagan, 'Notes on Folklore Objects collected in Argyleshire', *Folk-Lore*, Vol. 6. 1895.

[2] Wm. Henderson. *op. cit.*

doubly efficacious if they were applied to the diseased part or the wound by
an Irishman. One which belonged to the owner of Kyloe Hall was never
allowed to touch English soil. It was much used to cure sores or wounds in
the leg, and was carried to the patient's house in a basket where it was
rubbed on the sore place. The wound was then confidently expected to heal
very quickly.

In Northumberland, Irish stones were used as charms to prevent frogs,
toads, and snakes from entering the house. This seems to be connected with
an ancient belief, found in many parts of northern Europe, that earth brought
from the snakeless island could be used to destroy snakes in other places. The
same power was apparently enjoyed by St Patrick's compatriots, both animal
and human. Henderson records a north-country tradition that if an Irishman
drew a circle round a toad or adder, the creature would be imprisoned in it
and would die. It was also said that a sure way to cure a dog that had been
bitten by an adder was to wash the wound in the milk of an Irish cow.

In the *Denham Tracts* there is an account of a snake-averting Irish stone,
once the property of Thomas Hedley, of Woolaw in Redesdale, and afterwards of his son. Dr Denham describes it as being of a pale brown or dark
drab colour, 'of a cake form', three-and-a-quarter inches in diameter, and
about three-quarters of an inch thick in the middle. Unlike many charm-
stones, it was unperforated. It was subsequently given to the Museum of the
Society of Antiquaries in Newcastle-on-Tyne.

IRON

Iron was not used for tools and weapons until mankind had lived on Earth
for a very long time. When it was first so used, its superiority over stone and
bronze, especially in battle, caused it to be regarded as a magical metal, which
tribes who still clung to old ways and old materials had good reason to dread.
This belief in its wonder-working properties persisted long after it had passed
into general use, and still survives in many of our superstitions.

Fairies, witches and evil spirits were believed to fear it extremely and to be
powerless against it. In Egypt, a man entering a dark and unknown place will
often cry 'Iron, you devil!' before going in, in order to drive away any
malevolent jinn who may be lurking there. In Britain, horseshoes are still
hung up on houses to avert evil and bring good luck, or something made of
iron may be touched after making a rash boast instead of the more usual
wood. *See p.* 61. Nails used to be driven into cradles, or the beds of
women in childbirth, for the same protective purpose, and within this
century, scissors have been concealed under cushions or floor-coverings to
keep witches away from the house, or nullify their power when they came.

Iron and steel objects found on the roadway are usually thought to be
lucky to their finder. In a dairy, they prevent witches from enchanting the

churn, in a cowbyre, from casting spells on the cows or stealing their milk from a distance. When suicides were buried at the crossroads, an iron stake was often driven through their bodies to stop them from rising and haunting the place, and the same charm was occasionally resorted to when some notorious witch was buried. Bars laid across beer-barrels are said to prevent the beer from turning sour during a thunderstorm and the large spiral irons, single or crossed, which are sometimes seen in the walls of old houses, acted as charms to protect the building from lightning.

On the other hand, iron could be ill-omened in certain circumstances. When need-fire was kindled, the workers were not permitted to have any iron about them, for if they had, the spark would not come. See Need-fire. At Burghead, when the Clavie is burnt on Old New Year's Eve to bring good luck and fertility to all in the town, no iron or other metal must be used in its preparation, with the exception of one long nail with which the tar-filled barrel is fixed to the pole, or Spoke. This nail has to be specially forged for the occasion by the blacksmith, and hammered in with a stone, never with an iron hammer. To break this rule would be very unlucky, and might nullify the fertilizing and luck-bringing virtues of the ceremony.

Mrs Leather[1] records that in Herefordshire it was generally believed that a dead man could not rest if he had left behind him any hidden metal possessions, including money and iron tools. One of her informants stated that people in the Crasswall district were warned never to put bits of iron into walls, for fear they should die before they could remove them. He also told her that on one occasion a few years earlier, he heard a woman say she must go at once to search for her husband's tools which he had left under an archway. He was, she said, very ill, and was in great dread that he might die while they were still there, and so be forced to haunt the place after his death. See Horseshoes: Knife: Pins: Scissors, etc.

ITCHING OR TINGLING

The idea that any sudden and unexplained sensation in the human body had ominous significance was once very common, and it still survives in the well-known superstitions about itching, tingling, or burning in the face, hands and feet. Such sensations are supposed to foretell a coming event, or to warn the person concerned of some unseen happening connected with himself. The omens thus read vary slightly in different districts, but the most usual are as follows:

Right Ear: Someone is speaking well of you, or you mother is thinking of you.
Left Ear: Someone is maligning you, or your lover is thinking of you.
Eyes: A pleasant surprise is coming if the right eye itches, a disappointment if the left eye does so.

[1] E. M. Leather, *op. cit.*

Cheeks: Burning cheeks denote that someone is talking about you, probably unkindly. In an article contributed to *Folk-Lore* in 1913, Angelina Parker records an Oxfordshire charm recited when this happened as a protection against backbiting. It ran:

> Right cheek, left cheek, why do you burn?
> Cursed be she that doth me any harm.
> If it be a maid, let her be slayed,
> If it be a wife, let her lose her life,
> And if it be a widow, long let her mourn;
> But if it be my own true love, burn, cheek, burn.

Hands: If the palm of the right hand itches, money is coming to you, if that of the left hand, it will have to be paid out by you. It is customary to rub it on wood for luck in both cases.

Feet: If the underpart of the foot itches, you will soon tread on strange ground.

Knee: If the knee itches, you will kneel in a strange place.

Nose: An itching nose means you will be kissed, cursed, or vexed, run against a gatepost, or shake hands with a fool.

IVY

Ivy commonly appears in folk-belief as a kindly plant, which is perhaps to be expected in a bush anciently associated with Bacchus. In Christmas decorations it is lucky to the women of the household, as holly is to the men, and therefore it should never be omitted if all the family are to share alike in the blessings of the season. If it grows on a house, it protects those within from witchcraft and evil, but if it withers suddenly or falls away, misfortune of some kind will follow. In Wales, such a happening is said to predict the passing of the house into other hands, either through financial losses suffered by the owner, or through the failure of heirs.

A bush or garland of ivy was formerly hung outside taverns and vintners' shops as a sign that wine could be bought there. The wood of the plant was supposed to have the power of separating water from wine when these were mixed together in a bowl made from it. Its leaves and berries averted the effects of too heavy drinking. If a man desired to start on a drinking-bout, but feared the consequences, he could protect himself beforehand by drinking vinegar in which the berries had been dissolved, and later, when all was over, by drinking water in which the bruised leaves had been boiled.

Lupton describes in his *Notable Things* a form of divination with ivy-leaves. On New Year's Eve, at night, the enquirer put a green leaf into a basin of water, and left it there until Twelfth Night Eve. If it was then found to be still green and fresh, the coming year would be fortunate. Black spots on its surface foretold illness, in the head or neck if the spots were on the upper part, near the stalk, in the heart or stomach if they were in the middle, and in the feet or legs if they were near the pointed end. If the leaf was spotted all over, the enquirer would die within the year. 'You may prove this for many or few at one time,' says Lupton, 'by putting them in water, for everie one a leaf of green ivie (so that every leafe be dated or marked to whom it doth belong). This was credibly told me to be very certain.' A simpler form of the same charm was practised in Herefordshire on Hallowe'en at the beginning of this century. Each person marked a leaf so that it could be easily recognized, and left it all night in a basin of water. If any of the company was to die that year, a coffin-shaped mark would be found on his or her leaf next morning.

When an Oxfordshire girl desired to know whom she would marry, she picked an ivy leaf and put it in her pocket. The first man she met out walking thereafter would marry her eventually, even if at the time of the meeting he had a wife already. In southern Scotland, the girl had to put the leaf against her heart, saying

> Ivy, Ivy, I love you,
> In my bosom I put you.
> The first young man who speaks to me
> My future husband he shall be.

In Cardiganshire on Hallowe'en, ivy-leaves were thrown in pairs on to the fire, a pointed leaf for the man and a rounded one for the woman. If they jumped towards each other in the heat, the young people they represented would marry, but if they jumped apart, the affair would end in a quarrel and a parting.

The leaves, roots and wood of ivy were formerly used in a number of folk-remedies, some practical and some mainly magical. In Oxfordshire a cure for corns, still sometimes resorted to, is to soak the leaves in vinegar and bind them on the corn. Water in which such leaves had been steeped for a night and a day served as a lotion for sore eyes, and in Dorset, skin-rashes were treated in much the same way. The expressed juice of the leaves snuffed up the nostrils, stopped running at the nose in a bad cold. An ivy-leaf wreath worn on the head was supposed to prevent hair from falling out after an illness. For jaundice, the roots of ground-ivy were boiled in water, which the patient then had to drink. Food or drink taken from an ivy-wood bowl cured whooping-cough. In the seventeenth century the same wood, especially if cut from an old climbing plant, was thought to impart an infection-averting virtue to any wine that was left standing for some time in a vessel made from it.

J

JACKDAW

Jackdaws share some of the ominous traditions attaching to magpies. *See* p. 224. Of these, the commonest is that it is unlucky to see one by itself, and especially so if it is on the left of the person who sees it. In some districts, it is an omen of death in the house if one flies down a chimney.

If jackdaws are late coming home in the evening, it is a sign of bad weather to come, and if they flutter and caw round buildings, rain is foretold.

These birds, like magpies, were sometimes kept by farmers as watch-birds, to give warning by their chattering of the approach of strangers.

JUNIPER

In almost every country where it grows the Juniper appears as a protective tree. According to an Italian legend, it saved the life of the Infant Jesus during the Flight into Egypt. One day, Herod's agents came so close that capture seemed inevitable, and in desperation, the Virgin Mary besought the surrounding trees to hide her Child. A juniper bush at once opened its branches, and there Our Lord was hidden. When the pursuing soldiers came up, they saw only an old man walking with his wife, and so passed on without stopping. In 1 *Kings* xix, 4–7 we read that when Elijah fled from the vengeance of Queen Jezebel, he sheltered under a juniper, and was there visited and fed by an angel. Many other stories are told about this kindly tree, nearly all of them concerned with its merciful and protective nature.

The smoke rising from its burning wood was thought to keep away demons. In the Western Isles, sprigs of juniper were set about the byre to preserve the cows from the Evil Eye. The *buarach*, or fetter used to bind the animal's legs during milking, was sometimes fastened with a juniper stick for the same purpose. Country people say that foxes and hares often shelter under a juniper when hunted, because its strong smell obliterates their scent and confuses the hounds.

In Wales it is considered very unlucky to cut down one of these trees. Whoever does so will die within the year, or will lose a member of his family. Folkard, in his *Plant Lore, Legends and Lyrics* says it is unlucky to dream of juniper, and if the dreamer is already ill, he is unlikely to recover. On the other hand, to dream of the berries is fortunate, foretelling success and honours to come, or the birth of a male child.

During outbreaks of the plague or the sweating sickness, juniper wood used to be burnt on the hearth to keep away the infection. Infusions made from the plant were formerly given to cure rheumatism and fits, dropsy and liver troubles; and they were also believed to have the desirable property of restoring youthful vigour to the aged.

K

KINGFISHER

Legend says the kingfisher was once grey, and gained its lovely blue colour during the Flood. Noah let it out of the Ark and it immediately flew so high into the sky that it took on the true colour of the heavens. On the same journey it flew too near the sun and scorched its breast and rear feathers, which is why they now have a reddish tinge.

Another and far better known story is the Greek legend of Halcyone, whom the gods turned into a kingfisher. She was the wife of Ceyx, King of Trachis, who was drowned at sea when his ship was wrecked. Not knowing what had happened, she waited patiently for his return until, one night, his death was revealed to her in a dream. Wild with grief, she rushed down to the sea-shore and plunged into the water where his body was floating. The gods, touched by her fidelity, transformed her and her husband into kingfishers, so that they might live again happily as birds who love water and are always faithful to one mate. They also granted her and all her descendants the further boon that when the female bird sat to hatch her eggs in her floating, sea-borne nest, the sea should always be calm and untroubled by storms.

From this arose the tradition of the halcyon days. These were the seven days before and the seven days after the Winter Solstice, when kingfishers were supposed to brood, and consequently there were no storms at sea. In fact, of course, these birds nest on land, in tunnels in the overhanging banks of streams, but this was not known in antiquity, and it was commonly supposed that they built in a certain sponge-like floating zoophyte, which Linnaeus later called *halcyonium*.

In France, kingfishers were connected with St Martin, and were known as his birds. The period of fine weather which often comes round about his feast day (11 November) and is called St Martin's Summer, was there attributed to their brooding.

Sailors believed that if a dead kingfisher was hung up on board ship, it would always show in which direction the wind was blowing by turning towards it. In the seventeenth century, Sir Thomas Browne experimented with two birds and found that they turned in different directions. This discovery, however, had little or no effect upon the general belief.

Kingfishers moult like other birds, but so slightly that the process is almost imperceptible. Hence, many people thought that they did not moult at all, and that their skins never decayed. Such skins were supposed to have the power of preserving any material with which they come into contact, and for this reason, thrifty housewives often kept one in their linen or clothes chests to save the contents from decay.

KNIFE

Of the many cutting implements made of iron or steel which are in daily use, none has acquired more superstitions than the knife. This may be because at one time a knife was a very personal possession, constantly carried about by its owner, and used for every sort of purpose, from fighting or hunting to cutting up food at dinner. Being of steel, it served as a protection against evil of many kinds, including, of course, the once universally dreaded dangers of witchcraft and the onslaughts of fairies or demons. In Scotland, the sudden straw-laden eddies of wind that sometimes spring up on a calm day were believed to mark the passage of invisible fairies or witches. It was unlucky to see one, but the ill-luck could be averted by throwing a knife across the whirling dust and straws. A house could be protected from un-chancy visitants and influences by a knife thrust into the door, a baby by one stuck into the head of the cradle. Knives could also be used in divination and in healing-charms, or as a means of discovering how an absent person was faring. *See Life-Index.*

The word 'knife' must not be spoken at sea, but the thing itself is sometimes thrust for luck into the masts of fishing-boats when they are out on the *haaf*, or deep-sea fishing. If two knives are accidentally crossed on a table, or one is laid across a fork, bad luck or quarrels will follow unless they are straightened immediately. If one falls to the ground, it is a sign that a male visitor is coming. In Lincolnshire formerly, it was considered very unlucky to sharpen a knife after sunset, or to leave one on the table during the night. The first meant that a burglar or an enemy might enter the house, the second that some farm-animal would die before morning, and the knife would be needed to flay it.

To make toast on the point of a knife is ill-omened, and so is spinning one on a table. Sometimes, however, the latter was done as part of a charm to find out whether the charmer's future wife or husband would be fair or dark. For this, a table-knife with a white haft was needed. It was spun round, and the manner of its fall noted. If it fell with the blade towards the enquirer, the future mate would be dark, if with the haft, he or she would be fair.

The commonest modern superstition about knives is that, because they are sharp-cutting, they sever love or friendship when given as a present. They should never be accepted without something being given in exchange. Even today, it is quite usual for the recipient in such cases to tender a small coin, such as a penny or halfpenny, in order to prevent later quarrels or misfortune.

L

LADDER

It is widely held to be unlucky to pass through the angle formed by a ladder standing against a wall. Many people today carefully avoid doing so, even if avoidance involves stepping off the pavement into a busy town street, and so running a risk of being knocked down by a passing vehicle.

There are, however, several acknowledged methods of counteracting the bad luck incurred by such a passage. One is to cross the fingers and keep them crossed until a dog is seen or, in various districts, three, four, or five dogs, or three dogs and three horses. Another is to spit three times through the rungs, or once over the left shoulder. A third charm requires the person concerned to spit on his shoe and go straight on, taking care not to look back until the spittle has dried, or to make a cross on the shoe with the licked finger, and not look again at the shoe till the wet cross-mark has disappeared. In some places, silence is enjoined until a four-legged animal of some sort has been seen.

Yorkshire fishermen formerly believed that to reach through the rungs of a ladder for anything behind it was unlucky. It was permissible to reach round it, but not through it.

LADYBIRD

The bright scarlet ladybird is generally thought to be a luck-bringer, probably because it is traditionally associated by its colour with fire. It is a sign of good fortune if one lights on a person's hand or dress. It must, however, be allowed to fly away of its own accord, and must not be brushed off. It is permissible to speed it onwards by a gentle puff, and by the recitation of the rhyme which runs,

> Ladybird, ladybird, fly away home.
> Your house is on fire and your children are gone.

A variant of this couplet substitutes 'your true love' for the children, and this may perhaps be the older version. Other rhymes are sometimes recited. One in Northumberland seems to connect the insect with the weather. Children in that county pick it up as soon as they see it and throw it high in the air, saying,

> Reed, reed sodger, fly away,
> And make the morn a sunny day.

Young girls anxious to know where a future lover dwells, or if they will be married soon, gently blow the ladybird off the hand, or toss it into the air, with the words,

> Fly away east, fly away west,
> Show me where lives the one I love best,

or

> Bishop, Bishop Barnabee,
> Tell me when my wedding be;
> If it be tomorrow day,
> Take your wings and fly away.

The deeper the ladybird's colour, the better luck it brings. The number or spots on its back is also important. In Sussex, it is said that the person on whom the insect alights will have as many happy months as there are spots. In Dorset formerly, the same spots foretold the price of wheat, each one representing a shilling on the bushel.

It is exceedingly unlucky to kill a ladybird. In East Anglia, if one is accidentally killed, it is carefully buried, and the grave is stamped on three times, while the usual 'house on fire' rhyme is recited. In the West-country at one time, the yellowish liquid which the insect exudes when alarmed was considered a good remedy for toothache. The sufferer rubbed his finger on the ladybird's legs and then transferred the liquid so collected to his aching tooth.

LADY DAY

Lady Day is the name commonly given to the Feast of the Annunciation of Our Lady, which is celebrated on 25 March. This day, which for many centuries was reckoned through most of Christendom as the first day of the year, has a curious superstition attached to it. An old and well-known English rhyme says

> If Our Lord falls in Our Lady's lap,
> England will meet with a great mishap.

which means that if either Good Friday or Easter Sunday falls on 25 March and so coincides with Lady Day, some national misfortune will follow within twelve months.

It is not certain how old the belief in this form is, but that it is still alive has been proved twice within the present century. Good Friday fell on 25 March in 1910, and in the following May, Edward VII died after a short illness. In

1951 Easter Sunday fell on the same ominous date, and a little less than eleven months later, George VI died suddenly on 6 February 1952. On both these occasions, the old rhyming prophecy was widely remembered and quoted.

Ill-luck is supposed to follow either conjunction of festivals in other countries also, though not necessarily in the form of a national disaster. An ancient, but unproven tradition says that Our Lord was crucified on 25 March. No one really knows exactly when that great event occurred, but the tradition has evidently been strong enough to give rise to a widespread belief that it is ill-omened for Easter, the Day of Resurrection, to fall on that anniversary, or for Good Friday to coincide with its supposed original date.

LADY'S TREES

Small dried branches of seaweed, known as Lady's Trees, are sometimes seen in cottages near the coast, hanging above the hearth, or set in vases on the mantelpiece. They are believed to protect the house and its inmates from the perils of fire and the malice of evil spirits.

LAMB

The first lamb seen in Spring is widely believed to bring good luck, provided that its head is turned towards the observer. If it is turned the other way, the omen is bad. To have money in one's pocket then is a fortunate sign. It should be turned over at once, and then the owner need not fear any lack of ready cash in the following twelve months. In Lincolnshire, when farm-workers used to change their employment every year on May Day, they took care to notice which way the first lamb they saw was looking, for in that direction would their new work lie.

It is usually said to be lucky if the first-seen lamb is black, and that a wish made on seeing it is likely to be fulfilled. But the folklore of the black lamb varies. In many districts, it is held that a flock which does not contain one will not prosper. In Sussex, it is, or was formerly, fortunate to have one in a flock, but no more; if there are two or three, bad luck will follow. In Shropshire, old shepherds say it is very unlucky if the first lamb dropped in the lambing-season is black, and still more so if black twins are the first to appear. Almost everywhere, white twins are welcomed as the first-comers, for they bring good fortune to the whole flock. At Glaisdale, a large sheep-rearing parish in Yorkshire, it is customary to bless the flocks, the dogs, and the shepherds at the Evening Service on Good Shepherd Sunday. For this ceremony a black-faced lamb without blemish is chosen to represent all the sheep of the district, and is carried in the arms of a shepherd to be blessed at the altar rails.

The lamb without blemish has always typified innocence, and was a frequent sacrificial victim in pagan and Biblical times. In Christian thought it is a symbol of Christ, and consequently it was once believed that no witch or sorcerer could transform himself into a lamb (though he could appear as a sheep), nor could the Devil take that form. A widespread country tradition, lasting well into the nineteenth century, was that if anyone climbed to a hill-top at sunrise on Easter morning, he would see the image of the Lamb of God, the Lamb bearing a banner marked with a red cross, in the centre of the sun's disc.

Until 1858 a ceremony showing distinct pagan traces was annually per-formed at Kirtlington in Oxfordshire on Trinity Monday and the following few days. This was called the Lamb Ale. The best lamb in the parish was carried about in procession on the Monday and Tuesday, decked with rib-bons, and treated with great honour. On the Wednesday it was killed, and its flesh cooked in luck-bringing pies which were distributed to the people. The pie containing the head brought the greatest good luck and this, unlike the others, had to be paid for in cash.

In England, lamb is the traditional Easter Sunday dish, but no superstition seems to attach to its eating. In parts of Wales, however, no dog is allowed to share this food, for if a dog ate a lamb-bone on that day, it would go mad.

An old charm to recall a straying or faithless lover was to take the shoulder-blade of a lamb and stick a knife into it, saying,

> It's not this bone I wish to stick,
> But ——'s heart I wish to prick.
> Whether he be asleep or awake,
> I'd have him come to me and speak.

In some areas, this had to be repeated on three successive nights. If the charm worked, the unfortunate young man would be forced by an uncontrollable urge to come to the girl, however unwilling he might be to do so, and even if it meant travelling over a distance of many miles.

LAPWINGS

Lapwings are usually said to be ill-omened birds because they fly about continually crying 'Bewitched! Bewitched!' and so call down evil upon those who hear them. In Scotland and along the Welsh Border they were once greatly disliked for this reason, and in some districts it was considered un-lucky to handle, or even to see one. In his *Pictures of Nature around the Malvern Hills*, Edwin Lees tells the story of a boy living at Colwall in Herefordshire who, about the middle of last century, caught a young lapwing in a field. He showed it to the parish clerk's wife, and was earnestly advised by her to let it go, for if he kept it, some accident or misfortune would certainly befall him.

Another tradition says that these birds are departed human spirits, who cannot find rest and are doomed to haunt the earth in this form.

LAUGHTER

Laughter before breakfast means tears before night. A Lincolnshire variant of the tradition is that it is unlucky for anyone to laugh before he has said his prayers in the morning or after he has said them at night.

Excessive laughter or unusual gaiety at any time is often regarded as an evil omen, and for this reason children who show signs of either are usually checked at once. If an adult of normally sober temperament suddenly becomes very hilarious and continues so for some time, the omen is extremely bad. He is said to be *fey*, a condition recognized as perilous from remote antiquity. In most parts of Britain, as elsewhere, it is, or was, believed that such a man is doomed and will die very soon.

LAUNDRY

Certain days and seasons are commonly considered ill-omened for laundry-work. Clothes should never be washed on New Year's Day. To do this 'washes one of the family away', that is, it causes a death in the house. To wash blankets in May is equally dangerous and has the same effect.

The worst day of all for such work is Good Friday. Henderson[1] mentions a legend found in north Yorkshire which is sometimes given in that region as an explanation of the ban. When Our Lord was walking to Calvary, a woman, who was washing outside her house, derisively waved a wet garment in His face, whereupon He cursed her and all those who should in future wash upon that day. But the belief that it is unlucky and in a sense, sinful to do such work then is found in places where this legend is unknown. 'Never put your hands in lye on Good Friday' is a common saying, harking back to the time when housewives made their own lye from wood-ashes, and used it instead of soap. In some areas, it is said that clothes hung on the line then will be spotted with blood, in others, that the water itself will turn to blood. A Worcestershire superstition is that soap-suds must not be left in the boiler over Good Friday, even though no actual washing is done, or a death in the house will follow.

By custom, household laundry should always be done at the beginning of the week, in order to allow time for proper drying, ironing, and airing before Sunday. Saturday washing was formerly regarded as an indication of a bad housewife. A rhyme mentioning every weekday in this connexion ends with the lines,

> Wash on Friday, wash in need;
> Wash on Saturday, a slut indeed.

In Wales, it is considered a bad omen if water is spilt while being carried

[1] Wm. Henderson, *op. cit.*

from the spring to the wash-tub. It is unlucky also to splash water about too freely during the process of washing, or for the laundress to make her own apron over-wet. If an unmarried girl does this, it is a sign that her future husband will be a drunkard.

In some areas, it is thought unwise to wash new garments for the first time when the moon is new. They will not wear well.

The persistent appearance in ironed linen of a diamond-shaped mark, known as a 'coffin', is widely held to be a death omen. If it appears in a sheet, there will be a death soon in the bed on which the sheet is used, if in a table-cloth, a departure from the house, or the death of someone sitting at the table on which it is laid.

LEAVES

As many falling leaves as can be caught in the hand in autumn, so many happy months will follow. According to one version, even a single leaf caught before it touches the ground will preserve the person concerned from colds and similar ailments during the coming winter.

It is a bad sign if the trees in any districts shed their leaves in large quantities before the autumn. If elms or fruit-trees do this, it is, or was, said to foretell an outbreak of cattle disease. It is unlucky to keep withered leaves in the house, and especially so if, after being brought in green and fresh, they wither suddenly. A Welsh tradition says that dead leaves accidentally left in a church, or any other place where a baby is christened, denote the early death of the child.

Country people read weather signs in the behaviour of growing leaves. If they make a sudden rattling or rustling noise, rain is near, and so too if they turn their undersides uppermost. The best known of these traditions is probably that which concerns the appearance of new leaves in spring on the oak and the ash. If the former leafs first, the summer will be dry, if the latter it will be wet. An old and widespread rhyme says:

> If the Oak comes before the Ash,
> We shall only have a splash.
> If the Ash comes before the Oak,
> We are sure to have a soak.

LEE PENNY

The Lee Penny, or Lee Stone, is another, and perhaps the most famous, of those healing charm-objects which, like the Clach Dearg and the Black Penny, were greatly valued in Scotland and Northern England until well towards the end of the nineteenth century. It is a small, dark-red, triangular stone, set in the reverse side of a groat of Edward I's reign, and takes its name from the family of Lockhart of Lee, to whom it belongs. It is said to have been in their possession since the early fourteenth century, when Sir Simon Lockhart brought it home from the Holy Land.

Water in which it had been dipped and turned was believed to cure a variety of diseases, including rabies, haemorrhage, and the ailments of cattle. In 1645 the inhabitants of Newcastle-upon-Tyne borrowed the Lee Penny during an outbreak of plague, and gave a bond of £6,000 for its safe return. Its curative virtues proved such that they subsequently offered to buy it, but the owner would not sell.

A complaint of witchcraft having been made against Sir James Lockhart in connexion with this stone, the Glasgow Synod enquired into its properties in 1638. Their verdict was that, since no spoken charms were used in the cures, 'and considering that in nature there are mony things seen to work strange effects, whereof no human witt can give a reason, it having pleasit God to give to stones and herbes special virtues for the healing of mony infirmities in man and beast', the Synod 'advises the brethren to surcease their process, as wherein they perceive no ground of offence: and admonishes the said Laird of Lee, in the useing of the said stone, to take heed that it be used hereafter with the least scandal that possiblie may be'.

LETTUCE

Lettuces, both wild and cultivated, were formerly believed to have magical and healing properties, including the power of arousing love and counteracting the effects of wine. The Romans ate them at their banquets for the latter reason, and in medieval times they were often included in love-potions and charms. They were also said to promote child-bearing if eaten in salads by young women, or taken in the form of decoctions made from the juice or seeds.

Some years ago, what seems to be a confused and inverted version of this last belief was recorded at Richmond in Surrey, where it was stated that too many lettuces growing in a garden would stop a young wife having children. In 1951 the *Daily Mirror* printed some letters on this subject, in one of which (published on 20 July) the writer asked whether it was true that eating the plant was bad for brides. In another letter (26 July), a woman wrote: 'After being childless for a number of years, I was advised by a specialist to eat plenty of lettuce, and to give my husband some too. In less than six months, my first baby was on its way.'

The wild lettuce, which the Anglo-Saxons called Sleep-wort, is still used to help sufferers from insomnia. It was formerly recommended as a cure for headaches, stomach-pains, digestive troubles, and other ills.

LICE

Lice are unpleasant creatures in everyday life, and their significance in superstition is usually unpleasant also. To dream of becoming infested with them predicts illness in the dreamer's family. In northern England, the appearance of a single louse upon a person who does not normally suffer in this way is often regarded as a death omen. If a nurse finds one on her head, it is a sign that her patient will die. A writer in the *Sheffield and Rotherham Independent*[1] in 1874 recorded that, a few weeks earlier, a woman had told him she was very worried because she had found a louse in her hair. She feared that some serious misfortune was about to overtake a near relative or friend. She said the same thing had happened to her once before, and very soon afterwards, her father fell ill and died. On the other hand, the sudden disappearance for no apparent reason of such parasites from a person usually afflicted with them is also a death warning, in this case for the individual himself or herself.

A singularly spiteful and distressing form of magic, of which witches were often accused, was the sending of lice upon a hitherto clean person. In 1637 Mrs Rose, of Bedford, was charged with bewitching a man in this way, so that he became suddenly verminous and remained so. Again, in 1645 Alice Warner, of Rushmere in Suffolk. confessed that she had sent evil spirits to carry lice to two women who had offended her. The official deposition (now in the British Museum) adds briefly, 'and the sd women were lousie, according as she confessed'.

A somewhat drastic remedy for jaundice, recorded in Westmorland during last century, was to swallow a tablespoonful of live head-lice. The insects were supposed to find their way to the liver and clear it. A Dorset variant of the same remedy involved the magical number nine also, nine insects being placed on a piece of bread-and-butter, and so eaten.

LIFE-DEMANDING RIVERS

Just as the sea was held to demand its toll of human lives, *see Drowning*, so certain rivers were believed to require a definite number of lives every year or every three or seven years, and to take them without fail. Such stories are told still of streams in many parts of the world. They have their roots in ancient river-worship, which was once widespread. In primitive thought, a river was often regarded as a living and divine being, at once beneficent and dangerous. It brought fertility to the valleys through which it ran, and made possible the growing of crops and the rearing of flocks and herds. It provided men with the water that is essential to life, and also with fish, but it also drowned them occasionally, and destroyed lands and dwellings by sudden,

[1] Quoted by S. O. Addy, *op. cit.*

disastrous floods. It was always mysterious and uncontrollable, and therefore divine honours were paid to it, and sacrifices offered to avert its anger and secure a continuance of its gifts. These notions faded eventually from human minds, but they left their traces in the still-surviving traditions of streams which no longer have victims given to them, but take them all the same, either so many a year or, more dangerously, as many as they please.

Northern rivers and pools are often said to be haunted by a malevolent spirit known as Jenny Greenteeth, who drags down those who come too near. On the Tees, Peg Powler, a bloodthirsty being with green hair, does the same, especially in the vicinity of Pierse Bridge. The Yore has a kelpie who appears at evening by the water-meadows near Middleham and carries off the unwary. The unnamed spirit of the Tweed takes one life a year. Fishermen formerly used to throw a plaid into the water, in the hope that she would be satisfied with that, and spare the owner. Salt, too, was thrown into the river and over the nets to placate the spirit. The Devonshire Dart also takes one life a year, and so does the River Spey. The slow-running Dean in Forfarshire claims only one in seven years, but of another slow river, the Till, an ominous and well-known rhyme says,

> Tweed said to Till,
> What gars ye rin so still?
> Till said to Tweed,
> Though ye rin wi' speed,
> And I rin slaw,
> For ae man that ye droon,
> I droon twa.

Some rivers require more than a single life. The dangerous spring-tide on the Trent takes three every year. It is called the Eager, a name derived from that of the Norse Jotun, Aegir, who once informed the river, and is always spoken of as 'he', not 'it'. Of two Scottish rivers it is said:

> Bloodthirsty Dee, each year needs three,
> But bonny Don, she needs none.

In some places, the water-spirit has lost its divine nature and has become a mere human ghost, although remaining quite as vengeful and perilous to human beings as before. Peg o' Nell on the River Ribble has taken the place of the goddess Minerva, to whom the stream was sacred in Roman times. Local legend says she was a maid at Waddow Hall in the Middle Ages, and was drowned by her mistress's witchcraft at Bungerley Stepping-Stones. Since then, she has demanded a human life once in every seven years, and has taken it unless some cat, dog, or bird has been offered to her instead. The dangerous pool in the River Swale known as Hoggett's Hole is now said to be haunted by the ghost of Tom Hoggett, a highwayman who was drowned in it while escaping from arrest in the late eighteenth century. He seems to have inherited the legend of some forgotten water-spirit, for tradition says he dwells in the pool still, and drowns anyone who falls into it, no matter how powerful a swimmer that person may be.

It is probable that no one seriously believes in these tales today, yet they are still told, and some of the old nervousness seems to linger with them. Along Trent-side, it is frequently said that the Eager will take his three lives whatever happens, and figures seem to show that he (or the spring-tide) usually does so. And if conscious faith in such things is really dead now, it has not been so very long. In 1904 a story appeared in *Folk-Lore*[1] concerning the Derbyshire Derwent, which was recounted to the writer a few years earlier. 'There was a man drowned in Darrant,' said her informant, speaking quite naturally of the river as if it were a living person, 'He didna know Darrant, he said it were nought but a brook. But Darrant got 'im. They never saw his head; he threw up his arms, but Darrant wouldna let him go. Aye, its a sad pity, seven children – but he shouldna ha' made so light o' Darrant. He knows now.'

An even clearer state of belief is shown in an incident recorded by Mrs Leather[2] as having happened a few years before she wrote in 1912. A boy was drowned in the river at Ross-on-Wye and his brothers were told to keep away from its banks. An old man, hearing this, said, 'Let 'em go, let 'em go. No one else'll be drowned this year. The river has had its due.'

LIFE-INDEX

The Life-Index, or Life-Token, was a charm whereby the welfare of an absent person could be ascertained by those left behind at home. It consisted of something that had once belonged to him, or had been in vital association with him, and which was capable of showing changes in its appearance, and thus reflecting his present state in its own.

The urine of the absent man was often used for this purpose. A bottle was filled with it, securely corked, and hung up in some safe place in the house. If the liquid remained clear, it showed that he was safe and well. If it became cloudy, he was ill, or in danger, and if it wasted and dried away, he was dead.

Sometimes a knife he had once owned was employed instead of urine. So long as the blade remained bright, all was well, but if it dulled, the omen was bad. If it rusted badly or broke, his kinsfolk knew that he had died, and duly put on mourning for him.

[1] *Folk-Lore*, Vol. 15. 1904. Letter from M. A. Turner.   [2] E. M. Leather, *op. cit.*

The same idea appears in the superstition already mentioned, *see Clothes*, that if garments left behind by an absentee wear out or rot, it is a sign of his death.

Faith in the Life-Index was strong in times when communications were difficult, and few people could write, and when transportation to the colonies was the penalty for many offences in English law. A man once parted from his kindred then, willingly or otherwise, might be unheard of for years, and perhaps for ever. In such cases, the bereaved family turned to the Life-Index as the only means by which they could discover whether he still lived, and whether he was well or ill.

LILAC

In some parts of England, it is considered unlucky to bring lilac, especially white lilac, into the house. The purple and red varieties are usually less feared, but even they are sometimes excluded from house-decorations as bringers of misfortune. A few months before these words were written (1960), an Oxford florist strongly advised a customer not to buy white lilac for a friend in hospital, on the grounds that many people thought it foretold death if brought indoors. He did not know why this should be so, only that it was quite commonly believed. In fact it is almost certainly due to the widespread association of death and misfortune with 'drowsy-scented' flowers, and also with those which are white. An interesting detail about the lilac tradition is that, unlike that connected with white may and meadowsweet which is very general, it is found only in some English districts, especially in the midland counties, and is quite unknown elsewhere.

It is lucky to find a five-petalled lilac blossom of any colour. Along the Welsh Border, lilac trees are said to mourn if any of their kind are cut down, and to be flowerless in the following year.

LILY

From very early times, white lilies have been emblems of innocence, purity, and virginity. They are favourite flowers at weddings for this reason, and also at funerals, where they typify the shriven soul, freed from the marks of sin. In north European folklore there are stories of lilies, unplanted by any human hand, growing of themselves on the graves of innocent men unjustly executed for some crime they did not commit. If a man treads on a lily, he destroys the purity of his womenfolk. To dream of one is a sign of good luck. On the other hand, because of their heavy scent and their association with funerals, many people today dislike lilies in the house, and some consider their presence there is a death omen.

In Worcestershire it is said that when Madonna lilies are plentiful, bread will be cheap. These flowers keep away ghosts; if they are planted in a garden, the house that it surrounds will be free from such unwelcome visitants. Another and more practical reason for planting them, which may account for their frequent appearance in cottage gardens, is that they were, and indeed still are, used as first-aid remedy for boils, whitlows, and gatherings of various kinds. A well-known country cure for these afflictions is to take forty Madonna lily petals, steep them in brandy, and lay them on, the rough side for drawing and the smooth side for healing. In Lincolnshire the roots are sometimes pounded into a pulp and used as a poultice. Tiger lily leaves laid on the sore place serve the same purpose.

LILY OF THE VALLEY

A charming country name for lilies of the valley is Liriconfancy. Another is Our Lady's Tears, because tradition says they first sprang up where her tears fell to the ground. In Sussex, the legend of their origin is different. There they are supposed to have bloomed first where St Leonard's blood was shed during his three-day fight with the dragon. The plant still grows wild in St Leonard's Forest, the scene of that heroic contest.

In spite of their innocent appearance and sweet scent, lilies of the valley are sometimes thought to be ill-omened, probably because they are white and have hanging heads. Thistleton Dyer[1] mentions a West-country belief that it is dangerous to plant a bed of these lovely flowers in a garden. Whoever does so will die within the year.

Nicholas Culpeper, in his *English Physician and Complete Herbal*, says the distilled water of the flowers 'comforts the heart and vital spirits' restores the power of speech when it has been lost, helps in cases of palsy, and 'is excellently good in the apoplexy'. He also recommends the plant for a failing memory and inflammation of the eyes.

LIZARD

It was formerly believed that if a lizard saw a snake approaching any man or woman sleeping out of doors, it would at once waken the sleeper and so save him or her from peril. In Ireland it was thought that if anyone licked a lizard all over, his tongue would ever afterwards have healing properties, so that he could cure sores and relieve pain by licking the affected parts. Moreover, if at any time he fell asleep in a field with his mouth open, he could be sure that no lizard would crawl down his throat. That these creatures, and also snakes, were likely to do this when the opportunity occurred was once a very common belief; and as they were usually thought to be poisonous any charm which prevented their intrusion was obviously of value.

[1] T. Thistleton Dyer, *op. cit.*

In some parts of Britain it was considered a bad omen if a lizard crossed the path of a bridal party on the way to the church.

LOCKERBY PENNY

The Lockerby Penny, a flat piece of silver about the size of a half-crown piece, was formerly much esteemed as a remedy for hydrophobia and madness in cattle. It belonged to a family living at Lockerby in Dumfriesshire, and was frequently lent to farmers needing its help. It had to be dipped into water and turned about for some time at the end of a cleft stick, after which the water was given to the sick animal to drink, or was bottled and kept against emergencies.

William Henderson[1] mentions a Northumbrian farmer who borrowed it in the mid-nineteenth century after a mad dog had bitten a donkey on his farm, and the donkey had bitten a cow. He deposited £50 as security for its safe return. The donkey died, but the cow was saved by the charm. After the farmer's death, several bottles labelled 'Lockerby Water' were found among his effects, carefully sealed and stored away in a cupboard.

Dr Denham also refers to 'Lockerby Water' in the *Denham Tracts*. An acquaintance told him that a mad dog bit another dog and many cattle on a South Tynedale farm. 'Lockerby Water' (which his informant called 'Lockerlee') was at once sent for, and administered not only to the bitten beasts, but also to every other animal on the farm. As a result of these prompt measures, no evil effects followed the bites. Dr Denham also quotes from the *Gateshead Observer* of 23 March 1844, in which it is recorded that after the appearance of no less than seven mad dogs in one Northumberland district, 'Lockerlee Water' was sent for, 'a large supply having been procured by voluntary subscription'.

LOGAN STONES

Logan, or rocking stones were once thought to have magical powers, and to be frequented for this reason by witches, both black and white. This is not very surprising when we consider the awe-inspiring appearance of these great boulders, so lightly balanced on the tops of other stones that, notwithstanding their immense weight, they can rock backwards and forwards without falling. M. A. Courtney[2] says that in Cornwall such stones were believed to be the favourite meeting-places of local witches, who rode thither on ragwort stems. If anyone desired to become a witch, he or she could do so by going secretly at midnight to a logan rock and touching it nine times.

At Nancledra, near St Ives, there was formerly such a stone which could

---

[1] Wm. Henderson, *op. cit.*   [2] M. A. Courtney, *op. cit.*

only be moved at midnight. Children suffering from rickets could be cured if they were laid on it then and gently rocked, but only if they were born in wedlock. The stone would not rock for the illegitimate.

LUCK-FLOWER. *See Chicory.*

LUCKY BIRD. *See First Foot.*

LUCKY TIP. *See Calf.*

LYCHGATE

An old belief, now commonly disregarded, was that it was very unlucky for a bridal procession to pass through a lychgate on the way to the church. Either the marriage could be a failure or one of the pair would die within the year. This was because lychgates are closely associated, by their name and their original use, with funerals. The word 'lych' means 'corpse', and the name was given to the gate because it was there that the coffin was rested before being carried into the churchyard.

At Kneesall in Nottinghamshire, two separate entrances were used for funerals and marriages, one called the Corpse Gate and the other the Bride Gate. The former was never, in any circumstances, used by a bridal procession.

M

MACBETH

A strong tradition amongst actors and others connected with the theatre is that *Macbeth* is an exceedingly unlucky play, the presentation of which is almost invariably marked by a series of misfortunes and disasters affecting members of the cast, or anyone associated with the production. Many stories are told of accidents, some of them serious, outbreaks of fire, and other troubles which have occurred in various theatres while the play was running, including the death of Lilian Baylis, which occurred while *Macbeth* was being given at the Old Vic.

The reason usually given for the unlucky character of this play is that the Witches' Song in it has the power of working evil.

MAGPIE

The magpie, like many birds with pied plumage, bears a double-sided reputation in popular tradition. It is sometimes friendly to man, foretelling good luck or giving warning of danger, but far more often it is a creature of evil omen. Legend says that it has black and white plumage because it refused to go into full mourning with the rest of the birds at the time of the Crucifixion. Another story says it would not enter the Ark with Noah, preferring to stay outside and jabber maliciously over the drowning world. A widespread rural belief is that it can be made to desert its nest by carving a cross on the tree that contains it, and similarly, bad luck can be averted when meeting the bird by making the sign of the cross upon the person, or on the ground.

In Britain, it seems to have inherited some of the folklore of the now rare raven. In some parts of Europe, it is, or was, unlucky to kill it, and in Poitou formerly, it was honoured by bunches of heather and laurel tied to tree-tops, because it gave warning by its chattering of the approach of wolves. Swedish witches are said to take its form when they go on their secret errands, so that no one can be certain whether a magpie encountered in the open is really a bird or a witch. S. O. Addy[1] mentions a Nottinghamshire witch who was supposed to change herself thus, and was often seen by her neighbour in this shape. In Scotland, it is the Devil's bird, and has a drop of his blood under its tongue.

If a single magpie croaks persistently round the house, it is a death omen for someone dwelling within. If one hovers over a man's head, that man will die soon. In Scotland and northern England, it is very unlucky to see one flying away from the sun. Whoever does so should seize the first thing that comes to hand, throw it after the bird, and say 'Bad luck to the bird that flies widdershins.'

To encounter magpies on a journey is always ominous, but whether of good or evil depends on the number seen at once. A well-known north-country rhyme says,

> One sorrow, two mirth,
> Three a wedding, four a birth,
> Five Heaven, six Hell,
> Seven the De'ils ain sell.

There are many variants of this, but the first line remains more or less the same almost everywhere.

To meet a single magpie is still widely held to be an unfortunate omen, and many people who are not otherwise superstitious will bow to it, spit, or cross their fingers to avert the threatened misfortune. Or they may look hastily round for a single crow, in the belief that the two evils will cancel each other. In Staffordshire formerly, it was customary to remove the hat,

[1] S. O. Addy, *op. cit.*

spit towards the bird, and say 'Devil, devil, I defy thee.' In Yorkshire, the two thumbs had to be crossed while saying,

> I cross the magpie, the magpie crosses me,
> Bad luck to the magpie, good luck to me.

In the West of England, it was usual to spit three times over the right shoulder and say,

> Clean birds by sevens, unclean by twos,
> The dove in the heavens is the bird I choose.

Two magpies seen together are commonly supposed to foretell good luck. It is necessary, however, to salute the birds by bowing, and in some areas, by spitting, otherwise the good omen will not be fulfilled.

Farmers sometimes kept tame magpies as watch-birds because they could be relied upon to make a great noise whenever any intruder, animal or human, entered the farmyard. The chattering of wild magpies was sometimes thought to be a warning of coming trouble. Addy records a belief existing in Yorkshire and the northern midland counties that such a sound was always heard before a misfortune, whether any bird was near or not. In some country districts, it is still said that a magpie constantly perching on a roof is a guarantee that the building is sound. So too, if it makes its nest in any tree, it is a sign that the tree will never be uprooted, even in the most violent gale.

When cock-fighting was a popular pastime, game-fowl eggs were sometimes put to be hatched in a magpie's nest, in the belief that the young bird would acquire their foster-parents' bold nature, and so fight more fiercely than others.

MAIDEN'S GARLAND

It was formerly the custom in many districts for a Maiden's Garland to be carried in the funeral procession of an unmarried woman of unblemished reputation. The garland was made of white paper or linen, decorated with white and coloured rosettes and streamers, and usually had a white glove hanging from its centre as a symbol of the dead girl's innocence. It was carried before the coffin by young people dressed in white. After the funeral it was hung in the chancel, or over the dead person's customary seat, for a certain time. If during this period, no one challenged her right to be thus honoured, it was removed to another part of the church and left hanging there permanently.

Many such garlands have been removed by tidy churchwardens when they became old and dusty, or have been swept away by reforming vicars when changes of various kinds were made in the building. In popular belief, however, it is very unlucky to do this. The garlands should be left where they hang until they drop to pieces, and any bits that fall from them should be decently buried in the churchyard. It is perhaps this belief which has helped to preserve a number of garlands that still hang in various English churches, some dating from the early eighteenth century.

At Abbots Ann in Hampshire, the custom itself is still kept up, the latest occasion on which such a garland was carried being the funeral of an unmarried woman which took place in September 1953.

MALE FERN

Male Fern is called Lucky Hands in some parts of the English Midlands, a country name which preserves an old belief in the magical qualities of this plant. Like other varieties of fern, it had protective, healing, and love-inducing properties, and so was once used in charms and cures. Its most distinctive traditional use, however, was in the making of an amulet known as the Lucky Hand, or St John's Hand. If anyone dug up its root on Mid-summer Eve (which is also St John's Eve), and then cut away all but five of the unrolled fronds, he would have something that looked very much like a gnarled hand with hooked fingers. Such a hand, if smoked and hardened in one of the bonfires that formerly blazed everywhere on Midsummer Eve, would last a long time; and for so long as he kept it, the maker, his household and his cattle, would be protected from demons, witchcraft, the Evil Eye, and every kind of bad luck.

MANDRAKE

The mandrake is a plant of mystery and magic wherever it grows, and has been so from very remote times. Its root is bifurcated in such a way that it resembles the roughly-made figure of a man, and consequently it was believed to have powers of preventing sterility in men and animals, causing barren women to bear children, and compelling love. We read in the *Book of Genesis* (xxx, 14–17) how Reuben found some mandrakes in a wheat-field and brought them to his mother, Leah, and how Rachel, being childless, besought Leah to give them to her and bargained with her for them. Many centuries later, women were still employing the roots for the same purpose, and in some parts of Britain, where briony is often confused with the true mandrake, the former is credited with aphrodisiac and fertilizing properties even yet. *See Briony*.

The plant had other marvellous properties also. Clairvoyants used it to increase their visions and enable them to see strange and wonderful things.

Witches used it in image-magic. According to some, it could always be found at night because it shone in the darkness like a lamp. In France and Germany, it was supposed to spring up where criminals had polluted the earth, and to grow freely under or near a gallows. On the other hand, Apuleius Platonicus says in his *Herbarium* that it fled instantly when an unclean man approached it unless he prevented it from doing so by inscribing it with iron.

The most celebrated of its legends concerned the manner in which it was gathered. This was a very perilous operation, for when it was pulled from the earth, it gave a shriek so unearthly that all who heard it fell dead or, according to another version went mad. The wise man, therefore, never attempted to pull it up himself. He first loosened the earth round it with an implement of iron or ivory, and then tied a hungry dog to it, placing meat just a little beyond the animal's reach so that when it strained towards the food, it would jerk up the mandrake. The operator then retired hastily out of ear-shot, leaving the wretched dog to its inevitable fate. Thereafter, it was safe for him to pick up the root and use it for whatever good or evil purpose he had in mind.

In the Middle Ages, mandrake was used in syrups and other preparations as a cure for insomnia, and as a drug to relieve pain. The fruit, or Mandrake Apple, held in the hand on going to bed, was recommended to induce sleep. The root-bark and juice mixed with brandy was given as an anaesthetic before surgical operations.

MAPLE

Although the maple is not itself a very long-lived or strong tree, it was once believed that if a child was passed through its branches in infancy, he or she would have long life. Charlotte Latham[1] records that in the nineteenth century a certain maple growing in West Grinstead Park was constantly resorted to for this purpose. When, a few years before she wrote, a rumour spread that it was to be felled, great alarm was expressed by mothers in the locality, and several petitions that it might be spared were sent to the owner.

MARIGOLD

The bright yellow marigold used to be called Husbandman's Dial, or Summer's Bride, because it faithfully follows the sun, spreading its petals in the sun's light and closing them again as soon as that light is withdrawn. It symbolized constancy and endurance in love, and for that reason it was often used in wedding garlands, and sometimes in love-charms. In south-east Europe, a magical method of ensuring a lover's faithfulness was to dig earth

[1] Charlotte Latham, *op. cit.*

secretly from his footprints, put it in a pot, and sow marigold seeds therein. Like other plants with yellow petals, it served as a protection against witchcraft, and to dream of its flowers in full bloom was considered a certain sign of coming wealth.

In medicine and household crafts it had many uses, and still has in some country districts. The flower-head rubbed on a wasp- or bee-sting is said to cure the pain immediately. When ague was a common trouble, the seeds powdered in white wine were frequently given to the patient. In the sixteenth century, it was one of the herbs commonly used in the treatment of pestilence and fevers, both as a cure for the disease already present and to ward off infection. If a man looked long and carefully into the flowers first thing in the morning, he was deemed to be safe from the contagion of fever for the whole of that day. To smell at the plant removed 'evil humours' from the head. The distilled water of the blossoms cured heart-sickness, took away noises in the head, and eased inflammation of the eyes. In her *Gentlewoman's Companion* (1673) Hannah Woolley recommends a little conserve of marigolds, taken early in the morning whilst still fasting, as a remedy for depression of spirits.

Old-fashioned housewives still occasionally flavour their broths and soups with the flower-heads, as their Tudor and Stuart ancestors did before them. It is, however, unlikely that anyone now uses these flowers in the way noticed by William Turner in his *New Herbal* (1551), where he remarks, rather censoriously, that 'some use to make their heyre yelow wyth the floure of this herbe, not beynge content with the natural colour, which God hath gyven them'.

MARTIN

The martin is widely regarded as a sacred and luck-bringing bird which must never be harmed. 'The martin and the swallow', says a well-known country rhyme, 'are God's mate and marrow', or in some versions, 'God's bow and arrow,' or 'God Almighty's birds to hallow'. It is a sign of good luck if martins build their nests on a house, but needless to say, such nests must not be damaged or removed, nor must the eggs be stolen. Whoever does any of these things will meet with an accident or some other form of misfortune.

MAY KITTENS

Kittens born in May were formerly considered unlucky, and were often drowned for no better reason than the date of their birth. Like May-born babies, they were thought to be weakly, and unlikely to grow into strong mouse-catching cats. It was also said that they would bring snakes and slow-worms into the house when they were older, and that whenever possible, they would lie on the faces of babies in the cradle and suffocate them. In some districts, it was alleged that May cats sucked the breath of children and so caused their death. This false accusation was sometimes levied against other cats also, and was probably connected with old beliefs concerning witches and the cat-familiar.

MEADOWSWEET

In country districts today it is often considered unlucky to bring flowering meadowsweet into the house. An explanation of this belief recorded at Worcester in 1959 was that the drowsy scent induces a deep sleep from which the sleeper may never awaken. Here again we find the common association of heavy-scented blossoms with death. It is possible, however, that the inclusion of meadowsweet in the list of ominous plants may not be very old, for in Gerard's *Herbal* we read: 'The leaves and floures of Meadowsweet farre excelle all other strowing herbs for to decke up houses . . . for the smell thereof makes the heart merrie and joyful and delighteth the senses.'

MERRYTHOUGHT

The forked bone between the breast and neck of a fowl is often called the merrythought, and sometimes the wishing-bone. A well-known charm, now mainly used by children, is for two people to hold the ends of this bone and pull it between them, while forming a secret wish. The one who breaks off the larger part will gain his wish, providing that he neither speaks nor laughs during the proceedings, and that he does not reveal what his wish was before it has been fulfilled. In some areas, this is done to see which of the pair will marry first.

Another form of marriage-divination, recorded in Scotland, is for the enquirer to take an unbroken merrythought and drill a small hole in the flat piece at the top. He must then set the bone on his nose like a pair of spectacles, and while it is in that position, he must pass a thread through the hole. As many times as he fails to perform this quite difficult task, so many years will he have to wait before marriage.

MICE

If mice suddenly overrun a house previously free from them, or as suddenly leave an already infested house when nothing has been done to drive them away, it is a death omen for someone living within. So too, if one squeaks behind a sick-bed, the patient will not recover, and if one runs over any person, well or ill, he will die soon after. Another death omen is to see a ghostly white mouse running across the floor of a room.

These portents probably spring from the ancient belief that mice are connected with, and sometimes visible manifestations of, the soul. Many stories are told of sleepers whose souls have left them temporarily in the form of a mouse. The creature is seen to issue from the unconscious man's mouth, run off on some errand of its own, and eventually return by the same route. If the sleeper is roused too quickly, or is moved from the place where he lies, the mouse-soul cannot get home in time, and then the man dies. The same tale is also quite often told of souls wandering in the shape of bees, butterflies, snakes, and other small creatures.

Faith in the curative properties of mice was once very common, in Britain as elsewhere, and has only recently died out. There are old people still living who, as children, were given fried, roasted, baked or stewed mice to eat, either to strengthen them when they were weakly, or to cure them of coughs, colds, sore throats, fits, or infectious fevers. Persistent bed-wetting was treated in the same way. In 1936, an Oxfordshire woman stated that whooping-cough could be cured by skinning a mouse, removing all its bones, and giving the fried meat to the sick child. She said the taste was not at all unpleasant, and that if the dish was properly prepared, the patient need never know what he was eating.

Most people who used the cooked-mouse cure for any ailment did so because they thought mice really had natural medicinal virtues, although at one time there seems to have been a notion that some diseases, like whooping-cough and measles, were caused by mice, and therefore could be healed by charms which included parts of their bodies. A more definitely magical remedy for whooping-cough, recorded near Flamborough, was to wear a nest of mice in a bag round the neck. The cough would be transferred to them, and as they died inside the bag, so it would disappear.

Mouse-blood drove away warts, if dropped upon them. A seventeenth-century cure for quinsy was to dip a silk thread in the blood and then swallow it, or else to drink the water in which mice had been boiled. In Scotland, ailing cattle were given water in which the teeth, skin, or backbones of mice had been laid, and mouse-teeth were often worn as charms. A method of securing small, sharp teeth through the influence of mice is described under *Teeth. See also Shrew-Mouse.*

MILKY WAY. *See Stars.*

MINCE-PIES

Whoever eats one mince-pie on each of the Twelve Days of Christmas will have twelve happy months in the coming year. It is occasionally said that the charm will work if the twelve pies are eaten at any time during the wider

Christmas season, which ends on Candlemas Eve, but the more usual connexion with the Twelve Days is probably the older form of the belief.

There is, of course, no rule to prevent anyone from eating more than
twelve mince-pies at Christmas. In some districts, it is said to be very unlucky
to refuse an offered pie during that season, even if one or more have already
been eaten. The person who does so refuse something that typifies plenty,
is likely to be unfortunate or poverty-stricken throughout the year.

MIRROR

Primitive peoples believed that when a man saw his own image in a pool,
or any other reflecting surface, what he saw was not a mere reflection, but his
soul looking back at him. The notion that the soul could be separated from
the body without causing death, and that it was sometimes visible as a
reflection or a shadow, existed all over the world in early times, and appears
in many well-known folk-tales. So long as the separated spirit was unharmed,
the man in whose body it was normally contained was safe, but if it was
injured in any way, misfortune, evil, and very often death inevitably
followed. Basutos today believe that crocodiles can kill a man by snapping
at his reflection in water; and amongst Zulus, it is thought dangerous for
anyone to look into a dark pool, lest the spirit that dwells within it should
seize the reflection and so bear away the soul.

These ancient beliefs lie at the root of many of our modern mirror superstitions. It is still commonly said that to break a mirror means seven years'
bad luck, or else a misfortune of a particular kind, like the loss of a close
friend, or a death in the house. Many women will not allow a baby to see
itself in a looking-glass before it is twelve months old because they believe
that, if it does so, it will not thrive, or its growth will be stunted, or it will die
young. The custom of veiling mirrors after a death is partly due to the idea
that whoever sees his reflection then will die soon after or, if not he, then
someone else in the house. *See Death, Immediately After.* Brides, too, are
usually warned not to look at themselves in their wedding clothes, lest
something should happen to prevent the marriage. On the other hand, once
the ceremony is safely over, it is considered lucky for the married pair to
stand side by side before a mirror.

An actor will not usually look into a mirror over the shoulder of another,
so that the two reflections are seen together. To do this brings certain misfortune to the one overlooked. The worst of all mirror omens (fortunately
found more often in legend than in fact) is for someone to look into one and
see no reflection of himself. Death is certain then, and very near, for the soul
has already departed.

Mirrors were formerly used in divination, in much the same way as
scryers use a crystal ball. The diviner looked into the glass after the per-

formance of certain ceremonies, and saw the answer to his questions reflected therein. Thessalian magicians in antiquity held up a glass to the moon before reading the future in it, and so did English girls in the nineteenth century who wanted to know how many years must pass before they married. Addy[1] tells us that the method used was for the girl to stand upon a stone on which she had never stood before, with her back to the Full Moon, and a mirror in her hand. She would see the moon's reflection in the glass, and also a number of smaller 'moons', one for each year before her wedding.

Another very common form of divination was practised on Hallowe'en, and sometimes on other significant dates. The girl went at night to her bedroom and lit two candles on her dressing-table. Then, standing in silence before her mirror, she brushed her hair and ate an apple. The ghost of her future husband would be seen in the glass, looking over her shoulder.

MISTLETOE

Mistletoe, the Golden Bough of classical legend, was a sacred and wonder-working plant alike for the Celtic Druids, by whom it was ceremonially cut at the Winter and Summer Solstice festivals, and for the pagan Norsemen. For the latter, it was the holy and terrible plant which slew Baldur the Beautiful when all things in Heaven and Earth had sworn not to harm him. But the mistletoe was forgotten because, rooting on trees and not in the ground, it was not in Heaven or Earth, but only between them. Consequently Loki, the Norse evil deity, was able to use it to kill the Sun God when all other things had failed him.

It was also the plant of peace in ancient Scandinavia. A bunch hung outside a house denoted a safe welcome within, and if enemies happened to meet under a tree that bore it, they had to lay down their arms and fight no more on that day.

Being a thunder-plant, its presence in a house protected it from thunder and lightning, as well as from witches and evil spirits. In Britain, it was anciently called All Heal, because it cured many diseases, composed quarrels, and was an antidote to poison. It brought good luck and fertility. For all these reasons it was, and remains, an essential part of Christmas decorations in almost every house, though not in churches.

Its strong pagan associations probably caused it to be banned from churches at Christmas or any other season. This prohibition still prevails in most parishes, and if a sprig or branch is accidentally included in the general greenery, it is usually removed as soon as the clergyman sees it. In one Oxford parish a few years ago, permission was given to hang a bunch in the porch, but not inside the church itself. An exception to this rule in the Middle Ages was at York Minster, where a branch was ceremonially laid on the altar on

[1] S. O. Addy, *op. cit.*

Christmas Eve and left there throughout the Twelve Days of Christmas. A general pardon and liberty throughout the city was proclaimed for so long as it remained there. In the Black Country also, it seems to have been customary to include it in church decorations at one time, for payments for it appear in the churchwardens' accounts at Bilston in 1672 and at Darlaston in 1801.

In Worcestershire, where it grows very freely, it is said to be unlucky to cut mistletoe at any time but Christmas. Until very recently (and perhaps still in some households), it was usual to keep the Christmas bunch throughout the year for good luck, and then to replace it by a new one on Christmas Eve. In some districts, sprigs from such a bunch were given to the cow that calved first after New Year's Day, to ensure the prosperity of the herd in the following twelve months. In Herefordshire formerly, it was unlucky to bring mistletoe into the house before New Year's morning. It was not included in the Christmas decorations, but was brought in at the time of Burning the Bush. *See Hawthorn.*

Kissing under the mistletoe seems to be a purely English custom, of which no trace has been found in other countries unless Englishmen have settled there at some time. Strange as it may seem to us now, the English were once much given to kissing. Foreign visitors in the sixteenth and seventeenth centuries frequently remarked with surprise on the way in which men and women exchanged kisses without self-consciousness, even slight acquaintances and newly-introduced strangers being thus pleasantly greeted. The last shadow of this old freedom is now cast by the mistletoe bough at Christmas. If a girl stands under it, she cannot refuse to be kissed by anyone who claims the privilege. At one time, the young men had the right to pluck a berry from the bough for every kiss they took.

To cut down a mistletoe-bearing tree was once considered to be very unlucky. *See Oaks.* Many stories are told of misfortunes which fell upon those who did so. A curious tradition relating to the Hays of Errol, in Perthshire, is connected with this idea. The continued existence and prosperity of that family was bound up with an ancient mistletoe-bearing oak growing near the Falcon Stone. So long as the tree stood and the mistletoe grew on it, they would flourish, but, as we read in the verses traditionally ascribed to Thomas the Rhymer,

> . . . when the root of the aik decays,
> And the mistletoe dwines on its withered breast,
> The grass sall grow on Errol's hearthstone,
> And the corbie roup in the falcon's nest.

It was said that if a branch or sprig of the mistletoe was cut with a new dirk on Hallowe'en, after the cutter had walked three times round the oak sunwise, it was a sure guard in the day of battle, and a protection at all times against glamour and witchery. A similar sprig laid in the cradle protected the child from being stolen by the fairies and replaced by a changeling. Oak and mistletoe together have vanished now, and the estate no longer belongs to the Hays. Exactly when the tree was cut down is not now remembered, but local tradition says that it was before the lands were sold, and that it was because of that destruction that they were lost to the family.

Mistletoe tea was widely believed to cure the falling sickness or epilepsy, and is still recommended by herbalists for that purpose. The plant was also used in folk-medicine for a variety of other ills, including St Vitus' Dance, heart troubles and nerve complaints, sores, the bites of venomous creatures, and toothache.

MOLES

A well-known charm against cramp, used within this century, is to carry the feet of a mole about in the pocket. If the cramp is in the arms, the fore-feet must be used, if in the legs, the hind feet. To carry the wrong set is said not only to be useless for curative purposes, but likely to increase the trouble by driving the cramp into the corresponding human limbs, hitherto free, and so leaving the sufferer afflicted in both arms and legs. Another remedy for the same complaint is to take a mole's skin to bed at night, and sleep with it wrapped round, or laid against, the part affected.

A mole's foot is sometimes carried about to prevent rheumatism, and in some districts, to avert toothache. Henderson[1] says that in Staffordshire, during the mid-nineteenth century, the toothache charm was supposed to work only if the foot was cut off while the unhappy animal was still alive. This horrible idea has fortunately disappeared now, but there are traces of its existence formerly in other counties besides Staffordshire.

The blood of a freshly killed mole healed warts if it was dropped upon them while it was still warm. This cure has been tried, apparently with success, within living memory. Mrs Leather,[2] writing in 1912, tells us that Weobley people still treated wens by catching a mole, making its nose bleed, and smearing the blood with the finger nine times across the swelling. The mole was allowed to escape, and was supposed to take the wen away with it. Another equally magical treatment in use at the same place and time was to bind the two halves of a dead mole on to the swelling, leave them there all night, and bury them in the morning. As they decayed underground, so the wen was expected to diminish.

In some districts, the sudden appearance of a mole-hill in a garden formerly free from them foretells the death of someone in the family. Similarly, if a mole burrows under the wash-house, dairy, or other outhouse

[1] Wm. Henderson, *op. cit.*   [2] E. M. Leather, *op. cit.*

used for domestic work, it is an omen of death within the year for the mistress of the house.

In *The Antiquary* (Vol. XIV), a writer records how he was once shown a caterpillar of the death's-head moth in a Lincolnshire village, and was quite seriously informed that it would in due course turn into a mole.

MOLES (Human)

Moles, which may appear almost anywhere on the body, were supposed to show by their position the probable future of the person who bore them, and sometimes his or her most prominent characteristic. The omens were not always the same in every district, or at different times, but usually, as in so much else, those on the right side of the body were fortunate, and on the left side the reverse.

A mole on the chin seems to have been a sign of riches everywhere, or as a country saying has it, 'if you've a mole upon your chin, you'll never be beholden to any of your kin'. The front of the throat was also a lucky situation, but if a man had a mole on the back of his neck, he was likely to end on the gallows. One on the nose denoted a great traveller, one on the lip, a hearty eater or a fluent talker. On the right shoulder, arm or foot, it was lucky, but not on the left. On the stomach, it was variously said to show great strength, or gluttony, on the thighs, poverty and sorrow, on the wrist, a lively mind.

'A mole on the left side of the heart,' says Lupton in his *Thousand Notable Things*, 'denotes very ill qualities.' Something of the same sort may have been intended by the saying that a girl who had one on her left breast would have many lovers. On the right breast, such a mark meant poverty for men and women alike.

If a woman had a mole on her lower jaw, she could expect only misfortune, or on her left knee or on her hands, many children. One on the eyebrow meant an early marriage and a good husband.

A mole on the right side of the forehead was very fortunate, foretelling riches, honours, and the friendship of great men. On the left side, it was unlucky, although according to some, it showed keen wits and understanding. In the centre, it might mean a cruel disposition or, if it was raised like a wart, good luck. A woman with such a centre mole was held to be a slut, and if it was black, she was treacherous, and likely to consent to murder if the temptation to that crime ever came her way.

Many moles on the arm, between elbow and wrist, portended troubles in middle life, followed by prosperity and comfort in later years.

Misson remarks in his *Travels over England*[1] that 'when Englishmen, i.e.

[1] H. Misson de Valbourg, *Memoirs and Observations of M. Misson in his Travels over England*, trans. J. Ozell, 1719.

the common people, have warts or moles on their faces, they are very careful of the great hairs that grow out of these excrescences; and several have told me they look upon those hairs as tokens of good luck.'

MOLUCCA BEAN

In the Western Isles of Scotland, the Molucca, or Virgin Mary, Bean is worn or carried about as a charm against evil of various kinds, and especially as a protection against death by drowning. Such beans are often found on the seashore, and are supposed to be brought there by the Gulf Stream from the other side of the world. The white ones are the luckiest, but those of light or dark brown colour are also valued. If they turn black, it is an omen of misfortune or death.

Martin found the same beliefs in the same area two hundred and fifty years ago. In his *Description of the Western Islands of Scotland* (1703), he says that a 'variety of Nuts called *Molluka* Beans' were worn as amulets against witchcraft and the Evil Eye, the white ones being the most highly prized, and that they turned black if any secret evil was intended against the wearer. 'That they did change colour,' he remarks, 'I found true by my own observation, but cannot be positive as to the Cause of it.' He possessed one of these beans himself which Malcolm Campbell had given him after it had already proved its worth. Campbell told him that a few weeks earlier all his cows had given blood instead of milk for several days together. His wife was advised to put a white bean into the pail used for milking. This bean turned a dark brown when the first milk, still bloody, was drawn into the pail, as though it recognized the presence of a witch's evil; but thereafter, all the other cows gave pure good milk, and the affliction was ended.

MOON

Many moon-superstitions, past and present, show distinct traces of ancient moon-worship, and of astrological doctrines concerning the influence of heavenly bodies upon the lives of men.

It is, or was, widely thought to be unlucky to point at the moon. Misfortune of some kind will inevitably follow. In the north-midland counties, it is said that if anyone does so nine times, he will not go to Heaven when he dies.

When the new moon is seen for the first time, it should be respectfully greeted by bowing or curtseying, particularly if it happens to be the first moon of the year. In the Highlands and the Western Isles until very recently, women curtseyed and men doffed their bonnets to it, as if to some great personage. Shropshire people 'made their obedience' by bowing three or nine times, forming a wish as they did so, and turning round between the bows. In East Yorkshire, women used to go outside as soon as the crescent appeared in the sky, turn their aprons, and make a secret wish that would only be granted if they told no one what it was. On the north-eastern coasts, fishermen's children invoked protection for their fathers by saying,

> I see the moon and the moon sees me,
> God bless the sailors on the sea.

In Somerset, it was usual to bow and say,

> New Moon, New Moon, fust time I've seed 'ee,
> Hope before the week's out I'll ha' summat gi'ed me.

It is customary almost everywhere in Britain to turn over silver in the pocket when the new moon is first seen. Many who do not consider themselves particularly superstitious regularly do this for luck. In Scotland formerly, a special coin called the lucky penny was carried about and turned over three times when the moon appeared. To be without money then is unlucky, but if a man has some about him, and turns it over without taking it out of his pocket, he will have plenty during the coming month, and the wish he makes as he turns it will be fulfilled.

Many people strongly dislike seeing the new moon for the first time through glass. In Devonshire, it is unlucky to see it through trees. Both these ideas are connected with the wider belief that it should be first seen in the open air, with nothing between the observer and its light. If it appears on the right hand, or directly ahead, the omen is good, but if on the left, or behind, it is very bad. The right-hand rule is not, however, universal, for in East Anglia it is lucky to see the new moon over the left shoulder.

Mrs Leather[1] records that Herefordshire girls used to wait until the year's first moon was strong enough to 'shine shaddow', and then looked at its reflection in a bucket of water through a new silk handkerchief or a piece of smoked glass. As many 'moons' as were thus seen, so many months or years away was their wedding-day.

As the moon waxed and waned, so it affected all other growing and changing things. Planting is still quite often arranged to fit in with the moon's phases, some seeds being set always with the waxing moon, and others just after the full, so that by the time the plants are above ground, they will be growing with the new moon. If trees are cropped in the moon's increase, the new branches will grow straighter; if eggs are set under the hen then, they will not go bad. Wild animals are said to travel farther afield at this season, moles to throw up more hills, and rats to eat the poison put out for them more readily.

[1] E. M. Leather, *op. cit.*

Farm animals should not be castrated when the moon is declining, nor should pigs be killed then, for if they are, the meat will shrink in the boiling. In Oxfordshire, old-fashioned shepherds will not dock lambs' tails when the moon is 'southing', (that is, waning), because if they do, the lambs will die. Anything cut then will not grow again, or will do so only slowly; hence, it is a good time to cut hair which it is desired to keep short, or corns on the feet. Some housewives say that feather-beds are best made then, because the feathers will lie more smoothly in the ticking, and will not fall together in uncomfortable lumps.

As the moon influences daily work, so it is often supposed to affect the more serious events of life. A child born under a waning moon will be unlucky, and an animal born then will not thrive. In the Orkneys, a marriage celebrated at that season will not be happy and is unlikely to be fruitful. In some parts of Wales, it is said that if a death occurs with the new moon, three more may be expected shortly. On the other hand, to move to a new house then is fortunate, and those who do so will be free from the danger of hunger.

Lunacy takes its name from the moon, and was anciently believed to be caused by it. In some places, this notion still persists. Idiots and insane persons are commonly said to be worse when the moon is full. Sleeping in moonlight is very generally thought dangerous because it may cause lunacy, or blindness, or at best, a swollen and distorted face. In Germany, one of the crossbill's traditional services to mankind was that it always awakened children whom it found sleeping thus.

Similarly, the moon was once supposed to influence blood-flow as it influenced the tides, and blood-pressure was thought to increase with it. When blood-letting was a customary form of treatment, it had to be done when the moon was waning, for to let blood when the light was increasing and the tide flowing was very dangerous.

A country cure for whooping-cough was to take the child out of doors and let him look at the new moon. His mother, or some other woman, then rubbed his stomach with her right hand while fixing her eyes on the moon and saying,

> What I see, may it increase,
> What I feel, may it decrease,
> In the Name of the Father, Son, and Holy Ghost.
>
> Amen.

In Co. Durham, warts could be cured by blowing on them nine times when the moon was full. Another remedy, recorded in many parts of Britain, was to catch the moon's rays in a dry metal basin and 'wash' the hands in it. Cornish people said when doing this,

I wash my hands in this thy dish,
O man in the moon, do grant my wish,
And come and take away this.

Sir Kenelm Digby knew this charm. In his *Discourse on the Powder of Sympathy*, he speaks of a silver basin, and this probably, was the original requirement where now any reflecting metal is considered efficacious. He tells us that the hand-washing 'is an infallible way to take away warts from the hands, if it be often used'.

Certain omens attached to the moon at particular times. The Harvest Moon riding high meant dear bread; a full moon at Christmas foretold a poor harvest. In Worcestershire, this applied particularly to the hay-harvest. A new moon coming in on a Saturday or Sunday meant foul weather and bad luck almost everywhere. In Cornwall, a Saturday moon was called 'the sailor's curse'. In Norfolk, one on that day, 'if it comes once in seven years, comes too soon'. In Cheshire, there is a saying that

Saturday's Change and Sunday's Full
Never brought good and never wull.

Two moons in a single month are usually said to mean a month's bad weather, but two moons in May mean 'rain for a year and a day'. This last belief is still very general, as are numerous other weather signs connected with the moon, some based upon meteorological fact, and some on pure superstition or faulty observation.

MOONWORT

The inconspicuous little fern known as moonwort was once credited with a variety of magical powers, including that of turning mercury into silver, and of helping women in childbirth. It had also one special ability that must have endeared it to thieves. Like the elusive and mysterious springwort, it opened locks and drew out nails, and it had the useful advantage over springwort that it was easily recognizable and grew wild on English heaths. A leaf laid against a nail at once loosened the latter, so that it fell out easily; one thrust into the keyhole opened any lock, however secure. If horses accidentally stood upon the plant, it pulled off their shoes. Nicholas Culpeper tells us that country people in his time called it *Unshoo the Horse* for this reason; and he then repeats a story he had heard concerning the Earl of Essex's horses, thirty of which lost their shoes thus on one occasion when they were drawn up all together on White Down, near Tiverton.

Woodpeckers apparently knew of the moonwort's power as well as human beings. Tradition has it that if they found any nail obstructing their nests, they laid moonwort-leaves against it, and so drew it forth without difficulty. They also rubbed their beaks against the plant on Midsummer Eve, thereby making them so sharp that they could pierce anything, even iron spikes.

MUGWORT

Medieval travellers believed that if they carried mugwort about with them, they would not tire on their journeys, and that those already weary could be cured either by drinking an eggshellful of the expressed juice, or by laying an ointment made from the leaves beaten in hog's lard upon their feet. This belief goes back at least as far as the first century A.D., for Pliny records it, and it was still current in the seventeenth century. In his *Art of Simpling* (1656), William Coles tells us that 'if a footman take mugwort and put it in his shoes in the morning, he may goe forty miles before noon, and not be weary'.

The herb had other striking virtues also. It protected its owner against witchcraft and thunder, and was used in remedies for consumption, fever, and failing sight. Pliny says that whoever wore it could not be harmed by poisonous medicines, or by wild beasts, or the effects of sunstroke. In Lupton's *Notable Things* we read that if anyone digs under the root on Midsummer Eve, he will find there a coal which, when carried about, will save him 'from the plague, carbuncle, lightning, the quartan ague, and from burning'. Other seventeenth-century writers state that this miraculous coal can only be found during one hour of Midsummer Eve, variously given as noon or midnight. One, Paul Barbette, writing in 1675, says it cured or averted epilepsy as well as the evils mentioned above; but he adds that those who believe this are deceived, for the supposed coal is really only an old acid root, such as are often found under mugwort plants.

Similar legends were told of magical coals found on the same day under the roots of plantains.

MUSICAL AIRS

Certain songs and airs are considered by musicians and actors to be very unlucky, if they are sung, hummed, whistled or played in the theatre at any time except during the performance of the play or opera to which they belong. One of these is Tosti's 'Goodbye'. Another is 'I Dreamt that I Dwelt in Marble Halls', from *The Bohemian Girl*. The latter is so ill-omened that even to hum or whistle it without thinking may bring serious misfortune, perhaps death, to someone in the theatre, or the failure of the show itself. Moreover, this superstition is not confined to professional musicians and actors. Amateur singers dislike the song also, and it is very rarely performed by them. In 1949, it was sung at a concert given on three successive nights by members of the staff of a large London firm. Illness and bad luck overtook several of those concerned in the organization of the concert, including the singer, who lost a relative by death.[1]

Music from Macbeth is also very ill-omened, and should never be hummed during rehearsals. The Witches' Song in it is said by some to be the source of the ill-luck that so often attends this play. *See Macbeth.*

MYRTLE

Myrtle is usually regarded as a lucky plant in Britain. It is traditionally associated with love, marriage, and fertility and was widely used in bridal wreaths before orange-blossom became the fashionable flower for this purpose. If it blooms freely in a garden during any one season, it is a sign of a coming wedding. If it is grown indoors, it brings good luck to the household. According to a Welsh tradition, a bush set on either side of the main house-door secures harmony and peace for those within for so long as the two bushes remain there.

Like rosemary and parsley, it is said to grow best if it is planted by a woman. A writer in the *Athenaeum* (5 February 1848) said she was advised to spread her skirt over it and 'look proud' whilst planting it, otherwise it would not grow well.

Young girls formerly drank an infusion made from the leaves to increase their beauty. A similar infusion, or a flowering sprig, given by a lover to the object of his affection was held to be a sure way of securing and retaining her love.

In his *Household Tales and Traditional Remains*, S. O. Addy mentions a form of marriage-divination used in the English midland and northern counties. 'On Midsummer Eve,' he says, 'let a girl take a sprig of myrtle and lay it in her Prayer Book upon the words of the marriage service, "Wilt thou take this man to be thy wedded husband?" Then let her close the book, put it under her pillow, and sleep upon it. If her lover will marry her, the myrtle will be gone in the morning, but if it remains in the book, he will not marry her.'

N

NAILS

Nails, like almost everything else made of iron, were formerly used in charms of various kinds, both for protection and healing. The Romans are said to have driven them into the walls of houses as an antidote to the plague. Pliny remarks that an epileptic patient could be cured by driving a nail into

[1] Told to the Editor by one of the performers at the concert.

the ground on which he had fallen in his fit. He also says that a nail drawn from a sepulchre, if laid on the threshold of a bedroom, protected the sleeper from nightmares, phantoms, and terrifying visions. In the latter charm, of course, the power of the dead was involved, but doubtless that power was strengthened by the use of the magical iron implement.

In Britain it is said to be lucky to find a nail in the roadway, especially if it is rusty. It should be picked up at once and taken home. Carried in the pocket, or concealed about the house, nails serve as amulets against witch-craft and the Evil Eye. It was formerly believed that if any person was suspected of witchcraft, his (or her) guilt or innocence could be determined by secretly driving a tenpenny nail into his footprint. If he was indeed a witch, he would be compelled to return and draw it out, but if not, he would go peacefully on his way, unaware of the magical test that had been applied to him.

A Suffolk remedy for ague was to go at midnight to a cross-road, turn round three times, and drive a tenpenny nail up to its head in the ground. This had to be done while the clock was striking, and it was then necessary to walk away backwards before the last note died away. If all was accom-plished in due order, the ague would be left behind, and the next person to walk over the buried nail would take the disease.

Aubrey tells us in his *Miscellanies* that toothache could be cured by scratch-ing the gum till it bled with a new nail, and driving the latter into an oak-tree. 'This did cure William Neal's son,' he says, 'a most gallant gentleman, when he was almost mad with the pain, and had a mind to have pistolled himself.' In Islay during last century, nails were driven into a large boulder called the Clach Deide to prevent toothache in the future. Another charm used in the same island was to hammer a horse-nail into the upper lintel of the kitchen door. While it stayed there, the person on whose behalf it was hammered in would always be safe from tooth-pains. In Bernera, at the same period, when a coffin was closed over a corpse, the first nail used was some-times withdrawn and rubbed against an aching tooth as a sure remedy.

When a group of Cheshire men wished to bind themselves to do, or not to do, something, they went together to a wood some way from their homes, and there drove a nail into a tree, swearing to keep their engagement for so long as it remained there. It could not be withdrawn without the consent of all concerned; but if it was withdrawn, then all were released from their vow. Although this custom had died out now, the phrase 'to draw the nail' still means to break a vow or promise in Cheshire speech. *See also Wound-Treatment.*

NAMES

In primitive thought, a man's name was not merely a convenient label by which he could be distinguished from others. It was an integral part of himself, as important to him as, and indeed, more so than, his arms or legs or eyes. Knowledge of it by another gave that other power over him, as is clearly shown in many ancient folk-tales, such as *Tom Tit Tot*. A sorcerer knowing it could use it to bewitch him as surely as he could use his nail-parings and hair-clippings, or discarded parts of his clothing. Consequently it was, and still is, customary among some simple peoples to conceal the true name from all but those nearest to its owner, and to use instead a secondary, or nick-name for all ordinary purposes.

These beliefs survive in the custom, once quite general, of keeping a child's name secret from outsiders until he had been baptized. To let it be known to any stranger, or to use it before it had been sanctified by the Church, was to run the risk of witchcraft. Miss Burne[1] tells us that in Shropshire, when the father chose the name, it was not unusual for him to conceal it from everyone, even the mother, until he whispered it to the godparents in the church.

The choice of the name was also very important. Devout parents some-times sought Divine guidance by opening the Bible at random and adopting the first name of the right sex thus seen. It is now generally considered a compliment to call a baby after some loved or admired individual, but originally this was done in order to acquire the virtues, or the luck, of the person so honoured. Even today, names which have become associated with some notoriously evil or ill-starred individual tend to fall out of fashion for a time; and it would be hard to say for certain whether some dim notion of acquiring virtue does not underlie the custom of naming children after film stars, victorious generals, and other fortunate people.

To give a baby a name previously borne by a brother or sister who has died is commonly thought to be ill-omened. The dead child will call the living one away, so that he too dies; or, according to one north-country tradition, a child so christened will, if he survives, grow up to be a 'graceless prodigal'. In some districts it is said that if the two first children are named after their parents, they will die before them.

When two or three names are given, it is lucky if the initials form a com-plete word. Mrs Leather[2] mentions a Herefordshire belief that it is dangerous to give a child an animal's name. On one occasion, a farmer near Cusop called his baby daughter Chloe after a favourite mare. The child was burnt to death in the rickyard when she was three years old, and the mare broke her back on the same spot soon afterwards.

The couplet,

> Change the name and not the letter,
> Change for the worse and not for the better,

[1] C. S. Burne, *Shropshire Folk-Lore*, 1883.   [2] E. M. Leather, *op. cit.*

is now little more than a remembered saying among brides, though the superstition which it enshrines is extremely ancient, and probably has its roots in archaic tribal rulings concerning the intermarriage of related clans. A more active superstition is that which forbids the use of the married-name-to-be before the wedding day. If anyone addresses an engaged girl by it, or if she writes it down for the pleasure of seeing what it looks like, she may never bear it in fact. At one time, this idea extended even to the marking of clothes and house-linen in advance; they had either to be left unmarked until after the marriage, or marked with the girl's maiden name. If, immediately after the wedding, someone calls the bride by her old name, purposely or inadvertently, the omen is very bad. The marriage will be unfortunate from the start.

In some parts of England, a woman whose married and maiden names are the same, though she has not married a relation, is believed to have healing powers. In one Cheshire parish between the wars, such a woman was regularly applied to by children suffering from whooping-cough. The cure was effected by taking bread-and-butter from her hand and eating it immediately, without saying 'thank you'. Elsewhere, other diseases were curable in the same manner, and similar powers were ascribed to women who had been twice married to men whose names were the same, though they were unrelated to each other.

Sailors believe that it is unlucky to alter the name of a ship. Many tales are told of vessels which were lost after such a change. H.M.S. *Victoria*, which sank in a tragic accident in 1893, was one of these; so was H.M.S. *Cobra*. In both these cases, another seamen's superstition was also involved, which is that ships whose names end in 'a' are likely to be unlucky. This belief was remembered by sailors all over the world when the *Lusitania* was torpedoed in 1915.

Names have power. To speak them is to invoke that which bears them and to lend it strength. Hence, even today, many people use euphemisms for such ill-omened words as cancer or death, and in the hey-day of the fairy-belief, it was thought dangerous to speak of those spirits by name. They were referred to by other titles, such as the Good Neighbours, or the Gentle People or the Little Folk.

The tabued words of sailors and miners may perhaps spring from the same idea. Many things, some with evil associations like drowning or the Devil, witches or death, and some quite innocent, such as parts of the body or of the boat, are never named at sea; nor are certain animals, or things with a definitely Christian connexion, like churches or ministers. The subject is too complicated to discuss here, nor has any really satisfactory explanation of the custom's origin been as yet put forward; but that it is associated with the power of the spoken word to invoke the dangerous, or to attract attention to the thing spoken of, is at least very probable.

NEED-FIRE

Need-fire is the name commonly applied in Britain to the new fire, obtained by friction, which was ceremonially kindled in many European countries, either as part of the rites of certain sacred anniversaries, such as Beltane or Midsummer, or in order to avert particular evils, like cattle disease, plague, famine, or similar communal misfortunes. Other names for it were Bale, Wild, Will, or Neat fire. In Gaelic-speaking districts it was sometimes called Forlorn, or Forced fire, and in parts of Sweden, Running fire, because the new flame, when kindled, was carried by swift runners to all the houses in the parish.

Various methods were used to obtain it. In some places an oak spindle was turned in an oak log by relays of men, or an oaken peg was violently twisted against some other dry wood until the peg took fire. In Caithness a wooden axle was fixed horizontally between two upright posts, and four levers projecting from the centre were rapidly moved until the spark came. Elsewhere a wheel was turned unceasingly over oak spindles, usually nine in number. In most areas the turning had to be done *deiseil*, the way of the sun, but in some Swedish districts, the opposite rule obtained, and the spindle or wheel was turned widdershins. When the spark appeared, it was caught by dry straw, bracken, or other easily ignited material, and from this a previously prepared bonfire was set ablaze. As soon as this bonfire began to die down, young men le˜pt through the purifying flames for good luck and protection, and cattle were afterwards driven over the dying embers.

Because of the sacred nature of need-fire, certain rules had to be observed when kindling it, whether this was done as a ritual of renewal at some festival, or to destroy an already present evil. All household fires had to be put out beforehand; if this was not done, the spark would not come. In 1767, when new fire was raised in the Isle of Mull during a cattle epidemic, the work failed for several days because one man refused to put out his house-fire. When he was finally persuaded to do so, the desired flame appeared without further difficulty, and a heifer from the diseased herd was then sacrificed in the resulting bonfire.

The men who turned the wheel or spindle had to be free from the unexpiated guilt of any crime, known or secret, and they could not have any metal thing about them while they worked. If either of these conditions was broken, their labour was in vain. As soon as the new fire had come, it was carried by burning peats or torches to every house in turn. Wherever possible, the bearers travelled from east to west, like the sun; they were not allowed to stop anywhere, except outside the houses to which they were bound, and on no account might they carry the holy flame under any roof as they went. It was essential that the new fire be carried to the householders, not fetched by them from the bonfire; and in many districts it was thought very unlucky if a hearth-fire, after being thus renewed, was allowed to go out again before the next need-fire kindling.

In A.D. 742 the Church condemned the use of need-fire as a pagan practice, which indeed it was, but the custom continued for many centuries thereafter, almost to our own day. In 1834 a public kindling took place near Carlisle during an epidemic of foot-and-mouth disease. At Troutbeck in 1851, need-fire was made as a remedy for cattle-plague. The new fire was carried to every farm in the dale by relays of burning peats, each farmer lighting his own fire by means of a peat received and kindling another from it to send on to his neighbour. In a note to *The Gytrash of Goathland*, published in 1929, Michael Temple recorded that he saw need-fire made in the Vale of Mowbray only twenty years before he wrote. It was, he said, a festival fire, once lit at Beltane but now transferred to the Patronal Festival of a local church, which fell near that ancient anniversary. The method of kindling which he described was centuries old, and must have been well known to the remote ancestors of all those who took part in it. In this case, however, the custom had degenerated into real superstition, since its meaning had been forgotten, and it was continued only because 'it had always been done', and because of a confused feeling that it might be, in some unspecified way, unlucky to omit it.

NETTLE

The humble nettle, whose lavish growth is said to be a sign of good soil, was traditionally connected with thunder. It protected those who carried it against lightning, and it also gave them courage in times of danger. An old magical method of curing fever was for someone to grasp a nettle firmly and pull it up by the roots, saying at the same time the name of the patient and those of his parents. The plants which had the strongest protective and healing powers were those which grew in a place upon which the sun never shone. In Lincolnshire, it was supposed that nettles sprang up spontaneously wherever human urine had been deposited.

In Britain until quite recent times, nettles were much used in ordinary folk-medicine. The plants were gathered early in the morning during May or June, and made into a tea, or boiled and eaten as a vegetable, to purify the blood and cure nettle-rash. Nicholas Culpeper recommends the seeds for stings and poisons, and the effects of a mad dog's bite, and the juice of the leaves to stop bleeding at the mouth. A remedy for nose-bleeding, still remembered in many English districts, is to snuff stinging-nettles up the nostrils. Another is to bruise a dead-nettle and lay it on the nape of the neck. A common treatment for rheumatism formerly was to thrash the affected part with stinging-nettles, and one old way to make hair grow strongly was to comb it the wrong way every morning with a comb previously dipped in nettle-juice.

NEW YEAR WATER. *See First Foot.*

NIGHTJAR

Nightjars, like owls, are usually considered birds of evil omen because of their nocturnal habits and their strange-sounding cry. In some parts of northern and midland England, they are called Lychfowl, that is, Corpse-fowl. In Nidderdale, they were once thought to embody the wandering souls of children who had died unbaptized. It is unlucky to hear their call in the darkness, and if they perch on a house (which they do only rarely), it is a sign of misfortune or death for someone within.

Their Latin name *Caprimulgus*, or Goat-milker, springs from a very ancient belief that they suck the udders of goats and cause them to go blind. This idea, which is quite unfounded, existed in Aristotle's time, and was once very widespread. That it flourished in England formerly is shown by the fact that another country name for the nightjar, still sometimes used, is Goatsucker.

NIGHTSHADE

Deadly Nightshade (*Atropa Belladonna*) is a valuable medicinal herb and is cultivated today for this reason, but it has a very evil reputation in folk-tradition. This is easily understandable, since a plant which is highly poisonous, has a rather sinister appearance, and is often found growing near ruins is likely to be looked at askance by the superstitious. Witches were supposed to use it as one of the ingredients of their flying-ointments, and also in spells to induce madness and death. That they, and perhaps other evilly-disposed persons, did use it for the latter purpose is very probable, since it grows wild in most parts of England and can be relied upon to produce very unpleasant and often fatal results if eaten, or swallowed in decoctions.

It was also believed to induce clairvoyance, and preparations of the berries or roots were therefore used by those who desired to see spirits, good or evil, and to foretell the future.

Nevertheless, in spite of its sinister properties, nightshade, like most magical plants, was two-sided in its action, and could be employed against witches as well as by them. A chaplet of the leaves worn upon the head defeated spells, and a collar hung round the necks of cattle prevented witches gaining power over them. Woody nightshade, or bittersweet, was also supposed to have protective virtues. Aubrey tells us in his *Remaines* that when a horse was found to be exhausted and ill because it had been 'hag-ridden' by night, a garland of bittersweet and holly twisted together and hung round its neck would certainly cure it. And lest any one should doubt this, he firmly adds the word *probat* at the end of his account.

NINE. *See Numbers.*

NUMBERS

A very ancient belief which flowered in the time of Pythagoras into a complicated philosophical system was that all numbers and their multiples had mystical significance, and that certain numbers, particularly those between one and thirteen, had peculiar power. Traces of this conception still linger today in the form of quite strongly held superstitions concerning the virtues of odd numbers, and the good luck or otherwise of three, seven, nine, or thirteen.

It is commonly said that luck, good or bad, has a threefold aspect. If an accident occurs, two more of the same kind may be expected soon afterwards. If there is a funeral in a parish, there will be two others within a week, a month, or some other locally defined period. Letters, gifts, and unusual visitors come in threefold succession; three unexplained knocks heard in a house are a death omen; if anything is broken, so will two other objects be, and so on. Many old charms required certain actions to be performed, or a form of words to be repeated, three times before the magic would work. In Pagan antiquity, three was a sacred number, and for Christians, its sanctity was strengthened by its association with the Trinity. Hence, it has come down to us as a fortunate numeral, and we still say 'three times lucky'.

Four, which was once of great importance as a symbol of unity, endurance, and balance, seems to have left few traces on everyday superstition, but seven is almost everywhere thought to be lucky, or at least, significant. Astrologers taught that seven planets governed the universe and the life of man, and that life was divided into seven ages. A seventh child has gifts denied to others. Seven horseshoes on a house guard it from all evil, and seven ominous birds seen together foretell very good or very bad luck, according to the differing traditions of the districts in which they are seen.

Nine, being a multiple of three by three, is usually lucky, and was much used by our Anglo-Saxon forebearers in healing and spell-breaking charms.

At one time, every seventh and every ninth year in a man's life was believed to bring great change and great dangers. Sixty-three, which is seven multiplied by nine, was therefore the most perilous of all ages, and if a man survived his sixty-third year, he might hope to live to a good old age.

There is still a fairly general belief that an individual's whole body and mind change completely every seven years, and that quite dramatic alterations can sometimes be looked for at the end of such periods. Within this century, mothers of unmanageable naughty children have been heard to say that they were not worried because they knew there would be a great (and apparently, an automatic) improvement in the children's behaviour as soon as they reached the age of seven. In 1924, the secretary of a cripples' guild in Berkshire was told by two of the members that they expected a decided change for the better in their condition on their twenty-first birthdays, which were then not far off. They said that if no such improvement occurred then, they were uncertain whether this would mean they must be cripples for life, or only for another seven years.

The most widespread numerical superstition today is that thirteen is extremely unlucky. This belief is often attributed to the fact that thirteen were present at the Last Supper, but in fact it is far older than that event, and existed in pagan times. The ancient Romans disliked thirteen as much as we do, and regarded it as a symbol of death, destruction, and misfortune. Another explanation sometimes given is that witch-covens always consisted of thirteen persons. The records of the trials do not always bear this out, but it was generally believed, it might well help to strengthen the aversion in which this number was, and is, held, especially as the presiding member was supposed to represent the Devil, or even to be him in person.

It is very ill-omened for thirteen people to sit together at table. The person who rises first will die or meet with serious misfortune within the year. In some districts, it is the last to rise upon whom the penalty falls, in others, it may be any one of the company. In Oxfordshire, it is unlucky to be thirteen in a room, especially for the person nearest the door.

Hotel-keepers rarely have a room in their house which is numbered thirteen. They know they will have difficulty in letting it, and the thirteenth room is therefore usually labelled 12a or 14. Houses numbered thirteen are often hard to let or sell, and some town councils have been forced to take notice of this tradition and omit thirteens from their three-numerals. A famous English barrister is said to have refused all briefs marked thirteen guineas.

The thirteenth of the month is an inauspicious day on which to embark upon any new enterprise, including marriage, or to set out on a journey. It is doubly so if it happens to fall on a Friday. Probably the unluckiest of all dates for a wedding is Friday, 13 May, and few brides would choose it without some very strong reason. On the other hand, to be born on the thirteenth of the month does not seem to be particularly ill-omened anywhere and in some districts it is thought to be lucky. Where that is the case, a child born then is expected to prosper in anything he begins on that date in later life.

NUTMEG

To dream of nutmegs foretells coming changes in the dreamer's life. To carry one about the person cures or prevents rheumatism. The latter belief is still very common, and many people customarily keep one of these little nuts in their pockets as a precaution. An Oxfordshire woman who suffered badly from rheumatism between the two wars of this century made a garter of nutmegs and wore it round her leg; the remedy is said to have been entirely successful.

In Somerset, one carried in the pocket is also a charm against boils, but only if it has been given to the patient by a friend.

NUTS

Nuts, which were symbols of life and fertility in pagan antiquity, are traditionally associated still with love, marriage, and childbirth. In ancient Rome they were given to a newly-married couple on their wedding-day to ensure their fruitfulness. Baring-Gould tells us in *A Book of Folklore* that at Gaillac, in France, the bridal pair were showered with nuts while they were still kneeling at the altar, and that in Poitou, the floor of the room where the wedding-breakfast was held was strewn with them. In Devonshire formerly, the bride was met as she came out of the church by an old woman who gave her a bag of hazel-nuts.

These rites, like our modern confetti-throwing, were intended to promote child-bearing, the only difference between them and the present-day custom being that the nut-givers knew what they were doing, whereas the throwers of confetti have usually forgotten the underlying meaning of their action. In many English counties still, a plentiful crop of nuts in any parish is said to foretell numerous births there during the coming year. 'Good nutting year, plenty of boy-babies' is a well-known country saying, to which is sometimes added a rider that if the tree bear an unusually large crop of double nuts, a correspondingly large number of twins may be expected.

In Germany the phrase 'going a-nutting' was once a euphemism for love-making. It is perhaps because of some kindred idea that the Devil is often associated with nut-gathering in English tradition. He collects nuts himself, and carried a black bag for the purpose. If anyone goes nutting on a Sunday, he may appear to the Sabbath-breaker and bend the branches down to his hand. On Holy Rood Day (14 September), when young people used to do nutting in bands, there was always a risk that he might attach himself to the company as an uninvited and terrifying companion. Brand[1] quotes a rhyme printed in 1709 which says

> The devil, as the common people say,
> Doth go a-nutting on Holy-rood day;
> And sure such leachery in some doth lurk,
> Going a-nutting do the devil's work.

Hallowe'en was known as Nutcrack Night in some districts because nuts

[1] J. Brand, *op. cit.*

were often used then in charms and divination. When a girl wanted to be sure her lover was true, she took two hazel-nuts, named one for herself and one for him, and set them side by side on the bars of the grate. If they burnt away together, all was well, but if they flew apart, or failed to burn, she knew that he was faithless. A charm to know if a wish would be granted was to form it silently whilst throwing a nut on the fire. If the latter flared up in the heat, the desired end would be achieved, but not otherwise.

The most magical nut was, of course, one with two kernels in a single shell. If anybody found one, he made a wish, ate one kernel, and threw the other over his left shoulder. He had to do this in silence, and to refrain from speaking afterwards until someone asked him a question to which the right answer was 'yes'. A sure method of obtaining the love or friendship of some admired person was to divide a double hazel-nut with him. If he could be induced to eat one kernel while the finder of the nut ate the other, both being silent throughout, the charm would almost certainly succeed.

O

OAK

The oak was a holy tree for many Indo-European peoples, both because it was traditionally associated with thunder and lightning, and because it often serves as host for the sacred mistletoe. It was deeply venerated by the Druids, and also by the pagan Norsemen and Celts. It was one of the Seven Noble Trees of Irish law (the others being the apple, alder, birch, hazel, holly, and willow), for the destruction of which a fine of a cow had to be paid. In Ostrogoth law also, it 'had peace' and could not be felled. Legend says that when St Columcille founded his church at Derry, he burnt the town and the king's rath in order to obliterate the works of worldly men, but he spared the oak wood from which the place took its name,[1] and when it accidentally caught fire in the general conflagration, he saved it by pronouncing an invocation over it.

The idea that it was unlucky, and even sinful, to cut down oaks, especially those which bore mistletoe, persisted for many centuries. In Kelly's *Curiosities of Indo-European Folk-Lore* (1863) there is an account of the felling of a mistletoe-bearing oak at Norwood in 1657. The man who hewed down the tree broke his leg, and all concerned in the work met with bad luck thereafter, including the London apothecaries who bought the mistletoe. Near Oswestry, a very ancient oak, traditionally connected with St Oswald and known as the Mile Oak, was considered holy and inviolable during most of

[1] The name Derry comes from *doire*, an oakwood.

its long life. Charlotte Burne records in her *Shropshire Folk-Lore* that fire, sickness, or death was believed to follow the cutting of any of its branches; and when in 1824 the tree was felled by the Lord of the Manor's agent, the local people were horrified, expecting dire misfortune to fall upon the entire parish.

Aubrey remarks in his *Natural History of Wiltshire* that 'when an oake is felling, it gives a kind of shrieke or groanes, that may be heard a mile off, as if it were the genius of the oake lamenting. E. Wyld, Esq., hath heard it several times.'

Oaks are thunder-trees, once sacred to Thor, and as such they are thought to protect against lightning and thunderbolts. It is quite commonly thought that they are never struck by lightning, though in fact they sometimes are, and consequently that anyone who shelters under them is safe during a storm. Their branches, or their acorns, kept in a house protect that house from being struck. When 'pull-down' blinds were fashionable, the bobbins at the ends of the blind-cords were usually shaped like acorns for this reason. But if an oak was struck by lightning, its wood thereby gained additional protective powers. Charlotte Burne, writing in 1896 in *Folk-Lore* (Vol. 7) says that about three years earlier, an oak at Hanbury, in Needwood Forest, was so struck, 'and people came from all round to get pieces of the injured wood, to keep as charms to preserve their houses from a similar misfortune'.

Oaks also protected those who stood beneath them, or wore their leaves, from witchcraft and evil. Bede tells us in *Historia Ecclesiastica* that when St Augustine first preached before King Ethelbert of Kent in the Isle of Thanet, the King would not allow him to do so indoors, 'lest if they were skilful in sorcery, they might the rather deceive and prevail against him'. Instead, he arranged an open-air meeting under a large oak, beneath whose sacred branches he would be safe from any spell the strange newcomers might attempt to cast upon him.

In pagan times, marriages were sometimes celebrated under certain isolated trees, known as Marriage Oaks. This practice was naturally forbidden by the Christian Church, but traces of it lingered for a long time in some places. Newly-married couples, hoping to make the best of both worlds, often hurried from the church porch as soon as the wedding ceremony was ended, to dance three times round the bridal tree, and cut a cross upon it. A Marriage Oak survived at Brampton in Cumberland until the middle of last century. Although, needless to say, no one went to it to be married at that late date, a vague tradition of good luck for bridal couples clung about it to the end, and its final disappearance was greatly regretted by the local people.

Many old parishes have ancient single oaks growing at one or more points along their boundaries. These are usually known as Gospel Oaks, and numerous place-names suggest that they were once far commoner than they are now. It was formerly the custom for Rogation processions to halt beneath such boundary trees, and for a short service, including the reading of some part of the Gospel, to be held there. It may be that in this purely Christian ceremony we have a last memory of the veneration once so widely given to the thunder-tree.

Acorns and oak-apples have their significance in folk-belief also. Oak-apples became an English symbol of royalist sympathies after 1660, and were worn by the loyal on Royal Oak Day. Those found without either oak-apples or oak-leaves then were liable to be beaten with stinging-nettles. To find a worm or a spider in an oak-apple is unlucky. The first denotes poverty for the finder, the second a coming illness. An acorn carried about was a charm to preserve youthfulness. Young people, anxious to know if their sweethearts would marry them, sometimes took two acorns, named them for themselves and the lover, and dropped them into a basin of water. If they floated close to each other, marriage was certain, but if they drifted apart, the lover would be faithless, or something else would occur to prevent the wedding.

A somewhat less romantic use for acorns, current in the seventeenth century, was to distil a liquid from them and give it to the intemperate, either to control the craving for strong drink, or to offset the effects of prolonged drunkenness.

ONIONS

Onions have many uses in the world of superstition, quite apart from their normal use as food. Snakes are commonly believed to have a strong antipathy to their smell, and consequently a raw onion carried in the hand is a sure protection against their attacks. Witches also were thought at one time to dislike them, and for this reason they were often employed in anti-witch charms. Even to keep them in the house served as a protection, provided that they were not cut or peeled. Young people used them to induce dreams of the future husband or wife. A form of divination practised by girls who could not make up their minds without magical assistance was to take as many onions as there were possible suitors, scratch the name of one man on each, and set them all in the chimney-corner, or some other warm place. The man whose onion sprouted first would be, or at all events, should be, the chosen husband.

A charm of another sort was, and perhaps still is, resorted to by schoolboys about to be caned. A raw onion was rubbed on the palm of the hand in the belief that this would deaden the pain of the stroke, or better still, if it was possible to rub it on the cane itself, the latter would split as soon as it was used.

Onions are often employed to avert, or give warning of infection. It is a fact that peeled onions quickly attract germs, and from this grew the belief that diseases would fly to them and spare the inmates of the house. In

Oxfordshire, they are said to prevent the common cold, if left about in a room. It is still quite widely believed that their presence keeps off infectious fevers, and in some parts, they are thought to give warning, by turning black, that someone in the family has been infected. During the plague epidemics of the sixteenth and seventeenth centuries, they were used both to avert and treat the disease. In *Present Remedies against the Plague* (1594) it is stated that if three or four are peeled and left on the ground for ten days, they will gather all the infection in the neighbourhood, and in one of the official Plague Orders which were issued at such times, poultices of onions, butter, leven, cloves, and mallow are recommended for laying on the plague-sores. J. Harvey Bloom relates[1] that when scarlet fever broke out at Whitchurch in Warwickshire in 1915, one young mother tried to protect her family by paring an onion and burying the peelings in a secret place where they would not be disturbed. She believed that this would carry the fever from the house.

Onions were also used in folk-medicine to prevent insomnia, and to cure the after-effects of drunkenness. In *The Book of the Physicians of Myddvai*, we are told that patients who have been given sleeping-potions before an operation should afterwards be roused by having a compound of onion and vinegar poured down their throats. A nineteenth-century Lincolnshire charm against toothache, recorded in *Notes and Queries*, was to put the outer parings of an onion, thimblewise, on the great toe of the sufferer. In another number of the same journal, a clergyman in north Yorkshire described how, in 1889, he had been called to a house in the parish to baptize a baby who had had convulsions during the previous night. On his enquiring what had been done for the child, the mother told him that, on the advice of a neighbour, she had rubbed its hands with a raw onion. This, she said, had done good at the time, and there had been no second fit.

A cure for chilblains still used in many districts is to rub the affected part with raw onion and salt. For earache, a roasted onion held against the ear whilst still hot is often recommended. An Oxfordshire remedy for baldness is to rub the bare patch with a raw onion until the skin is quite red, and then smear it thickly with honey.

ORANGE

In countries where it is a native, the orange-tree has been regarded for many centuries as a fertility-inducing plant, of which both the white blossoms and the golden fruit were used in charms to secure love, and to make marriages fruitful. In Britain, it is, of course, an alien, never seen by the untravelled until it appeared in the orangeries of great Stuart houses. Its magical traditions, however, seem to have been imported with it and, in some extent at least, to have taken root and flourished in popular superstition. Orange-blossom

[1] J. Harvey Bloom, *Folk Lore, Old Customs and Superstitions in Shakespeare Land*, 1929.

is now by far the most usual flower for wedding wreaths, and has quite super-
seded the older myrtle or rosemary. In this connexion, it has exactly the same
meaning as had the English flowers and, though the modern bride does not
always remember the fact, its presence in her wreath is, or was originally,
intended to ensure that the marriage shall not be childless.

In *I Walk at Night* (1935) Lilias Rider Haggard records an interesting
Norfolk survival of the use of oranges in love-charms. The poacher whose
sayings form the basis of this book told her that if a man desired a girl's love,
he must take an orange and prick it all over in the pits of the skin with a
needle. He must then sleep with it under his armpit. Next day, he must give
it to the girl, presumably without telling her the reason for the gift, or where
it has been all night, and see that she eats it. If she did so, he could be sure that
she would return his love.

ORPINE

Orpine is often called Live-Long because it remains green a long time after
it is cut, and will sometimes continue to grow if watered occasionally, or even
without this attention. It was formerly the custom to gather it on Midsummer
Eve and hang it up in the house as a protection against lightning and disease.
Tournefort remarks in his *Compleat Herbal* (1719–30) that those who hang it
thus have 'this Persuasion, that they shall be troubled with no Distemper, so
long as it continues green'.

Another country name for the plant is Midsummer Men. It was once much
used in love-divinations on Midsummer Eve. An enquiring girl would bring
in a stalk or cutting and fix it in clay upon a shell, a slate, or piece of potsherd,
or in some convenient crack in the door. If next morning the stalk inclined
towards the right, she knew that her lover was true, if to the left, that he was
false. Another method was to bring in two pieces, naming one for the man
and the other for the girl. If they were found bending towards each other
next day, the love-affair would prosper, but if they had turned in opposite
directions, there would be no marriage. If either of the two named stalks
withered, it was a sign that the person it represented would die before long.

OWLS

Almost all night-birds, and especially those with eerie-sounding cries, are
objects of superstitious fear, and none more so than the owl. In antiquity this
bird was hated by the Romans, who associated it with death and disaster, but
in Greece it was greatly respected because it was the bird of Athene, the
Goddess of Wisdom. If one flew before or over Greek soldiers in war, it was
a sign of victory. In Britain, as in most parts of Europe, it has always been
considered an unlucky fowl, and there are still many people who hate to hear

it hooting at night. Country people say it lives in churches and drinks lamp-oil, or that it nests in ruins, not because it likes the shelter of ivy, but because such places are haunted and ill-omened. To meet one in daylight is often thought to be unlucky, and in Cheshire there is a belief that if a man looks into an owl's nest, he will be melancholy all the rest of his life.

An owl entering, or flying round a house, or perching on the roof, is a death omen, and so too if it attempts to come down the chimney. In Sussex, if one perches on the church-roof, there will be a death in the parish shortly afterwards. The appearance of two large white owls on the house-roof was said to warn the Wardours of Arundel of a coming death in the family. In some parts of Ireland an entering owl is killed at once, for if it flies away, it will take the luck of the household with it.

Constant hooting near a dwelling, and especially the cry of a screech-owl many times repeated, is widely thought to foretell a death. In Oxfordshire, this is certain if the bird does it for three nights running. But owls may also be concerned with childbirth. If one shrieks at a birth, the child will have an unhappy life. In France, if a pregnant woman hears one, it is a sign that her baby will be a girl; in Wales, continued hooting round a village means that some girl will lose her virginity. If the bird cries by day, the omen is doubly evil, for then the terror of the unusual is added to a portent already sufficiently unlucky in itself.

The witches in *Macbeth* used an owlet's wing 'for a charm of powerful trouble', and much farther back in time Horace (*Epode*, V. 15, 16) mentions a screech-owl's feather as part of a witch's brew. But the power that could thus be used for evil purposes could also be used for good. In England, owl-broth was given to children suffering from whooping-cough, and the crushed and powdered eggs of the bird that can see in the dark were used to strengthen failing eyesight. Swan in his *Speculum Mundi* (1643) says that if an habitual drunkard was given owl's eggs broken in a cup, he would henceforth detest strong drink as much as he had formerly loved it. A similar idea existed in ancient Greece, where it was thought that if a child was given such an egg, he would never be a drunkard. A remedy for gout, which is encouraged by too much drinking, was to eat salted owl, and both epilepsy and madness were treated with various forms of owl-preparations. In Germany a charm against the terrible consequences of being bitten by a mad dog was to carry the heart and right foot of the bird under the left armpit. Of these cures, the first two were purely magical, but the others sprang originally from the owl's connexion with Athene who, as Goddess of Wisdom, was opposed to anything that caused frenzy and unreason.

P

PANTOMIMES

Most actors consider *Cinderella* a lucky pantomime, likely to be successful, and to bring good luck to those who act in it. On the other hand, *Robin Hood* and *The Babes in the Wood* are both very unlucky. Something unfortunate may be expected to occur in the theatre, either during the run of the pantomime, or during rehearsals.

PARSLEY

Although parsley is a valuable culinary herb, grown in innumerable gardens, it has a curiously unlucky reputation in folk-tradition. In ancient Greece, it was associated with death. It was said to have sprung from the blood of the hero, Archemorus. Graves were strewn with it, and the wreaths worn by the victors in funeral games were made from it. In Rome also it had an ominous significance, and if, as many suppose, the plant was introduced into this country by the Romans, it is probable that some of our superstitions concerning it have grown out of their beliefs.

Because it germinates slowly, it is often said to go nine times to the Devil (or twice, or three, or seven times) before it comes up. To prevent this, it should be sown on Good Friday, when the soil is redeemed from the power of Satan. Sowing it on any other day is considered unlucky in some areas, and likely to cause death in the family of the sower within the year. A further extension of this belief is that it is unlucky to have it in the garden at all, though in view of its long-established usefulness in cooking and medicine, this idea can hardly have been very widespread at any time. Thistleton Dyer[1] quotes two proverbs which seem to support it. One is 'A parsley field will bring a man to his saddle and a woman to her grave.' The other, which he ascribes to the English southern counties, is 'When parsley's grown in the garden, there'll be a death before the year's out.'

It is variously said to grow best for the wicked, for an honest man, or where the 'mistress is master', provided, of course, that she sows it herself. In Lincolnshire, if a young woman plants it, she will have a child soon afterwards. In that county, as in some other parts of England, the parsley-bed sometimes takes the place of the gooseberry-bush as the alleged source of new-born babies. Children are told that the doctor, or someone else, digs them up there with a golden spade. On the other hand, E. M. Porter[2]

---

[1] T. Thistleton Dyer, *op. cit.*
[2] E. M. Porter, 'Some Folk Beliefs of the Fens', *Folklore*, Vol. 69, 1958.

records that in the Cambridgeshire Fens, unmarried girls who became pregnant used to eat parsley three times a day for three weeks in the hope of escaping from their predicament.

It is very unlucky to give away parsley-roots, and on no account must they ever be given directly. The only safe method of making such a gift is for the owner to indicate the site of the bed and allow the recipient to help himself. One of the strongest superstitions about the plant is that it is dangerous to transplant it. A death will follow, or at best, serious misfortune. John Jones relates in his *Notes on Certain Superstitions Prevalent in the Vale of Gloucester* that he once visited a friend, and found him telling his gardener to move a parsley-bed. The man flatly refused, saying he was quite willing to destroy the bed, but transplant it he would not, and moreover, he knew of no one in the neighbourhood who would undertake so unlucky a task. In the end, his employer had to give way, and the bed remained where it was. This happened at the close of last century, but the underlying idea is not quite dead yet. Even today, some gardeners are reluctant to transplant the roots because of the tradition (now usually rather vague in detail) of following bad luck.

Parsley was formerly thought to be an antidote to poison, and its presence upon any dish was a sign of good faith. According to Tournefort,[1] it also had the curious property of weakening glass. He says that if a glass is rinsed in water wherein parsley has been washed, and in which some of the leaves still float, it will break in pieces as soon as the slightest pressure is applied to it.

Farmers at one time grew parsley in large quantities and gave it to their sheep to prevent certain diseases to which they were liable. Pliny states that if the fish in a fish-pond are sick, parsley thrown into the water will heal them. It was also used to cure or prevent some human ailments. In Turner's *New Herball* we read that 'the sede taken beforehand helpeth men that have weyke braynes to beare drinke better'. The same seeds sprinkled over the head three times in a year were supposed to prevent baldness. It is still believed in many country districts that to chew parsley regularly keeps off rheumatism. An old Cambridgeshire method of ensuring good eyesight for a baby, mentioned by Miss Porter, was to steep parsley in rainwater collected after a thunderstorm, and apply it to the child's eyes during the first week of its life.

PASQUE FLOWER

The lovely purple anemone known as the Pasque Flower, which grows on chalk downs and blooms in April, is said in Berkshire to flower only where Saxon blood has been shed. In Hertfordshire, however, it is called Dane's Flower, and is supposed to have sprung originally from the blood of the

[1] J. P. de Tournefort, *op. cit.*

invading Danes. It is traditionally said to bloom most plentifully on the sites of ancient battles between the Saxons and the Danes.

Its more usual name was given to it because it blooms at Eastertide, and was once used to produce a bright green dye for Easter eggs.

PEACOCK

The peacock, perhaps because of its beauty and its proud demeanour, has always had a prominent place in mythology and tradition. In ancient Greece, it was sacred to Here, in Rome, to Juno. In many countries, including medieval England, it was a royal bird. Amongst the early Christians it was a symbol of immortality because its flesh was thought to be incorruptible. In southern Asia, which is its true home, it is greatly valued because it gives warning of tigers, snakes, and coming rain. This last belief obtains in England also, where its persistent cries are said to be a sure sign of wet weather.

The commonest English superstition about the bird is that it is very unlucky to have its tail feathers in the house. Some disaster will befall the owner, or the daughters of the house will not marry. Many people think it unlucky to wear these feathers, although in Lincolnshire formerly, agricultural labourers often wore them in their hats when they went to the Statute Fairs to find work. Hawkers sold them for this purpose in the streets at such fairs. Actors strongly dislike them on the stage, or in any part of the theatre. They believe their presence will cause the play to be a failure, or that something will go seriously wrong during its run.

Various reasons have been given for these superstitions, but the most probable is that the ever-open 'eyes' on the feathers have become associated with the Evil Eye, and therefore with the worst forms of bad luck.

PEAS

It is a sign of good luck, when shelling peas, to find a pod containing only a single pea or, conversely, more than the usual number. It is still more fortunate to find one with nine perfect peas in it, especially if it happens to be the first one opened. If an unmarried girl puts such a pod on the lintel of the outer door, the first man to cross the threshold thereafter will be her future husband; or if when laying it on the lintel she murmurs the name of another woman in the house, the next male visitor will be that woman's destined mate.

It was formerly the custom in northern England to eat carlins, or grey peas boiled, or fried in butter, on Carling Sunday, the fifth in Lent. A form of marriage-divination was practised in Northumberland on that day. Each person present helped himself in turn from the dish of carlins, taking successive spoonfuls until only a few peas remained. These were then taken one at a time. The man or woman to whose lot the last pea fell would be the first of the company to marry. Another way of discovering the same thing was to put a bean among the carlins, the person who got it in his or her portion being the lucky individual who would marry first.

Brand refers in his *Popular Antiquities* to a 'peascod wooing'. The young man chose a pod still growing on the stem, tore it away roughly, and then looked to see if the peas still adhered to the husk. If they did, his courtship was likely to prosper, and the pod was then presented to the girl of his choice as a love-token. On both sides of the Scottish Border, a girl deserted by her lover was rubbed down with pease-straw by the lads of the parish, and the same derisory consolation was given by the village girls to a youth who had lost his sweetheart to another. In Derbyshire not so long ago, any girl who had not been kissed or visited by a young man on St Valentine's Day was similarly 'dusted' with pease-straw or, if none was available, with a broom.

A Cornish method of curing warts was to take a pod containing nine peas, rub it on the warts, and then throw it away, saying 'Wart, wart, dry away'. Another very old remedy, mentioned by Pliny in his *Natural History*, was to touch each wart with a different pea on the first day of the new moon, wrap the peas in a cloth, and throw them away backwards. Although Pliny does not say so, it is probable that whoever picked up the cloth was expected to get the warts. A modern Buckinghamshire variant of this remedy requires that each pea be separately wrapped in paper and then buried. As it decays, so will the wart that was touched with it disappear.

PEONY

The peony was venerated as a magical and healing plant from very early times almost down to our own day. It was named after Paeon, God of Healing, who used its roots to cure the wounds of Hercules, and through him it was associated with Apollo. The ancient Greeks believed that its roots could only be safely gathered by night, and then only, like the mandrake, with the aid of a dog tethered to it and tempted to pull it up by a bait of meat placed just beyond his reach. It was necessary for the human being concerned in the operation to retire to a distance, leaving the unhappy dog to its fate, because again like the mandrake, the plant uttered a cry as it was torn from the ground which was fatal to all who heard it. But once gathered, the roots were powerful antidotes to evil of many kinds, and especially valuable as a cure for lunacy, nightmares, epilepsy, and similar ills.

Pythagoras tells us that if sufferers from epilepsy carried the root about with them, or wore a necklace of the seeds, they need not fear a recurrence of their fits; and many centuries later, Parkinson remarks in his *Paradisi in Sole, Paradisus Terrestis* (1629) that peony-roots were 'a most singular approved remedie for all Epileptical diseases, in Englische, The falling sicknesse'. Seednecklaces (or beads turned from the roots) were still being worn as late as the mid-nineteenth century in many English rural districts as a charm against fits of various kinds, and also to prevent convulsions in babies and to ease teething troubles. An Irish remedy for the after-pains of childbirth, recorded by Maura Laverty in 1942,[1] was to powder nine single peony-seeds, mix them with borax and nutmeg and give them to the mother in white aniseed water.

In addition to their healing properties, peonies were long considered to have protective powers, and their seeds and roots, especially those of the male plant, were used in amulets and anti-witch charms.

PERAMBULATOR

To bring a new perambulator into the house before the birth of the child for whom it is intended is widely held to be very unlucky. The baby will never ride in it if this is done, for either the mother will have a miscarriage, or the child itself will die. Like the similar superstition about new cradles, from which it seems to be directly descended, this idea is rooted in the age-old fear of assuming beforehand that something which is yet in the future will go well. Oddly enough, it does not appear to apply to clothes made in readiness for the birth, or to bassinettes or other necessities bought in advance. In the case of perambulators, however, the belief is so firmly held that sellers of baby-carriages have been forced to take notice of it. It is now quite usual for them to offer to store the perambulator for the purchaser until the birth is safely over.

PERIWINKLE

The pleasant blue periwinkle which adorns so many English flower-borders has no connexion, real or legendary, with the shell-fish that shares its name. It was once called pervink or parvenke, and its fishy name is probably a corruption of these. In the past, it had other names also, springing from its traditional association with death and witchcraft. The Italians called it *Fiore di morte*, and used it to make garlands for dead babies. The French had an even more ominous name for it, which was *Violette des Sorciers*. In the Middle Ages, criminals on their way to execution were often crowned with it. It is perhaps a dim memory of these dark traditions that lies at the root of a superstition still found in some parts of Wales. It is said there to be unlucky to uproot a periwinkle that grows on a grave. Whoever does so runs the risk of being haunted by the dead man whose grave he has robbed or, at best, of suffering from evil dreams throughout the year that follows.

Culpeper tells us that 'the leaves of periwinkle eaten by man and wife

[1] Maura Laverty, *Never No More*, 1942.

together, cause love between them'. The plant was also valued for its healing properties. The leaves, held in the mouth or chewed, were used to stay bleeding of the mouth or nose, and to stop toothache. Sir Francis Bacon recommended bands of the green stems to be tied round the leg in order to ease the pains of cramp. In Oxfordshire still, the dark, cool leaves are some-times laid upon boils and gatherings to draw their venom, and are said by those who cling to this practice to effect a swift and efficacious cure.

PETTING STONE. *See Barring the Way*.

PHOTOGRAPH

Photography is a comparatively new art, but it has inherited some very ancient superstitions. There are people even today who dislike being photo-graphed because they believe it will bring them bad luck. If an engaged couple are photographed together, something will happen to prevent the marriage. In the *Transactions of the Devonshire Association* (Vol. 90, 1958) it is recorded that in March of that year, two Devonshire football teams refused to allow a Press photographer to take a picture of them before the game, on the grounds that it was very unlucky to be photographed before a match.

A similar prejudice exists among many Eastern and African peoples. Arabs rarely, if ever, allow themselves to be photographed, and often cover their faces as soon as a camera is produced. This dislike of what seems on the face of it so harmless a proceeding is rooted in the ancient notion that a picture of a man is more than a mere representation of his face. It is a part of him, closely connected with his soul. If anyone possesses such a picture, he gains power over its original thereby, and may use it to work evil upon him. Practically all primitive races held this belief once, and it is almost certainly the forgotten origin of the aversion to being photographed still felt by some, even in civilized countries. It may also account for the curious reluctance which most people have experienced at some time in their lives to tearing up or burning an unwanted photograph, if the person depicted is still living.

In most cases, the fear survives without any conscious recollection of its original cause, and all that is expected is some vague and unspecified ill-luck. Yet even in England, the age-old use of pictures in magical practice seems to be still dimly remembered. In *Moonrakings*, a collection of Wiltshire folklore edited by Edith Olivier, there is a record of a very curious incident in that county which happened in 1922. A certain woman was approached by the relatives of a man who had suffered for some years from neurasthenia in so advanced a form that he was unable either to work or to take any interest in the affairs of daily life. Witchcraft was suspected, and this was confirmed by the wisewoman. Two witches, both men, were involved. The woman procured a photograph of one of these men, and with it she was able to break the spell laid upon the patient. How she did it is not related, but probably she treated the photograph as older magicians would have treated a wax or clay image, that is, by injuring or destroying it. Soon afterwards, the original of the picture died, and a little later, the second man died also. The patient then recovered with startling rapidity. No doubt coincidence can explain all these somewhat odd events; but the fact remains that, in the England of 1922, the magical use of an image (in this case in the modern form of a photograph) was apparently as well understood and as simply put into practice, as in the hey-day of the witch-belief centuries ago.

PICTURE

It is still quite commonly believed that if a picture falls from the wall for no apparent reason, it foretells the death of someone in the house. In some districts it is said that the omen will not be fulfilled unless the glass is broken, but more usually, the fall of the picture alone, even if it and the protecting glass are undamaged, is deemed to be enough.

In this well-known superstition we see an extension of an older belief. It is still thought that a falling portrait means the death of its subject. Originally, however, it was *only* a portrait which thus foretold a death, because it, like a photograph, was held to be magically connected with the person depicted. If it fell suddenly, without the excuse of a frayed cord, or anything likely to shake it from its position, that was a sign of death or, at least, great evil, for the individual concerned. Today, when the ancient connexion between a man's soul and any pictorial or photographic representation of him is largely (though not entirely) forgotten, the fall of any painting or drawing is regarded as ominous. And since no one easily imagines the 'death' of a landscape or a material object, the omen is now transferred to someone living in the house at the time.

It should be added that the victim may be anyone in the house, not necessarily the owner of the picture or the occupant of the room in which it hangs. In the case of a portrait, the portent is valid whether its original is living there or elsewhere at the time of its fall.

PIG

The fierce and dangerous wild boar was associated in antiquity with the rushing storm-winds, and with thunder and lightning. It was sacred to almost all the Indo-European peoples, including our Norse and Celtic ancestors, and traces of this sanctity still linger in superstitions attached to the ordinary pig.

In some parts of the Highlands, there was formerly a strong prejudice against eating pork. It is still very generally said to be a bad omen if a pig crosses the path of a bridal procession. Fishermen on many parts of our coasts will not use the word 'pig' to this day, either on sea or on shore. The creature is usually referred to as 'the thing', both by the seamen themselves and by their friends and relatives. To meet a pig on the way to the boats is exceedingly unlucky, and few fishermen will put to sea after having done so. 'Soo's tail to ye!' is an insult sometimes hurled at Fifeshire seamen (though not by any member of the fishing community, however spiteful, for he or she would not dare to say the tabued word). The tail itself, if carried on board, will bring serious bad luck. At Buckhaven on one occasion, a mischievous boy flung a pig's tail on to an outgoing boat, and the crew immediately returned to the harbour, and did not sail again that day.

Pigs are supposed to be able to see or smell the wind, and if they run about with straws in their mouths, it is a sure sign of windy weather to come. In the not very distant days when dancing bears were common in England, the breeding of these animals was thought to have adverse effects on that of pigs. In Sussex, when captive lions bred, which was said to be once in seven years, the effect on the piggery was the same.

Pigs must be killed with the waxing moon, otherwise the meat will shrink in the pot, or will not take the salt. In some areas, they are never killed on a Monday for the same reason. When they are being cured, no woman must touch the meat if she is pregnant, or during her monthly periods, because if she does, it will go bad. In the *Denham Tracts*, it is stated that north-country women, when making black or white puddings after a pig-killing, silently dedicated each string, as it was put into the pot, to some absent person. This had nothing to do with the subsequent disposal of the puddings, but was intended to prevent them from bursting as they boiled.

In the Isle of Man, there are several legends of fairy pigs, some friendly and some not, which haunt certain roads and bridges. One near Glenfaba rather charmingly wears a red hat, and is apparently harmless. Another known as the Ark Sonney is lucky to meet. But the large white boar which haunts Grenaby bridge shows clearer traces of its divine lineage, for it is a dangerous creature which sometimes seizes unhappy mortals and carries them up the river and through a cave near Barrule to the Underworld.

At Andover in Hampshire there is, or was, a spectral pig which is visible on New Year's Eve, and first appeared, rather significantly, during a very bad thunderstorm. In Lancashire, the sites of the parish churches at Winwick and Burnley were determined by the actions of a demon pig. The masons in both cases had chosen a suitable spot, but the pig had other views. Every morning, when they came to work, the men found that it had moved all the stones and scaffolding to another place. Finally, deeming it useless to fight the will of the demon, they built the churches on their present sites. A small figure of a pig carved upon the walls of both buildings is supposed to commemorate these curious happenings.

PIGEONS. *See Doves and Pigeons.*

PINS

Pins were used in numerous charms formerly, both good and evil, and also in divination. Being at once sharp-pointed and made of metal, they could be dangerous or protective according to the circumstances and the manner in which they were used. Witches could be kept from a house by thrusting pins into the door-post, but they sometimes employed them themselves in spells, particularly in image-magic. A bent or crooked pin was a favourite offering at wishing- or healing-wells, and apparently it still is, since quite new ones can often be seen at the bottom of such wells today.

It is commonly said to be lucky to find a pin lying on the ground, provided that it is picked up immediately. In some districts, this is only so if the point is away from the finder. If it is towards him, it should be left lying where it is, for to pick it up would be 'to pick up sorrow'. In Sussex, a yellow crooked pin should never be picked up by an unmarried woman, or she will die an old maid.

Their sharp points make pins ill-omened gifts between friends, unless something is given in exchange for them. In some places, it is considered unlucky even to lend them. It is, however, safe if the giver or lender refrains from handing them over, and simply invites the person needing them to help himself. Sailors often dislike them on board ship, because of a belief that their presence there will cause the vessel to spring a leak, or the fishermen's nets to be torn.

A dressmaker will not, as a rule, use black pins when fitting a dress. If she accidentally fastens the new garment to the customer's other clothes, the number of pins she uses in doing so foretells the number of years before her marriage.

When it was part of the bridesmaids' functions to undress the bride on the wedding night, the girl who drew out the first pin was thought to be lucky, for she would be the first of her company to marry. She could not keep it, however, for all such pins had to be thrown away. Misson, in his *Travels over England*, says that, after the wedding feast,

'the bridesmaids carry the bride into the bedchamber, where they undress her, and lay her in the bed. They must throw away and lose all pins. Woe be to the bride if a single one is left about her; nothing will go right. Woe also to the bridesmaids if they keep one of them, for they will not be married before Whitsontide.'

In some parts of Britain, it is said that if any single woman, not necessarily one of the bridesmaids, can secure a pin from a bride's dress on her return from the church, she will marry within the year; but she must not keep it, for either the charm will not work if she does, or the marriage just celebrated will not prosper.

Similarly, pins that have been used in a shroud, or in any other way about a corpse, must never be used again by the living. When they have been withdrawn from the grave-clothes, they must be carefully deposited in the coffin and buried with the dead man.

One of the many charms to recall a faithless or absent lover was to throw twelve new pins on the fire at midnight and say,

> 'Tis not these pins I wish to burn,
> But ——'s heart I wish to turn.
> May he neither sleep nor rest,
> Till he has granted my request.

Another method was to stick two pins into a lighted candle, so that they pierced the wick, while repeating the same verse. Addy[1] says that in the north midland counties it was believed that a woman could torture her husband or lover simply by wearing nine pins concealed inside her dress.

Pins were once very frequently used as a protection against witches, and in charms to break a spell. Charlotte Latham[2] records how, when a house at Pulborough was being repaired during the latter half of the nineteenth century, a bottle containing more than two hundred bent pins was found under the hearthstone of one of the rooms. The workmen said they often found such bottles in old houses, and that they were intended to guard the place from witchcraft.

In the same account of Sussex beliefs, it is related that Mrs Paxton, of Westdean, when visiting a cottage, saw a quart bottle full of pins on the hearth. She was told not to touch it because it was red hot, and also because if she did so, she would spoil the charm. It was then explained to her by the woman of the house that her daughter suffered from epilepsy. As the local doctors seemed unable to cure the girl, the mother had consulted a wise-woman, and had been told by the latter that the fits were due to witchcraft. She had then been instructed to fill a quart bottle with pins and put it by the fire until the pins were red hot. They would then prick the heart of the witch who had cast the spell and force her to remove it. Accordingly, she had done as she was told, and was now hoping that before very long, her daughter would be cured.

PLANTS IN MOURNING

The ancient conception of close sympathy between man and nature which

[1] S. O. Addy, *op. cit.*   [2] Charlotte Latham, *op. cit.*

underlies the custom of telling bees or rooks of a death in the family was sometimes extended to include favourite plants also. These too had to be told of the death, and put into mourning by having pieces of crêpe tied upon them, or their flowerpots draped in black. If this was not done, it was thought that the plants would begin to wither and, if left too long, they would die. M. A. Courtney[1] relates how, some time after the death of a near relative, she missed a fine maidenhair fern from the house, and asked what had become of it. She was told that no one had remembered to tell it of the death, or put it into mourning, and so it had gradually pined away.

In her *Walks about St. Hilary* (1838), Mrs Pascoe wrote: 'I saw with my own eyes a little black flag attached to our church-woman's bit of mignonette, which she assured me had begun to quail away since her poor grandson was burnt to death, but had revived after she put on it the piece of mourning.' Moreover, it was not only this woman's plants which had suffered in sympathy with the grandson's death. Her daughter in Penzance had, she said, twenty-two plants which were the admiration of passers-by. All began to droop from the time of the accident, but were saved by having black material tied upon each one.

Nearly a century later, and on the other side of England, Mrs Hood saw and admired a large geranium in a Norfolk cottage. The owner said it had belonged to her father, and when he died, it began to fail. But, she added, she had been advised 'to tie a bit o' black on that, and that'll grow; and arter a bit that did'. [2]

PLAYING-CARDS

Playing-cards have always been something more than mere innocent bits of pasteboard in popular belief. The first known in Europe were the mysterious Tarot packs, of which every card has a symbolic meaning. These packs are believed by some scholars to be derived from an ancient Egyptian book of initiation, the Book of Thoth. They were used in fortune-telling and divination, as their modern successors still are today. For this reason, and also because they are associated with gambling and games of chance, cards were hated and feared by many devout persons, and their use was strictly forbidden by the rules of several sects, including the constitution of the Methodist Church, as laid down by John Wesley.

The skippers of some fishing-vessels will not allow 'the Devil's picture-books' on board their boats. Others tolerate them, to while away a waiting-period, but they are always slightly suspect at sea, and if anything goes wrong, the packs are usually thrown overboard as a precaution. Miners frequently consider them unlucky in the pit, and will take care to remove any

[1] M. A. Courtney, *op. cit.*
[2] C. M. Hood, 'Scraps of English Folklore: North Norfolk', *Folk-Lore*, Vol. 37. 1926.

pack from their pockets before going down. Thieves will never voluntarily steal playing-cards, for fear of following misfortune or detection. Even to do so accidentally, as, for instance, by finding a pack inside a stolen box, is believed to be extremely ill-omened.

Superstitions connected with the cards themselves, and with their use in games and fortune-telling, are so numerous that it would be impossible to list them here in full. The following may give some idea of their nature and variety.

To be lucky at cards is to be unlucky in love. The knave and four of clubs, the knave and ace of spades, and the nine of diamonds are all ill-omened cards. Although divination systems vary, the ace of hearts usually denotes wealth, the two black knaves poverty and unhappiness, and the two red ones a hidden enemy.

Beginners' luck in gambling is well known, and so is that of borrowed money, which 'cannot lose'. To meet a woman on the way to the gaming-house, or to be touched by one while playing, is a bad sign, as is the presence of a cross-eyed person at the table. If luck goes against a player, he can change it by getting up and turning round three times with his chair. To lose one's temper or to sing while playing are both said to be unlucky, and certainly the latter is unlikely to be popular with either partner or opponents. A simple method of making a man lose is to wait until he has thrown a used match-stick into the ashtray, and then put another crosswise over it. His luck is thus 'crossed out', and presumably a cross made in any other way would do as well, provided that it included something that belonged to him or that he had used during the game.

POINTING

It is ill-omened, as well as ill-mannered, to point directly at any person. The attention of something better avoided may be thus attracted to him. To point at a ship out at sea, or leaving the harbour, will bring bad luck to those on board, and may cause a shipwreck.

In many countries of the world, including Britain, it is considered extremely unlucky to point at the sun or the moon, the stars, and the rainbow. In such cases, of course, it is not the thing pointed at which is harmed, but the person who thus affronts the celestial entities.

POPLAR

The poplar shares with the aspen the country name of Shivver-tree because like those of the latter, its leaves tremble. It also shares, and for the same reason, the aspen's power to cure agues and fevers. R. M. Heanley[1] records

[1] R. M. Heanley, *op. cit.*

a Lincolnshire charm in which the patient cut off a lock of his hair and wrapped it round a black poplar branch, saying as he did so:

> When Christ Our Lord was on the Cross,
> Then didst thou sadly shivver and toss.
> My aches and pains thou now must take,
> Instead of me I bid thee shake.

He then had to go straight home, speaking to no one on the way, after which he would be free from ague for ever. Heanley adds that some people considered it necessary to fast for twelve hours before attempting this charm.

The constant shaking of the poplar is often accounted for by the legend that its wood was used in the construction of the Cross. A. S. Rappoport in *Mediaeval Legends of Christ* (1934) mentions two other explanatory legends. One is that it was under a poplar that Our Lord prayed during His agony in the Garden of Gethsemane, and that the tree has trembled in sympathy ever since. The other is that it was cursed because, alone among trees, it refused to mourn at the Crucifixion, saying that Christ died for sinners, 'but I am innocent, and His suffering is no concern of mine'.

Poplar-leaves were supposed to be one of the ingredients of the witches' flying ointments.

POPPY

The poppy is a plant with many associations running back into very remote times. It is the flower of sleep and oblivion because of the narcotic properties of some varieties and, far more than the plant which bears that name, it is the true corn-flower. An ancient Greek legend says it was created by Somnus, God of Sleep, to give to Ceres, the Corn-Goddess, when she was so wearied by the search for her lost daughter that she could not make the corn grow. To save mankind from starvation, Somnus gave her poppies to make her sleep, and after she had rested, her strength returned, and the corn grew again. Hence in antiquity it was thought that the presence of poppies in a cornfield was essential to the welfare of the corn, a comforting belief with which modern farmers would hardly agree.

Poppies were also associated with fertility because of their many seeds, and the same seeds were used to flavour foods, and given with wine and honey to athletes training for the Olympic Games. Yet in spite of these traditional virtues, the plant is often ill-omened in popular belief. In Oxfordshire today, it is said to be unlucky to bring wild poppies into the house and, according to some, it is better not to pick them at all. The ban on their presence indoors does not seem to be general elsewhere, but the flower has an evil reputation in many areas as a cause of minor ills. Children almost everywhere say that if anyone looks into its heart, he or she will go blind, if only temporarily. In Yorkshire, where it is sometimes called *Blind Buff*, this is said to be due to the dazzling effect of the intense scarlet colour. Another Yorkshire name is *Head-waak*, because the smell of the flower is supposed to cause headaches.

Poppies are also said to produce violent earache if they are held against the ear. In folk-medicine, however, the heads are often used as poultices to cure earache, toothache, and similar pains, and a remedy for neuralgic pains in the face is to lay on the warmed leaves. Medieval physicians pounded the seeds with those of eryngo and mixed them with wine to make a lotion with which they washed the ears, eyes, and nostrils of sufferers from insomnia. Another cure for this trouble was to mingle the juice of the two plants with milk and other materials, and make them up into sleeping-pills.

Poppies, like water-lilies, were formerly considered a potent remedy against the passion of love, and were used for this purpose both in magic and in medicine.

Since the 1914–18 war, the poppy has acquired a new symbolism as the flower of remembrance because of its growth on the devastated fields of Flanders, and the annual buying and wearing by almost everyone in Britain of artificial poppies on Remembrance Day.

PORPOISE

Seamen regarded porpoises as fortunate creatures which must never be harmed. They are said to keep away sharks in water where those dangerous pests abound, and if they accompany, or play round, a ship at sea, it is a good omen for the voyage.

By tradition, they are connected with the wind, and may once have been thought to control it. Their gambols are often said to foretell a storm, but if they play about wildly when the storm is already raging, calm weather will soon follow. East Anglian fishermen say that if a porpoise is seen travelling swiftly northwards, it is a sign of fine weather, if southwards, of a gale.

POSTHUMOUS CHILD

A child born after the death of its father is thought to have healing powers, by virtue of the peculiar circumstances of its birth. This belief still lingers in many rural districts, and instances of posthumous children being asked to cure certain ailments, particularly thrush or whooping-cough, have occurred within comparatively recent years.

The most usual method is for the healer to breathe down the throat of the sufferer, while still fasting, on nine successive mornings. Sometimes a single 'breathing' is thought to be enough. In 1935 a Cheshire woman told the Editor that her sister had been posthumously born, and that consequently she was often asked to cure cases of thrush in this way. Her mother was at

first unwilling to let her do it, but the requests were so many, and refusal
was so obviously regarded as both unreasonable and unfriendly, that she had
to give way in the end.

Whooping-cough was cured in the same way in many parts of England.
In Ireland another method, rather less trying for the healer, was often used.
This was to take some hair from his or her head, wrap it in red cloth, and
make the patient wear it round his neck until the trouble vanished.

POTATO

A new potato carried about in the pocket until it has turned quite black
and as hard as old wood is said to be a sure cure for rheumatism. This belief
is widely held today in most parts of Britain, and is shared by both country
people and town-dwellers.

Two directly opposed superstitions exist about the planting of potatoes.
In many districts, it is customary to set the main crop on Good Friday, not
only because the holiday falls in the right season, but also because it is considered a fortunate day for the work. The crop will do well, for the Devil
has no power over the soil then. On the other hand, some people believe it
to be a most unlucky day; the potatoes so planted will never prosper. Not
everyone who holds the latter view is able to give a reason for it, but probably
it is connected with the once strong aversion to using any iron implement,
and particularly to breaking the ground with iron, on the anniversary of the
Crucifixion.

In Oxfordshire, both traditions have been recorded, in places within a few
miles from each other, and also a third which says that it is safe to plant
potatoes on Good Friday, but only if the person planting them has been to
church first.

POWDER OF SYMPATHY. *See Wound Treatment.*

PREGNANCY

A woman during her pregnancy was formerly thought to be surrounded
by spiritual and material perils which threatened both her and the unborn
child, and also, to a lesser extent, those about her. Among primitive peoples,
she was often required to go into ceremonial seclusion until after the birth
of her baby, and was forbidden to eat or touch certain things, or do particular kinds of work. She was not restored to ordinary life after the birth
until she had been freed of ritual uncleanness by some purifying ceremony.

Traces of these archaic ideas lingered for a very long time in the birth-
customs and superstitions of civilized races. In Britain and most European
countries, a pregnant woman was considered, until comparatively recently,

to be specially vulnerable to demons, witches, and other evil agencies. Charms and amulets of various kinds were needed to protect her. Certain actions were forbidden to her, and she had to be carefully guarded from any ill-omened encounter or sudden fright which might, by magic or by pre-natal influence, affect the coming child.

If she stepped over a grave, the baby would die. In Wales, she could not spin, or the child would be hanged with a hempen or flaxen rope. Even to tie a cord round her waist might make him unlucky in life. If she dipped her hands in dirty water, the child would have coarse hands, and if she handled flowers too much, his sense of smell would be poor. In many parts of England, no expectant mother ever acted as godmother to a friend's child, for this would result in the early death of the godchild.

In some districts, she was forbidden to wash clothes in the river, for her presence would drive away the fish. Within living memory, her touch was considered pernicious, and consequently she was debarred from making butter or doing any other work in the dairy, salting bacon, or touching any part of a slaughtered pig.

Although the ancient notion of ritual uncleanness in connexion with childbirth has long since faded from the minds of civilized people, it is still very often said that a woman after childbirth is unlucky to others until she has been churched. See Churching of Women: and Pre-Natal Influence.

PRE-NATAL INFLUENCES

It is very commonly believed that a baby can be physically marked or otherwise affected by things seen by its mother during her pregnancy, and especially by anything that frightened her then. Birthmarks, see page 53, are often said to be so caused, and to show by their shape what it was she saw. Eyes that are oddly set or strangely coloured, nervous twitches, defects of speech, and sometimes more serious troubles, are frequently ascribed to pre-natal influences. Thus, in 1933 a Berkshire woman, whose child suffered from a throat affection which prevented him from swallowing or speaking easily, said this was so because she had been startled by a snake before his birth. He had a snake's throat in consequence, which was too small for a human being, and also his eyes were green, like those of a reptile. She was quite prepared to believe that doctors could cure the child eventually, but she had no doubt at all that the trouble was due in the first place to the snake that had frightened her.

A very old superstition, not yet quite extinct, is that if a pregnant woman meets a hare, the baby will have a hare-lip. Formerly, the fear inspired by such an encounter was heightened by the idea that the hare might not be the innocent animal it seemed, but a witch in that form. To save the baby from a hare-lip, or possibly worse forms of bad luck, some sort of anti-witch charm had to be performed at once. A Warwickshire method was for the woman to stop as soon as she saw the hare and make three slits in her clothing. This charm was evidently well known in the seventeenth century, for in his *Daemonologie* (1650) Nathaniel Home records how, when a hare was seen, 'some in company with a woman great with childe have ... cut or torne some of the clothes off that woman with childe, to prevent (as they imagine) the ill luck that might befall her'.

PRIMROSE

The commonest superstition concerning primroses is that it is unlucky to bring less than a handful at a time into the house. Amongst poultry-breeders, this is thought to imperil the young stock. Either the broods will be very small, or the existing birds will die. In some areas, they are forbidden altogether when hens are sitting, but usually, their presence is considered safe provided there are enough of them. In Sussex, it is the first bunch brought in that is important. If this contains less than thirteen blossoms, the hens and geese will lay only as many eggs as there are flowers. A single primrose carried indoors, or given to any person, is the worst of all, for not only will this make the hens hatch only one egg out of each clutch, but it may also foretell or cause the death of a human member of the family. Untimely blooming is also a death omen, especially if it occurs in winter.

In spite of all this, the primrose has its fortunate characteristics, and was once valued as a protection against witchcraft and the malice of fairies. In the Isle of Man, little bunches used to be laid on the doorsteps of houses and cowbyres on May Eve, a night when witches were thought to be specially powerful, and many strange and evil influences were abroad.

The flowers and leaves of the plant are still used occasionally in country households for medicinal purposes. An infusion of the heads, taken just before going to bed, prevents insomnia. An ointment for chilblains, well known in Hampshire, is made by boiling the flowers with lard till the mixture turns yellow. In the New Forest, the woodmen treat small cuts by covering them immediately with primrose leaves; no further treatment is then considered necessary. A writer in *Notes and Queries* (Vol. VII) states that in Lincolnshire a decoction of the leaves was once given to people suffering from failing memory. In this remedy, which is not common elsewhere, the primrose seems to have taken the place of the more usual cowslip.

PROPHETIC WATERS

Just as certain rivers were formerly believed to demand and take a periodic tribute of human or animal lives, *see Life-demanding Rivers*, so particular streams, springs, pools, and other waters were thought to be endowed with foreknowledge, and to predict the future by their rise or fall, or by the manner in which they flowed.

The Drumming Well at Oundle was one of these. It has now disappeared, but in its day it gave warning of important national changes or misfortune by loud drumming noises in its depths. These were audible for a considerable distance, and sometimes continued for several days together. Baxter records in his *Certainty of the World of Spirits* (1691) how he heard them when he was a schoolboy, just before the Scots came to England during the Civil War. Many years later, he was told by the Oundle carrier, whom he met in London, that the well had drummed again before the death of Charles II.

St Helen's Well at Rushton Spencer in Staffordshire dried up in any weather, however rainy, before a calamity. Tradition says it did so before the outbreak of the Civil War, before the death of Charles I, and again at the beginning of the Popish Plot in 1679. Marvel Sike Spring in Northampton-shire predicted similar disasters by running in great gouts and jerks, which it never did at any other time. In Warksworth's *Chronicle* we read that a certain spring in Langley Park, Kent, dried up before a battle, however wet the season; but, says the chronicler, 'if there be no batayle toward he will be full of watere, but it never so drye a wethere'.

Similar stories were told of numerous other waters, and some are still repeated today. An uncertain stream in Oxfordshire, known as Assenden Spring, traditionally runs before a war. It is said to have done so in 1914, and again in 1939. At North Tawton in Devon, Bathe Pool, which is normally dry, is supposed to fill only before some national calamity. It did so fill in November 1951, and overflowed at the beginning of December, remaining in that state for some weeks, and then reverting to its usual dry condition. Subsequent correspondence in the newspapers showed that many people associated this occurrence with the sudden death of George VI in February, 1952.

Uncertain springs in chalk country, which run occasionally and are dry at other times, are still sometimes called Cornsprings, because they were formerly thought to foretell the price of corn. Another name for them is Levants. When they ran freely, farmers expected a good price for their crops, and poor people feared a rise in the cost of bread. In his *Natural History of Selborne*, Gilbert White remarks that 'the country people say, when the levants do rise, corn will always be dear'. Some other waters also predicted corn-prices by their rise and fall, as Dudley's Spring did at Allesley in Warwickshire, and Barton Mere, near Bury St Edmunds. The latter varied in size from a mere pond to a sheet of water covering several acres. It was supposed to expand to its full width only when corn was going to be excep-tionally dear.

R

RABBIT

Rabbits share many of the superstitions which attach to hares. They must not be mentioned by name at sea, or in any gathering, afloat or ashore, which includes sailors. For a fisherman to meet one on his way to the boats, or a miner on his way to the pit, is very ill-omened. In his *Magic in Modern London* Edward Lovett records how, when two fishing families quarrelled, the members of one secretly nailed a rabbit-skin to the mast of the boat belonging to the other. Every inch of the skin was tacked down, so that the victims had to spend a considerable time in getting it off. This, of course, meant that they wasted valuable hours when they ought to have been out fishing but, for no consideration whatever, would they have put to sea while the skin, or any part of it, was still on board the vessel.

To see or meet a rabbit is sometimes thought unlucky by landsmen also. A variant of this belief is that it is a sign of good luck if the animal crosses one's path in front, and of bad luck if it passes behind.

In some parts of Lancashire and the adjacent counties, it is unwise to shoot a black rabbit. This is because they were once believed to be ancestral spirits returning in that form. In Somerset, white rabbits are said to be witches. That anyone really believes this now is improbable; nevertheless, white rabbits are not popular as children's pets, and they are usually left severely alone, and are not shot.

A luck-bringing custom found all over Great Britain is to say 'Rabbits' or 'White Rabbits' once or three times on the first day of the month. It must be said early in the morning, before any other word has been uttered, otherwise the charm loses its force. In some districts it is considered necessary to say 'Hares' or 'Black Rabbits' when going to bed on the night before, as well as 'Rabbits' or 'White Rabbits' in the morning. If, however, the speaker becomes muddled and says 'Black Rabbits' on rising, bad luck will follow. The looked-for result of all this is variously given as general good luck during the ensuing four weeks, or the receipt of a gift within a few days.

To carry a rabbit's foot about is generally thought to be lucky. In *The Lore and Language of Schoolchildren*, Iona and Peter Opie record that children sitting for an examination often put one in their pockets as an amulet to ensure success. If an actor loses his from his make-up box, he will meet with some misfortune, professional or otherwise. One placed in a perambulator guards the baby from evil while it is out, and in Wales it is said that if a new-born child is brushed all over with such a foot, he will be lucky in life.

A country method of preventing pleurisy and kindred ills is to wear rabbit-skin socks inside the shoes.

In America, the Easter Rabbit has taken the place of the European Easter Hare, and it is he who is supposed to produce the Easter eggs.

RAIN

One of the best known English weather-rhymes runs:

> St Swithun's Day, if thou be fair,
> For forty days 'twill rain nae mair;
> St Swithun's Day, if thou bring rain,
> For forty days it will remain.

Legend says that when St Swithun was dying in A.D. 862, he asked to be buried in the common graveyard, where the rain could fall upon him, and the feet of ordinary men could pass over his head. After his death, he was so buried, but nine years later the monks of Winchester, feeling that so great a saint deserved a better tomb, attempted to move his remains to a more honourable place. The work began on 15 July, but it was not finished then, or for many years afterwards. Fierce rains made it impossible on the first day, and these continued unabated for forty days and nights. In A.D. 963, another attempt was made, and this time with success, but the tradition that St Swithun is a rain-saint was by then firmly established, and still lingers today. Most people scan the skies anxiously on 15 July, hoping for sunshine and fearing to see the rain that foretells forty days of bad weather. In fact, things rarely work out quite like that; but changes in the weather do often occur about the middle of July, and this may have helped to keep the old legend alive.

Prophecies concerning the crops are sometimes read from rainfall, or the lack of it, on particular festivals. Apple-growers hope for rain on St Swithun's Day, or on St Peter's Day (29 June) and say that the saints are watering the orchards then. If they fail to do so, the apple-crop will be a poor one. Easter rain foretells 'plenty of grass and little good hay', and a wet St Paul's Day (25 January) predicts a shortage of corn and consequent high prices. A rather charming tradition about St Mary Magdalen says that if it rains on her feast (22 July), or near it, she is washing her kerchief in readiness for the fair on 25 July, the festival of her cousin, St James the Great.

The belief that cutting or burning fern brought down rain was once very general, *see Ferns*, and in some districts, heather-burning was thought to have the same effect. Various magical methods of inducing badly-needed rain were often used in the past, most of them based on the notion of sympathy. Sprinkling water on stones while reciting certain incantations was one such. Another, well known in Normandy, was to throw flour into a spring, and then stir up the water with a hazel-rod. A mist would arise and condense into a rain-bearing cloud. On Snowdon, if anyone stood on the stepping-stones in Tarn Dulyn and threw water on to the farthest stone, which was known as the Red Altar, he could be sure of rainfall before night, even in the dryest season. On Uist in the Hebrides, a stone cross, called the Water Cross, stood opposite St Mary's Church, and was used to control the weather. It was raised when rain was needed, and lowered again when the need had passed.

In the Middle Ages, images of the saints were often dipped in water during a drought, either as a magical rite, or as a punishment for not answering the prayers of the people. Sir James Frazer mentions in *The Magic Art* a very late survival of this custom in Sicily. In 1893 there was a severe drought in the island. When it had lasted for six months, and all prayers had proved unavailing, the infuriated peasants threw the statues of their local saints into horse-ponds, tore off their splendid garments, insulted them, and finally pushed them into the parched gardens, 'to see for themselves' how serious were the results of their failure to send rain.

Perhaps the last survivals of these rain-controlling charms are the rhymes still used by children to secure fine weather. 'Rain, rain, go to Spain, and never come here again' is a common version, and so is the less optimistic 'Rain, rain, go away, come again another day'. Some variants direct the bad weather to a neighbouring town or district. One, recorded in the *Denham Tracts*, offers the rain-spirit a bribe. It says

> Rain, rain, go away,
> Come again tomorrow day.
> When I brew and when I bake,
> I'll give you a little cake.

Rainwater which falls on Ascension Day was formerly believed to have healing properties, provided that it was caught in some clean vessel as it fell from the heavens. It was useless to collect it if it had lain, even temporarily, on any roof or tree, or had dripped from the eaves. It is stated in *The Worcestershire Book* (a collection of local lore published by the Worcestershire Federation of Women's Institutes in 1932) that as late as 1927, basins were regularly put out at Elmley Castle to catch Ascension Day water. When caught, it was bottled, and was believed to remain pure indefinitely. It could be used for a variety of ailments, and was especially good for weak or sore eyes.

In Lincolnshire, these virtues were ascribed to rain falling at any time in the month of June, without regard to any particular festival. The method of collection was the same as on Ascension Day.

In Wales, babies bathed in rainwater were said to talk earlier than others. Another Welsh superstition was that money which had been washed in such water would never be stolen.

RAINBOW

In Biblical tradition, the rainbow is God's sign in the sky, set there after the Flood as a promise that the world would never again be destroyed by water. Pagan mythologies have seen it as a spirit (in Burma and among the Zulus, as a dangerous demon), or a weapon used by the gods, or as a soul-bridge. In India, and also in Finland, it was the bow from which the thunder-god shot his lightning-arrows. In ancient Scandinavia, it was Bifröst, the bridge that Odin built from Midgard, the home of men, to Asgard, where the gods dwelt. Along it passed the souls of the dead, if they were worthy to do so. If they were not, they were destroyed by a fierce fire which is visible to us here below as the red colour in the bow. Long after the establishment of Christianity, this idea persisted in a German and Austrian legend that souls, especially those of children, passed into Heaven along the rainbow, and were guided across it by their guardian angels.

The soul-bridge tradition has been forgotten in Britain, but shreds of holiness and mystery still cling to the rainbow in folk-belief. It is lucky to see one, and many people wish when they do so. It is very unlucky to point at it. Misfortune of some kind will befall the pointer, and the very least that can happen is that the rain will return. North-country children sometimes 'cross it out' by making a cross of sticks or straws on the ground with a small stone at the end of each stick. This is supposed to make it vanish, though few children can say why they wish to do so. Dim memories of its ancient death-association as a soul-bridge may perhaps lie at the root of this custom.

In Ireland, it is said that if anyone could find the place where the bow ends and touches the ground, he would discover a pot of gold at its foot.

Weather signs are still very commonly read from the time and manner of its appearances. A rainbow in the morning is 'the shepherd's warning' no less than a red sky then, but 'a rainbow at night, the rain is gone quite'. This is often true because, as weather normally travels from west to east, a morning bow shows rain coming up from the west, and an evening one shows that the rain has passed away. The broken parts of rainbows seen on a cloudy sky, sometimes called Wind-dogs or Weather-galls, denote stormy, blustery weather to come.

RATS

Rats, like mice, were anciently associated with the souls of men, and consequently they were regarded as ominous creatures, having foreknowledge of what was to come, and sometimes warning their human neighbours of death or misfortune. Sailors almost everywhere believe that if all the rats suddenly desert a ship just before she sails, that ship is doomed. Although rats are not now as common on board ship as they used to be, the tradition persists, and many stories, some quite modern, are told of vessels. thus abandoned beforehand by their rats which have been lost in storms at sea, or by enemy action during the two wars of the present century. Fishermen in most districts consider it unlucky to mention them by name whilst afloat, and a substitute word is commonly used if it is necessary to speak of them.

Inland also, it is a bad omen if rats leave a house for no apparent reason. Either the building is unsound and likely to fall, or some dire misfortune threatens someone living within. If they gnaw the hangings of a room, there will be a death in the family before long.

Rats and mice appear in several old legends as agents of Divine retribution, or as the souls of murdered persons avenging their own deaths. The best known of these tales is that of Bishop Hatto of Mayence, who is said to have confined many starving people in a barn during a famine in 970, and then to have set fire to the building in order to reduce the number of hungry mouths. He was pursued and finally destroyed by an army of rats. There is no historical evidence for the Bishop's crime, nor for his terrible death, but the story was long believed all over Germany.

It is not the only one of its kind. A Scandinavian legend tells how Earl Asbjorn was attacked and eaten by rats after he had murdered St Knut at Odense in 1086, and there are similar tales in Switzerland and Poland. It is curious to find an echo of this medieval tradition in nineteenth-century Sussex. Charlotte Latham[1] records how a man of notoriously bad character who lived alone was said by his neighbours to be haunted by evil spirits in the form of rats. Her informant said that those who passed his cottage after nightfall could hear him cursing them and begging them to leave him in peace. It was generally believed that one night they would carry him off, as a punishment for his many sins.

Rats seem specially susceptible to certain kinds of music and to magical charms. The most famous rat-charmer was, of course, the Pied Piper of Hamelyn who, in 1284, emptied that town first of its rats and then, by the same magical playing, of its children. He was not, however, the last of his kind, and rat-charmers exist to this day. In a letter published in *Folk-Lore* (Vol. 64, 1953) it is stated that one such practises in a West Cornish town still. He whistles to the rats, which come to him, and he is then able to pick them up and subsequently dispose of them. In another letter to the same journal (Vol. 66, 1955), it is recorded that an Irish farm had been cleared of these pests a few years earlier by a man who thrust pieces of paper bearing Erse incantations into their holes. They all left the farm together and did not return.

A variant of the custom of putting a fallen milk-tooth into a mouse-hole, *see Teeth*, was to place it in a rat-hole, at the same time adjuring the rat to

[1] Charlotte Latham, *op. cit.*

send a better one in return. In this way it was hoped that the child's second teeth would be made sharp and strong like those of a rat.

RAVEN

In Norse mythology the raven was sacred to Odin, who had two attendant birds, Hugin and Munin. These flew every day over the world and saw all that happened there, and at night they returned to tell the god what they had seen. In other mythologies also, the raven acted as a messenger for gods or heroes, and knew more than ordinary birds. In Ireland, the saying 'The raven told it, the grey crow told it' is still applied to news deemed to be true. The Celtic gods were thought to take its form sometimes, and in Wales and Cornwall, it shared with the chough the belief that Arthur dwelt in it. Hunt[1] relates a story about a man who shot at a raven on Marazion Green. An old man standing nearby at once reproved him, saying he should not have done so, 'for that King Arthur was still alive in the form of that bird'.

Perhaps because it is a carrion-eater, the raven has always been associated with death, battle, and destruction. It is also connected in folk-tradition with storm and flood. The fact that it was held sacred by the marauding Norsemen in the ninth and tenth centuries, and appeared on their banners, may have helped to confirm it as a bird of doom in the minds of Englishmen. Certainly, it was for centuries considered ominous of misfortune and death, and these traditions still linger in the districts where the birds, rarer now than they once were, are yet to be found.

Thus, to hear one croaking on the left is a very bad sign, especially if it happens early in the morning. If it croaks near a house where a sick person lies, that person will die. In Scotland, if it does so just as the fishing fleet leaves harbour, the voyage will be unlucky. To see two together is an evil omen, to see three is far worse. In *The Jew of Malta*, Marlowe mentions a contemporary belief that the bird carried contagion on its wings, and shed disease on places formerly free from it.

On the other hand, like most creatures that were once sacred, ravens had their fortunate side. Elijah was fed by them in the wilderness, and so was Paul the Hermit. In the *Denham Tracts* we read that the fortune of Sir John Duck, a rich burgher of Durham in the seventeenth century, was founded by a piece of silver dropped at his feet by a raven, though whether the bird did this on purpose or by accident is not clear. Highland deer-stalkers think it lucky to hear one croaking when they set out, and in many places it is fortunate to meet one by itself, though very much the reverse to meet two or three together. In Wales, a blind person who is kind to a raven will regain his sight. This seems to be connected with the widespread belief that these birds peck out the eyes of their victims. Because they eat eyes, it is argued,

[1] R. Hunt, *Popular Romances of the West of England*, 1881.

they acquire keen sight, and with it, the magical power of curing blindness in those who are their friends.

One of the most interesting surviving superstitions concerns the tame birds kept at the Tower of London. This is that if these birds are ever lost, or fly away, the Crown will fall, and Britain with it. This belief may not be very old, as age runs with such traditions, but it is not the first that connects ravens with that part of London. In the *Mabinogion* we are told that on the death of Bran the Blessed (who in some legends is a Celtic god, in others a virtuous king), his head was cut off and buried on Tower Hill with the face towards France. So long as it remained there, Britain would be safe from invasion. The name Bran means raven.

RED-HOT POKER

If the brilliant red or yellow flower known as the Red-Hot Poker, or Torch Lily, blooms twice in one year, it is an omen of death for someone in the family of the garden's owner.

REHEARSAL

Professional actors consider it a bad sign if a rehearsal is quite perfect. The play will go badly when it is produced, or will have only a short run. Similarly, it is very unlucky to speak the tag, or last line, during rehearsals. This, which completes the play, must not be spoken until the first night.

ROBINS

It is extremely unlucky to harm or kill a robin, to steal or break its eggs, or to injure its nest. The consequences of such actions vary in different districts, but they are all bad. Whoever robs a nest will not thrive thereafter, or he will fall into the power of witches or the Devil. If he breaks the eggs, something valuable of his own will be broken soon after; if he breaks the bird's wing or leg, he will break his own arm or leg. To kill a robin deliberately is so great a crime that no one who does it can expect good fortune afterwards. His cows will give bloody milk, or his house and barns will catch fire. His hand will shake perpetually or, in Ireland, a swelling will appear on it so that he can neither work nor play. Even cats will lose a limb if they kill and eat a robin; but cats usually have more sense, and very rarely do so.

Robins are, in fact, fairly safe all over Britain, for they are among the best loved and respected of our native birds. Even schoolboys leave them alone as a rule. In his *Folk-Speech of East Yorkshire* (1889), Nicholson records how, when a boy had robbed a robin's nest, his companions gathered round him, hissing and pointing with their fingers, and chanting over and over again,

Robin takker, robin takker,
Sin, sin, sin!

after which they often attacked him with their caps and knotted handker-
chiefs until he was forced to fly.

Various legends are told to account for the bird's red breast. One is that
on the first Good Friday, it tried to draw a thorn from the Crown of Thorns
and was stained by Christ's blood. Another says it scorched its feathers in the
flames of Purgatory when carrying water to the suffering souls there. A third
tale is that when the wren flew to Hell to fetch fire for mankind, it returned
with all its feathers blazing, and was saved by the robin who came to its aid
and was thus scorched itself. Guernsey people say the robin itself was a fire-
fetcher, and that there was no fire on that island until the bird brought it
there.

The well-known story of *The Babes in the Wood* enshrines another belief
concerning the robin's helpfulness to mankind. The old ballad relates that,
after the death of the children,

> No burial this pretty pair
> From any man receives,
> Till robin redbreast piously
> Did cover them with leaves.

In the north-midland counties, the bird is said to have rendered the same
service to Our Lord, covering His body with leaves, and dyeing its breast
feathers with His blood as it moved about Him. Lupton remarks in his
Notable Things that 'A Robbyn read breast, fynding the dead body of a man
or woman wyll cover the face of the same with Mosse. And as some holdes
opinion, he will cover also the whole body.' In Brittany, there is a tradition
that the bird sings sorrowfully beside a corpse until it is buried.

Beloved as it is, the robin is often feared as a death omen. One entering a
house or tapping at a window foretells a death in that house before long. If
anyone is already ill there, he will not recover. In Gloucestershire and
Oxfordshire, this omen is sometimes said to be true only for eleven months
of the year. If a robin comes indoors in November, it is a sign of good luck.
No satisfactory reason for this distinction has so far been given, but it is
possible that it may have something to do with the fact that November is the
traditional month of the dead.

It is also a death omen if a robin flies into a church and sings there. One of
the parishioners will die soon. In a footnote to Henderson's *Folk-Lore of the
Northern Counties*, Sabine Baring-Gould records how, being one evening in
the chapel of St John's College at Hurstpierpoint, he saw a robin come
through the open east window, alight on the altar and begin to chirp. 'A few

minutes later,' he adds, 'the passing bell began to toll for a boy who had just died.'

In Wales, if a robin sings on the threshold of a house, illness or death will follow, and its presence in or near a mine foretells a disaster below. In the *South Wales Weekly News* of 14 September 1901, it is stated that after an explosion in the pit at Llanbradach, several colliers blamed the disaster on to a robin which, some days before, had been found to have nested in the pump-house.

In Oxfordshire, a robin singing near the house means bad news, and one perching on a chair when someone is sitting in it foretells that person's death within the year. A curious extension of these ancient fears was recorded near Lechlade in 1950, where it was said that to receive a Christmas card with a robin on it was a sign of death or misfortune within the year. This superstition cannot be very old, for such cards were not invented until the middle of the nineteenth century, and it does not seem to have been found elsewhere. Certainly the designers of our Christmas cards do not appear to have heard of it.

ROOKS

Rooks, which dwell in colonies that are often quite close to houses, are usually considered friendly to man, and are rarely thought unlucky, except when they are confused with crows. But if they suddenly forsake the rookery, it is a sign of very bad luck for the owner or the tenant of the land on which the trees stand. In the case of inherited property, it is thought to foretell the loss of the estate and the downfall of the family, either through poverty or other misfortune, or from lack of heirs.

In Oxfordshire, the sudden desertion of an elm-tree by these birds denotes that the tree is unsound and will soon be blown down.

Rooks, like bees, were formerly told of a death in the family, especially that of the master. The new owner stood under the trees to convey the news, and usually added a promise that only he and his friends would be allowed to shoot them in future. If this was not done, it was thought they would leave the rookery. This custom is still observed in some families, though not as often as the companion custom of telling the bees.

In rural areas, rooks are regarded as weather-prophets. If they build high when nesting, the following summer will be fine, if low, it will be wet and cold. When they perch close together on a high tree, facing the wind, bad weather is coming. When they hurtle wildly downwards or, in country parlance, 'break their necks', strong gales or storms will follow.

ROSE

The rose is a symbol of love almost everywhere, and was once much used in love-charms and divinations. To dream of roses is fortunate, foretelling success in love, though according to one version, this is only true if the roses are red. To dream of white ones is as unlucky as to dream of any other white flowers.

If a girl desired to know whom she would marry, she plucked a rosebud on Midsummer Day, wrapped it in white paper, and put it away in some secret place until Christmas Day. It would then be found as fresh and sweet as ever, and if she wore it to church, the man destined to be her husband would come and take it from her. If, however, the rosebud had faded and turned brown, the charm failed, and the omen was very bad.

An errant lover could be recalled by a complicated rite involving three roses gathered on Midsummer Eve, one of which had to be buried in the small hours of Midsummer morning under a yew-tree, another in a newly-made grave, and the third laid under the girl's pillow. If she left it there for three nights and then burnt it, she would haunt her lover's dreams, and he would know no peace until he returned to her.

Roses, especially white ones, are emblems of silence, being the flowers of Harpocrates, God of Silence. This is the origin of the phrase 'under the rose', used in reference to things said that must not be repeated. In antiquity chaplets of roses are said to have been worn by those who desired to talk freely, without fear of having their words retold elsewhere, and in old Germany, a rose was often painted or carved on the roof of the banqueting-hall or council-chamber for the same reason. This latter custom was not, apparently, confined to Germany, for Peacham tells us in his *Truths o' our Times* (1638) that 'in many places, as well in England as in the Low Countries, they have over their tables a rose painted, and what is spoken under the rose must not be revealed'. He goes on to explain that 'The reason is this: the rose being sacred to Venus, whose amorous and stolen sports, that they might never be revealed, her sonne Cupid would neede dedicate it to Harpocrates, the God of Silence'.

According to an ancient and widespread tradition, the first roses were all white, but some turned red when they were stained by blood. Whose blood varies with the beliefs of the country where the tale is told. In ancient Greece, it was that of Adonis, wounded by a wild boar, or of Aphrodite, whose foot was pierced by a rose-briar as she ran to help him. For Moslems, it was the blood of Mahommed. An old Christian legend says that the Crown of Thorns was made from rose-briars, and that when Our Lord's blood fell from His forehead to the ground, red roses sprang up at the foot of the Cross.

The rose is dedicated in Christian thought to Our Lady, and is a symbol of virginity. In Wales formerly, a white rose was often planted on the grave of a virgin, and a red one on that of any person distinguished for his or her good-ness and kindness. Aubrey refers to the custom of planting red roses on the graves of dead sweethearts, and he tells us in his *Antiquities of Surrey* that in the churchyard at Ockley 'are many red rose-trees planted among the graves, which have been there beyond man's memory. The sweetheart (male or female) plants roses at the head of the grave of the lover deceased; a maid that lost her dear twenty years since, yearly hath the grave new turf'd, and continues yet unmarried.' There are legends of star-crossed lovers, dead untimely and buried near each other, upon whose graves rose-briars (and sometimes other trees) have sprung up and, growing towards each other, have become entwined, in proof of the undying fidelity of those who lay beneath them.

It is exceedingly unlucky to scatter the petals of a rose worn upon the person or carried in the hand. This does not, of course, apply to rose-leaves ceremonially scattered on the ground, or over a grave. Roses, like other flowers, are ill-omened if they bloom out of season. In Worcestershire, if leaves appear among the petals of a red rose, it is an omen of death for someone in the family of the tree's owner.

ROSEMARY

Many legends are told of rosemary, which was at once a holy and a magical plant in popular tradition. Its flowers are said to have been white originally, but when, during the Flight into Egypt, the Virgin Mary spread the Christ-Child's linen to dry on a rosemary bush, they turned blue and have remained so ever since. Another tradition says that the plant grows for thirty-three years, until it is as tall as Our Lord was when He was crucified. After that it broadens, but no longer grows upwards. In some districts, it is supposed to bloom at midnight on Old Christmas Eve, a proof of holiness which it shares with the Glastonbury Thorn and its cuttings, and also, according to one legend, with the blackthorn.

It is variously said to grow well only for the righteous, or for a woman who rules her husband as well as her houshold. It flourishes most strongly within sound of the ocean, whence comes its name, *Ros Marinus*, dew of the sea. It is a symbol of fidelity in love, and also of remembrance, and consequently it was formerly used both at weddings and funerals. Seventeenth-century brides wove its flowers and leaves into their bridal wreaths, and gilded branches were carried before them in the procession by the brides-maids and groomsmen. Before the newly-married pair drank at the wedding feast, sprigs of rosemary were dipped into the wine, as a charm to ensure their happiness and the continuance of love between them. At funerals, until fairly recently, the mourners often carried small pieces of the plant to the graveside. As the coffin was lowered into the earth, these were dropped upon it, as a token that the dead person would not be quickly forgotten.

Its magical and healing powers were many and various. Those who wore it were protected against evil spirits, witches and fairies, against thunder and lightning, and the danger of assault and physical injury. It was used in charms to secure success in enterprises or to renew youth, and also in love-charms and divination. If a girl put a sprig and a silver sixpence under her pillow on All Hallows' Eve, she would see her future husband in a dream. If she set a plate of flour under a rosemary bush on Midsummer Eve, she would find his initials traced in the flour next morning. A curious old tradition said that if a thief could somehow be induced, by persuasion or trickery, to wash his feet in wine vinegar in which a rosemary root had been seethed, he would never again have the power or strength to steal.

In the seventeenth century, rosemary was thought to be good against the plague, and was sold for this reason during epidemics. In the *Book of the Physicians of Myddvai* we read that it was useful for the treatment of numerous ills, including insanity, anxiety of mind, bad dreams, nausea, and 'any other noxious condition'. In the same book it is stated that those who drink their broth from a spoon made of the wood need have no fear of poison. Bancke's *Herball* (1525) says that the pains of gout could be eased by boiling the leaves and tying them, wrapped in linen, round the afflicted members, and also that teeth could be preserved from various evils by rubbing the burnt and powdered wood upon them. The plant was widely used in hair-lotions at one time, because it was supposed to make hair grow vigorously, and in France, giddiness was prevented by daily combing of the hair with a comb made of the wood. Country people in England still make rosemary teas or decoctions occasionally to cure coughs and colds, and also to strengthen weak hearts and failing memory.

ROUGH MUSIC

Rough Music is one of the many names given to a form of communal punishment for individual offences, especially those of a sexual nature, which was practised in towns and villages from a very early period down to quite recent times. This punishment took various forms, and was known in different districts as Riding the Stang, Riding Skimmerton, Low-belling, Shallal, Stag- or Hare-hunting, or simply as a Riding. The term Rough Music, though often used to cover any of these different forms, really applied to the appalling noise made during the proceedings. The origin of the custom lies far back in time, when primitive peoples believed that any sexual crime could blight the crops and bring famine or disaster upon the whole tribe. Because of this belief, offences which for us are mainly private were considered public crimes, for the prevention or punishment of which drastic action had to be taken by all concerned.

In its later manifestations, this punishment usually took the form of a noisy procession by night, during which all the men and boys of the parish beat upon kettles, frying-pans and iron pots, blew horns and whistles, and generally made as much raucous din as possible. Originally, no doubt, this noise was intended not only to signify disapproval but also, perhaps primarily, to drive away the demons of ill-luck and evil that had been evoked by the offence. Every so often, a halt was called, and the leader recited a doggerel rhyme, setting forth the name and crimes of the culprit. Any breach of the local moral code might be included, but normally Rough Music was made in cases of adultery, incest, wife- or husband-beating, marriage with a woman known to be immoral, or the too blatant domination of a husband by a wife. It was also made in some places for the re-marriage of widows or widowers, and sometimes for dishonesty in trade, or black-legging in a strike. Unpopularity for any reason might be enough to provoke such a demonstration, and it cannot be doubted that in many instances spite, malice, and simple love of a row played a large part.

Frequently, effigies of the offenders, made as life-like as possible, were carried on a pole, or in a cart drawn by donkeys and these were burnt at the end of the Riding, sometimes outside the victim's door, sometimes at the church, or in some nearby open space. In earlier times, doubtless, the offender himself would have been ridden round on a pole or cart instead of an image. As late as 1887, the *Liverpool Mercury* (15 March 1887) reported the case of a man accused of adultery who was thus carried by an angry crowd at Langefni, and had to be rescued by the police. Occasionally the demonstrators visited some house other than that of the victim, and either swept the doorstep, or strewed chaff upon it. This was a hint to those within that their conduct was disapproved of, and that the next Riding might be for them if they did not mend their ways.

When Rough Music had been made for anyone, that person rarely regained the good opinion of his neighbours, and very often he was forced to leave the district. Yet the custom was extremely difficult to stop. In a footnote to *Red Spider*, Baring-Gould relates how he once saw a notice of a Stag-hunt pasted up for all to see at a Devonshire crossroads. He tore it down and appealed to the police, but they could not, or would not, do anything because, as yet, no breach of the peace had been committed. Hamilton Jenkin records in *Cornwall and the Cornish* how, about 1880, six men of Stockeclimsland were prosecuted for causing an obstruction by a 'Mock Hunt', but their lawyer pleaded ancient custom, and only small fines were imposed.

It was a common belief that Rough Music was quite legal provided that it was made on three successive nights, and that the procession either circuited the church, or crossed the boundaries of three parishes. In one Oxfordshire case in the late nineteenth century, the demonstrators made a wide circle outwards from the home village, so as to cover a short distance in each of two adjacent parishes as well as their own. That they had done so was afterwards triumphantly pointed out as proof that nothing in their avenging ceremony was contrary to law, nor had they in any way exceeded what they believed to be their ancient and inalienable right to express their anger in this way.

Rough Music is fortunately less often heard in the twentieth century than in the nineteenth, or earlier, but it would be unwise to assume that it has ceased for ever. Old ideas die hard, and there is always someone in a parish who remembers how the ancient ceremony should be carried out. In 1930 Rough Music was made for a woman accused of immorality in a village close to Oxford, and even this late example is not the last recorded case. A writer in *Folklore* (Vol. 69, 1958)[1] states that about seven years earlier, that is, about 1951, there was a similar demonstration in a parish on the Surrey-Sussex borders where she was then living. A little boy hit a neighbour's little girl with a brick, and was promptly smacked by the latter's father. Soon afterwards, he developed pneumonia, and his mother claimed that the illness was due to the smacking. She took the matter to court where, not very surprisingly, the case was dismissed.

Unable to obtain any satisfaction from the Law, the villagers took their own revenge by making Rough Music for the unfortunate man and his family. There were no effigies in this instance, but every Saturday night for several weeks the traditional procession wound its way round the parish, with all the customary shouting, accusations, beating on pans, and other noises. The unfortunate family bore the demonstrations, and the subsequent general enmity, as long as they could; but in the end it was too much for them, and they were forced to sell their house and leave the district.

ROWAN

The rowan, or mountain ash, is a fortunate tree wherever it grows. It is known in some districts as the wicken-tree, or the witch-tree, and almost everywhere it is, or was, credited with the power of averting witchcraft, fairies, disease, and the Evil Eye.

In Scotland, its wood was often used to make the crossbeam of the chimney, as well as parts of agricultural implements and the tackle of water-mills. On Quarter Days, a wand was laid over the lintels of the house as an extra protection, and at one time, two crossed twigs tied with red thread were frequently hung over the doorways of cow-byres and stables. 'Rowan tree and red threid gar the witches tyne their speed' is a well-known Scottish saying. A necklace made from the scarlet berries protected the wearer from magical perils of all kinds, and the same berries given to mares and other animals helped them to drop their young easily and without mishap.

In the Isle of Man, rowan crosses made without the use of a knife were fastened to the tails of cattle on May Eve, that night of special danger from fairies and evil spirits. In Yorkshire, there was a saying that 'if your whip-stock's made of rowan, you may ride your nag through any town'. Carters and riders in many areas used such whips, or wore sprigs of rowan in their

[1] S. O. Woolley, 'Rough Music in Sussex', *Folklore*, Vol. 69. 1958.

hats, in order to prevent witches bespelling their horses and either making them restive and unmanageable, or keeping them standing in one place, sometimes for hours. In Lincolnshire, small twigs were often thrust into the roof-thatch, or into haystacks, to protect them from fire.

If a churn-staff was made of rowan, witches could not stop the butter from 'coming', nor could they harm a child lying in a cradle with rowan-wood rockers. The same wood was used for stakes and binders, the pins of ploughs, and the pegs of the tethers with which cows were shackled. If, when a pig was first put to fatten, a rowan-garland was hung round its neck, it would be sure to thrive. Similarly, a small sprig carried about by any human being was a certain charm against enchantment, bad luck, and the onset of rheumatism.

Rowan-tree Day is a name given in some areas to 3 May, or Holy Rood Day, the feast of the Invention of the Holy Cross. On that day (or sometimes on 13 May, Old Holy Rood Day), branches and sprigs of rowan were ceremonially brought in to safeguard the house and farm buildings during the following twelve months. In his *Forty Years in a Moorland Parish*, the Reverend J. C. Atkinson describes the custom as it was in Cleveland during his time there. It was necessary to find a tree which the seeker had never seen before, and of whose existence he or she had previously been unaware. This often involved a lengthy search, which grew longer and more difficult with every year that passed. When found, the twigs and branches had to be cut with a household knife, and then brought home by a route other than that which had been followed on the outward journey. Many pieces were needed, for not only had they to be hung over the doors of the house, stable, cow-byres and other places where stock was kept, but also over the bedhead and in the houseplace, while others were required to carry in the pocket or the purse. But no one doubted that it was worth the trouble involved, for in this way the house and outbuildings, with their inhabitants, human and otherwise, were preserved from evil until next Rowan-tree Day came round.

It is still often thought lucky to have a rowan growing near the house, and unwise to cut one down unless it is absolutely necessary. If such a tree suddenly withers without obvious cause the omen is bad. It is sometimes said that rowans, more than any other tree, flourish near ancient stone circles and old burial places, and that the Druids used their wood and berries in their magical arts.

ROYAL STORMS. *See Storms.*

RUE

Rue symbolizes sorrow and repentance, but its associations in folk-tradition are not all sorrowful. It could be used to bless or to curse, to heal or to harm.

It was believed to protect those who wore it against evil spells, but equally, it could be used in such spells and, being the plant of sorrow, it was a handy agent for a curse. Mrs Leather[1] cites an instance of such use of the plant which occurred only a few years before she wrote in 1912. A girl was jilted by her lover in favour of another young woman. On the day of the man's marriage, she waited for him in the church porch and threw a handful of rue at him as he came out, saying 'May you rue this day as long as you live'. The local people said this curse would certainly be fulfilled because the rue had been taken straight from the place where it grew to the church, and had been thrown 'between holy and unholy ground', that is, between the church and the churchyard. Had the girl been unable to obtain the right herb, rue-fern would have done as well, provided she had plucked it from a plant growing on the churchyard wall.

Rue could be used to cure a variety of ills, but according to one country tradition, it could only be safely employed medicinally if it was gathered in the morning. It was then Herb of Grace, or Herby-grass, and was beneficial, but once noon was passed, it turned into real rue and was poisonous. A variant of this belief was that it was Herb of Grace on Sundays and rue all the rest of the week. Why it should be so called is not clear, unless it is because of its association with repentance, a state of mind for which Divine grace is needed. Another suggested explanation is that the name comes from the fact that holy water was often sprinkled with a bunch of rue, both in church services, and during exorcisms.

In antiquity, the chief virtues of rue were that it strengthened the sight and was an antidote to poison. Pliny tells us that engravers, carvers and painters ate it to preserve their eyesight. It counteracted the effect of poisons that had been inadvertently swallowed, and it was also thought an efficient remedy for bites of serpents and venomous beasts of all sorts. Apparently, even weasels knew this, for Gerard tells us in his *Herbal* that when a weasel fought a snake, 'she armeth hir selfe by the eating of Rue, against the might of the serpent'.

In the days before Pasteur made his great discoveries, rue-leaves were sometimes used in semi-magical remedies for hydrophobia caused by the bites of mad dogs. An interesting cure of this kind is mentioned by a writer in *Notes and Queries* (Series 10, Vol. II), who found it in a manuscript book dated 1752. It consists of a compound of bruised rue-leaves, garlic, Venice treacle, and pewter scrapings, boiled all together in strong ale. Nine spoonfuls had to be given to a bitten man or woman for seven successive mornings while the patient was still fasting, and six to a bitten dog. For greater safety, some of the ingredients (of which the rue-leaves would probably be the easiest to handle) had to be applied, after the liquor had been strained off, to the bitten place. A note in the manuscript book states that the receipt was 'taken out of

[1] E. M. Leather, *op. cit.*

Cathorpe Church in Lincolnshire, the whole Town being bitten with a Mad Dog, all those who took the medicine did well, the Rest died mad'.

A country remedy for fits or convulsions was to drink rue-tea. Another was to tie the leaves round the patient's hands, wrists and ankles. In the *Book of the Physicians of Myddvai*, those who fear to talk in their sleep are advised to take a concoction of the pounded seeds or leaves, vinegar, and old ale before going to bed. Thereafter they will slumber in safe silence. The leaves averted infection if strewn about the floor and window-sills of a house, and they were widely used for this purpose during the plague epidemics of the sixteenth and seventeenth centuries. Assize Judges carried posies containing rue to save them from catching gaol-fever from the wretched prisoners, and they still do so today, although this disease has now happily disappeared from our prisons.

Two other traditions about rue may be mentioned. One is that it grows best if the plant has been stolen. The other is that toads detest it, and that when sage is set in a garden, it is wise to plant rue round it, to keep away the toads who might otherwise poison it with their venom.

RUSHES

An Irish legend says that rushes go brown and die from the top downwards because St Patrick cursed them. Nevertheless, they have luck-bringing and protective powers. It is still a custom in some parts of Ireland to gather them on St Bride's Eve (31 January), without the aid of any iron cutting instrument, and make them into small crosses, known as St Bride's Crosses. These are blessed in the church, and are then set over the doors of houses and cow-byres, in the thatch of roofs, and over beds, to bring good fortune and protection from evil to men and beasts alike.

It is lucky to find a green-topped rush. There is an old rhyme which says:

> With a four-leaved Clover, a double-leaved Ash,
> And a green-topped Seave,
> You may go before the Queen's daughter
> Without asking leave.

A Devonshire charm to cure thrush consisted in taking three rushes from a running stream, drawing each one separately through the child's mouth, and then throwing them back into the water so that they, and the ailment with them, might be carried away by the current. In Somerset, an ulcerated mouth was treated by passing a peeled rush very gently, three or four times, between the lips. A Cheshire method of healing warts was to tie three knots in a long straight rush, make it into a ring, and draw it nine times downwards over the warts. A form of words had to be repeated at the same time, but what this was could not be revealed, for if it was not kept secret, the charm would not work. If all was done in order, the warts would vanish within three months.

S

SACRAMENT MONEY

Sacrament Money was the name given to money offered at Holy Communion. It was once very generally believed to acquire curative powers by its association with the sacred rite, and was used to heal ailments of various kinds, particularly epilepsy and rheumatism. Twelve or thirty pennies were collected by the patient, or one of his friends, and presented to the parish clergyman in exchange for a shilling or half a crown from the Communion offertory. The coin so obtained was then made into a ring, or a hole was bored in it so that it could be worn round the neck on a ribbon.

The ritual associated with this half-religious, half-magical cure was often quite elaborate. In the neighbourhood of Whitby, the patient begged thirty pence from thirty poor widows and, having exchanged these for a half-crown piece, carried the latter nine times up and down the church aisle. Thereafter, it was worn round the neck to prevent epilepsy or other fits. Elsewhere, the place of the widows was supplied by twelve or thirty young people of opposite sex to the sufferer, all unmarried. In some districts, the healing coin was carried three times round the Communion Table (a part of the rite of which the clergyman must surely have been unaware) instead of up and down the aisle. In others, the 'walking' ceremony was omitted altogether, and the coin was taken at once to the blacksmith who hammered it into a ring, or bored a hole in it, usually without charging for this service. J. E. Vaux[1] records that at West Bromwich, about the end of last century, rheumatism was cured by rubbing a Sacrament shilling directly on the affected part.

What seems to be a broken-down version of this tradition is recorded in *The New Suffolk Garland* as a cure for hysteria or epilepsy. A collection was made from a dozen unmarried people (young men, if the patient was a woman, girls in the case of a man) who were each asked to give a penny and a small piece of silver of any kind. A sixpence or a threepenny bit was sometimes given, but broken bits of brooches, spoons, or buckles would do, always provided that they were real silver. Those who gave them were not told for what purpose they were required, though it can hardly be supposed that they did not know. The silver oddments were then taken to a smith, who made them into a ring to be worn on the patient's left hand, and received

[1] J. E. Vaux, *op. cit.*

the twelve pennies as his fee. If any silver was left over, he was allowed to keep this for himself, but he could not be directly paid any more than the twelve given pence.

In this custom, the main point of the cure seems to have been lost. It is true that silver in itself is traditionally supposed to have magical virtues, but evidently the rite described above was once connected with Sacrament money which gained its healing powers, not from the material of which it was made, but from the sacred use to which it had been dedicated. This power, presumably, would be absent from the Suffolk charm, since the metal used was not associated with any church service.

SAGE

There is a country tradition that just as rosemary grows best for the righteous, so sage grows best for the wise. Another belief is that it will flourish most strongly if it is planted by a woman who rules her household firmly, and her husband as well. In consequence, its vigorous growth in a married couple's garden is sometimes regarded as a sign that the wife is the dominant partner. In the manuscript collection of the Oxfordshire Folklore Society, it is recorded that in 1948 a man living in the north of the county chopped down a fine sage bush because, as he explained, it was doing too well, and he did not want the neighbours to think that he was not master in his own house.

In some areas, wild sage is believed to have been brought to this country by the Romans and dropped by them as they marched across Britain. Where it grows freely, especially along the sides of roads or lanes, there the Roman legions are thought to have passed long ago.

Sage-leaves were formerly used in marriage-divination, and in remedies for numerous ills. A charm to enable a young person to see his or her future mate, either in bodily form or as a vision, required the charmer to pluck twelve leaves at midnight on Midsummer Eve, or on St Mark's Eve, pulling one for each note of the striking clock and taking care not to break any. The destined wife or husband would then be seen coming up behind. In some districts, this rite could be equally well performed at noon on St Mark's Day. There is a well-known story about a maidservant who did this at the suggestion of her mistress. When asked by the latter if the charm had worked, she innocently replied that it had not, for she had seen no one at all, only her master coming up to the door. It had worked, however, for a few weeks later her mistress died, and the widower married the servant within the year.

Sage was once highly valued for its medicinal virtues, and especially as a means of obtaining long life. 'He that would live for aye must eat sage in May', says an old proverb, meaning that the plant should be eaten, regularly every year, just before it blooms, when its life-lengthening powers are strongest. It was also used to strengthen the sight, restore failing memory, and to heal throat-troubles, the after-effects of wounds, and the ailment known as St Anthony's Fire. A semi-magical remedy for ague involved the eating of seven sage-leaves before breakfast on seven successive mornings or, according to another version, two leaves on nine successive mornings. Country people still pluck a sage-leaf occasionally and rub their teeth with it, probably without knowing that this was an accepted method of whitening and cleaning teeth before the introduction of tooth-powders.

Sage, like rosemary, was sometimes strewn on graves as a sign that the dead man would be long remembered by those left behind. This was because the plant lives a long time after being picked, and is therefore a symbol of endurance. The fact that, medicinally, it was used to strengthen the memory may also have had something to do with it.

SAILOR'S COLLAR

It is lucky to touch a sailor's collar, especially if it can be done without his knowledge. This belief is more often found in inland towns, where sailors in uniform are comparatively rare, than in ports; but that it is still very common in most parts of Britain, any seaman on leave can testify from his own experience.

ST AGNES'S FAST. *See Dumb Cake.*

ST ELMO'S FIRE

St Elmo's Fire is the name commonly given by seafarers to the bright glowing light, caused by electrical discharge during storms, which often appears on the masts and yards of ships. It can also be seen round aeroplanes flying through chargèd clouds, and sometimes in mountainous country when thunder-storms are passing over high peaks. Its appearance is always startling at first sight, for the objects touched by it seem to be enveloped in spectral fire, and this phenomenon is frequently accompanied by a crackling noise, like the sound of twigs or dry grasses burning. It is not very surprising, therefore, that St Elmo's Fire has been regarded with superstitious awe by sailors and travellers from time immemorial.

Legend connects it with St Elmo (or Erasmus), the patron saint of Mediterranean seamen, who is said to have died at sea during a severe storm. In his last moments he promised the crew he would return and show himself to them in some form, if they were destined to survive the storm. Soon after his death, a strange light appeared at the masthead, and this was assumed to be the saint himself, or fire sent by him in fulfilment of his promise.

He was not, however, the first holy individual to be associated in tradition with this discharge, which has had many names, and has been attributed at various times to several gods or saints. The pagan Greeks and Romans believed the lights were manifestations of the Divine Twins, Castor and Pollux, and they called them Helen, after the sister of these gods. Pliny tells us that voyagers in his day thought it a good omen if the glow was double, for then the ship was clearly under the protection of the Twins; if it was single, the portent was bad and foretold shipwreck. Christian Greeks, by an easy transition, called it St Helena's Fire, after the empress who travelled to the Holy Land in search of the True Cross. In Spain and Portugal, it was known as *Corpus Santo*, meaning the body of St Elmo, a name which was sometimes rendered by English sailors as 'corposant', or 'composite'.

Because the light usually appears when the worst of the storm is over, sailors have almost always welcomed it and considered it a fortunate sign. Christopher Columbus is said to have cheered his disgruntled crew on the voyage to America by pointing to the holy fire at the masthead and predicting an early end to their perils. Yet St Elmo's Fire could be extremely ill-omened in certain circumstances. In the days of sail, it was thought lucky if it remained high up among the masts, but very unlucky if it came down on the deck. Some seamen believed it to be the ghost of a drowned comrade, returning to warn the living of shipwreck or disaster. It was dangerous to go too near it, or to attempt to touch it, and if (as has been known to happen) it shone like a halo round a man's head, that man's speedy death was certain.

ST JOHN'S WORT

St John's Wort, which looks like a little sun and blooms round about Midsummer Day, was a magical plant in almost every country where it was known. It was once called *Fuga Daemonum* because it drove away evil spirits and prevented ghosts from haunting or entering a house. It was used in love charms and to induce fertility in women, to defeat witches and fairies, and to protect dwelling-houses from fire and lightning. The red spots on its leaves symbolized the blood of St John the Baptist, and were supposed to appear every year on 27 August, the anniversary of the day on which he was beheaded.

Although, like most yellow flowers, it always had magical properties, it was at Midsummer that its powers were greatest. It had to be gathered ceremonially on St John's Eve, very early in the morning before the dew was off it, and while the gatherer was still fasting. If a young girl did this, she could be certain of marriage within the year, and if she slept with it under her pillow that night, she would see in a dream the man she was to marry. If a childless wife walked naked in her garden and picked the flower, she would have a child before next Midsummer came round. Similarly, anyone afflicted by evil spirits had only to gather it then to be cured of his trouble.

In folk-medicine, it was used to cure melancholy, delusions, and nervous disorders, and also as a pain-killer.

Since magic always worked both ways, witches could, and did, employ it in their spells, but usually it was considered to be more dangerous to them than helpful. An old rhyme says:

> Trefoil, vervain, john's wort, dill,
> Hinder witches of their will,

and of this quartette, the golden 'Herbe Jon' was generally considered to be the most powerful.

In some areas, it was held to be perilous to step on St John's wort when it was growing. If anyone did so, a fairy horse would rise under him and carry him away. He would be forced to ride wildly about all through the night, and in the morning the horse would vanish, leaving the exhausted rider stranded wherever he might happen to be, often miles from home. Another tradition said it was difficult to gather the plant at the proper season because it sought to escape, and moved about from place to place, to avoid the seeker.

In many parts of Britain, St John's wort is still considered a lucky plant, though its traditional importance has waned with the decline of the great Midsummer festival. Although it often came first in popular estimations formerly, it was not the only herb used in charms and divinations at the Summer Solstice. St John had many plants in his care, including fennel, bracken, male fern, orpine, ivy, plantain, daisy, vervain, corn marigold, mugwort, and yarrow. Stow tells us in his *Survey of London* that houses in that city were commonly decorated on Midsummer Eve with lilies, birch, fennel, orpine and, of course, St John's wort itself. All these plants had magical properties of one kind or another, and were doubly powerful at this season. In addition, flowers gathered then were said to last a very long time, and the seeds to thrive better than others.

SALT

Salt has many meanings. It is incorruptible itself, and preserves other things from decay, and hence it is an emblem of eternity and immortal life. It typifies wisdom and friendship. It was included in pagan sacrificial rites, and also in those of the Jews, and from time immemorial it has been used as a protection against all the forces of evil.

To eat another man's salt is to establish a mystical bond between host and guest which neither can afterwards ignore with safety. The First Foot in Scotland and northern England often brings salt with him, signifying prosperity, *see First Foot*, and it is still quite usual in many districts to put a pinch of salt and one of sugar into a baby's mouth when he first visits another house, or to include a little among the first gifts made to him. *See Child's First Days*. On the other hand, to help anyone to salt is to 'help him to sorrow', and a witch's spell to make fruitful land barren was to curse it and sprinkle it with salt.

Addy[1] records that in the English north-midlands, oaths were sometimes taken on salt instead of on the Bible, and that it was confidently believed that a prayer offered near salt would be answered. If a plateful was brought by the parents to a baby's baptism and held near him during the service, he would be certain of Heaven when he died. In some areas, it was thought that the first things carried into a new house, before any of the furniture was brought in, must be a box of coal and a plate of salt. Mrs Leather[2] says that at Eastnor people leaving a house were warned that they must leave bread and salt behind them, otherwise bad luck would follow both for them and for the new tenants. It is unlucky to borrow salt, and still more so to return it; if the lender wants it back, she must 'borrow' it from the original borrower.

To spill salt is very ill-omened. In Yorkshire, it is said that a tear must be shed for every grain spilt. It must not be scraped up, but a little should be thrown three times over the left shoulder to avert the misfortune. If it scatters in the direction of another person, bad luck will come to him, or to a member of his family. A salt-cellar overset between two friends is a sign that they will quarrel.

In his *Description of the Isle of Man*, Waldron says that Manxmen in his time would not 'go out on any material affair without taking some salt in their pockets, much less remove from one house to another, marry, put out a child, or take one to nurse without salt being mutually exchanged.' A Hallowe'en divination practised in the island was to upset a thimbleful of salt on the plates of all present, and leave it there until the morning. If any of the little mounds were then found to have fallen, the person on whose plate it stood would die within the year. Elsewhere, small heaps were made on Christmas Eve or St Agnes's Eve, and the omen was read from their dryness or moisture next day.

Cattle were sained with salt in the Outer Hebrides before being moved from one pasture to another. Dairymaids dropped a pinch into their pails when they began milking, and buttermakers into their churns, to avert the spells of witches. A little in a cradle protected an unbaptized child, a heap in a pewter plate set on a corpse kept away demons and prevented swelling. In the English midlands, salt-and-water, mixed three times, signed with the cross-sign, and sprinkled over any unlucky thing, would remove the bad luck. At sea, the word 'salt' must not be spoken, and on Trentside, the stuff itself must never under any circumstances be thrown overboard. The fisher-

[1] S. O. Addy, *op. cit.*   [2] E. M. Leather, *op. cit.*

men of the Tweed sprinkle their nets with salt, and throw it into the water, to placate the river-spirit and ensure the safety of the boats.

SCISSORS

Scissors share with knives the traditional protective powers arising from the steel of which they are made, and also the perils associated with most sharp cutting instruments.

A dislike of receiving scissors as a free gift from a friend is still quite common. A coin, however small, is usually given in exchange, otherwise the friendship will be cut. The same reluctance is often felt when receiving them from a stranger, as for instance, when a pair is given as a prize at a whist drive or some other competition. The person who distributes the prizes must take a coin from the winner, otherwise bad luck will follow.

To drop a pair of scissors by accident is unlucky, especially if they are picked up by the person who dropped them. Someone else should be asked to do this. If they fall points downwards, there will be a death shortly in the house, or in the near neighbourhood. Dressmakers say that to drop a pair is a sign that more work may be expected soon, very often an order for mourning clothes.

Like other iron or steel objects, scissors were formerly used in charms against evil. A pair, opened so as to form a cross, and laid on the threshold, or thrust closed into the doorpost, prevented the entry of witches. A charm against a visiting witch, or person suspected to be such, used in Somerset during the present century, was to conceal an opened pair behind a cushion, or under a mat. The supposed witch could then be safely admitted, but he or she would be uneasy throughout the visit, and would leave soon, without being able to do any harm.

SEA-ANEMONES

A curious Yorkshire belief is recorded by a writer in *Notes and Queries* (5th Series, Vol. V). In 1854 a Bridlington fisherman told him that sea-anemones turned into herrings in the course of time, and for that reason they were called 'Herring-shine'.

SEAGULLS

In many coastal areas of Great Britain and Ireland, seagulls were, and sometimes still are, thought to embody the souls of dead fishermen and sailors, especially those of men who have been drowned at sea. P.H. Emerson relates in his *English Idylls* (1889) how in certain parts of the east coast he found a belief, rarely expressed in words, but firmly held, that old fishermen turn into gulls when they die. For this reason, it is quite often thought unlucky to kill a seagull, although Emerson was told by one East-coast man that it did not matter. 'They have been dead oncet,' he said, 'they have been on earth oncet, and we hev got quite enough old men now.'

A single gull flying steadily on a straight and undeviating course is sometimes said to be following an unseen corpse which is drifting along the seafloor. It is the soul of the dead man which cannot rest, and thus attends the unburied body that once housed it.

If a seagull flies against the window of a house, it is a warning of danger to some member of the family then at sea. To see three gulls flying together overhead is a death omen, either for the man who sees them, or for someone connected with him.

When gulls come far inland, it is a sign of bad weather. There are storms at sea, and soon there will be storms and high winds on land also. A Yorkshire rhyme recited on seeing them runs:

> Seagull, seagull, get thi on t' sand.
> It'll nivver be fine while thou'rt on t' land.

SEAMEN'S GOODS

Sailors commonly consider it very unlucky to lose a mop or a bucket overboard. Welsh seamen strongly dislike anything being stolen from their vessel, not only for the obvious reason, but also because some part of the ship's luck is felt to have gone with it. Very strong measures are sometimes taken, or high prices paid, in order to get it back. Similarly, anything lent from one ship to another detracts from the lender's luck unless the article is first damaged a little, however slightly, or otherwise rendered imperfect before being handed over.

Along the north-eastern coast, it is a bad omen if a seaman finds his earthenware basin upside down in the morning. Many men will not go to sea at all that day, for fear of some disaster. It is recorded that young boys have sometimes turned this superstition to advantage by secretly overturning their basins in order to gain a day's holiday ashore.

SEVEN. *See Numbers.*

SEVEN WHISTLERS

'The Seven Whistlers' is the name given to certain birds whose cries foretell a disaster at sea, in mines, or elsewhere. What they are cannot be precisely stated because at various times, and in different places, they have been identified as plovers, curlews, whimbrels, widgeon, and other birds which have a whistling note. In legend, they are sometimes said to be the souls of the dead, sometimes the undying spirits of Jews to whom death is denied because they shared in the sin of the Crucifixion. In south Shropshire and Worcestershire, they are six birds in search of a seventh; when that seventh is found, the end of the world will come. In some local traditions they seem to have become confused with the 'gabble-ratchets', the death-hounds that run with the Wild Hunt. In every version of the tale, their cry is an omen of death and disaster which can only be disregarded at the hearer's peril.

This belief was once very widespread amongst men who followed a dangerous calling. Soldiers thought the birds cried before a battle which would involve great slaughter. Seamen believed them to be the souls of drowned comrades, crying to warn the living of coming storm or peril. R. M. Heanley[1] relates that he was once on a trawler in Boston Deeps when these birds were heard. The fishermen at once took up the trawl and went home, explaining that disaster would surely follow if they neglected this clear warning from the dead.

Miners also feared the Seven Whistlers greatly, and often refused to go down the pit when they had been heard. The *Leicester Chronicle* on 24 March 1855, recorded that a few days earlier a collier had been asked why he was not working that day. He replied that not only he, but all his comrades also had stayed away from work because the Seven Whistlers had been heard. They would go back on the morrow but not before. He added that on two previous occasions, some of the men had disregarded similar warnings, and each time two lives had been lost.

A contributor to *Notes and Queries* (21 October 1871) said that on 6 September of the same year he, being then in Yorkshire, had seen immense flocks of birds flying about and crying during a storm. His servant told him these were the Seven Whistlers, and that they foretold some calamity. The man said that the last time he had seen them was just before the terrible explosion at Hartley Colliery, Northumberland, in 1862. On the following morning, news reached the writer of a serious mine disaster at Wigan.

SEVENTH CHILD

The seventh son of a seventh son, or the seventh daughter of a seventh daughter, is commonly said to have magical gifts, particularly the gift of healing. This old and very widespread belief is sometimes stretched to include any seventh child of a family, whether the parent of the same sex was similarly born or not. More usually, however, the magical gifts are looked for only in the second generation of sevens. In some districts, it is thought necessary for the child's birth to be preceded by those of six brothers (or sisters) in an unbroken line, with no child of opposite sex intervening.

[1] R. M. Heanley, *op. cit.*

A person so born is, or was until very recently, believed to share with kings the power of curing the King's Evil, or scrofula, by touch. He or she can also cure goitre, ringworm, and the pain of burns in the same way. In the Scottish Highlands, a seventh son is said to have 'the power of the Magic Foot', which enables him to cure foot-troubles in others by placing his own foot on that of the sufferer. In most parts of Scotland, seventh children are credited with Second Sight and the ability to foretell the future. Almost everywhere, they are believed to make good doctors, quite apart from their power to heal certain diseases magically by touch.

Traditionally, the seventh child heals by laying his hand on the diseased part, sometimes, but not always, murmuring a secret prayer or charm as he does so. The rite is usually performed in the early morning, while the healer is still fasting. In the early years of this century, a Somerset man cured scrofulous patients in the Brendon Hills district by touching, when thus fasting, on a Sunday morning, repeating at the same time certain words which no one was ever allowed to hear. He would not attempt a cure on any day but Sunday. Near Dulverton, at about the same period, a seventh daughter healed goitre by stroking the swelling.

Alexander Polson, in his *Highland Heritage of Folklore* (1926), records a more elaborate rite. The healer visited the sick person before breakfast on seven consecutive mornings, and washed the afflicted part with water drawn from a north-facing well. Here too, a secret incantation was used, and also spittle, for the seventh son spat in the water before it was applied. On the Isle of Lewis, after touching his patient, he hung a sixpence on a string round the latter's neck. If this was afterwards removed, the malady returned. The same belief attached to the gold angels formerly hung on white ribbons round the necks of people who had been touched for scrofula by the King.

The actual presence of the seventh child was not always necessary. It was believed that he could convey his healing powers to water, which could then be bottled and taken away. To do this, he first dropped a gold sovereign into the water, dipped his hand into it, and pronounced a blessing over it. If the patient was subsequently washed or sprinkled with the water so prepared, a cure was expected without any further rites.

Henderson[1] mentions a Scottish Border belief which does not seem to be general in other parts of Britain. This was that the magical cures effected by a seventh child had to be paid for by a loss of his own vital energy. If he was required to perform such cures too often, he pined away and eventually died of exhaustion.

SHADOWS

A very ancient and widespread belief which still exists in some parts of the

[1] Wm. Henderson, *op. cit.*

world, was that a man's shadow, like his reflection, *see Mirrors*, was a visible manifestation of his soul, or of that mysterious entity, his double. Consequently, whatever happened to it affected him vitally, and he could be harmed, or even killed, if any malicious person injured it.

This notion survives today in a superstition that to walk or trample on a man's shadow brings him bad luck. Baring-Gould remarks in his *Book of Folk-Lore* that he had known children to cry with rage if another child stamped on their shadows, saying that it hurt them, or that it was an insult. In one of the legendary tales of Ireland we are told how Fionn relentlessly pursued his enemy, Cuirrech, and killed him at last by thrusting a spear through his shadow. In Eastern Europe, a very long-lived tradition connected the soul-shade with the ancient belief that a new building would not stand unless something alive had been laid in the foundations. When actual sacrifice for this purpose was no longer possible, builders sometimes supplied the lack of living victims by secretly measuring a man's shadow with a piece of string and burying the latter under the foundation-stone. Another way of achieving the same end was to entice some unsuspecting individual on to the site and make him stand in the sunlight so that his shadow fell across the place where the stone was to be laid. In either case, the unfortunate man died within twelve months because his soul had been captured, and the earth-spirits disturbed by the building operations were thus appeased.

A Welsh method of finding out whether any member of the household was to die during the coming year was to observe the shadows of those present as they were thrown upon the wall by the firelight on Christmas Day. If any appeared without heads, their owners would not live to see another Christmas.

A curious shadow-tradition of another type centres round the Ragged-stone on the Malvern Hills. At certain times, but not at any regular or predictable periods, the shadow of its rocky summit is thrown upon the valley below. Legend says that if it falls directly upon any person, he or she is marked for death or, at best, for some dire misfortune. It is said to have fallen upon Cardinal Wolsey when he was staying at Birtsmorton Court, and upon various other people, all of whom came to melancholy ends.

The origin of this long-lived tradition is obscure. The warning nature of the shadow is sometimes ascribed to a curse laid by a medieval monk upon the Raggedstone, but probably it is far older than the Middle Ages. It may well date from pre-Christian times, when it would not have been difficult to see in this unpredictable and sinister shadow a manifestation of some death-dealing god or spirit.

SHARKS

Seamen believe that sharks know when death is coming to anyone on board a ship, and that they will follow such a ship for miles, waiting for the moment when the dead body will be consigned to the sea. A persistently following shark is therefore held to be a certain death omen, and the fact that it is there is usually concealed from any sick person on board.

SHEEP

To meet a flock of sheep when on a journey is commonly thought to be a sign of good luck, a belief which may or may not console the hurrying motorist delayed by such an encounter.

In some districts, sheep are said to recognize the sanctity of Christmas, as cattle do, and to acknowledge it in their own fashion by rising at dawn and bowing three times towards the east. Sometimes they are said to do this at Easter. An old Manx tradition says it is impossible to count them properly unless the eyes of the counter have been washed in running water beforehand. Like most animals closely observed by men, they are weather prophets. When they lie down peacefully in the field, fine weather may be looked for, but when they become restless and baa loudly for no apparent reason, country people expect heavy rain before long.

Scottish seers sometimes used the blade-bone of a black sheep in divination. All the flesh had first to be scraped off it without the aid of iron; if a knife, or any other steel or iron object touched it during the process, its magic was lost. In Lewis, the seer read the future from marks on the bone, holding it lengthwise before him in the direction of the island's greatest length. In some parts of the Highlands, two persons were needed for the divination, one to hold the bone over his left shoulder, and the other to look through the thin part of the broad end, where the answers to the enquirer's questions could be read by those who knew how to interpret them.

It is unlucky to throw a mutton-bone on the fire. If the knuckle-bone from a leg of mutton is saved and carried in the pocket, its owner will be free from rheumatic pains and sciatica. In many parts of Britain, it was once believed that a small T-shaped bone from a sheep's head, similarly carried about, protected its owner from evil and bad luck. In Lincolnshire, during the present century, a strip of sheepskin suspended from a horse's collar was used to avert the Evil Eye. A well-known method of breaking a spell cast upon any person or animal was to take a sheep's heart, stick it full of pins, and roast it at midnight in a room with all doors, windows, and other openings tightly closed.

Many old folk-remedies are connected with sheep. A cure for adder-bites which involved wrapping the bitten person in the pelt of a newly-killed sheep has already been described in the section dealing with *Adders*. Mrs Leather[1] mentions the use in Herefordshire of a sheep's lung in cases of

[1] E. M. Leather, *op. cit.*

pneumonia. It was applied to the patient's feet, and was supposed to draw the disease down from the lungs into itself. A somewhat similar remedy for the same illness was used with success in Cheshire in 1935, but in this case a bullock's milt was employed instead of a sheep's lung.

A well-known cure for whooping-cough was to take the child to the fold at dawn, let a sheep breathe on him, and then lay him down in the place which the animal had just vacated. Similarly, consumptive people were once advised to walk round a sheepfold early in the morning, and again during the day, as many times as possible. A poultice of sheep's dung was sometimes used for erysipelas, and the same material, boiled and dissolved in new milk and taken internally, was thought to cure gall-stones. In Oxfordshire, 'sheep's bumbles', rolled into pills and swallowed, were said to promote general health. This idea was so firmly held that as late as 1936, many people genuinely believed that a certain highly successful brand of pills was invented by a shepherd who used the material thus ready to his hand as a basis. A decidedly repulsive remedy for ague, recorded in the same county about 1904, was to swallow a live sheep-tick on nine successive mornings. *See Lamb*.

SHIVER

It is usually thought to be a bad omen if anyone shivers suddenly without any obvious reason, or if an apparently causeless shudder runs through his body. Some spirit is passing close to him, or Death, though he may not be near, is looking towards him. In England, it is commonly said that someone is walking over his grave, that is, over the place where his grave will one day be. In Brittany a strong and unexplained shudder, particularly when it happens at night, is sometimes ascribed to the touch of the Ankou, *see Churchyard Watcher*, and in that case, it is a direct and certain death omen.

SHOES

Superstitions about shoes and boots are very numerous. It is unlucky to put them on a table, especially if they are new. In some areas, this is supposed to foretell a quarrel, in others, the death of the owner or the person who does it, and occasionally, death by hanging. This last may have something to do with the old phrase 'to die in one's shoes', which meant to be hanged. If a woman does it, it is sometimes said to foretell the birth of a child within the year, her own, or that of some other member of the family.

It is also unlucky to thrust the right foot into the left shoe by accident, or to put the left shoe on first when dressing. Long before the cobbler sang his famous song in *Chu Chin Chow*, country people knew that character could be judged by the way boots and shoes wore down, and so could the likely future of the wearer. An old Suffolk rhyme runs,

Tip at the toe, live to see woe,
Wear at the side, live to be a bride,
Wear at the ball, live to spend all,
Wear at the heel, live to save a deal.

Creaking shoes are often said to denote that the shoemaker has not yet been paid. To find a knot in the shoelace is lucky, however tiresome it may be if the wearer is in a hurry. When waiting for anyone who is late, the laggard can be forced to come quickly by taking off the shoes, crossing them over and back again, and then replacing them and tying them up. It is unlucky to leave a pair crossed on the floor, but to put them in the form of a T at night, or with the soles uppermost, keeps away cramp, nightmare, and rheumatism. Similarly, the T-charm can be used by young people wishing to dream of their lovers, provided that the appropriate rhyme is said while arranging them. Nerve pains and tingling in the foot can be healed by making a cross on the shoe with the finger.

The smell of burning shoes keeps off demons and serpents, and during the plague epidemics of the sixteenth and seventeenth centuries, it was considered an antidote to infection. In Herefordshire, it was thought lucky to burn old boots before a journey. Hop-pickers are said to have done this regularly during last century just before they returned to their homes.

Jockeys consider it a bad sign if anyone inadvertently places their boots on the floor before a race. They should be left on the shelf on which they are kept until the rider is ready to put them on. Fishermen's sea-boots should always be brought to them under the bearer's arm; if the messenger forgets this rule and carries them on his shoulder, the omen is very bad. Staffordshire miners think it ominous to dream of broken shoes; such a dream is a sure sign of a disaster in the pit. In an article on Staffordshire contributed to *Folk-Lore* (Vol. 7. 1896), Charlotte Burne relates the story of a curious warning received by a collier's wife at Bilston. When alone in the house, she heard her husband's hobnailed boots thrown down violently three times in the room above. Since there was no one in the house but herself, she took this to be an evil portent. She begged her husband not to go to work next day, but he insisted on doing so, and was fatally injured by a fall of coal.

If an actor's shoes squeak when he makes his first entrance, he will be well received. If, when he kicks them off in the dressing-room, they fall upright, it is a lucky sign, but if they fall over on their sides, or if he or anyone else put them on a chair, bad luck will follow.

Old shoes are still very usually thrown after a bridal couple for luck when they leave for the honeymoon, or tied to the back of the car. It is a sign of special good fortune if someone, when throwing, manages to hit one of the pair. This has been variously explained as a relic of ancient bride-capture and its attendant fight, or as a token of transfer of authority over the bride from her father to her husband. At Anglo-Saxon weddings, it was the custom for the father to give one of the girl's shoes to the bridegroom, who then lightly touched her on the head with it. In other parts of the world also, shoes figure conspicuously at weddings, either as gifts from the groom to the bride or her relations, or from her kin to the young man. Among the ancient Hebrews, when a widow refused to marry her brother-in-law as custom dictated, she unloosed his shoe from his foot. Again, in *The Book of Ruth*[1], we read that it was 'the manner in former times in Israel concerning redeeming and concerning changing, for to confirm all things; a man plucked off his shoe and gave it to his neighbour; and this was a testimony to Israel'.

These decorous ceremonies do not, however, account for the violent throwing of shoes by wedding-guests, nor do they explain the notion that if the bride stands at the head of the staircase and throws her right shoe among the unmarried guests, the one that catches it will be the first to marry. Shoes did in fact symbolize authority in many cases, but they seem also to have had some connexion with the life-essence, or soul, of the person to whom they belonged.

Thus, if a man was found murdered, his shoes were sometimes removed to prevent him from walking after death. In 1889, when a man had been murdered in Arran, his clothes were produced in court, but not his shoes. When these were asked for, it was explained that the constable had buried them on the foreshore, between high and low water marks, presumably to prevent the ghost from haunting the scene of the murder. In a Scottish witchcraft case at Strathbogie in 1644, the sorcerer, Patrick Malcolm, was accused, among other things, of trying to persuade a woman to give him her left shoe. Had he succeeded, he would have had power over her and could have forced her to follow him.

Until very recently, shoes were often thrown after ships leaving port, or people beginning a journey or a new enterprise, or taking up new work. By doing this, the throwers conveyed luck to ship or individual concerned, probably because they were endowing them with a little of their own life-essence or strength. The same idea may well underlie the modern shoe-throwing at weddings. Nowadays, of course, it is not, as it may have been once, a man's own shoes that are thrown; but it is significant that in every case it has to be old shoes, which have been worn by someone, and never new ones.

SHOT IN LARD

A country remedy for the internal disturbance known as 'rising of the lights' was to mix gunshot with lard and swallow the concoction. This was

[1] *Ruth*, IV, 7.

said to 'sink the lights' and cure the nauseous condition. The remedy was once quite well known, and has been used within this century.

SHREW-MOUSE

Until well towards the end of last century, the shrew-mouse was believed to cause a painful disease of the limbs, resulting in lameness, if it crept over any person or animal. Cattle, horses, and sheep were, of course, most liable to this evil because they frequently spent their nights out of doors, but human beings were not immune. Charlotte Latham[1] records how a Sussex farmer, finding a valuable horse unaccountably lame after being out in a field all night, at once blamed the shrew-mice. Another man, at about the same period, warned a new servant not to put the cows in a particular meadow, for fear that 'some harm will come to them, for the field's full of those picked-nosed mice'.

The remedies for this evil were twofold. One was the well-known rite (used for other diseases also) of passing the sufferer through a bramble that had rooted at both ends. The other, and more usual cure, was to take a living shrew-mouse and bury it alive in a hole bored in an ash-tree. The tree was thereafter known as a Shrew-Ash, and was believed to have the power of curing the ailment if its leaves or twigs were rubbed upon the afflicted parts. Such a tree, called the Sheen Ash, stood in Richmond Park, in Surrey, until about 1895, and to it sick cattle, horses, and weakly children were brought for healing. Another famous tree of this kind grew at Warton in Lancashire. Gilbert White tells us in his *Natural History of Selborne* (1789) that an ancient shrew-ash once grew by the parsonage there, but the Vicar of the parish destroyed it, in the pious hope that by uprooting the tree, he would also uproot the superstition.

In Northamptonshire, it was considered unlucky to meet a shrew-mouse when starting out on a journey. In most districts, it was firmly believed that this little beast could not cross any path trodden by man. If it attempted to do so, it died at once. This theory, which was sometimes extended to field mice in general, was thought to account for the number of mice found dead by the side of paths, without any visible signs of disease or injury.

SIEVE AND SHEARS

The charm known as the Sieve and Shears, or Turning the Riddle, was employed to detect thieves or other suspected persons. When anything had been stolen, the points of the shears were thrust into the wooden rim of the sieve in such a way that the handles stood upright, and the sieve hung down from the points. Two persons of opposite sex supported the handles with the

[1] Charlotte Latham, *op. cit.*

middle fingers of their right hands. Aubrey[1] tells us that the supporters should be two maidens, but this does not seem to have been a general requirement, and in some instances, one person alone appears to have been sufficient. The sieve being thus prepared and suspended from the shears, the names of the suspected individuals were repeated in turn, with the words:

> By St Peter and By St Paul,
> If (such a person) has stolen (so-and-so's) goods,
> Turn about riddle and shears and all.

When the thief's name was mentioned, the sieve turned or fell to the ground.

Faith in this form of divination was formerly strong enough to leave an indelible stain on the reputation of anyone who had been a victim of it. Henderson[2] mentions a nineteenth-century case in Yorkshire, in which a man was accused of stealing a feather-boa. The sieve turned against him, and so complete was the general belief in his guilt that he was obliged to give up his work and leave the district. He was subsequently cleared by the discovery of the boa in a local stream. Another Yorkshire case in the same century was described by a writer in *Notes and Queries* (8th Series, Vol. II) who was told the story by someone who had been present at the time. This man said that in his youth some money had been stolen at the Hall. The entire household being gathered together, the sieve and shears were carried round by one individual (probably the owner of the money, though this is not stated). He stopped in front of each person, saying 'Bless St Peter, bless St Paul, bless the God that made us all. If so-and-so' (naming the man or woman before whom he stood) 'stole this money, turn sieve.' The sieve did turn in front of the schoolmistress, who was living at the Hall at the time. The prejudice created against her by this happening was so strong that she had to leave the village. She died about four months later, and on her deathbed, confessed that she had stolen the money.

In antiquity, the sieve was a sacred and magical instrument, symbolizing the clouds through which the life-giving rain fell upon the earth. Like many other things originally sacred in pagan belief, it was afterwards associated with witches, who were supposed to be able to sail in it through the air or over water.

SIN-EATING

The belief that it was possible to transfer a dead man's sins to a living individual willing to receive them was once very widespread. This notion, which seems so strange to us now, is akin to the ancient conception of the

[1] J. Aubrey, *Remaines of Gentilisme and Judaisme*, 1686–7.
[2] Wm. Henderson, *op. cit.*

Scapegoat, upon whom the guilt and sorrows of primitive communities were laid, and notwithstanding its distinctly pagan characteristics, it seems to have lingered on in many Christian countries until a very late date.

In Britain formerly, the transfer of guilt was effected by the ritual eating of food which had been in contact with the corpse. The classic description of this rite, which was known as Sin-eating, is that given by Aubrey in his *Remaines of Gentilisme and Judaisme*. He tells us that in Herefordshire, and also in Wales, when a death had occurred, the relatives summoned a sin-eater, and then carried the corpse outside and laid it upon a bier in front of the house. A loaf of bread and a mazar-bowl full of beer was handed across the body to the sin-eater, who also received sixpence in cash, 'in consideration whereof he tooke upon him (*ipso facto*) all the Sinnes of the Defunct, and freed him (or her) from walking after they were dead.'

Aubrey says that 'in our dayes', that is, when he wrote at the end of the seventeenth century, the custom was declining, 'yet by some people was observed even in the strictest time of ye Presbyterian government'. He mentions an instance at Dynder where 'volens nolens the Parson of ye Parish, the kindred of a woman deceased there had this ceremonie punctually performed according to her Will'; and he adds that 'the like was donne at ye City of Hereford in these times, when a woman kept many yeares before her death a Mazard-bowle for the Sinne-eater; and the like in other places in this Countie; as also in Brecon, e.g. at Llangors, where Mr Gwin the minister about 1640 could not hinder ye performing of this ancient custome.'

The Herefordshire sin-eaters were apparently poor people who performed the required service for the sake of the food and money. 'One of them I remember,' says Aubrey, 'lived in a cottage on Rosse-high way. (He was a long, leane, ugly, lamentable poor raskal).' In Wales and Scotland also there was often a recognized practitioner in a parish who, for a small fee, played his gruesome part in the ceremony. A letter printed in the *Sunday Times* on 5 March 1950, states that the writer's father (who had died ten years before, aged eighty-eight) remembered a sin-eater in the Carmarthenshire village where he lived as a boy. This was an old man who, when requested, went to funerals and ate a piece of bread which had been placed on the breast of the corpse, 'thus signifying that he took to himself the sins of that person'.

If there was no regular sin-eater available, it seems to have been thought possible, at least in some districts, for others to take his place by means of a semi-sacramental eating and drinking across, or in the presence of, the corpse. S. O. Addy[1] mentions a Derbyshire belief, still alive in the late nineteenth century, that every drop of wine taken at a funeral was a sin committed by the dead man, which was thus taken away by the drinker. Mrs Leather[2] records a story, told to her by the person concerned, of a man who was

[1] S. O. Addy, *op. cit.*   [2] E. M. Leather, *op. cit.*

invited to the funeral of a farmer's sister near Hay. On being taken upstairs to the room where the corpse lay, he observed at the foot of the coffin a box covered by a white cloth, with a bottle of wine and six glasses upon it. He was asked to drink, but refused, saying that he never took wine, whereupon the farmer exclaimed, 'But you must drink, sir. It is like the Sacrament. It is to kill the sins of my sister.'

In these, and most other recorded instances, the eating and drinking was voluntary, and those who took part in it knew what they were doing. But in an article published in *Folk-Lore*[1] L. F. Newman says that in the Eastern Counties, this was not always so. Although the practice was rare, or at least, rarely mentioned, by the end of last century, it was not unknown for relatives to put part of a loaf and some salt on the corpse, and then to give the food to some unsuspecting tramp or other person, who ate it without being aware of the burden of guilt he thus acquired. 'Even now,' adds Mr Newman, writing in 1945, 'wayfarers avoid a house where a death has recently taken place, and there is a distinct reluctance to take a solitary meal in a house where there is an unburied body. The funeral feast is quite safe, as all present partake of the same food.'

SINGING BEFORE BREAKFAST

To sing before breakfast is a sure sign of sorrow before nightfall. This belief is still very common, and in some districts is extended to include laughter, or any other sign of gaiety before the morning fast has been broken. *See Laughter.*

SMOCK WEDDINGS

A curious belief concerning a husband's liability for his wife's premarital debts prevailed in many districts until at least as late as the first half of the nineteenth century. It was said, and firmly believed, that if a girl had contracted debts before her marriage, her husband would not be liable for them if she came to her wedding barefoot, and clad only in her smock, or shift.

Another, and perhaps earlier form of the belief was that the same end could be achieved if she walked naked from her own home to that of her future husband. In *Notes and Queries* (Vol. VII), it is recorded that at Kirton-in-Lindsey during the nineteenth century, a woman attempted to do this by climbing naked out of her bedroom window. Presumably she lacked the courage to make the full journey thus to the man's house, for she put on some clothes while standing at the top of the ladder by which she descended.

[1] L. F. Newman, 'Some Notes on the Folk-Lore of Cambridgeshire and the Eastern Counties', *Folk-Lore*, Vol. 56, 1945.

Probably few girls at any time dared to do even as much as she did, as far as complete nudity was concerned. 'Smock weddings', however, that is, weddings in which the bride wore only a single undergarment, are recorded in a number of parishes in Yorkshire, Lincolnshire, Cumberland, and else-where. Sometimes a sheet was worn instead of a smock. A writer in *Notes and Queries* (Vol. XII) mentions by name a widow who, at Gedney in Lincolnshire, came to the church in a sheet, stitched up like a bag, with slits at the sides for her bare arms. She had been told that if she did this, neither she nor her husband would be liable for the debts she had run up during her impoverished widowhood. In another volume of the same journal, a clergy-man recounted how he had once been confronted by a bride dressed only in her chemise. He was, he said, somewhat startled, but he felt obliged to perform the ceremony, since nothing is said in the rubric about the woman's attire on such occasions.

The origin of this belief is obscure, but the underlying idea seems to be that the girl sheds her debts with her clothes, and so comes to her new life naked and unencumbered, the shift or sheet worn at the wedding being no more than a slight concession to decency. In his *Confessions of an Uncommon Attorney* (1945), R. L. Hine remarks that the custom was 'based on an old law that a husband is only responsible for his wife's ante-nuptial debts to the extent of the fortune she brought him'. A smock wedding served as a public announcement that she brought him nothing, and therefore no claim could be made upon him or her past debts.

SNAILS

Snails have long been credited with the power of healing various ailments, and they are still used today in some semi-magical cures. One very well-known remedy for warts is to stroke them with a black snail and then impale the creature on a thorn-tree. As it dissolves and dies, the warts will disappear. Another method, for which strict secrecy is usually enjoined, is to prick the snail with a thorn, once for each wart, and anoint the latter with the froth or juice that exudes from the pricks. The snail must then be buried with the thorn left in it. The same froth, similarly obtained and dropped into the ear, has been recorded in Gloucestershire as a cure for earache.

Whooping-cough charms include the burial of a snail, or hanging it up in the chimney, or on a tree, to die. A gypsy remedy for the same complaint is to let a black snail crawl over brown sugar and, when the sugar is thoroughly mixed with the slime, give it to the patient to eat. When ague was prevalent, its onset could be prevented by wearing a snail in a bag round the neck for nine days and then throwing it on the fire. Aubrey[1] mentions a plaster of pounded snails, taken from their shells, which healed gout if applied to the

[1] J. Aubrey, *Royal Soc. MS.* fol. 168.

affected part. This, he says, was recommended to Elias Ashmole by the Moroccan Ambassador, who stated that it was widely used in Africa.

Snail-slime was formerly considered a cure for consumption, and was quite seriously recommended for that purpose in the seventeenth century. The creatures were removed from their shells, mixed with barley, eryngo, sugar and spring water, and taken daily in the milk of a red cow. In his *Nunwell Symphony* (1945) C. Aspinall Oglander gives a variant of this receipt taken from a household book belonging to his family, in which chopped-up earthworms were added to the concoction.

Faith in the slime remedy for consumption was not, however, confined to people in the seventeenth century. In 1954, a Berkshire district nurse stated that when she worked in a downland village in that county, she found consumptive patients, or those troubled with persistent coughs, using a preparation of common snails dissolved in salt and mixed with cream and sugar to make an emulsion. In the same year, an Oxfordshire woman in the Wychwood area said she used a similar medicine whenever she had a bad cough and always found it efficacious. A more drastic remedy employed in Westmorland during last century was to gather small white shell-less snails while the dew was on the grass and swallow them alive, so that they might eat the slime that was thought to cause the disease from off the lungs. In 1929, some American social workers in the Virginian Blue Ridge Mountains were told by the local people that a general cure for tuberculosis and chest complaints was to swallow a live snail every evening for nine days. If the treatment was not immediately successful, it could be repeated for a further nine days, four or five times, if necessary. The snails lived on in the stomach for some time, and the slime they exuded healed the lung irritation.[1]

A charm to know who the future wife or husband would be was to catch a snail on Hallowe'en and shut it up in a flat dish for the night. Next morning, the initials of the future lover would be seen, traced in slime, on the surface of the dish. Sometimes a box-lid was substituted for the dish, or the creature was allowed to wander on the hearth and trace the initials in the ashes.

A black snail crossing anyone's path is a sure sign of rain in some districts, but in others, it foretells bad luck. In northern England, whoever sees one on first leaving his house should seize it by one of its horns and throw it over the left shoulder. This ensures a prosperous journey; but if it is thrown over the right shoulder, misfortune will follow. The distinction appears to be somewhat academic, since the number of people quick enough to catch hold of the horns before they are withdrawn must be extremely small.

In the Isle of Man, when children see one, they say, 'Snail, snail, put out your horn and give me your good wish this morn.' M. A. Courtney[2] records that Cornish miners, if they meet a snail (or 'bulhorn') on the way to their

---

[1] Mandel Sherman and T. R. Henry, *Hollow Folk*, 1933.
[2] M. A. Courtney, *op. cit.*

work, will propitiate the creature, and so avoid ill-luck by giving it some of their dinner, or a little tallow from their lanthorns.

SNEEZING

When anyone sneezes, it is still quite usual for some person standing nearby to say 'God bless you'. At one time, it was considered very impolite to withhold this blessing, and Aubrey[1] tells us that in seventeenth-century England it was customary to doff the hat and bow while pronouncing it. The ancient Greeks also, and the Romans, wished the sneezer health or good fortune. This custom they explained by various legends, but its true origin, and that of the numerous other sneezing superstitions, is probably to be found in the belief of primitive peoples all over the world that a sneeze, that little explosion in the head, is a direct sign from the gods, foretelling good or evil fortune according to the circumstances in which it occurs.

Thus, to sneeze three times before breakfast is often said to predict a present before the week is out. In Cornwall, it is lucky to do so once, but not twice; in North Yorkshire, sneezing after a meal, and especially after dinner, is a sign of good health and a man who does so regularly can expect to live to a ripe old age. Like birth and marriage, sneezing has its weekday rhymes, one version of which says,

> Monday for danger, Tuesday kiss a stranger,
> Wednesday for a letter, Thursday for something better,
> Friday for sorrow, Saturday, see your lover tomorrow.

A Cornish addition to this says

> Sneeze on Sunday morning fasting,
> Enjoy your true love for everlasting.

The number of successive sneezes at any one time also foretells the future. In some districts, a rhyme often applied to seeing magpies is used for sneezing, and runs,

> One for a kiss, two for a wish,
> Three for a letter, four for a better,
> Five for silver, six for gold,
> Seven for a secret never to be told.

In Scotland formerly, a new-born baby's first sneeze was awaited with anxiety because the child was thought to be in the fairies' power until it

[1] J. Aubrey, *Remaines of Gentilisme and Judaisme*, 1686-7.

sneezed. It was also held to be a proof that he or she was mentally normal, since there was a widespread idea that no idiot could sneeze. These two notions were probably allied, because defective children were often believed to be fairy changelings, the human child having been stolen away and the changeling substituted by the fairy mother so that it might have the benefit of human milk and care.

To sneeze towards the right is fortunate, especially at the start of a journey or sea-voyage, but to do so towards the left, or near a grave, is very unlucky.

SNOWDROP

The snowdrop, or February-Fair-Maid, is a symbol of hope because it is one of the earliest heralds of coming Spring, and of purity because of its virgin whiteness. Legend says it first appeared on Earth when Adam and Eve were driven out of the Garden of Eden. Winter reigned then in the world outside. Snow was falling fast, and everything was dark, barren, and lifeless. But the Angel consoled our unhappy first parents by promising them that even here, in the land of their exile, Spring would follow Winter, and as a token that this would indeed be so, he breathed upon some of the falling snowflakes. Where these touched the ground, snowdrops sprang up, and ever since then, these delicate-seeming but hardy little flowers have appeared in the darkest winter weeks as a sign of better times to come.

They are also associated with Our Lady, and especially with Candlemas Day, the feast of her Purification. Since they are in bloom then, they are often used in church decorations on that festival, and are called by a variety of charming names, such as Purification Flowers, Mary's Tapers, or Candlemas Bells. In the district round the Herefordshire Beacon, where they grow very freely and are thought to be true natives, bunches used to be brought indoors at Candlemas, to protect the house from evil influences and give it what was known as 'the white purification'.

Yet in spite of these sacred and hopeful associations, the commonest modern superstition about snowdrops connects them with death and misfortune. In country belief they 'wear shrouds', and consequently they are unlucky flowers indoors. If they are brought in, and especially if one blossom alone is brought in, a death in the house will soon follow. In some districts, this belief extends to all snowdrops, in others, only to the first flower seen in Spring.

Charlotte Latham[1] tells us how she once heard a Sussex child sharply scolded for bringing home a 'death-token', that is, a single snowdrop. On asking why this was considered unlucky, she was told by the child's mother that 'it looked for all the world like a corpse in its shroud', and that 'it always kept itself quite close to the earth, seeming to belong more to the dead, than

[1] Charlotte Latham, *op. cit.*

to the living'. The woman added that it was quite safe to bring in handfuls of the flowers. It was the single blossom only that was ominous. The same idea applies to single primroses also, and probably represents the older form of the superstition.

Nowadays, however, this distinction is often forgotten. Many people dislike snowdrops in any quantity indoors, and February deaths are not infrequently blamed upon some ill-omened gift of a basketful or large bunch. In one Oxfordshire village very recently, a lady was advised by her charwoman to throw away the flowers with which she had filled numerous bowls and vases because their presence was 'a sure sign of a funeral'. She kept them, however, and shortly afterwards, her mother-in-law died. Although the latter was ninety-one, the charwoman insisted that it was the snowdrops that had caused her death.

Along the Welsh border, snowdrops, like some other Spring flowers, are considered harmful to poultry as well as human beings. They must never be brought indoors while hens are sitting or the eggs will not hatch.

SORTES VIRGILIANAE. *See Bible.*

SPADE

To carry a spade on the shoulder through a house is very unlucky. It is a sign that a grave will soon be dug, most probably for someone living in the house.

It is equally ill-omened to try to attract a distant person's attention by waving a spade at him. His death will follow soon, unless he instantly seizes a handful of earth and throws it in the direction of the person so hailing him.

SPARROW

The cheerful and inoffensive sparrow bears a curiously bad reputation in the folk-tradition of many parts of Europe. A Lancashire rhyme about birds includes the couplet,

> The spink and the sparrow
> Are the Devil's bow and arrow.

In a Lettish legend mentioned by E. A. Armstrong in *The Folklore of Birds*, sparrows guard the Devil's fire, and chase the swallows who come to carry away fire for the benefit of mankind. An old Russian tale says that when Our Lord was in the Garden of Gethsemane, all the other birds tried to mislead His pursuers, but the sparrows betrayed Him by chirruping loudly round the place where He was. So too, on Calvary, when swallows flew away with the executioners' nails, the sparrows went after them and brought the nails back. Later on, when Christ hung on the Cross, the kindly swallows tried to protect Him from further torment by crying 'He is dead! He is dead!', but the sparrows retorted 'He is alive! He is alive!', and so urged His persecutors on to still greater cruelties. Because of all this, they are accursed birds, whose flesh men must not eat, and their legs are fastened by invisible bonds, so that they can never run, but only hop.

It is an omen of death, or at least, of misfortune, if a sparrow flies into a house. Aubrey tells a curious tale in his *Miscellanies* which seems to connect the bird with illness. When in 1643, Major John Morgan lay dangerously ill in the house of Aubrey's father, a sparrow came every day to the sick-room window and pecked at the lead of a particular panel. This it did during the whole time that the Major was ill, but when he was sufficiently recovered to leave the house, the sparrow went also and was not seen again.

Like many other birds, sparrows were sometimes thought to contain the souls of the dead, and consequently it was very unlucky to kill them. A superstitious reluctance to do so is still fairly common, even when the ancient connexion between birds and human souls has been forgotten. In Kent, however, if a sparrow is caught, it must not be kept in the house, but must be destroyed at once, otherwise the person who caught it will die.

SPIDER

Spiders are lucky, however terrifying the larger ones may seem to some people, and they should never be killed. 'If you wish to live and thrive, let the spider run alive' is a well-known saying which has probably saved the lives of millions of these insects since it was first coined. A reason often given for sparing it is that it once protected the Infant Jesus during the Flight into Egypt. Legend says that during that perilous journey, the Holy Family took refuge in a cave. A spider came and wove a thick web across the entrance, and soon afterwards a dove appeared and laid an egg in its threads. When the pursuing soldiers came up, they saw the unbroken web and, concluding that no one had entered the cave for some time, they passed on without searching it.

Almost exactly similar tales are told of King David and of Mahomet when they were flying from their enemies. But these legends are the result, rather than the origin, of the very general respect for the spider which is found in many parts of the world, including places to which Christianity and Mahommedanism have never penetrated. In pagan antiquity, and among heathen tribes in Africa and Asia today, it was and is regarded as a wonder-working insect, wise and endowed with healing gifts and, except perhaps in the case of poisonous varieties, helpful and friendly to mankind.

A spider in the house is a good sign, foretelling prosperity and happiness. If one drops on anybody from the roof, that person will soon receive a legacy, or money from some other source. A money-spider running over garments while they are being worn denotes that they will soon be replaced by new ones; if it is caught and kept in the pocket, that pocket will never be empty of ready cash. To see a spider when out is usually considered a good omen, though in some parts of the Scottish Highlands, this is only so in the evening. A spider seen there in the morning is unlucky, but one seen in the evening is very fortunate, especially if it is coming towards the observer.

The webs and bodies of spiders figure in many ancient cures. Sufferers from ague and jaundice swallowed the living insect rolled up in butter, although in some parts of northern England, spiders were thought to be poisonous, and to swallow them very dangerous. Ague could also be cured by shutting one up in a box and leaving it there to die, or by wearing one or more in a bag round the neck. 'I took early this morning a good dose of elixir,' wrote Elias Ashmole in his *Diary* during the seventeenth century, 'and hung three spiders round my neck, and they drove my ague away.' In Suffolk, when a child had whooping-cough, his mother looked for a dark spider lurking somewhere in her house, and held it over the child's head, saying,

> Spider, as you waste away,
> Whooping-cough, no longer stay,

after which she hung it over the fireplace in a bag to perish. A more merciful variant of this charm found in Herefordshire was to hold the insect to the child's mouth, repeat the same words, and then let it run away, taking the disease with it. Another method was to bore a hole in the doorpost of the house and immure the creature therein. The use of spiders' webs in cures for bleeding, asthma, ague, warts and insomnia has already been described under *Cobwebs*.

A Herefordshire superstition, inspired by memories of St Patrick, was that spiders do not spin their webs on Irish wood. Mrs Leather[1] records that at Goodrich Castle, the timber was said to have been brought from Ireland to avoid the annoyance of cobwebs, and the cellars floored with Irish earth, so that no toads could live there.

SPITTLE

Spittle, like blood, was once thought to be a centre of soul-power, and therefore a potent agent of magic and protection. To spit averted evil, and it also increased the beneficent virtue of that which was fortunate. It is still

[1] E. M. Leather, *op. cit.*

customary in many parts of the world to spit on meeting a piebald horse or a magpie, a cross-eyed person or a chimneysweep, or when making a wish, or seeing the new moon for the first time. All these, and many other things and persons similarly greeted, have power of one kind or another, and spitting nullifies their evil and enhances their good effects.

Reginald Scot tells us in his *Discoverie of Witchcraft* that if a man spits into his right shoe before putting it on, or into his own urine, he will be safe from spells, and so too, if he spits before going into any dangerous place. In some districts, it is usual to spit after any dispute or unpleasantness, and if two people wash in the same hand-basin, they can avoid the quarrel that such an action is supposed to produce by spitting into the water. *See Washing*.

Spitting on any person before he sets out on a journey, or begins some important new task, will protect him and bring him good luck. An Oxford-shire woman said a few years ago that she always spat on her daughter, then a schoolgirl, before she sat for an examination, on her husband before he went to a bowls match, and on any letters applying for contracts or other business which she wrote on her husband's behalf. Dressmakers sometimes spit on the outside wrappings of finished work when returning it to the customer, in order to ensure that it will give satisfaction.

To spit on the hands before a fight, or before beginning to dig, gives greater strength and makes victory or good work more likely. Handsel money, that is the first money received in a market or other place of sale, should be spat upon, or placed in the mouth, and then transferred to a pocket by itself. This protects it from being overlooked and ensures that more will come. Misson[1] remarks that London market-women in his day did this 'to make it tenacious, that it may remain with them and not vanish away like a fairy gift, or else to render it propitious and lucky, that it may draw more money to it'. The 'fastenpenny', or money given to a newly-engaged servant at a Hiring Fair as a token of wages to come, was similarly treated.

Children still spit when they make a promise which they mean to keep, or as a proof that what they say is true. This is 'spitting their faith' or, in the significant north-country variant of the phrase, 'spitting their soul'. To say 'finger wet, finger dry, cut my throat if I tell a lie' after wetting the finger with spittle is a serious affirmation which few children will risk if what they have just said, or are about to say, is untrue. Nor would their primitive ancestors have risked it, for to them, a lie in such circumstances would have involved a real danger to the vital soul-essence contained in the spittle, and therefore to life itself.

Fasting spittle is sometimes used to cure warts and swellings and to disperse birthmarks (*see p. 53*). Ringworm and skin blemishes are treated by having spittle laid upon them. A cure for obstinate corns is to spit on a piece of washing soda and lay it on the corn. In 1954, a North Oxfordshire woman

[1] H. Misson de Valbourg, *op. cit.*

stated that when her child was born with a crooked leg, she was advised to massage it with spittle on the palm of her hand. She did so regularly for about two years, at the end of which time the leg was quite straight, no other treatment having been used. In the past, it was frequently employed by charmers and cunning-men to heal ailments of all sorts in men and cattle, including scrofula, tumours, muscular affections, skin diseases, and the bites of reptiles and insects.

SPOON

To drop a spoon is usually said to mean that a child will soon visit the house or, in some districts, a fool. Where the latter superstition prevails, the visitor nowadays expected is merely someone rather tiresomely stupid, but it seems probable that originally a 'natural' was meant, one of those innocent and witless individuals who were deemed to be under God's special protection. *See Afflicted Persons.* In Leicestershire, C. J. Billson[1] was once told that a falling spoon foretold the coming of a woman. As this event is connected almost everywhere else with a dropped fork, his informant may merely have confused the two implements. On the other hand, since spoons were in everyday use in Britain long before forks, it is just possible that this version represents an older form of the belief.

Spoon-omens are not all concerned with visitors. Mrs Rudkin[2] tells us that round Gainsborough a spoon dropped with the bowl uppermost means a surprise coming, but if it falls with the bowl downwards, the person dropping it will suffer a disappointment. In the Midlands, a dropped tablespoon means a quarrel in the house shortly, and in the West-country, the same result is expected if anyone pours gravy or other liquids 'back-handed' from any type of spoon.

If two teaspoons are accidentally put into one saucer, it is a sign of a wedding. A Herefordshire variant of this omen is that if the two spoons are set in a girl's saucer, it denotes that she will marry twice. In Wales formerly, young men sometimes made elaborately carved wooden spoons, known as love-spoons, and gave them to the girls of their choice as love-tokens.

The *Wilkie MS*. mentions a Scottish belief that a child's future could be foretold by the manner in which he first used a spoon to sup. If he took it up with his right hand, the omen was good, but if he used his left hand, it meant he would be unlucky in life.

SPRINGWORT

Springwort is, or was, the name given to a magical plant associated with fire and lightning. In ancient Greece and Rome, amongst Jews and Arabs, and

---

[1] C. J. Billson (ed.) County Folk-Lore, Vol. 1. *Leicestershire and Rutland*, 1895.
[2] E. Rudkin, *Lincolnshire Folklore*, 1936.

all over medieval Europe, it was credited with a great variety of wonder-working properties. It endowed its possessor with the power of discovering secrets and hidden treasure, opening locks, and making himself invisible. When eaten, it made human beings fertile, and in France, it was said to give superhuman strength to any man who rubbed his limbs with it. If buried on a mountain-top, it drew down the lightning and divided the storm. It could pierce the heart of the strongest oak, and legend says that woodpeckers (themselves thunder-birds) used it for this purpose.

Unfortunately, no one now knows exactly what springwort was, although in *Teutonic Mythology* (1884) Grimm identified it with *Euphorbia lathyris*, the Caper Spurge. It could be recognized by the fact that it was always covered with dew, winter and summer alike. One way of finding it was to watch a woodpecker in flight. If the bird stopped to rub its beak on a certain plant, that was the springwort. The seeker could then take up the herb, but he had to do so with wood, or with his bare hands, never with an iron tool.

Another traditional method of obtaining it was to plug up a woodpecker's nest (or in Germany, a hoopoe's), and then light a small fire, or spread a red cloth, on the ground below. The bird, finding its nest blocked, would fetch a sprig of springwort and hold it before the obstruction, which would immediately fall out. Then, seeing the fire below, or mistaking the red cloth for flames, the woodpecker would drop the fire-plant into its native element, and the watcher had to be ready to catch it as it fell. Sometimes a pan of water was used instead of fire or cloth, the connexion here being with the storm-clouds which produce the lightning.

STAIRS

If two people cross on the stairs, bad luck will follow. Superstition, no less than good manners, demands that a person standing at the head or foot of the staircase should wait until someone descending or ascending has completed his journey. When a meeting is unavoidable, the two people concerned should cross their fingers as they pass, to avert the threatened misfortune. An Oxfordshire tradition says they should touch each other and speak; to pass in silence is very unlucky.

Stumbling on the stairs, as elsewhere, has ominous significance. To do so when going down is very unlucky, but if the person concerned is going up, it is a sign of good fortune, or of a wedding, either his own or that of some other inmate of the house.

STAMP STAINER

In Northumberland formerly, sprains and swellings could be cured with the help of the Stamp Stainer, or Stamp Steener. This was an individual who by acquired art or innate gift, could heal by stamping on the affected part with his foot. After the first sharp twinge, the operation was said to be painless. To complete the cure, the sprained limb or swelling had afterwards to be bound up with an eel's skin.

STARS

In some pagan mythologies, stars and planets were thought to be human souls; in others, they were gods, or great heroes raised after death to dwell in glory in the skies. Astrologers, both pagan and Christian, regarded them as the governors of men's lives, whose influence was seen in everything that an individual might be or do. Traces of these ancient notions can still be seen in superstitious beliefs concerning stars, which are found all over the world, in Britain no less than elsewhere.

It is very unlucky to point at a star, as it is to point at the moon, or the rainbow. It is also unlucky to attempt to count those visible in the sky. If, however, any young unmarried person wishes to find out whom he or she will marry, seven stars (and no more) may be counted on seven successive nights. The first person of opposite sex with whom he or she shakes hands on the eighth day will be the future wife or husband.

If a wish is made when the first star of evening is seen, it will be granted. This belief is general in England, but in the Midlands and Yorkshire it is thought necessary to say, while forming the wish,

> Star light, star bright,
> The first star I've seen tonight.
> Would it were that I might
> Have the wish I wish tonight.

In East Anglia, it is a bad omen for farmers if the Evening Star rides low in summer, with the leading star of the Bear's tail above it. The harvest will be a poor one.

The connexion between falling stars and human souls is very widespread, and is found amongst peoples of very varying stages of culture. In some parts of Britain, such a star foretells a birth; the soul is passing from Heaven to animate the coming child. Elsewhere, it is thought to be a soul released from Purgatory.

If a falling star is seen on the right hand of the observer, it is a sign of good luck, if on the left, it foretells misfortune. Any wish made while it is visible will be granted, but it must be made very quickly, or the charm will not work. An old cure for pimples recorded by Marcellus of Bordeaux was to pass a cloth over them while a shooting star flashed by. It had to be done with a cloth, for if the bare hand was used, the pimples would simply be transferred to the hand.

An old country name for the Milky Way was Walsingham Way, because it seemed to point towards the famous shrine of Our Lady at Walsingham. It was also called Watling Street, because it was believed to be the road along which souls passed to Heaven. The same idea existed in Lithuania, where it was known as the Road of Birds, for it was in that form that the souls travelled along it to the next world. Some Red Indian tribes also thought it a soul-road, the brighter stars in the galaxy being the camp-fires which the dead lit and rested by on their long journey to the land beyond the grave. In Spain, it was called Santiago Way because it guided pilgrims to the shrine of St James of Compostella.

STILLBORN CHILD. *See Unbaptized Child.*

STOCKINGS

In most parts of Britain, it is thought lucky to put on the left stocking before the right when dressing in the morning. In some areas, the opposite rule obtains, and the right one must go on first. In Suffolk, if a woman makes a practice of putting on her left glove and her left stocking before their companions, she will not suffer from toothache.

To wear odd socks or stockings is fortunate, especially if they differ in colour and pattern. As with other garments, it is a good sign if stockings are accidentally put on inside out. They must, of course, be left as they are, for to correct the mistake is to change the luck. Here too there are regional differences of opinion. In some northern districts, it is only the reversed left stocking which brings good luck, in others, to put either or both on the wrong way is ill-omened.

A pair pinned crosswise at the head or foot of the bed keeps away nightmare, and sometimes acts as a charm in cases of acute and serious illness. If anyone suffering from sore throat ties his (or her) left stocking round his throat on going to bed, he will be better in the morning.

The custom of 'flinging the stocking' was observed at town and country weddings until the introduction of honeymoons made it impossible by taking the bride and groom away from home on their wedding night. As soon as the married pair were put to bed, the bridesmaids and groomsmen sat on either side of the bed, the girls holding the wife's stockings and the young men those of the husband. At a given signal, these were thrown backwards over their shoulders. If one thrown by a bridesmaid hit the groom, or one thrown by a groomsman hit the bride, it was a sign that the thrower would be married very soon. A quieter Yorkshire charm of the same type was for the bride's stockings to be laid crosswise on her bed when she retired. If this was not done, she would have no children.

STONECROP

Stonecrop, like houseleek, protected a house from fire and lightning if it grew upon the roof. It also kept away witches. A charming country name for the yellow variety was Welcome-home-husband-though-never-so-drunk.

The white-flowered plant was valued from Anglo-Saxon times onwards for its medicinal properties. Decoctions made from it cured the ague, expelled poison, prevented infection, and healed sores and ulcers. The plant itself, bruised and laid upon the afflicted part, helped sufferers from the King's Evil, piles, and eye-troubles. 'It is so harmless a herb,' says Culpeper, 'you can scarce use it amiss.'

STORMS

Great storms have from time immemorial been regarded as something far more than mere natural phenomena. In almost every ancient mythology, thunder, lightning, and fierce winds have been thought of as manifestations of the gods, and usually of their anger. In many parts of the world, a person killed by lightning was deemed to have been directly overwhelmed by Divine wrath. Among some Bantu tribes today, such a man is hastily buried where he lies, without rites or mourning, and if an animal perishes thus, its flesh cannot be eaten. Exactly the same ideas prevailed in ancient Rome, where it was also unlawful to repair or rebuild any house that had been damaged in a thunder-storm.

In Britain formerly, a bad storm of any kind was often ascribed to the Devil and his hosts, or to the action of witches. The latter were supposed to be able to raise them at will, and during the period of the witch-trials, they were frequently charged with doing so in order to wreck ships at sea or damage property on land. 'The raising of Storme by Witches,' said Baxter in 1691[1] 'is attested by so many, that I think it needs less to recite them.' Winds, hail, snow, and thunder were all at their command; if they whistled, the wind sprang up, *see Whistling*, and they could, and did, sell knotted threads to sailors, to enable the latter to have what wind they needed on their voyages. As the knots were loosened, so the wind increased, until with the freeing of the last knot, a dangerous gale arose. There were other and more unpleasant methods of raising storms, including that practised in 1590 by the witches of North Berwick. They christened a cat with diabolical rites, tied parts of a dead man's body on to it, and flung the poor creature into the sea. This they did in order to produce a storm which would wreck the ship in which James VI was returning from Denmark, but in this case they failed to do more than raise a delaying wind.

There is an old belief that if a storm rages during the Assizes, many prisoners

[1] R. Baxter, *The Certainty of the World of Spirits*, 1691.

will be condemned to death. This may well have seemed to be true in the days when people were hanged for quite small offences, though it is improbable that the weather had anything to do with it. Another common belief, still firmly held by many, is that the lightning never strikes twice in the same place. It could be a very comforting thought in some circumstances, but unfortunately, it is not true. Many high buildings, including the campanile of St Mark in Venice, have been struck more than once, and B. F. Schonland records in his *Flight of the Thunderbolt* (1950) that the Empire State Building in New York was hit sixty-eight times in three years.

Many people cover their mirrors and put away all metal objects during a thunder-storm. In some districts, it is said that doors and windows should be left open, so that if the thunder gets in, it can get out again without doing any damage. The oak is usually thought to be the safest tree to shelter under, if caught by the storm out of doors, but in Sussex, there is a contrary rhyme which says:

> Beware of the oak; it draws the stroke.
> Avoid the ash; it courts the flash;
> Creep under a thorn; it can save you from harm.

It has already been mentioned that bells used to be rung during storms because they were believed to have power over the demons of the air, *see Bells*. It is for this reason that the words *Fulgura Frango* are often found inscribed on bells of medieval date.

In Oxfordshire, they say that thunder in the winter foretells 'a casualty summer', and that 'a storm out of season is a summer's glory or a great man's death'. A somewhat similar Welsh tradition is that a winter thunder-storm means the death of the most important man in the parish. Fierce storms have often been said to occur when a great man dies. Such a storm raged when Oliver Cromwell died, and the Royalists, perhaps naturally, said it was caused by the Devil who had come to fetch his own. But his followers, if they had been Scots, might have explained it as a Royal Storm, one of those which come for the souls of the great, and only for them.

A very curious story is recounted by Otta Swire in *Skye: The Island and Its Legends* (1952). She was at Kingsburgh during George V's illness in 1928 and every night an old man came to the house to hear the latest wireless news of the King. He had been a stalker in his youth, and had served the King in that capacity when the latter was a boy. There came a day of wild storm, with strong winds, snow and thunder, which raged all day long until the evening, and then the wind abated. The old man came as usual and asked if the King was still alive. On being told that he was, he went away. He did not come again, and when news was taken to him that the King had taken a turn for the better, he said he knew that would be so, because he had not gone with the storm. He said it was a Royal Storm which blew only for the truly great. He had seen one come for Lord Kitchener, and he had gone away with it, but this one had gone back without the King, a most rare thing, he said, and consequently he knew that his recovery was certain.

STRAW-CART

The traditional lore of the straw-cart is uncertain and contradictory. In some districts, it is said to be lucky to meet one, in others unlucky. The commonest belief is that if seen by itself, it foretells a pleasant surprise, and a wish formed by the observer as it passes will be granted. But if it is immediately behind a loaded hay-cart, it nullifies the good luck of the latter, *see Hay-cart*, and the two together become an omen of misfortune.

STRAW GARTER

A curious fertility charm formerly used in Yorkshire is recorded by Richard Blakeborough in his book, *T' Hunt o' Yatton Brigg* (1899).

A girl about to marry could make sure of the children she desired by going secretly to the harvest fields on a Friday night, and drawing straws from the stooks. For every hoped-for son, she took a wheaten straw, for every daughter, an oat straw. She then plaited them into a garter and wore it round her leg, repeating certain words as she did so. Blakeborough was unable to learn what the exact words were, only that they referred to the straw on which the Infant Jesus lay in the manger.

The garter had to be worn from the Friday evening to the following Monday morning. If it remained in position all that time, the omen was good, but if it broke or fell off, the charm would not work. It was also essential that the husband-to-be should know nothing about it.

The most interesting belief connected with this charm was that only a virgin could use it with safety. If it was used by a girl who had lapsed from virtue at any time in her life, it brought evil of some sort to every child of her coming marriage.

STRAW HAT

Oxfordshire children sometimes watch in early summer for the first man to be seen wearing a straw hat. As soon as he appears, they 'touch elbows, touch hands' alternately, and sing,

> Strawberry Man, Strawberry Man,
> Bring me good luck,
> Today or tomorrow,
> To pick something up.

They then pick up a stone or some other small object, and throw it over the left shoulder. This charm is supposed to ensure general good luck and, more particularly, the acquisition of a gift or a 'find' within a few days.

In their magnificent collection of schoolchildren's customs and beliefs, Iona and Peter Opie[1] record many similar charms, still extant in various parts of England. The words vary, and in some places, it is necessary to spit, or lick finger or thumb, or keep the fingers crossed until three dogs are seen. The underlying belief in the luck-bringing nature of the first straw-hatted man seen seems to be everywhere the same, whatever the ritual employed.

STUMBLING

Stumbling is usually thought to be unlucky, especially if it happens early in the day, at the start of a journey, or at the beginning of an enterprise. This belief is very ancient, and probably springs from memories of a rougher and more dangerous world than ours, when any lack of physical co-ordination or carelessness in observation might have fatal results in a moment of sudden peril. For a soldier to stumble before a battle, for a ruler to do so on a state occasion, or a traveller when he started out or landed on a new shore, was always a bad omen. So was it if a man tripped on the threshold of a house entered for the first time, or if a bride did so when she came to her new home. In Yorkshire, if either the bridegroom or the bride stumbled as they approached the altar rails during the wedding ceremony, it was thought to be a sure sign of a pre-marital moral lapse.

Stumbling on a staircase has its own lore, see Stairs, foretelling bad luck when going down, a wedding when going up. To stumble near the open grave at a funeral is a death omen. If an actor trips as he makes his first entrance, he will miss a cue, or forget his lines at some time during the performance, unless he is able to retrace his steps and make a fresh start. To fall on the stage (as distinct from mere stumbling) is a good sign and foretells a long engagement.

SUN

Ancient sun-worship has left many traces in superstition and custom. The still living association of the right-hand circuit with good luck is connected with it, see Sunwise Turn, and so were the bonfires that once blazed everywhere at Beltane, Midsummer and Hallowe'en. These were luck-bringing and fertilizing fires in their later days, but in pagan times they were imitative rituals to strengthen the sun on the first day of Summer, at the turn of the year, and at the beginning of Winter. Those which burn so merrily now on 5 November, only five days later than their Hallowe'en predecessors, probably have the same roots, in spite of the fact that they actually celebrate

[1] Iona and Peter Opie, The Lore and Language of Schoolchildren, 1959.

the failure of the Gunpowder Plot in 1605. Protestant fervour and a civic holiday established by Parliament in 1606 helped to keep them alive; but the fact that they have persisted to our own day may be due less to historical factors than to subconscious memories of bonfires lit about this season from time immemorial.

Because the sun was anciently divine, it is unlucky to point at it, as it is to point at other heavenly bodies. In Hungary formerly, it was said that if a girl threw sweepings in the sun's direction, she would never marry. There is a Cornish tradition that the sun never shines upon a perjuror, or at least, when it does, he cannot feel its warmth or see its light.

It has already been noted elsewhere in this book that it is fortunate to be born at sunrise, and the reverse to be born at sunset, that it is a good sign if sunshine falls about a bride, and a death omen if a direct ray strikes upon a mourner at a funeral. If the sun's heat is unseasonably strong on Christmas morning, many fires in the district are foretold in the following twelve months, but if it shines through the apple-trees then, or on Easter Day, the next crop will be a heavy one, and the owner of the trees will have a fortunate year.

The belief that the sun dances at its rising on Easter morning, for joy that Our Lord is risen, was once very widespread. As late as the end of last century, many people used to rise early and go to some hill-top or open space to see it leap and change colour, or swing round and round like a wheel. This lovely sight could not always be seen, but many firmly believed that they had seen it at least once or twice, a quite genuine belief that may in some cases have been partly due to the flickering effect that is sometimes visible in a sunrise viewed from a high place. The explanation often given for not seeing it was that the Devil always tried to put some obstruction between the dancing sun and the observer.

In 1864, a Devonshire clergyman[1] was told by one of his parishioners how, three or four years before, she and a party of friends went to the end of a local lane, and 'there was the sun whirling round and round, and every now and then jumping up'. One of the most beautiful descriptions of the sun's Easter dance was given by an old Scotswoman who had seen it only once in her life to the author of *Carmina Gaedelica*. 'The glorious gold-bright sun was after rising on the crests of the great hills,' she said, 'and it was changing colour – green, purple, red, blood-red, white, intense-white, and gold-white, like the glory of the God of the elements to the children of men. It was dancing up and down in exultation at the joyous resurrection of the beloved Saviour of victory.'

A less usual tradition, found mostly in Devon and Somerset, was that the image of the Lamb and Flag appeared in the centre of the sun's disc for a few minutes after its rising. *See Lamb.*

[1] *Notes and Queries*, 1864. Vol. III.

A form of weather-divination known as Wading of the Sun was formerly practised on Easter Sunday in the Lincolnshire marshes. A bucket of water was so placed that it caught the first rays of the rising sun. If the light shone clearly and steadily in the water, the coming season would be good, but if it trembled and glimmered uncertainly, a bad, wet season was to be expected.

Primitive peoples feared an eclipse of the sun because they believed that the encroaching shadow was some devouring dragon or demon who was destroying the source of all light and warmth. A later form of this dread was the superstition that an eclipse foretold some great disaster, such as war or pestilence, famine, or the deaths of kings. In Herefordshire, it was unlucky (as well as bad for the sight) to watch it directly. It could only be safely observed through the reflection in a bucket of water.

A country tradition says that the sun always shines on Saturday, if only for a few moments. If it shines on Easter Day, it will do so again on Whit-Sunday.

SUNWISE TURN

The custom of turning the way of the sun, or *deiseil*, when performing any important ceremony or luck-bringing rite, is very old, and has its roots in ancient sun-worship. The sun, the source of all earthly life and fertility, seems to go from east to west, and its worshippers did likewise on every ritual occasion. To go widdershins, or against the sun, strengthened the powers of darkness and brought dire misfortune; and even today, many people believe the left hand or 'anti-clockwise' turn to be ill-omened.

Rites or charms involving a circular movement were almost always performed *deiseil*, and many still are. When processions circuit holy wells or beat the parish bounds, or young people join hands in a wide ring to 'clip' the church, they go in a sunwise direction. Most circular dances and games swing first to the right. Passing port 'clockwise' round the table is so general a practice that it has now become a convention, the magical origin of which has been forgotten. When every parish had its own mill, the millstones were always set to run with the sun. It is still a belief of some housewives that if jams, sauces, and other liquids are not so stirred, the cooking will be a failure.

In the Isle of Lewis formerly, the cattle brought down from the shielings at the beginning of winter were guarded from disease by a man who went three times round them, bearing fire in his right hand and travelling from east to west. If any beast had injured its foot, it could be cured by being driven sunwise round a stone. Until well into the nineteenth century, Lancashire people fertilized their fields at Hallowtide by lighting bonfires on hills and cairns, and carrying flaming brands about the fields. In some parishes, the bonfires were allowed to burn out, and their ashes were strewn over the ground next morning. In both cases, it was necessary to travel right-handed, or the magic would not work.

In many fishing ports also, vessels made a wide *deiseil* turn, or three such turns, as they left the harbour for the fishing-ground, in order to ensure a good catch and a safe home-coming.

An old Gaelic method of calling down a blessing upon some loved or respected person was to walk *deiseil* round him whilst invoking God and the saints on his behalf. Scottish wedding-parties often walked sunwise round the church for luck immediately after the ceremony. During the dangerous period between a birth and the baptism, and before the mother was churched, the father or the midwife would protect the woman and the child by carrying a lighted candle round the bed in an east-west direction. Sometimes more devout householders substituted an open Bible for the pagan fire, waving it three times round in the name of each Person of the Holy Trinity, but always carrying it the way of the sun.

The dead also went to their last rest thus. When walking funerals were more usual than they are now, the coffin was often taken once or three times round the graveyard before the burial or, in some parishes, round the churchyard cross. To omit this ceremony, or to go the wrong way, imperilled the dead man's soul. At Brilley in Herefordshire, a stone which stood in an open space outside the churchyard was so encircled. It was known as the Funeral Stone, and is believed by some to have been the base of a vanished cross. The local people said that if the coffin was carried three times round it, the Devil would be prevented from seizing the soul of the corpse.

To go widdershins deliberately was usually done for some dark purpose, such as evoking evil spirits or casting a spell upon some person or thing. Charles Plummer, in his *Lives of the Irish Saints*, tells an odd tale about St Maedoc who, wishing to prevent one of the O'Rourkes from gaining the throne, forced the nobles of Ireland to go the wrong way round Tara. As a result, neither O'Rourke himself nor any of his descendants ever reigned over Ireland. In *Thorfinn's Saga*, it is related that a woman brought down an avalanche on an Icelandic farm by running round it widdershins and looking in every direction. When she began, it was a night of keen frost, but as she ran round and round, there came first fog, then an icy wind, and finally the avalanche which thundered down upon the house and killed twelve men.

In northern England, there is a still remembered tradition that if a man runs widdershins three times round a church at night, he will see the Devil looking out at him from the porch.

SWALLOW

The swallow is a bird of blessing in most parts of Britain and Europe. Its arrival foretells the coming of Summer, the season of plenty, and it is traditionally associated with water, which brings life, and with fertility. In some legends, it shares with the wren the honour of being the bird that brought fire to mankind. By this perilous service it gained its red markings and its smoky blue feathers.

It is widely held to be a very good sign if a swallow builds its nest upon a house. Such a dwelling is protected from fire and lightning and will be fortunate in other ways. If, however, the birds desert the nest later on, or fail to return to the same house next year, the omen is bad.

To destroy such a nest is very unlucky. Many people today would be reluctant to do so, and formerly it was thought to be almost sinful. Bloody milk from the cows was one of the least of the disasters likely to follow such an act. Henderson[1] relates how, when a certain banker of Hull acquired a farm, his sons pulled down all the swallows' nests from the eaves. 'The bank broke soon after,' said Henderson's informant, 'and, poor things, the family have had nought but trouble since.'

To kill a swallow is still more unlucky, a belief of which even cats seem to be aware, for they seldom or never eat one. According to one tradition, it is an omen of evil if one dies while being held in the hand, whether the person holding it has caused its death or not.

In spite of its luck-bringing virtues, the swallow has its darker side. In Ireland, it is said to be the Devil's bird, and there is a Scottish tradition that, like the magpie, it has a drop of the Devil's blood under its tongue. Swallows flying over the house are fortunate, but if one comes down the chimney, or enters a room, it foretells a death. In Germany, if many perch on the roof, it is a sign of coming poverty. In some districts, if one flies under a horse or a cow, the animal will die, and if it alights on a man's shoulder or hand, that man will not live long.

Aubrey relates in his *Miscellanies* how in 1648, when the tide of events was running strongly against the Royalists and Charles I was a prisoner, the Rector of Stretton in Herefordshire stood in the bay-window of the Manor House to drink the King's health. As he raised the cup to his lips, a swallow flew through the window, perched on the cup's brim, sipped a little of the cider, and then flew out again. Aubrey does not attempt to explain this happening, but it could have been, and perhaps was by some, construed as a death-warning only too well fulfilled by the execution of the King in the following January.

Swallows were supposed to cure dim sight in their young by using the herb Swallow-wort, *see Celandine*, and also by means of a stone contained in their bodies. This stone, if taken from the bird about the time of the August full moon (or, according to Winstanley's *Book of Knowledge*, on a Wednesday), cured epilepsy and blindness in human beings, protected them from peril, secured the love of a desired woman and, if placed under the tongue, made its owner eloquent. Another cure for epilepsy recommended in the seventeenth century was swallow-broth, or a concoction of the birds' bodies,

---

[1] Wm. Henderson, *op. cit.*

pounded with their feathers on, mixed with white wine. These preparations also healed hysteria, palsy, and kidney troubles.

At one time, it was believed that swallows did not migrate in winter, but slept in holes in cliffs or in the ground. Aristotle alleged that this was so, and even Gilbert White, though he knew that some birds migrated, thought that others sheltered in holes, coming out in warm weather. Another theory propounded by Olaus Magnus[1] was that on the approach of Winter, all the swallows of the district flew together, joined leg to leg and wing to wing and, after a most sweet singing, submerged themselves in ponds and lakes, from which they rose again in Spring.

SWAN

The swan was a sacred bird all over northern Europe and in Siberia. In Scandinavia, it was associated with Freyr and with the white cirrus clouds that formed his chariot, and also with the Valkyries who summoned to Valhalla those who died in battle. In ancient Greece, too, it was connected with the gods. Apollo's chariot was drawn by swans when he flew north-wards to the land of youth, and he himself, with his twin sister, Artemis, was born from the union of Leto with the great God, Zeus, who came to her in the form of a swan. In another version of this story, Leda was visited by Jupiter in swan-form and laid two eggs, from one of which sprang the Divine Twins, Castor and Pollux, and from the other, Clytemnestra and Helena.

A very well-known folk-tale is that of the Swan-maiden who becomes the wife of a human being. It has many variants, but in its most usual form it concerns a flock of swans who alight by some lake or river, and there divest themselves of their feather robes and bathe as women in the water. A man steals the feathers of one and so gains power over her. She becomes his wife and remains with him, often for years, until one day she discovers the place where he has hidden the robe. She puts it on, becomes a swan once more, and flies away, never to be seen by her husband again.

In parts of Scotland and Ireland, it is considered very unlucky to kill a swan because these birds embody human souls. Misfortune will befall whoever does so; in some districts, it is said that he will die within a year, in others that if not the slayer, then someone else in the parish will die.

Tradition says that swans' eggs are hatched only during storms, and that it is the thunder and lightning which breaks the shells. In his *Defensative against the Poyson of Supposed Superstition* (1538), Lord Northampton remarks that 'It chanceth sometimes to thunder about that time and season of the yeare when Swannes hatch their young; and yet no doubt it is a paradox of simple men to think that a Swanne cannot hatch without a crack of thunder'.

[1] *Historia de gentibus septentrionalibus*, 1555.

One of the most persistent legends about swans is that they sing before they die. Plato mentioned it, and so does Aristotle, who says that when death approaches, the birds fly out to sea, and that sailors along the Libyan coast had heard them singing mournfully in their last moments. Shakespeare refers to the tradition, and so does Sir Thomas Browne in his *Vulgar Errors*, though he did not believe it. But if their death-song was the most famous, it was not their only music. They could also sing at other times, and in one Irish story we are told that once, when a great company of swans wearing silver chains and gold coronets alighted on Lough Bel Dragon, they sang so sweetly that all who heard them fell into a deep sleep for three nights and days.

SWEARING

Superstitions about swearing are a curious blend of genuine religious dislike of cursing and blasphemy, and a strong fear that bad luck will follow. To swear is not only to speak lightly of that which should only be spoken of with reverence; it is also quite often thought to be a direct evocation of the powers of evil. It is perhaps because of this latter belief that some skippers of fishing-vessels sternly forbid any kind of profanity when at sea. Ethel Rudkin[1] records that on Trentside the river boatmen would swear quite freely in their ordinary talk, but they would never under any circumstances curse the keel or the nets. Serious misfortune of some kind would inevitably follow.

SWEEPING

When a woman sweeps her house, tradition requires that she should always sweep the dust inwards, or bad luck will follow. If she sweeps it outwards through the door, it will carry away all the money and good fortune of the family. The omen is particularly bad if such outward-sweeping is done by a bride when she cleans the rooms of her new home for the first time or, in Yorkshire, if it is done by a man.

This association of household dust with wealth and prosperity was once widespread in Europe. One of the charges made in 1323 against the Irish witch, Alice Kyteler, was that she had attempted to rob the citizens of Kilkenny for the benefit of her son, by sweeping the dust from before their doors, saying as she did so,

> To the house of William my son,
> Hie all the wealth of Kilkenny town.

When a room has been correctly swept inwards, it is quite safe to gather

[1] E. Rudkin, *op. cit.*

the dust into some receptacle and carry it outside thus. In the case of upper rooms, however, this must always be done before twelve o'clock (noon). If dust is carried down the stairs after that time, a corpse will shortly be carried down the same stairs.

To sweep the house in any direction on New Year's Day, or on Good Friday, is very unlucky, for it will cause the death of someone in the family. A besom made of birch-twigs, or of green broom, should never be used during the month of May for the same reason. An old rhyme says,

> If you sweep the house with broom in May,
> You'll sweep the head of that house away.

See Besom.

SWIFTS

Swifts are usually included among the sacred or luck-bringing birds whose persons or nests must never be harmed. In Herefordshire, they are associated with the robin, wren, and swallow in a rhyme which runs:

> The Robin and the Wren,
> Are God Almighty's cock and hen.
> The Swallow and the Swift
> Are God Almighty's gift.

In some areas, however, they are said to be the Devil's birds, and elsewhere they are connected with the dead. R. M. Heanley[1] says that in Lincolnshire they were believed to be the souls of the lost, 'vainly bewailing the opportunities of grace which during their lifetime they had neglected'. It seems odd that the excited cries of these birds, one of the happiest of summer sounds, should ever have suggested so melancholy an idea to anybody, but this belief is not peculiar to Lincolnshire, and has been found in other parts of Britain also.

T

TABLE LINEN

The conventional custom whereby a casual visitor, invited to a single meal in another man's house, does not fold his napkin at the meal's end has its roots in a superstition. Tradition says that whoever does so, especially if the

---

[1] R. M. Heanley, *op. cit.*

meal happens to be the first he has eaten in that house, will never again return there. Fate will prevent his doing so, however welcome he may be. Guests staying for a longer period are not affected by this superstition, for they have become, even though only temporarily, part of their host's household.

In some districts, it is said to be unlucky to leave a white tablecloth on the table overnight.

A 'coffin' in an ironed tablecloth denotes a coming parting or a death. *See Laundry.*

TABUED WORDS AT SEA. *See Names.*

TAXI-CAB NUMBERS

Taxi-cab drivers believe it is lucky for the index numbers of their cabs to contain a seven, or multiples of seven. It is also lucky if they contain the letter U, because this resembles a horseshoe. Herbert Hodge in his *Cab, Sir?* (1939) says that a driver who has two U's in his number 'feels he cannot possibly go wrong'.

TEA

In Worcestershire formerly, it was said that tea-leaves strewn in front of a house kept away evil spirits. This is a rare instance of belief in the protective powers of the plant, which is more usually associated with divination and omens.

Divination by tea-leaves is still quite common. An elaborate system of fortune-telling is based on the shapes and figures formed by leaves left at the bottom of an emptied cup, after the user of the cup has swung it round three times and then turned it upside down to drain off the last drops of liquid. A single stalk floating on top of the tea foretells the coming of a stranger, a man if the stalk is hard, a woman if it is soft. To find out when he or she may be expected, the stalk is laid on the back of the left hand and hit with the right hand until it falls off. As many blows as are needed to move it, so many days will elapse before the visitor arrives. In some districts, such a stalk represents a lover, and the hitting charm is used to see how many months or years must pass before marriage.

If the lid is accidentally left off the teapot, this also foretells a coming stranger or, in some places, bad luck. It is unlucky to stir the tea in the pot; to do so causes quarrels. If two women pour out of the same pot, one of them will have a baby within the year, or some member of her family will do so. Another version is that one or both will meet with misfortune soon afterwards.

TEARS

Although anything even faintly suggestive of sorrow or misfortune is thought unlucky at a wedding, tears shed then seem to be an exception to the general rule. No one prophesies evil if the bride's mother cries on parting with her daughter, and in some districts, it is said to be a good omen if the bride herself weeps freely. At christenings also, it is a good sign if the baby cries. *See Baptism.* It is, in fact, unlucky if he does not, and nurses and godparents have been known to give the poor child a surreptitious pinch or slap to make him do so.

Tears at a death are another matter. If they are shed over a dying person, they hinder his peaceful departure and force him to 'die hard'. Those who give way to extreme grief at such times are said to be 'crying back the dying'. In some areas it is believed that they will suffer for this cruel selfishness later on by the loss of a faculty, or some other misfortune. According to an Irish tradition mentioned by Lady Wilde, no one should weep for at least three hours after a death, lest the soul be held back on its journey to the next world.

Grief too long continued is also said to injure the departed. If the living will not resign themselves to their loss, the dead cannot break free of earthly ties, which the tears of the mourners constantly renew, and so they are unable to pass onwards in peace.

TEETH

It is commonly supposed to be a very bad sign if a child is born with a tooth, or teeth, already in his head. Such a happening foretells different things in different districts, but all of them are bad. The child will be unlucky in life, or he will have an ungovernable temper, or he will die by violence. What may well be an older version of these beliefs was recorded in Oxfordshire about 1951. A midwife, asked about the superstition, said, 'I never speak of it, and if anyone asks me, I deny it for the sake of the mother; but it means that the child will grow up to be a murderer.'

The difficult period of teething has its own omens, and also its own dangers, which are, or were, guarded against by the use of numerous charms. The coral-and-bells often given still as a christening present was one of these, *see Coral*, and so was a necklet of nine strands of scarlet silk, knotted at regular intervals, which some midwives hung round the baby's neck as soon as he was washed, and left there until teething was over. Another protective charm, also worn round the neck, was a bag containing nine or seven woodlice, put in alive, or a few hairs drawn from a donkey's cross. All these, and many more, were supposed to make the teeth come more easily, and also to guard the child from evil influences during the dangerous period of change.

If the first tooth appears in the lower jaw, the child will die in infancy, and so too, if the teeth are irregularly spaced. In some areas, teething earlier than usual is also thought to be a death omen. Yorkshire people say 'soon todd, soon with God', and the same notion is found in other parts of northern England and in Scotland. Elsewhere, however, early teething by the existing baby means another birth in the family before long. 'Soon teeth, soon toes' is a well-known country saying expressing this belief. In Northamptonshire, it is a lucky sign, foretelling wealth and prosperity, if the two front teeth are sufficiently far apart for a small coin to be inserted between them; but in north-eastern Scotland, this predicts 'a lichtsome character', and a too great fondness for the opposite sex.

Until at least as late as the end of last century, fallen or extracted teeth were often carefully saved until the death of the owner, and were then buried with him in his coffin. Even the milk-teeth of children were sometimes so preserved by mothers, and given into the care of the children when they had grown up. This custom was connected with the ancient and persistent notion that a man's body must be complete on burial, see Burial, Complete, but another and particular reason was often given for it. This was that the teeth must be placed ready to the dead man's hand because when he reached Heaven, he would have to account for all the teeth he had had in this life. If he could not do so, he would have to search for them on Judgement Day. In some areas, it was believed that this wearisome task could be avoided, even without the burial rite, if each tooth, as it came out, was sprinkled with salt and thrown on to the fire. It was necessary to say whilst doing this,

> Good tooth, bad tooth,
> Pray God, send me a good tooth,

or

> Fire, burn; burn tooth (or bëan)
> And give me another;
> Not a cruck's one,
> But a straight one,

or yet another of the many variants of the same incantation.

A second reason for burning extracted or fallen teeth was to prevent witchcraft. It was considered extremely unwise to throw a tooth away, for a witch might find it and work evil through it on its former owner. Although few people today admit to a belief in witchcraft, it is still customary in many families for the milk-teeth of children to be salted and burnt in the traditional manner as soon as they fall out. If possible, this rite should be performed by the mother. Round Oxford it is, or was until very recently, a fixed rule among schoolchildren that if a tooth comes out during school-hours, it must not be burnt then and there, but must be taken home for the mother to put on the fire. It may be added that the sentimental custom of setting children's first teeth in a brooch would once have been regarded as extremely dangerous, since the brooch might be lost and perhaps found by a witch, with consequent evil results for the child.

In some parts of England, the reason given for destroying milk-teeth by fire is not witchcraft, or even a vague idea of bad luck, but to prevent any animal getting hold of them. If this happens, the child's second teeth will resemble those of the animal concerned, or some of them may. Charlotte Latham[1] mentions the Sussex case of 'old Master Simmons, who had a very large pig's tooth in his upper jaw'. Her informant said this was due to the fact that his mother had accidentally thrown one of his milk-teeth into a pig's trough. On the other hand, milk-teeth were sometimes buried in a mouse-hole, so that the new ones should be small and sharp, like those of a mouse. Harvey Bloom[2] records this as a Warwickshire custom when he wrote in 1929. Three hundred years earlier, Aubrey was told of something very like it in seventeenth-century Germany. 'Cramer saith,' he observes in *Remaines of Gentilisme and Judaisme*, 'that in Germany, in his native Country, some women will bid their Children to take the Tooth, which is fallen or taken out, and goe to a dark corner of the house or Parlour, and cast the same into it thereby saying these words:

> Mouse! Here I give thee a tooth of bone,
> But give thou me an Iron-on,

(or Iron Tooth), beleeving, that another good tooth will grow in its place.'

It is unlucky to count one's own teeth, or to dream of them, especially if they seem to fall out in the dream. This is an omen of coming sorrow, or the loss of a near friend.

A tooth taken from a dead man's skull and worn on the person was once held to be a sure method of protecting the wearer from toothache. Another was to hang a bag containing the feet of a mole over the mantelpiece, or on the person. Written charms were also used for this purpose. One such 'scriven', found all over England, had many variants, both in prose and verse, and was supposed to be worn by its owner, who would not suffer from tooth-ache as long as he did so. One version, recorded in the *Denham Tracts*, is as follows:

> Peter was sitting on a marble stone,
> And Jesus passed by:
> Peter said, 'My Lord! My God!
> How my tooth doth ache!'
> Jesus said, 'Peter art whole!
> And whosoever keeps these words for my sake
> Shall never have the toothache.' Amen.

[1] Charlotte Latham, *op. cit.*   [2] J. Harvey Bloom, *op. cit.*

Written charms of this sort were often sold by wisemen and white witches, although in one case mentioned by Francis Havergal in *Herefordshire Words and Phrases* (1887), the charm failed because sixpence in money was given for it.

Many other magical cures for toothache, or methods of preventing its onset, were known formerly, and some of them are described elsewhere in this book, under the headings of the herb or object used. Two semi-magical methods of extracting a decayed tooth are given in *Arcana Fairfaxiana Manuscripta*. One was to mix wheat-flour with the milk of spurge and fill the hollow tooth with the resulting paste. The other was to 'take wormes when they be a gendering together; dry them upon a hott tyle stone, then make a powder of them, and what tooth ye touch with it will fall out'. No doubt, either method was preferable to the rough-and-ready practices of seventeenth-century dentists.

TENCH

A common country tradition says that the skin of the tench contains healing oils, and that other freshwater fish know this, and rub themselves against it when they are sick. Because of this belief, the tench is sometimes called the Doctor Fish.

Aubrey[1] mentions 'an approved receipt for the yellow jaundise' in which tenches slit in two were applied to the soles of the sufferer's feet and round the region of his heart. He remarks cheerfully that they will 'stinke within an hower', but nevertheless, they had to be left in position for twelve hours, after which they were removed and buried in the earth, and others were laid on in their place. 'A matter of five applications,' says Aubrey, 'will doe the cure, if not too late.' He adds that the backbone must be taken out beforehand, and the head cut off 'because it will be uneasy on the patient'.

In the seventeenth century, it was a common practice to apply various things, such as pigeons, sheep's lungs, or bullock's milts, to the feet or to plague sores, in order to reduce fever or extract the venom. Since the tench's skin, besides being thought of medicinal value in itself, is yellowish, the fish would obviously be suitable for treating the yellow disease. The additional requirement in this case of immediate burial in earth suggests that there was a magical element also in this cure, the ailment being transferred by contact from the patient to the tench, and safely buried with it.

THEATRE ATTENDANTS

Theatre attendants, like actors, have a number of superstitions connected with their work. In the Box Office it is said that if the first person to buy seats for a new production is old, the play will have a long run, but if he or she

[1] J. Aubrey, *Royal Soc. MSS.* fol. 157.

is young, the omen is bad. If a torn banknote is proffered in payment for tickets, it is a sign that the girl in the office will soon change her work.

It is lucky for an usher to seat the first patron to arrive on any night, unless that patron happens to hold a ticket numbered thirteen. If this is the case, everything will go wrong for the usher during the rest of the performance. Similarly, bad luck will follow if she does not hear the first words of the play, or if a woman faints in the section of which she is in charge.

It is unlucky to accept a tip from a woman buying a programme, though not from a man in the same circumstances. The first tip received at the beginning of a new season should not be spent. It should be vigorously rubbed against the recipient's legs, and then kept in the pocket for the rest of the run to ensure that it will be followed by many others.

THIRTEEN. *See Numbers.*

THYME

The souls of the dead were once thought to dwell in the flowers of thyme, as they did also in bean-blossoms and in foxgloves. In English tradition, the scent of thyme is specially associated with the ghosts of the murdered. If it clings persistently about a particular place where no plants grow to account for it, it is a sign that a murder has been committed there at some period. A Lancashire legend says that a traveller was once killed under a tree near Staining Hall, and that ever since that day the tree has given out a sweet odour of thyme. S. O. Addy tells a similar story in his *Household Tales* concerning a footpath near Dronfield, in Derbyshire. A young man murdered his sweetheart there when she was carrying a bunch of blossoming thyme, and thereafter the scent of the flowers was always noticeable at that spot.

In Derbyshire formerly, it was usual to bring thyme and southernwood into the house after a death, and to keep them there until the corpse was carried out for burial. But when the coffin was dressed with flowers, thyme was always omitted, 'for the dead have nothing to do with time'. This curious punning superstition is found in other counties also. In some districts, however, sprigs of the plant were taken to the churchyard and dropped upon the coffin as it was lowered into the grave.

Notwithstanding these associations with death, thyme was believed to give courage to those who used it, and in folk-medicine it was included in remedies for melancholy and depression.

TIDES

In many coastal areas still, the state of the tide is believed to affect the lives and actions of those who live by the sea. Births are thought most likely to occur with the flowing tide, and death with the ebb. *See Birth, Times of, and Death, Times of.* In *The People of the Sea* (1954), David Thomson records an Orkney belief that a marriage celebrated during the ebb will not be fruitful. Along the eastern coasts of England, children suffering from whooping-cough were formerly taken down to the shore to meet the incoming tide, in the belief that when it ebbed again, it would take the cough with it.

Butter is often said to form more quickly in the churn when the tide is flowing. In Brittany, water boils faster then, and any sea-birds' feathers that may be contained in mattresses or eiderdowns will swell up. Pigs are killed and, in some districts, clover is planted with the rising tide, but human hair should not be cut then, on pain of catching cold, nor should wounds be dressed or baths taken. In Scotland, if a poultry-farmer desires cockerels, he will set his eggs at the flood, if hens, at the ebb.

Children who live by the sea are frequently warned that if they make faces at the moment when the tide turns (or in some parts, at any time during the flow) they run the risk of finding the grimace is permanently fixed.

TOAD

Toads have a very mixed reputation in folk-belief. They are sometimes lucky and very often unlucky. They can be used in healing-charms and as a poison, and they are closely associated with witchcraft and black magic.

It is lucky to meet a toad. To kill one brings down rain or may cause a storm. A dried toad's heart carried about by a thief ensures him against detection, or if beaten to a powder and swallowed in a drink, it prevents epilepsy. In *Arcana Fairfaxiana Manuscripta* it is stated that a toad, killed and dried in March and worn in a silk bag next to the skin, will stop bleeding at the nose; 'by God's grace', says the pious writer, 'it will stanch presently.'

Dropsy, rheumatism, and the plague could be healed or averted by wearing the ashes of a burnt toad. A charm against the King's Evil was to hang a living reptile in a bag round the neck until it died, or to cut off the creature's hind leg and wear that. Tumours, swellings, warts, skin diseases, and various other ills were thought to be curable by the same cruel device. Mrs Leather[1] records that a man at Walford in Herefordshire told her that he had been advised by a gypsy to try it for an obstinate abcess in his arm. Having severed the leg, he cut a turf from beneath a hedge and placed the still living toad under it. He then wrapped the leg in a silk handkerchief and hung it round his neck. Next morning, he looked to see if the toad had gone. It had, presumably taking the trouble with it, for his abcess dried up within three weeks.

Witches were sometimes thought to have familiar spirits in the form of toads, and occasionally to take that shape themselves. In 1879, the *Leigh*

[1] E. M. Leather, *op. cit.*

Chronicle (19 April 1879) reported that a man was charged at East Dereham Petty Sessions with assaulting a young woman. His defence was that she and her mother had bewitched him, depriving him of rest and sleep, by burying a walking-toad in his garden.

Heanley[1] describes a peculiarly horrible Lincolnshire charm whereby a girl could force an unwilling man to marry her. She had to go to a Communion Service and keep the holy bread in her mouth until the service was over. When she came out of the church, she would find a toad waiting for her. She had then to spit out the bread, which the toad would eat, and the next time she met her lover, he would be ready to marry her. The same rite could be employed by those who desired to become witches. Evidently the reptile in both these cases was the Devil himself. The return of a dead man in toad-shape to his old home, also in Lincolnshire, has already been described under *Burial Preparations*.

A Yorkshire method of acquiring the power of the Evil Eye is recorded in *Notes and Queries* (Vol. I, 1849). A Catterick woman told the writer that all that was necessary was to go out at night on as many nights as were needed for the task, and find nine toads, hang them up on a string to die, and then bury them in a hole in the ground. The charmer's eye would thus become evil, and if he looked at anyone with intent to injure him, that person would pine away as the toads decayed, 'without any desease at all', and eventually die.

Toad-magic could be used against witches as well as by them. A Devonshire charm to destroy their power was to take three small-necked jars and place in each the heart of a toad studded with thorns and the liver of a frog full of new pins. The jars, carefully corked and sealed, had then to be buried in three separate churchyards, seven inches below ground-surface, and seven feet from the church porch. While this was being done, the Lord's Prayer had to be repeated backwards, an evil and dangerous proceeding which must surely have prevented the charm's use by any but the very determined or the very frightened. The operator was supposed thereafter to be safe from witch-craft for ever.

The frog-bone control charm already mentioned, *see Frog*, had even greater force when the bone used was that of a toad. The same ritual was needed to obtain it, although in some accounts, there were other and more terrifying features. The bone was said to scream as it floated upstream in so horrible a manner that only a brave man could endure the sound. Nor was it enough merely to withdraw it from the water. The operator had afterwards to go with it to the stable on three successive nights, on the third of which he would see the Devil in person, and be forced to fight with him.

If he had the courage to go through all this, he became a Toadman, having power over horses and pigs and, in some cases, over human beings, especially

[1] R. M. Heanley, *op. cit.*

women. Like the possessors of the Horseman's Word (see p. 195), he could do anything he liked with horses, and his services were always in demand on any farm where they were kept. Toadmen seem to have flourished particularly in eastern England, and faith in their powers existed until a very late date in the Isle of Ely, South Lincolnshire, and the Soke of Peterborough. A contributor to *Folk-Lore*[1] says that in 1950 he was told in the March, Peterborough and Stamford districts that they were well known between the two wars. One man said he had worked on the same farm with one, and others spoke of them either from their own personal knowledge, or from the information of friends and relatives. All agreed that the charm, though potent with animals and living beings, would not work with tractors and machinery.

TOADSTONE

The dark grey or light brown stone often called a Toadstone was formerly supposed to come from the heads of very old toads, and to be taken from them when they were dying. They were thought to be lucky, and were often worn in rings or personal ornaments. One of their special virtues was to change colour, or sweat, if their wearer was bewitched, or if any liquid standing near them contained poison. They were also used as amulets to protect houses and boats, and were supposed to bring victory to those who carried them in a fight.

In Lupton's *Notable Things*, we read that a sure method of knowing whether a supposed toadstone really is one is to 'holde the stone before a tode, so that he may see it; and if it be a right and true stone, the tode will leape towarde it, and make as though he would snatch it. He envieth so much that man should have that stone'.

TOUCHING THE DEAD

In many households, when a corpse lies in the house awaiting burial, it is customary to invite any visitor or chance caller into the death-chamber to pay his last respects to the departed, whether he knew the dead man in life or not. Such a visitor is usually expected to touch the corpse, and great offence is often taken if he refuses to do so.

This custom is still quite common in numerous districts. In 1959 a Birmingham man whose employment caused him to visit houses regularly stated that he and his colleagues were instructed by their employers to miss from their rounds any house where a death was known to have occurred recently. This was because they would certainly be asked to visit the dead, and it was felt that such a request 'might cause embarrassment'. Mrs Leather[2]

[1] G. W. Pattinson, 'Adult Education and Folklore', *Folk-Lore*, Vol. 64, 1953.
[2] E. M. Leather, *op. cit.*

mentions the case of a Herefordshire child who died of diphtheria in the early years of this century. Almost everyone in the immediate neighbourhood came to touch the corpse, to the great fury of the local doctor when he heard of it.

Various reasons are given for the practice. The most usual is that it prevents the person touching from dreaming of the dead man. In Scotland, it is said to prevent haunting. Cornish people say that the toucher gains the strength of the departed. In some parts of northern England, it is supposed to show that no ill-will existed between the visitor and the dead. Often no reason at all is given, except that it is an act of courtesy. Thus, in one Cheshire village just before the 1939 War, children were carefully trained to perform the rite simply because it was held to be polite to do so.

In earlier times, however, touching the dead had a deeper significance, and it is probably from dim memories of this that the modern custom sprang. It was widely believed that the corpse of a murdered man would bleed at the touch of the murderer. Willingness to take part in what was actually a form of Ordeal was thus an indication of innocence, as refusal to do so was, if not quite a proof of guilt, at least a source of strong suspicion. Prisoners charged with murder were sometimes forced to touch their supposed victims, as part of the evidence for or against them. Thomas Potts relates in *The Wonderfull Discoverie of Witches in the Countie of Lancaster* (1613) that when Jennet Preston was tried at York for the murder by witchcraft of Mr Lister, she was made to touch his body, which bled as soon as she laid her hand upon it. This, says Potts, 'hath euer beene held a great argument to induce a Iurie to hold him guiltie that shall be accused of Murther, and hath seldome, or neuer, fayled in the Tryall'.

Two centuries later, the same belief evidently existed in Oxfordshire, for when in 1828 William Edden was murdered near Thame, his widow summoned the man she suspected to touch the corpse. He refused to come, thereby confirming her suspicions. Some time afterwards his accomplice made a full confession, which also implicated him, and both men were hanged for the murder two years later at Aylesbury.

TOUCHING WOOD OR IRON. *See Boasting.*

TWINS

It is a very common belief that twins, especially identical twins, are united by so strong a bond of sympathy that each knows when danger or misfortune threatens the other, even when they are separated. In the same mysterious way, any special state of happiness or well-being in one of the pair is reflected in the feelings of the other. It is often said that if one twin dies, the other will not live long thereafter, and if the corpse does not stiffen as rapidly as usual, it is a sign that the dead man is waiting for his companion.

If, however, a twin does survive his fellow, the vitality of the latter passes to him, and he becomes stronger and more vigorous than heretofore. In Sussex, such a 'left twin' acquires healing powers and, like the posthumous child, can cure thrush by breathing down the throat of the sufferer. A male 'left twin' is, or was, called in to blow three times into a woman's mouth, a female into that of a man.

In the counties on both sides of the Scottish Border, it was formerly believed that if a woman bore a girl and a boy at one birth, she would never have another child.

U

UMBRELLA

To open an umbrella in the house is generally said to be unlucky, and likely to bring misfortune either to the person who does it or to the household as a whole. In the North Riding of Yorkshire, it is unlucky to lay one on a bed. An umbrella unnecessarily opened during fine weather may bring down the rain. If anyone drops one, he must not pick it up himself, but must allow someone else to do so. In some districts, an umbrella is considered to be a rather ill-omened gift.

Although these beliefs are themselves trifling, it is interesting that they should exist at all in Britain, in view of the late appearance of the umbrella there. In the East, it was a symbol of majesty and was held over the heads of rulers on ceremonial occasions. Only those of royal blood had the right to use it, or those upon whom the King had conferred the privilege as a particular honour. In England, it seems to have been known in its utilitarian form in the seventeenth century, but its use then was not widespread and was confined to women. It was not adopted by Englishmen until after Jonas Hanway had had the courage to appear with one in 1778 in London, where he was at first jeered and hooted at in the streets for using anything so outlandish. How soon the superstitions mentioned above attached themselves to the umbrella is uncertain, but they are now quite well known and seem to be well established.

UNBAPTIZED CHILD

When a baby died unbaptized, the grief of the parents was often greatly increased by the belief that his soul would not be able to enter Heaven. He

was not yet a Christian, and therefore his body had to be buried in unconse-
crated ground on the north side of the churchyard, while his soul, though
safe from Hell, was doomed to wander restlessly in the air until Doomsday.
A more merciful belief was that it dwelt in some intermediate spiritual region
which was not Heaven, but was nevertheless happy, or that it became a
butterfly or a moth, or joined the ranks of the fairies. In parts of Yorkshire,
it was thought to live on as a nightjar, in Devonshire, to become one of the
Yeth Hounds which hunted with the Devil across Dartmoor. Hence, quite
apart from all religious considerations, early baptism was of the utmost
importance and, if the child was weakly or likely to die, the ceremony was
often performed at home by some member of the family, without waiting for
the arrival of a clergyman.

To step on the grave of an unbaptized child was very unlucky. Whoever
did so ran the risk of contracting a fatal disease known as grave-merels, or
grave-scab, the symptoms of which were a burning skin, difficulty in breathing, and trembling of the limbs. The same peril attached in Scotland and
northern England to the grave of a stillborn baby, or, rather oddly, one who
had been overlaid by his nurse.

Sometimes a stillborn or unbaptized child was buried with an adult, the
little coffin being laid at the foot of the larger one during the burial service,
and then in a space at the grave-foot specially made to receive it. In southern
England, it was a fortunate circumstance if a stillborn child was buried in an
open or common grave, because its innocence and sinlessness served as a
passport to Heaven for the next person buried there.

Until the end of last century, the stillborn were often interred in Derbyshire, without any funeral service, at night, or just before sunrise. It was
believed there that if such a child was so buried it would go to Heaven, but
not if it was laid to rest in daylight.

A curious belief which cut across those mentioned above, and also across
self-evident facts, was that an unbaptized child could not die. The *Morning
Herald* of 18 June 1860 reported that a woman accused of attempting to kill
her baby, by abandoning it in a garden near Liverpool, confessed that she had
done so, and added that she had had him baptized first, because otherwise
he would not have died. In fact, he did not, for he was found and rescued in
time to save his life.

URINE

Urine, like blood and spittle, was formerly believed to have magical and
healing powers. Its use as a Life-Index has already been described, *see Life-
Index*. If any person or animal was bewitched, the spell could be broken by
boiling some of the patient's urine. This had to be done with certain ceremonies, the details of which varied slightly in different places. Very often the

nail-parings of human patients, or tufts of hair from animals, had to be added, and almost everywhere the rite was performed at night in a room to which every possible entry had been carefully closed and sealed.

In Suffolk, nine nails drawn from as many horseshoes were boiled in the urine. Two people took part in the ceremony, working in complete silence and communicating with each other only by signs. If any word was spoken, either by them or by anyone else present, the charm would not work. The proceedings began exactly at midnight, and went on until the force of the boiling liquid was strong enough to set three, five, or seven nails in motion at once. If at this point the patient cried out, it was a sign that the spell had been broken. This antidote was often used in cases of ague, wasting diseases and worms in children, and also to heal some cattle ailments supposed to be produced by witchcraft.

Sir Thomas Browne in his *Vulgar Errors* mentions a charm used by young women whose monthly periods were delayed. If they made water upon a newly thrown-up mole-hill, their trouble would cease immediately. A seventeenth-century remedy for ague or fevers, mentioned by Aubrey,[1] was to boil an egg in 'the morning urine of the sick party before it is cold', prick holes all over the shell, and bury it in an ants' nest. Recovery was expected to follow in a few days. 'The receipt,' says Aubrey, 'I had from Captain Hamdon, who hath tried it several times with good success.'

Country people say there is an acid in urine which heals chilblains and chapped hands. The patient should dip his hands (or feet) in his own water while it is still warm, and then gently massage them until they are dry. This must be done night and morning until a cure is effected, which will be quite soon. Warts are said to yield to similar treatment. Another quite widespread belief is that if a young child's gums are regularly rubbed with his own water, he will never suffer from toothache in later life.

A magical cure for persistent bed-wetting in children is to take the patient to the churchyard, and let him make water on the grave of a child of opposite sex. *See also Ash-keys: Eggshells: Mice.*

V

VALERIAN

Valerian was once believed to provoke love, and consequently it was used in love-philtres and aphrodisiacs. Its scent, which Topsell[2] says is like that of a

[1] J. Aubrey, *Royal Soc. MS.* fol. 168.   [2] E. Topsell, *op. cit.*

cat, is now usually disliked, but in the Middle Ages it was considered pleasing, and perfumes were made from the plant for personal use, and to sweeten linen. It is possible that a vague memory of its use in love-charms and perfumery is preserved in the superstition, still sometimes found in Wales and western England, that if a girl wears a spring of valerian, she will never lack suitors.

It is sometimes called Cats' Valerian because cats delight in it and love to roll about on it. Topsell says they dig up the root which 'is very like the eye of a cat', and that he often saw them doing it in his own garden. Rats also like the scent so much that some rat-catchers formerly used the root as a bait for their traps. It has even been suggested that the use of valerian, rather than his magical music, was the secret of the Pied Piper's success with the rats of Hamelyn.

An old name for the plant (which it shares with mistletoe) was All Heal, because it cured so many diseases. It was included in remedies for nervous disorders, insomnia, convulsive coughs, and numerous other ills, and is still used for some of them.

One Eastern variety, *V. Jatamansi*, which grows in the Himalayas, is said to have been the spikenard mentioned in the Bible, the plant from which the precious ointment which St Mary Magdalen brought to Our Lord was made.

VERVAIN

The belief that vervain is a holy and magical herb is very old. In Norse mythology, it was sacred to Thor, and in ancient Persia to the sun. By the Druids, it was venerated almost as much as mistletoe and, when gathered under the Dog Star with appropriate rites, was used by them for magical and healing purposes. In Christian legend, it is said to have been first found growing under the Cross on Calvary, and to have been used to staunch the bleeding of Our Lord's wounds. For this reason, it was sometimes called the Holy Herb, and was believed to have the power of averting evil of all kinds, arresting haemorrhage, and healing serious wounds.

It had, however, to be gathered with great care, during certain phases of the moon and while repeating secret words or incantations. If this was not done, its full strength and virtues were lost. One method of gathering it is described in an Elizabethan manuscript kept in Chetham's Library in Manchester.[1] The seeker went to the place where the herb grew and said:

> All-hele, thou holy herb, Vervin,
> Growing on the ground;
> In the Mount of Calvary,
> There wast thou found.

[1]See J. Harland and T. T. Wilkinson, *Lancashire Folk-Lore*, 1867.

Thou helpest many a grief,
And stanchest many a wound.
In the name of sweet Jesus
I take thee from the ground.
O Lord, effect the same
That I do now go about.

While actually plucking it, he said,

In the name of God, on Mount Olivet
First I thee found.
In the name of Jesus,
I pull thee from the ground.

Vervain, like St John's wort and dill, 'hindered witches of their will', and guarded its owner from the effects of overlooking and many other misfortunes. Nevertheless, it was sometimes said to be an 'enchanter's herb', and witches, if they were often defeated by it, were also supposed to use it in their spells. In Hungary, it was beloved of thieves because, like moonwort in England, it had power over locks and bolts. If a man made a small cut in his hand and pressed a fragment of the leaf into it, that hand would afterwards be able to open any locked door or chest-lid simply by touching it. It was also used in love-charms and aphrodisiacs. In Germany, a wreath made from it was often presented to a bride on her wedding day, both to bring her good luck and to ensure the fertility of the marriage.

The roots hung about a man's neck when he went to bed kept away bad dreams, and a tea made from the leaves soothed nervous excitement and prevented insomnia. In the *Supplement ot the London Pharmocopaeia* (1837) it is stated that a necklace of vervain roots, tied with a yard of white satin ribbon, would help to cure the King's Evil.

Marcellus of Bordeaux mentions a magical remedy for a tumour in *De Medicamentis* (XV). A root of vervain had to be cut in two, and one half had to be hung round the patient's neck. The other was smoked in a fire. As it dried in the heat, so would the tumour dry up and vanish. A sinister rider to this receipt says that if it was desired to bring the tumour back again, all that was necessary was to throw the smoked portion into a basin of water. As it swelled with the moisture, the tumour would return.

VIOLET

In country districts, it is considered unlucky to bring less than a handful ot wild violets indoors at a time. On poultry-rearing farms, to do so is injurious to the young birds, and has the same effect upon them as too few primroses.

If they bloom in autumn, it is a death omen or, in some areas, a sign that an epidemic is threatened.

To dream of violets is fortunate, foretelling a change for the better in the dreamer's circumstances.

In *The Book of the Physicians of Myddvai* it is stated that a sure way to discover whether an injured man would recover was to bind a bruised violet to his forefinger and watch to see whether he slept thereafter. If he did, he would live, if not, he would die.

In the past, violets were used in a number of ways. They were included in some love-charms and philtres. They were candied and eaten as sweetmeats, put into salads, and made into syrups, preserves and cordials. Decoctions of the flowers or leaves were used to cure agues, fevers, jaundice, pleurisy and colds. Plasters of the leaves allayed pain, reduced swellings and ulcers, and healed sore throats. Such remedies have mostly disappeared from official medicine now, but country people still remember them, and occasionally use them. In Oxfordshire, within recent years, an infusion of twenty violet leaves in boiling water was recommended as a drink to allay the pains of cancer. In another part of the same county, a man suffering from an ulcer in the cheek asked his doctor's permission to treat it with a plaster made from the leaves. Permission being given, he did so, and the ulcer healed up and did not return.

A Greek legend of the violet says it sprang up first when Orpheus laid his lute down on a mossy bank. In France, at one time it was the emblem of the Bonapartists because, when Napoleon I was banished to Elba, he said he would return with the violets in the spring.

WASHING

The washing or bathing of the human body has always had a ritual or magical significance, quite apart from any desire for physical cleanliness. From time immemorial men have believed that they could free themselves by ceremonial washing from the spiritual stains of murder and other crimes, and the ritual uncleanness incurred by childbirth, contact with the dead, or the breaking of a *tabu*. When Pilate washed his hands at Our Lord's trial, saying, 'I am innocent of the blood of this just person', he was performing a rite which everyone who saw him do it recognized for what it was, a symbolic and magical act intended to free him from the guilt of shedding Christ's blood. Similarly, when a priest touched sacred things, he washed before he did so to purify himself, and afterwards to remove the contagion of power and holiness which otherwise would make him dangerous to anything he touched in the everyday world.

Ordinary washing had significance also. When a man washed himself, a little of his spiritual essence passed into the water along with the dirt of his body, and he was thus subtly altered for the moment. If due care was not taken, bad luck might follow.

Beliefs of this kind were very long-lived. It is commonly said today that if two people wash their hands in the same water, they will quarrel before night, or some misfortune will befall one or both, unless the cross-sign is first made on the water with the forefinger. Another method of averting the evil is for one of the pair to spit into the water. In some districts it is considered safe to omit these precautions if the two people concerned have known each other intimately for seven years or more, but not otherwise.

Henderson[1] records a Durham superstition which required a man to wash his face before killing anything, perhaps from a vague memory of purification from blood-guilt. Older miners in Wales and elsewhere often dislike washing their backs, and do so only rarely, because of a belief that it will cause the mine-roof to fall upon them. In some mining districts, it is said to weaken the back. It was recently stated in a B.B.C. broadcast that the fishermen of the Milford Haven district abstain from washing during a period of good catches for fear of washing their luck away.

It used to be very generally supposed that a child's right hand should never be thoroughly washed until he was twelve months old, otherwise he would not be able to gather riches in later life. The hand could be wiped with a damp cloth during the early months, but no more.

One of the many methods of curing disease by transferring it from the patient to some other person or thing was to take the water in which the sick man had been washed and throw it down on the road outside the gate of the house. The first living creature to pass over the damp patch would take the illness and the original sufferer would recover. Another method was to entice a stray cat into the house, throw the water over it, and then drive it out again, taking care that it was not allowed to return. The disease would go with it.

WATCHING IN THE CHURCH PORCH

Watching in the Church Porch was a form of death or marriage divination that was well known in most parts of England until at least as late as the latter half of the nineteenth century. It could be performed only on certain significant nights. The most usual date was St Mark's Eve (24 April), but watching on All Souls' Eve or Day, Christmas Eve, and Mid-summer Eve was not uncommon.

[1] Wm. Henderson, *op. cit.*

If a man wished to know who would die in the parish within the coming year, he went to the church porch and waited there for an hour before and an hour after midnight. It was essential that he should remain awake during this time, for if he fell asleep, he would die soon afterwards. At some moment during the two-hour vigil, usually at midnight or a little later, the forms of those destined to die in the ensuing twelve months would appear and pass, one by one into the church. If anyone turned back at the door, or having entered, came out again, it was a sign that he or she would have a dangerous illness, but would recover.

A variant of this belief, found in some parts of Lincolnshire, was that *all* the parishioners would be seen entering the church, and that only those who failed to return were doomed. If a man and a woman came out arm-in-arm, they would marry within the year.

If the watcher was himself fated to die within the period, he would see his own form among the others. In 1899, R. M. Heanley[1] was told at Wainfleet that the parish sexton had watched in the porch some years before in order to see how many burials he might expect in the near future. He saw his own wraith passing into the church and died within a fortnight. Heanley's informant said he had intended to try this divination himself, but had decided against it because he was told that if he watched once, he would be compelled to continue doing so, year after year, until he was finally warned of his own death. Belief in this curious compulsion seems to have been widespread in Lincolnshire, but it was not general elsewhere. In *Folk-Lore concerning Lincoln-shire*, it is said that on the last occasion, the watcher would be unable to keep awake, and thus his death would be certainly foretold.

In some areas, it was thought that the ghostly procession could be seen on the first night of watching. In others, especially in the north of England, it was considered necessary to watch for three successive years, the vision first appearing in the third year.

For marriage divination, the inquirer went at 11 p.m. to the porch and laid a flower there. He (or more often she) then went away, returning at midnight just before the clock struck. If a bridal procession was seen passing into the church, marriage was foretold within the year, the number of bridesmaids denoting how many months must elapse before the wedding. If nothing happened, it meant simply that the watcher would not marry in that particular year; but if he or she was destined to die unwed, a coffin covered by a white cloth would be carried into the church by spectral bearers.

WAXWINGS

The appearance of an unusually large number of waxwings in any one year is said to foretell war, pestilence, and very cold weather.

[1] R. M. Heanley, *op. cit.*

WEANING

To wean a child is to set his feet firmly on the long road to manhood, and consequently, tradition demands that great care should be taken at the beginning of the process. The choice of the season is important, as with all first steps. It is good to begin on a holy or fortunate day. In some districts, Good Friday is considered the most auspicious date, and children who are first weaned then are expected to prosper and be healthy in later life. Ordinary Fridays should be avoided and so, needless to say, should Childermas, or the day of the week on which that ominous festival last fell. *See Childermas.* In Wales formerly, it was believed that a child first weaned when the birds are migrating would grow up to be restless and changeable.

All young things, including human children, are best weaned when the moon is waning, because then the flow of the mother's milk is more easily reduced. Another way of achieving this end is for the woman to throw a little of her milk on to the fire, or into a running stream. As it vanishes in the flames, or is carried away by the water, so the rest will diminish in sympathy and rapidly dry off.

It is, or was, widely held to be extremely unlucky to begin weaning a child and then suckle him again. The effect upon his character or prospects, or both, is disastrous.

WEASEL

The weasel is a beast of evil omen in most countries, including Britain, and especially so if it is white. Witches were formerly supposed to take its form, and so did evil spirits. Hence, the appearance of the creature near a house was an unfortunate sign, and to hear one squeaking nearby was a death omen.

Running across anyone's path, it foretells misfortune and sometimes death, and is an extremely bad omen at the start of any journey. If it runs towards the left, the omen is still worse, and so too, if it runs in front of the traveller and then turns backwards in its path.

In Wales, a weasel going before a person without turning back is sometimes said to denote triumph over enemies, but here also it is unlucky if it veers towards the left, denoting that the observer has enemies in his own household.

Stories are told in some areas of the apparitions of ghostly weasels, usually white. These are almost invariably followed by disaster of some kind.

WEDDING CAKE

The wedding cake is a very ancient feature of the marriage feast, symbolizing fertility and good fortune. By tradition, it should be made of fine wheaten flour, and of as rich a mixture as possible, to indicate abundance. The first slice must always be cut by the bride, otherwise the marriage will be childless. Normally, the husband helps by laying his hand over hers while she is cutting, and sometimes by lending his own knife, or his sword if he is a soldier.

When the rest of the cake has been cut up, all present must eat a little. To refuse is very unlucky, both for the bridal pair and for the person concerned. If a young girl keeps part of her share and sleeps with it under her pillow that night, she will dream of her future husband. This is still done by many, but without the more elaborate ritual of the past, which involved passing a fragment of the cake three times, or in some districts, nine times, through a wedding ring before sleeping on it. The bride also should keep a portion, though for a different reason. If she does so, her husband will be faithful to her. At one time, such portions were kept until the first child was baptized, and then eaten at the christening feast.

In Yorkshire and Lincolnshire formerly, a plate of bride-cake was flung over the new wife's head as she returned from the church, and omens were read from the way the plate broke. The more pieces there were, the happier would the marriage be. In some places, the number of broken bits indicated the number of children. If the plate remained intact, it was a bad sign, and usually some quick-witted person stamped on it with all possible speed to avert the evil omen. The cake itself was scrambled for by the guests and torn into luck-bringing fragments. On both sides of the Scottish Border, a somewhat similar custom was observed, but with shortbread instead of bride-cake. Here the scramble and the omen-reading took place when the married pair reached their new home which, before honeymoons were the rule, was on the evening of the wedding-day.

The modern custom of sending pieces of wedding-cake to friends not present at the marriage, though now mainly a conventional compliment, has its roots in a desire that they too should share in its luck-bringing properties.

WEDDING DRESS

The choice and making of the wedding dress is surrounded by traditional beliefs and strict rules, many of which are still very much alive today. Because she is entering on a new state of life, every item of a bride's clothing should be entirely new. The only exception to this rule is the customary inclusion of 'something borrowed' and 'something old'. Nowadays, a borrowed veil often provides both these necessities in one; formerly, the 'old' item was frequently the shoes. Charlotte Burne[1] says that Shropshire girls used to undress completely on the wedding morning and start afresh, with new, unlaundered garments from head to foot. Even pins that had been used before were sometimes rejected.

[1] C. S. Burne, op. cit.

It is generally considered unlucky for the bride to make her own dress, and even professional dressmakers rarely do so. It is still more unlucky for her to put on her full bridal array too soon, and particularly if she sees herself in the mirror when thus prematurely clad. Anticipation of this sort may cause something to happen that will prevent the marriage. Only when she is on the point of leaving for the ceremony is it safe for her to look at herself fully robed and veiled, and even then, it is often thought wiser for some small item, such as the gloves to be omitted. When the dress is being fitted, it should be put on in sections, never all at once, and if possible, it should not be completely finished before the actual day. In some districts, it is customary for a short length of the hem to be left unsewn, so that a few stitches can be put in at the very last moment.

The colour of the dress is very important. White, silver, blue, pink, and gold are now considered the luckiest shades. Grey, stone-colour, or fawn were often chosen formerly by simple brides who did not aspire to the full glory of bridal white, but preferred something that could be worn afterwards on Sundays and high-days. Blue has always been popular because it signifies constancy, although in some parts of Yorkshire it seems to have been considered unlucky at one time. M. C. Morris, in his *Yorkshire Folk-Talk*, records a local saying that 'if dressed in blue, she's sure to rue'.

More generally, however, it is so excellent a shade that 'something blue' has to be included for luck, even if the dress is of another colour. In the seventeenth century, one or two of the bride-favours were always blue.

These were knots of coloured ribbons loosely stitched on to the wedding gown, which were plucked off by the guests at the wedding feast, and worn as luck-bringers in the young men's hats. Now that bride-favours are out of fashion, the necessary 'something blue' often takes the form of a pair of garters made and given by a particular friend.

Nothing black should ever be worn by a bride, for obvious reasons. Green is always an unlucky colour, connected with fairies, and believed by many people still to foretell a change into mourning clothes whenever it is worn. It is therefore very clearly unsuitable for weddings, and even today, few girls would choose it deliberately. In Lowland Scotland once, it was thought so ill-omened that not only the bride but the wedding guests also were forbidden to wear it. Nothing green was permitted in the decorations, and no green vegetables were served at the feast. 'Those dressed in blue have lovers true,' says a north-country rhyme, 'but green and white, forsaken quite.'

Brown is avoided in Oxfordshire because those who are married in it 'will never live in a town'. This appears to mean that their husbands will not rise in life or acquire riches. Yellow is widely disliked, since in country tradition it signifies 'forsworn', and so is purple because it is a mourning colour. *See Wedding Veil.*

WEDDING PROCESSION

Superstitions of many kinds surround the bride's journey to and from the wedding, and to a lesser extent, that of the bridegroom and the guests.

It is now generally considered extremely unlucky for the bride and groom to see each other on the wedding morning before they meet in the church. At one time, however, this rule was by no means universal, and was usually disregarded by simple folk who favoured a 'walking wedding'. Sixty or seventy years ago, it was still a common practice for the two people most concerned to walk to the church, the bride going first with the best man and the groom following with the bridesmaid. On the return journey, the married pair walked together in front, followed by the bridesmaid and the best man. No ill-luck was expected from this pre-marital meeting, though some superstitious customs which have now died out, such as the absence of the parents from the procession or the ceremony, were then carefully observed.

The bride must leave her home by the front door, stepping over the threshold with her right foot foremost. It is lucky if the sun shines on her, or if she sees a rainbow on the way. It is most fortunate if she, or any member of the party, meets a black cat, or a chimney-sweep 'in his blacks', especially if the latter offers good wishes, or walks a little way beside the bridal carriage. It is also a good omen for either bride or groom to meet an elephant, a rare occurrence, perhaps, at British weddings, but not unknown when there is a circus in the town. On the other hand, a pig running across the road is a sign of evil. The worst of all omens is for the bride to meet a funeral, or even to catch sight of one from a distance.

Before the advent of motor-cars, the bridal carriage was always drawn by grey horses, if these could possibly be obtained. It is still thought to be lucky for the bride or groom to encounter a grey horse on the way to church. It was, of course, a bad sign if the horses refused to start, either on the outward or the return journey. By an easily understood transition, the modern car has inherited this superstition, so that a breakdown, or difficulty in starting, is now an unlucky omen. When the bride had been set down at the church door, the coachman was expected to drive on for some way before turning, since to turn the horses' heads immediately outside the building would bring bad luck to one or both of the married pair.

In some districts, it was thought unlucky, until fairly recently, for a bridal procession to pass through a lychgate, see *Lychgates*, or through the north door of the church. In many parishes, the latter was reserved for funerals, wedding and baptismal parties always entering by the south or west doors.

A superstition peculiar to Hoxne in Suffolk is recorded in *The Suffolk Garland*, published in 1818, as one of the beliefs still flourishing at that date. No bridal procession ever passed over Gold Bridge on its way to or from the church. To do so would be extremely unlucky, and a marriage so begun would be unlikely to bring happiness.

The reason for this strongly-held belief was that, according to a local legend, St Edmund, King and Martyr, hid under this bridge when he fled from the victorious Danes in A.D. 870. A newly-married couple, passing that way by moonlight, saw the reflection of his gilt spurs in the water, and betrayed him to the Danes, by whom he was murdered. As a punishment for their treachery, the King laid a powerful curse upon every bridal pair who should henceforth cross the bridge on their way to or from their wedding. The editor of *The Suffolk Garland* states that marriage processions always carefully avoided passing over it, even when doing so involved going a long and inconvenient way round to the church. *See Barring the Way: Confetti.*

WEDDING RING

The wedding ring, which in some non-European marriage ceremonies is absent altogether, has in Britain and most parts of Europe so deep a significance that its loss or breaking foreshadows the destruction of the marriage, through the death of the husband, or the loss of his affection, or some other disaster. It is usually considered unlucky to remove it once it has been put on in church. If it falls off, or is accidentally removed, then the husband must replace it in order to avert the threatened evil. In some districts, it is thought safe to take it off after the birth of the first child, but not before. Charlotte Burne[1] records that in the Oswestry area formerly, it was believed that if a husband failed to maintain his wife, she could divorce him simply by giving him back his ring. She was then thought to be quite free to marry again.

The rule against removing the ring, though well known and still quite commonly observed, does not seem to have prevailed everywhere in the past. The fact that wedding rings were used in divination and love-charms, and sometimes in cures, shows that they must often have been taken off, presumably without ill-effects. Moreover, extreme poverty occasionally forced a girl to be married in a borrowed ring which she could not keep. If her husband could not afford to buy one, a neighbour might lend hers for the ceremony. John Kibble tells us in his *Wychwood Forest* (1928) that his grandmother once lent her ring to an impecunious young couple, and received it back after the ceremony. He also records that during the nineteenth century, when times were hard and it proved impossible to borrow a ring, it was not unknown in the Forest villages for the ringed top of the church door-key to be pressed into service. In Ireland, where a gold ring was thought essential for a legal marriage, the parish priest, or some other person, often kept one in readiness, to be hired out for a small fee and afterwards returned.

To drop the ring before or during the wedding service was very unlucky.

[1] C. S. Burne, *op. cit.*

If either the groom or the bride dropped it, it was a sign that he or she would be the first to die. If it rolled away from the altar steps, the omen was extremely bad, and if it came to rest on a gravestone in the floor, it foretold an early death for one of the pair, the bride if the person buried beneath the stone was a woman, the groom if it was a man.

WEDDING TIMES

Certain days and seasons were, and some still are, thought to be unlucky for marriages. One of these is the month of May. It is still quite often avoided by modern brides, as it was nearly two thousand years ago, when Plutarch inquired why the men of Rome did not take wives then. He answered his own question by pointing out that May was the month when offerings were made to the dead and mourning was worn. This would, of course, make it inappropriate for weddings, but we cannot be sure that it was the true, or only, reason for a reluctance which seems to have been already old when he wrote, and which was destined to linger on for so many subsequent centuries.

'Marry in May, rue for aye', is a common saying in Scotland and northern England, and it is matched by others with the same meaning elsewhere. Another, found all over Great Britain, is 'Marry in Lent, you'll live to repent'. Many people, of course, dislike Lent weddings for purely religious reasons, but they are also said to be unlucky by others who are not conspicuously devout. The same applies, though less now than formerly, to Advent and, in some cases, to Easter Week. All these periods, except the month of May, were included in the Church's prohibited marriage-seasons, as laid down in the Sarum Missal, and probably this fact is enough to explain the lingering tradition of bad luck attaching to them. Before the Reformation, the rule forbidding marriages then was strictly enforced, and one celebrated without special permission during such seasons might well be thought to be a tempting of Providence, and unlikely to bring happiness to those most nearly concerned.

Some holy days were also considered ill-omened. Childermas was an unfortunate day for any enterprise, including marriage. Maundy Thursday was unlucky in itself, as well as being part of Holy Week. In East Anglia even now, St Swithun's Day (15 July) is often avoided. Opinions varied about St Thomas's Day (21 December). In Yorkshire, it was said that if a girl married then, she would soon be a widow, but in Lincolnshire, it was considered an auspicious date because, being the shortest day in the year, it 'left less time for repentance'. The bride and groom would be less likely than others to repent of their marriage later on.

Ordinary weekdays had their significance also. An old and well-known rhyme says,

Monday for wealth,
Tuesday for health,
Wednesday the best day of all.
Thursday for losses,
Friday for crosses,
And Saturday no luck at all.

These prophecies, however, like those concerning birth on particular days, were not universal. Monday and Tuesday were lucky in most districts, but Wednesday was disliked in some parts of the Midlands because those who married then would come to poverty. Thursday was often unfortunate, but not in all counties. In Shropshire and Northamptonshire, it was a good day to choose. Friday is still considered ill-omened for weddings by many people, as it is for most other enterprises, but in a few districts, it is, or was, lucky. The reason given for this belief was that the day is holy because of its association with Good Friday, and consequently a marriage begun then is likely to be happy. It is, however, possible that this notion is derived less from Christian thought than from the fact that in Norse mythology, Friday was sacred to the goddess Freya, and hence it was fortunate to lovers. Saturday is now a favourite day for the purely practical reason that it is usually a holiday, or half-holiday, and therefore convenient, but formerly, it was greatly disliked because of a belief that marriage then would be followed by the early death of one of the partners.

In addition to all this, a now almost forgotten superstition once demanded that the day of the week on which the previous Childermas had fallen should be carefully avoided. The sinister influence of that ill-starred anniversary affected the corresponding weekday throughout the year that followed.

WEDDING VEIL

An old bridal veil is often thought luckier than a new one, particularly if it is borrowed from a woman who is known to be happily married, or if it is an heirloom in the bride's family. The good fortune and fertility of the earlier marriages passes with the veil to its new wearer.

The belief that it is unlucky to wear, or see oneself in, bridal clothes too soon, see Wedding Dress, applies with double force to the veil. This should never be put on before the wedding morning except during necessary fittings, and then it must be tried on separately, not with the dress. If a girl looks at herself in the mirror whilst wearing it on any other occasion, the marriage will be unhappy, or the young man may desert her, or die before the wedding day. When she is dressing for the ceremony, the veil should not be donned until she is otherwise completely ready, nor should she see herself in it until she takes her last look in the mirror just before starting for the church.

In a letter printed in *Answers* in January 1939, a Nottingham veil-embroideress described a form of divination often used by her fellow-workers. They took a long fair hair from the head of one of the girls, attached it to the silk, and worked it through the veil they were embroidering. If it went right through without breaking, a long and happy married life was foretold for the couple concerned. If it broke at the beginning, the wife would die early, if at the end, the husband. The writer said she had twice performed this rite when embroidering veils for girls she knew, and on both occasions the prophecy was fulfilled to the letter. She added that she did not really believe in such things; but in spite of her disbelief, she lacked the courage to try the experiment on her own bridal veil.

WEEDS

Just as stones were sometimes thought to grow like plants, so that it was useless to try to clear them permanently from the fields, *see Growing Stones*, so in some rural areas it was formerly believed that weeds could never be successfully eradicated from any land because they were natural to it. Unlike other plants, they did not need the help of seeds, but were spawned by the soil itself. Zincke[1] tells us that when he wrote in the late nineteenth century, Suffolk people ascribed this spawning to a curse laid upon the ground as a punishment for Adam's first disobedience. By this curse, God ordained that thistles, speargrass, and other weeds should flourish while the world lasts. Consequently it was hopeless, and to some extent impious, to attempt to clean land thoroughly, for by Divine command, the weeds would always return.

WEIGHING BABIES

Until a very few years ago, it was widely held that to weigh a baby before he or she was twelve months old was very unlucky. If this was done, the child would not thrive, and would probably die young. This belief is rapidly disappearing now under the influence of health visitors and child-welfare clinics, but it was once very strong, and is not quite dead even yet. Most women nowadays are quite willing to have their children weighed before the year is out, but some dislike the practice, and cases have been recorded in fairly recent years of subsequent ailments being blamed upon it. An Oxfordshire midwife stated in 1935 that one woman in her district firmly refused to have her latest baby weighed, giving as her reason that an older child, who was mentally backward, had been so weighed, and 'that was why he went funny'.

[1] B. Zincke, *Some Materials for the History of Wherstead*, 1887.

Since a baby's progress is to some extent marked by his steady increase in weight, it seems probable that the root-idea of this superstition is the age-old dread of boasting and making too sure. Good fortune, in traditional belief, must never be too openly acknowledged, or it will cease, and bad luck will follow. To know how a child is improving, and more especially to record it each time he is weighed, involves a kind of boasting that might be expected to call down some illness or disaster upon one so young and vulnerable. It is, however, usually considered safe to weigh him once the twelve-month mark is passed.

WHEATEAR

In Scottish and northern English tradition, the wheatear was usually an unlucky bird, connected with the Devil, and also with toads. The latter were supposed to hatch out its eggs, as they were also said to hatch those of the stonechat and, in some districts, the yellowhammer. This curious item of natural history was used as a justification for the persecution and destruction of wheatears by young men and children.

To hear a wheatear crying was a sign of bad luck. In some areas, to meet one was a death omen; in others, this was only the case if the bird was perching on a stone at the time of seeing it. If the observer happened to be sitting on grass when he first saw it, the omen was fortunate, and good luck might be expected.

In Oxfordshire, the wheatear is sometimes called Horsematch because it flies along the road beside horse-drawn traps and carriages, and is supposed to be racing them.

WHISTLING

Seamen usually consider whistling to be an ill-omened act, and so do most miners, and many people connected with the theatre. In the case of sailors, this is very understandable, for to whistle is to imitate the wind and so, by imitative magic, to raise it. It is particularly unlucky if a woman does it. Henderson[1] relates the story of a Scarborough sea-captain in the mid-nineteenth century who refused to allow one member of a party to board his ship. 'Not that young lady,' he is reported to have said, 'she whistles.' This tale is well known, but there must have been many other incidents of the same kind in the days of sail.

A woman who whistles is always ill-omened, on land as well as at sea. 'A whistling woman and a crowing hen are neither fit for God nor men' is a widespread proverb, and in many districts, both are believed to bring misfortune or death to those about them. Along the coast, a female whistler is a

[1] Wm. Henderson, *op. cit.*

wind-raiser. Witches were formerly supposed to produce storms by whistling, and consequently any woman doing so could be suspected of raising a gale, intentionally or otherwise, that might be dangerous to shipping, especially to small vessels such as those owned by fishermen.

This anti-feminine prejudice has its roots in the remote times when women were thought to be the guardians of secret knowledge, and in the later period when, as the records of the sixteenth- and seventeenth-century trials show, female witches were more numerous than their male counterparts. Nevertheless, when afloat, the act of whistling in itself is deemed to have the power of raising winds and storms, whether it is done by a man or a woman. Aubrey tells us[1] how Cramer, when sailing on the River Elbe, 'began accidentally to whistle, which the Watermen presently disliked, and would have him rather to forbeare'. On the other hand, sailors are said to whistle sometimes, gently and softly, to raise a breeze during an unwanted calm.

Whistling down a mine is also unlucky, though the reason for this is less obvious. M. A. Courtney[2] says it is supposed to annoy the Knockers, those curious spirits who inhabit the Cornish tin mines, and so to bring misfortune. In some districts, it is said to cause an explosion or some other disaster in the pit. Whatever the explanation given, whistling while underground is usually forbidden, and any inexperienced lad who starts to do so is at once silenced by the older men.

It is also disliked in a theatre, except when it is part of an act. This applies to every part of the building, and especially to the dressing-rooms, where it means that someone, not necessarily the whistler, will soon be out of work. When a room is shared by more than one performer, the culprit is usually turned out of it at once, and made to turn round three times outside before being readmitted.

In many places it is considered dangerous to whistle after dark. Hunt[3] says that 'to whistle by night is one of the unpardonable sins amongst the fishermen of St Ives'. In Yorkshire formerly, this belief was found inland as well as on the coast, and the offender was driven out of the house and made to walk three times round it to break the spell.

It was, apparently, not only the wind or a general bad luck, that could be raised by this ill-omened act, but sometimes entities far more dangerous. L. F. Newman[4] records that in the East Anglian fens sportsmen out shooting on the marshes at night never whistle to their dogs, for fear of calling up the Lantern Man. This is a local form of fire-fiend, rather like a Will o' the Wisp, who haunts the marshes and is perilous to those who see it. If anyone is rash enough to whistle in the dark and so call it up, he must at once fling himself

[1] J. Aubrey, *Remaines of Gentilisme and Judaisme*, 1686-7.
[2] M. A. Courtney, *op. cit.*   [3] R. Hunt, *op. cit.*
[4] L. F. Newman, 'Some Notes on the Folklore of Cambridgeshire and the Eastern Counties', *Folk-Lore*, Vol. 56, 1945.

face downwards on the ground, with his mouth in the mud. The spirit will then pass over his body, presumably without noticing him.

WIDDERSHINS. *See Sunwise Turn.*

WIFE-SELLING

A common popular delusion, once very widespread, was that it was legal for a man to sell his wife, provided that this was done publicly, and according to certain generally accepted rules. The woman's consent was necessary, and seems to have been freely given in most recorded cases. She had to be brought to the place of sale, usually the market, with a halter round her neck, and she could not be sold for less than a shilling. If these conditions were fulfilled, the sale was held to constitute a true divorce. The woman became the 'wife' of her purchaser, and the original husband was thought to be free to marry again.

Numerous instances of such sales are recorded in the eighteenth and nineteenth centuries. The usual causes were disagreements between the married pair, the shrewish or idle nature of the woman, or the husband's poverty, which made him unable or unwilling to maintain her. It was generally supposed that a woman, once sold, had no further claim on her husband for support. At Bolton in Lancashire, a man sold his wife in 1831 for 3s 6d and a gallon of ale; on the following day he sent the bellman round to announce that he was no longer responsible for any debts she might incur.

The *Annual Record* for 1832 describes the sale of a farmer's wife in Carlisle market in April of that year. The husband placed her in a chair, with a straw halter round her neck, and offered her for sale, with the warning that she had been a 'tormentor' and a 'domestic curse' to him during their three years of married life. In spite of this unflattering description, he sold her to a local man for 20s and a Newfoundland dog. The account states that the pair, now free, as they supposed, of the bond that had held them together, parted in perfect amity. In 1858, a young and pretty girl was sold at a beershop in Little Horton, Yorkshire, because her husband could not get on with her. In this case, an odd touch of delicacy caused him to lead her there by a ribbon instead of the customary rope.

The origin of this widespread delusion is obscure, since at no time in our history did English law permit the sale of wives. It may possibly spring from confused memories of the bride-price, or payment commonly made in Anglo-Saxon times by the husband to the father of the bride. This did not, however, represent an actual purchase-price for the girl, but rather, a form of compensation to the father for the loss of a daughter's services, nor did the payment confer any supposed right to sell her to someone else should the marriage prove a failure. Yet the general belief in the legality of wife-sales was so persistent amongst simple people that in 1913 an old Oxfordshire man, relating how he had once seen a woman sold for 5s in Witney market, could say with complete conviction that such a transaction was quite legal if the husband remembered to bring his wife to the market with a halter round her neck.

In 1881 a woman stated in a London County Court that she had been sold for 25s some years before, and could produce a stamped receipt to prove that she was not living in adultery, but had been lawfully bought by her 'second husband'. Similar sales have occurred even as recently as the period between the two great wars of this century. In his *English Folklore* (1928) A. R. Wright mentions several such transfers, evidence of which was preserved in the records of various courts. The latest occurred a few months before the publication of his book. In May 1928, a man told the magistrates at Blackwood in Monmouthshire, that he had sold his wife for £1, but had kept the child of the marriage, a baby, because 'it was my own flesh and blood'. He also said he had given the buyer a written document, presumably to regularize the wife's position in case of future inquiries.

WILLOW

The willow is a traditional emblem of grief, and of those who have been forsaken in love. Deserted lovers were said 'to wear the green willow'. Swan remarks in his *Speculum Mundi* (1635) that 'it is yet a custom that he which is deprived of his love must wear a willow garland'. In a note to Aubrey's *Remaines of Gentilisme and Judaisme*, Dr White Kennet tells us that 'the young man whose late sweetheart is married to some other person does often in a frolique literally wear a willow garland, as I have seen in some parts of Oxfordshire'. It seems also to have been the custom at one time to send a willow garland to a jilted girl or young man on the occasion of a former sweetheart's marriage to someone else. In Wales, this malicious reminder of lost happiness usually took the form of a peeled hazel rod, known as the 'white stick', or a piece of ginger, or both, sent anonymously to the victim, and sometimes accompanied by derisive and spiteful verses.

Willow catkins are still thought unlucky by some if brought into the house. In Herefordshire, where they are called gulls (meaning goslings), they bring bad luck to the young stock. In some districts, however, willow-branches brought in on May-day morning are fortunate and protect those in the house from the Evil Eye. This is especially so if they are given by a friend.

Because willows decay early and are said to 'perish at the heart', it is, or was until recently, very widely believed that to beat a child with a willow-rod stunts his growth. To beat an animal thus causes it to suffer internal pains. In northern England, if a girl desired to know whom she would marry, she took a willow-branch or stick in her left hand, left the house secretly, and ran three times round it, saying, 'He that's to be my gude man, come and grip the end o't'. On the third time round, the wraith of the future husband would be seen grasping the other end of the stick.

Willow withes were often used to bind up split trees through which children had been passed to cure them of rupture or rickets. Occasionally, the willow-tree itself was used in such cures, either one split intentionally or one with a natural hole in it.

In sixteenth-century medical theory, and later, in folk-medicine, willows were thought good for rheumatism because they grow in damp places, and rheumatism is caused or affected by damp. This idea was based on the semi-magical Doctrine of Signatures; but it is interesting to note than in modern times salicin, found in the bark of willows and unknown in the sixteenth century, is used in the treatment of rheumatic fever.

WILLS

Many people still believe it is unlucky to make a will because to do so hastens the death of the testator. This belief has often resulted in strong resentment felt at any suggestion that a will should be made, and still more often in continual postponements of the necessary arrangements until it is too late, the person concerned dying intestate at last.

In some parts of the country, it was formerly usual to read the will over the coffin before the funeral procession left the house. The dead man was thus made a witness to the proceedings, and might be expected to testify in some manner if anything contrary to his wishes was done. In one case cited by Mrs Leather[1] this was done in order to settle a dispute. A Longtown man named the heir to his small property in his will, but two other men claimed superior rights to it, one as next-of-kin and the other as the holder of a note-of-hand for a sum equivalent to the value of the property. No agreement was reached before the funeral, and an appeal was therefore made to the dead man. The coffin was placed on a bier outside the house, and each claimant in turn stated his case over it, believing that the corpse would bleed, or make some other sign, if a false claim was made. The appeal failed because no such sign appeared, and the dispute had subsequently to be settled by more ordinary means.

WINDOW BLINDS

A blind falling down suddenly over a window is sometimes held to foretell a death in the house. Hanging objects which fall without warning are often considered ominous, and in this case there is an additional death-association

[1] E. M. Leather, *op. cit.*

through the custom of drawing blinds while a corpse lies in the house, or when a funeral is passing. The superstition is less common now than it used to be, because of the modern preference for curtains as window coverings.

For the significance of bobbins on blind-cords, *see Oak.*

WOUND TREATMENT

The idea that a wound can be healed by treating the knife, nail, or whatever else inflicted it, is very ancient, and was once widespread. Sir Francis Bacon remarks in his *Natural History* that 'it is constantly received and avouched that the anointing of the weapon that maketh the wound will heal the wound itself'. The treatment applied to the agent was expected to react upon the flesh of the wounded person, and it was generally supposed that if the instrument was kept well greased or polished, the wound would heal up without further attention.

It was a common practice on many farms, when a horse ran a nail into its foot, to cover the nail with lard or oil, and put it away in a safe place. If this was done at once, it was considered unnecessary to do anything to the foot. Sir J. G. Frazer records in his *Magic Art* how a veterinary surgeon was called to a farm where a horse had ripped its side on a gate-hinge. He found that nothing at all had been done to the actual injury, but several men were busily engaged in taking down the gate, so that the offending hinge might be removed and thoroughly greased.

Heanley[1] mentions the case of a farmworker in Lincolnshire who was so badly cut by the knives of a mechanical reaper that he died the next day. He had received what we should consider proper medical treatment, but not according to the ideas of the local people. One man remarked that if the victim had insisted that the knives be taken off the reaper and treated in the traditional manner, he might not have died; but he was 'nobbutt one of them iggnerent Irishmen, and they knaws nowt'. Similarly, when Heanley himself was cut about the face by a bolt that flew out of some old ship's wood he was chopping, his gardener advised him to have all the dirt and rust rubbed off the edges of the bolt in order to make the wound heal quicker.

In 1902 a Norwich woman named Martha Henry died of tetanus after running a rusty nail into her foot. It was subsequently learnt that the wound had not been dressed in any way, but the nail had been carefully greased. Charlotte Latham[2] relates how the servant of one of her friends injured his back by falling upon a sword-stick. He was in bed for several days, and during that time the sword-stick was hung over the bed-head, polished at stated intervals both night and day, and anxiously examined to see that no spot of rust appeared upon it. If one had done so, it would have been a sure sign of his death, but fortunately none did, and he recovered.

[1] R. M. Heanley, *op. cit.*   [2] Charlotte Latham, *op. cit.*

Sympathy between the wound-agent and its victim was held to be both acute and lasting. Sir Walter Scott refers to this belief in *The Lay of the Last Minstrel*. When Walter of Deloraine was wounded by a lance, the broken weapon was washed, and the splinter left in the wound was removed and anointed with a salve. Each time the woman treating it turned the splinter round, the unconscious man 'twisted, as if she galled the wound'. In *Folk-Lore of the North Riding of Yorkshire*,[1] there is an account of a ship carpenter's wife who kept a brightly polished nail on her chimney-piece. With this nail, her husband had once been injured in the leg, and she believed that if she failed to polish it and allowed it to become dull, his wound would break out afresh.

Anything that had been in contact with a wound was thought to remain in sympathy with it, and therefore to affect the progress of the cure, adversely or otherwise. In East Anglia, it was believed that the old plaster removed from a cut or burn must never be thrown on the fire, but always buried. If it was burnt, the wound would not heal. When Sir Kenelm Digby lectured on his famous Powder of Sympathy at Montpellier in 1657,[2] he told his audience how he had cured James Howell with the aid of the powder and a garter. Howell had been badly wounded in the hand when trying to separate two duellers. The cut was hastily bound up with one of his garters. It subsequently became inflamed and very painful, and seemed likely to turn gangrenous in spite of all the doctors could do. Digby was consulted, and treated the wound by immersing the bloodstained garter in a basin of water wherein some Powder of Sympathy had been dissolved. Within a very short time the pain ceased, and Howell was sent home with instructions to keep the cut clean, but not to do anything else to it. Later in the day, however, Digby took the garter out of the basin and hung it before the fire to dry. Almost immediately afterwards, he received a message that the pain had returned with as much violence as before. The garter was replaced in the water and left there, and within five or six days the wound was completely healed.

The Powder of Sympathy was highly esteemed by many in the seventeenth century, though a few questioned its efficacy. Its virtue did not lie in its composition, which was that of a simple vitriol consisting of a fixed and a volatile salt, but in the fact that it could cure at a distance, either by application to the weapon or, as in Howell's case, to something which had been in contact with the wound. Its reputed success may have been partly due to a general faith in remedies based on sympathy, and partly to Digby's insistence that wounds treated through it should be kept closed and clean, and that none of the usual salves and decoctions (some of which were rather more harmful than otherwise) should be used upon them.

[1] *County Folk-Lore*, Vol. II, ed. Mrs Gutch, 1901.
[2] Sir Kenelm Digby, *A late Discourse . . . touching the Cure of Wounds by the Powder of Sympathy*, 1658.

Weapon salves did much the same work as the Powder, and were very popular at one time. They were intended for use on the weapon and not on the wound, which was perhaps just as well, for their ingredients were sometimes decidedly curious. One receipt, preserved in a book of household lore dated 1688, requires bear's fat, grease from 'the flick of the Boar, the staler the better', powdered bloodstones, red saunders, dried and powdered worms, and an ounce-and-three-quarters of moss from a dead man's skull, 'or more if you can get it'.

Y

YARROW

Yarrow (or Milfoil) is sometimes called Nose-bleed, Bloodwort or, in Scotland, Stanch-girss, because it was formerly used to stop bleeding at the nose. It could also cause such bleeding if a leaf was thrust up the nostril and gently moved about there. Gerard tells us in his *Herbal* that this was sometimes done to ease the pains of migraine. East Anglian girls did it as a form of love-divination, saying as they moved the leaf about,

> Yarroway, Yarroway, bear a white blow.
> If my love loves me, my nose will bleed now.
> If my love don't love me, it won't bleed a drop.
> If my love do love me, 'twill bleed every drop.

A charm to induce dreams of the future husband, well known throughout southern England, was as follows. The girl gathered yarrow from a young man's grave, saying as she did so,

> Yarrow, sweet yarrow, the first that I have found,
> In the name of Jesus Christ, I pluck it from the ground.
> As Jesus loved sweet Mary, and took her for his dear,
> So in a dream this night, I hope my true love will appear.

She then slept with it under her pillow, and the desired dream followed.

Yarrow strewn upon the threshold kept witches from entering the house and, if worn on the person, protected the wearer from their spells. Tied on to a cradle, it similarly protected the baby. Its presence at a wedding ensured that the married pair would love each other truly for at least seven years. In folk-medicine it was used in remedies for various ills, including ague, wounds, cramp and internal upsets.

YELLOWHAMMER

The yellowhammer is one of several birds which are associated in folk-belief with the Devil. In Scotland and northern England, and also in Czecho-slovakia, it is said to drink a drop of the Devil's blood every May Day morning. For this reason, it used to be persecuted by gangs of boys who destroyed its nest and its eggs, and killed the nestlings. In his *Folklore of Birds*, E. A. Armstrong suggests that one reason for the diabolic reputation of this harmless little bird may have been the fancied resemblance of its song to human speech. In Scotland, this is translated as: 'Whetil te, whetil te, whee! Harry my nest and the de'il tak ye'. Another possible reason suggested by Mr Armstrong is that the markings on the eggs are rather like scribbled writings, and may once have been taken for cabbalistic signs.

Because of these markings, the yellowhammer is sometimes called the 'writing lark', or 'writing master'. In Wales, it is called *Gwas y Neidr*, the servant of the snake, because it is supposed to warn snakes of approaching enemies. Another version of this legend is that snakes are hatched in its nest. This is thought to be proved by the same marks, which are here seen as those of serpents. Elsewhere the bird is associated with the toad rather than with snakes. A Northumberland rhyme sung by children when destroying the nests ran:

> Half a paddock, half a toad,
> Half a drop o' de'il's blood,
> Horrid yellow yorling.

YEW

The evergreen yew, which lives to an immense age, extending over many generations of men, is a natural symbol of life everlasting, and seems to have been so regarded from time immemorial, alike by pagans and by Christians. At English country funerals formerly, the mourners often carried branches of yew, which they laid with the dead man in the grave. Small sprigs were also inserted in the folds of his shroud in some districts, before the coffin was nailed down. These typified, not the end of life, but its continuance in the resurrection to come. Similarly, yew-boughs are usually included today in church decorations at Easter (though not at Christmas), because they symbolize the triumph of life over death, and so are fitting emblems of the Resurrection.

To cut down a yew-tree growing in a churchyard, or to burn or damage its branches, is very unlucky. It is also said to be unlucky to bring yew branches into the house, and most people are careful to omit them from the evergreens used for Christmas decorations.

Like most plants with a long history of pagan as well as Christian sanctity, the yew has certain magical properties. In Herefordshire, a girl who wished to dream of her future husband went to a churchyard that she had never visited before and plucked a sprig, which she laid under her pillow at night. Addy[1] tells us that in the north-midland counties, lost goods could be found if the seeker took a branch of yew and held it out before him as he walked. He would be led straight to the place where the lost things were, and when he reached it, the branch would turn in his hand.

In the Scottish Highlands, in the days of clan warfare, there was a curious tradition which said that if a chief took a piece of churchyard yew in his left hand, and then denounced or threatened his enemy, the latter, though present, would hear nothing, though all around could hear quite clearly what was said. This, presumably, enabled the speaker to claim afterwards that he had given due warning of his intentions, whilst at the same time retaining the advantages of a surprise attack on a totally unprepared victim.

[1] S. O. Addy, *op. cit.*

SELECT BIBLIOGRAPHY

ADDY, S. O. *Household Tales, with Other Traditional Remains collected in the Counties of York, Lincoln, Derby and Nottingham, 1895.*

ALEXANDER, R. G. *A Plain Plantain, 1922.*

ALFORD, V. *Introduction to English Folklore, 1952. Pyranean Festivals, 1937.*

ALLIES, JABEZ. *On the Ancient British, Roman and Saxon Antiquities and Folk Lore of Worcestershire, 1852.*

ANDREWS, W. *Church History, Customs and Folk Lore, 1881. Curious Church Customs, 1895. Curious Church Gleanings, 1896.*

Arcana Fairfaxiana Manuscripta. Facsimile Reproduction, 1890. Introduction by George Weddell.

ARMSTRONG, E. A. *The Folklore of Birds, 1958.*

ATKINSON, J. C. *Forty Years in a Moorland Parish, 1891. Glossary of the Cleveland Dialect, 1868.*

AUBREY, J. *Remaines of Gentilisme and Judaisme,* ed. J. Britten, 1881. *Miscellanies upon Various Subjects,* 1857. Fourth ed. *The Natural Historie of Wiltshire,* ed. J. Britten, 1847. *The Natural History and Antiquities of the County of Surrey, 1718–19.*

AXON, W. E. *Cheshire Gleanings, 1894.*

BALFOUR, M. C. and THOMAS, N. W. *Northumberland. County Folk-Lore,* Vol. IV. 1904.

BANKES, M. M. *British Calendar Customs – Scotland, 1937–41.* 3 vols. *British Calendar Customs – Orkney and Shetland, 1946.*

BARING-GOULD, S. *A Book of Folk Lore,* n.d. *A Book of the West,* 1899. *Curious Myths of the Middle Ages,* 1869. *Cornish Characters and Strange Events,* 1925. *Early Reminiscences,* 1923. *Strange Survivals,* 1892. *Yorkshire Oddities, Incidents and Strange Events,* 1890.

BAXTER, R. *Certainty of the World of Spirits, 1691.*

BEDDINGTON, W. and CHRISTY, E. *It Happened in Hampshire,* n.d.

BERKELEY, M. and JENKINS, C. E. *A Worcestershire Book,* n.d.

BILLSON, C. J. *Leicestershire and Rutland. County Folk-Lore,* Vol. I. 1895.

BLACK, G. F. *Orkney and Shetland Folk-Lore, 1901.*

BLACK, W. G. *Folk-Medicine: A Chapter in the History of Culture, 1883.*

BLAKEBOROUGH, J. FAIRFAX. *The Hand of Glory, 1924.*

BLAKEBOROUGH, R. *Wit, Character, Folk Lore and Customs of the North Riding of Yorkshire,* 1898. *T' Hunt o' Yatton Brigg, 1899.*

BLOOM, J. HARVEY. *Folk Lore, Old Customs and Superstitions in Shakespeare Land, 1929.*

BORLASE, W. *Antiquities of Cornwall, 1784.*

BOTTRELL, W. *Traditions and Hearthside Stories of West Cornwall, 1873.*

BOVET, R. *Pandaemonium, 1684.*

BOWKER, J. *Goblin Tales of Lancashire.*

BRAND, J. *Observations on the Popular Antiquities of Great Britain,* ed. Sir Henry Ellis, 1849.

BRAY, MRS A. E. *The Borders of the Tamar and the Tavy. Their Natural History, Manners, Customs, Superstitions, etc.* 1879. Second ed.

BRIDGES, J. C. *Cheshire Proverbs and Other Sayings and Rhymes connected with the County Palatine of Chester,* 1910.

BRIGGS, K. M. *The Anatomy of Puck,* 1959. *The Personnel of Fairyland,* 1953.

BROCKIE, J. *Legends and Superstitions of the County of Durham,* 1886.

BROWN, W. J. *The Gods have Wings,* 1936.

BROWNE, THOMAS. *The Works of Sir Thomas Browne,* ed. Geoffrey Keynes, 1928–31.

BULLOCK, E. A. *Folk Lore of the Isle of Man,* 1816.

BURNE, C. S. *The Handbook of Folk-Lore,* 1914. *Shropshire Folk-Lore,* 1883.

BURTON, R. *The Anatomy of Melancholy,* 1638. Fifth edition.

CAMERON, I. *A Highland Chapbook,* 1928.

CAMPBELL, J. F. *Popular Tales of the Western Highlands,* 1890–3.

CAMPBELL, J. G. *Clan Traditions and Popular Tales of the Western Highlands and Islands,* 1895. *Witchcraft and Second Sight in the Highlands and Islands,* 1902.

CAREW, R. *Survey of Cornwall,* 1602.

CARMICHAEL, A. *Carmina Gaedelica,* 1900.

CASHEN, W. *Manx Folklore,* 1912.

CAUDWELL, I. *Ceremonies of Holy Church,* 1948.

CHAMBERS, R. *The Book of Days,* 1864. *Popular Rhymes of Scotland,* 1890.

Cheshire Notes and Queries.

Cheshire Sheaf, The. Reprinted from the *Chester Courant.*

CLODD, E. *Tom Tit Tot,* 1898.

COBHAM-BREWER, E. *Dictionary of Phrase and Fable,* n.d.

COCKAIGNE, O. *Leechdoms, Wortcunning and Starcraft in Early England,* 1865.

COLES, W. *The Art of Simpling,* 1656.

Countryman, The.

COURTNEY, M. A. *Cornish Feasts and Folk-Lore,* 1890.

COX, M. R. *Introduction to the Study of Folk-Lore,* 1893.

CROKER, T. CROFTON. *Fairy Legends and Traditions of the South of Ireland,* 1825–8.

CROWE, MRS C. *The Night Side of Nature,* 1848.

CULPEPER, N. *The English Physician and Complete Herbal.*

DACOMBE, M. R. *Dorset Up Along and Down Along,* n.d.

DALYELL, GRAHAM. *The Darker Superstitions of Scotland,* 1835.

DAVIES, J. CEREDIG. *Folklore of West and Mid-Wales,* 1911.

DEENEY, D. *Peasant Lore from Gaelic Ireland,* 1900.

DENHAM, M. A. *The Denham Tracts,* ed. J. Hardy, 1892. 1895. Two vols.

Devon and Cornwall Notes and Queries.

Devonshire Association Transactions.

DITCHFIELD, P. H. *Old English Customs,* 1896.

DYER, T. THISTLETON. *British Popular Customs,* 1876. *English Folk-Lore,* 1880. *The Folk-Lore of Plants,* 1889.

ELWORTHY, F. T. *The Evil Eye,* 1895. *Horns of Honour,* 1900.

EVANS, G. EWART. *The Horse in the Furrow,* 1960.

FARRER, J. A. *Primitive Manners and Customs,* 1879.

FOLKARD, R. *Plant Lore, Legends and Lyrics,* 1884.

Folklore. Journal of the Folk-Lore Society.

Folk-Lore Record, The, 1878-82.

FORBY, R. *The Vocabulary of East Anglia, 1830.*

FRAZER, SIR J. G. *The Golden Bough, 1913-15.* Abridged Edition, 1922. *The Fear of the Dead in Primitive Religion, 1933-6.* Three vols. *Psyche's Task. A Discourse concerning the Influence of Superstition on the Growth of Institutions, 1913.*

Gentleman's Magazine Library. Dialect, Proverbs, Word-Lore, 1884. English Traditions, 1885. Manners and Customs, 1883. Popular Superstitions, 1884.

GERARD, J. *Herbal, 1597.*

Gloucestershire Notes and Queries.

GOMME, G. L. *Ethnology in Folk Lore, 1892.*

GRANVILLE, W. *Dictionary of Theatrical Terms, 1952.*

GRATTON, J. G. H. and SQUIRE, C. *Anglo-Saxon Magic and Medicine, 1952.*

GREGOR, WALTER. *Notes on the Folk-Lore of the North-East of Scotland, 1881.*

GRIGSON, G. *A Herbal of All Sorts, 1959.*

GRIMM, J. *Teutonic Mythology.* Trans. J. Stallybrass, 1880-9. Four vols.

GROSE, F. *A Provincial Glossary: with a Collection of Local Proverbs and Popular Superstitions, 1790.*

GURDON, E. C. *Suffolk. County Folk-Lore,* Vol. I. 1893.

GUTCH, M. *The East Riding of Yorkshire. County Folk-Lore,* Vol. VI. 1912. *The North Riding of Yorkshire, York, and the Ainsty. County Folk-Lore,* Vol. II. 1899.

GUTCH, M. and PEACOCK, M. *Folk-Lore concerning Lincolnshire. County Folk-Lore,* Vol. V. 1908.

GUTHRIE, E. J. *Old Scottish Customs, Local and General, 1886.*

HADFIELD, R. L. *The Phantom Ship, 1937.*

HAGGARD, L. RIDER. *I Walk at Night, 1935.*

HALLIDAY, W. J. and UMPLEBY, A. S. *The White Rose Garland, 1949.*

HARDWICK, C. *Traditions, Superstitions and Folk-Lore, 1872.*

HARLAND, J. and WILKINSON, T. T. *Lancashire Folk-Lore, 1867. Lancashire Legends, 1873.*

HARRISON, F. *Medieval Man and his Notions, 1947.*

HARRISON, J. *Ancient Art and Ritual, n.d.*

HARTLAND, E. S. *Gloucestershire. County Folk-Lore,* Vol. I. 1895. *The Science of Fairy-Tales, 1891.*

HAVERGAL, F. T. *Herefordshire Words and Phrases, 1887.*

HEANLEY, R. M. The Vikings: Traces of their Folk-Lore in Marshland. *Saga Book of the Viking Club, 1902.*

HENDERSON, G. *Survivals of Belief among the Celts.*

HENDERSON, W. *Notes on the Folk-Lore of the Northern Counties of England and the Borders, 1879.* Second ed.

HEWITT, S. *Nummits and Crummits, 1900. The Peasant Speech of Devon, 1892.*

HOLE, C. *English Folklore, 1940. English Custom and Usage, 1942. English Folk-Heroes, 1948. English Shrines and Sanctuaries, 1954. Christmas and Its Customs, 1957. A Mirror of Witchcraft, 1957. Tradition and Customs of Cheshire, 1937.*

HONE, W. *The Everyday Book, 1826. The Table Book, 1827. The Year Book, 1829.*

HOPE, R. C. *The Legendary Lore of the Holy Wells of England, 1893.*

HOWELLS, W. *Cambrian Superstitions, 1831.*

HOWEY, M. OLDFIELD. *The Cat in the Mysteries of Magic and Religion, n.d. The Horse in Magic and Myth, n.d.*

HULL, E. *Folklore of the British Isles, 1928.*

HULME, F. E. *Natural History Lore and Legend.*

HUNT, R. *Popular Romances of the West of England, 1881.* Third ed.

JEFFREYS, C. *Whitby Lore and Legend.*

JENKIN, A. HAMILTON. *Cornwall and the Cornish, 1932.*

JOHNSON, W. *Folk-Memory, 1908.*

JONES, F. *The Holy Wells of Wales, 1955.*

JONES, J. *Notes on Certain Superstitions Prevalent in the Vale of Gloucester.*

JONES, T. GWYN. *Welsh Folklore and Folk-Custom, 1930.*

JONES, W. *Finger-Ring Lore, Historical, Legendary and Anecdotal, 1877.*

KEIGHTLEY, T. *The Fairy Mythology, 1850.*

KELLY, W. *Curiosities of Indo-European Folk-Lore, 1863.*

KENNEDY, P. *Legendary Fictions of the Irish Celts, 1866.*

KITTREDGE, G. L. *Witchcraft in Old and New England, 1929.*

LATHAM, C. *Some West Sussex Superstitions Lingering in 1868. Folk-Lore Record,* Vol. I. 1878.

LEATHER, E. M. *The Folk-Lore of Herefordshire, 1912.*

Lincolnshire Notes and Queries.

LOVETT, E. *Magic in Modern London, 1925.*

LUPTON, J. *A Thousand Notable Things, 1660.*

Mabinogion, The. Trans. Gwynn Jones and T. Jones, 1948.

MACINNES, D. *Waifs and Strays of Celtic Tradition, 1890.*

MACKENZIE, D. *Scottish Folk Lore and Folk Life, 1935.*

MACKINLAY, J. E. *Folk-Lore of the Scottish Lakes and Springs, 1883.*

MACPHERSON, J. M. *Primitive Beliefs ir. the North-East of Scotland, 1929.*

MACQUOID, T. and K. *About Yorkshire, 1883.*

MARTIN, M. *Description of the Western Islands of Scotland, 1703.*

MAYO, H. *Letters on the Truths contained in Popular Superstitions, 1840.*

McNEILL, F. M. *The Silver Bough,* Vol. I. 1957.

MILES, C. A. *Christmas in Ritual and Tradition, 1912.*

MITCHELL, A. *The Past in the Present, 1880.*

MOOR, E. *Suffolk Words and Phrases, 1823.*

MORRIS, M. C. *Yorkshire Folk-Talk, 1892.*

MURRAY, M. A. *The God of the Witches, 1933.*

NAPIER, J. *Folk Lore: or Superstitious Beliefs in the West of Scotland within this Century, 1879.*

NEVILLE, C. *A Corner of the North, 1911.*

NICHOLSON, J. *The Folk-Lore of East Yorkshire, 1890. The Folk-Speech of East Yorkshire, 1889.*

NORTHALL, G. F. *English Folk-Rhymes, 1892.*

Notes and Queries.

OLIVIER, E. *Moonrakings,* n.d.

OPIE, I. and P. *The Lore and Language of Schoolchildren, 1959.*

OWEN, M. TREFOR. *Welsh Folk Customs, 1959.*

PARKINSON, T. *Yorkshire Legends and Traditions. 1889.*

PATON, C. I. *Manx Calendar Customs, 1939.*

PAYNE, J. F. *English Medicine in Anglo-Saxon Times, 1904.*

PEACOCK, E. *A Glossary of Words used in the Wapentakes of Manley and Corringham, Lincolnshire, 1877.*

PENNY, J. E. *Folklore round Horncastle, 1922.*

PETTIGREW, T. J. *On Superstitions connected with the History and Practice of Medicine and Surgery, 1844.*

POLSON, A. *Our Highland Folklore Heritage, 1926.*

POOLE, C. H. *Customs, Superstitions and Legends of the County of Somerset, 1877.*

PUGHE, J. *The Physicians of Myddvai, 1861.*

QUILLER COUCH, M. and L. *Ancient and Holy Wells of Cornwall, 1894.*

RAPPOPORT, A. S. *Medieval Legends of Christ, 1934.*

RHYS, SIR J. *Celtic Folk Lore, Welsh and Manx, 1901.*

ROBERTS, P. *Cambrian Popular Antiquities, 1815.*

ROBINSON, F. K. *A Glossary of Words used in the Neighbourhood of Whitby, 1876.*

RUDKIN, E. *Lincolnshire Folklore, 1836.*

SALMON, L. *Untravelled Berkshire, 1909.*

SCOT, R. *The Discoverie of Witches, 1584.*

Shropshire Notes and Queries.

SIKES, WIRT. *British Goblins: Welsh Folk-Lore, Fairy Mythology, Legends and Traditions, 1880.*

SIMPSON, E. B. *Folklore in Scotland, 1908.*

SINGER, CHARLES. *From Magic to Science, 1928.*

Somerset and Dorset Notes and Queries.

SPENCE, J. *Shetland Folk-Lore, 1899.*

SPENCE, L. *British Fairy Origins, 1946.*

STERNBERG, T. *The Dialect and Folk-Lore of Northamptonshire, 1851.*

STEWART, W. G. *Popular Superstitions of the Highlands, 1823.*

Suffolk Garland, The.

Suffolk Notes and Queries.

SWAINSON, C. *The Folk-Lore of British Birds, 1886.*

SWAN, J. *Speculum Mundi, 1635.*

TEBBUTT, C. F. *Huntingdonshire Folk and Their Folklore, n.d.*

The Times (various dates).

THOMSON, D. *People of the Sea, 1954.*

THORPE, B. *Northern Mythology, 1851–2.* Three vols.

TOPSEL, E. *History of Four-Footed Beasts and Serpents, 1607.*

TREVELYAN, M. *Folk-Lore and Folk-Stories of Wales, 1909.*

TYLOR, E. B. *Primitive Culture, 1903.* Fourth ed. Two vols.

UDALL, L. S. *Dorsetshire Folklore, 1922.*

URLIN, E. *Festivals, Holy Days and Saints' Days, n.d.*

VAUX, J. E. *Church Folk Lore, 1902.*

WALDRON, G. *A Description of the Isle of Man.* ed. W. Harrison, 1865.

WHISTLER, L. *The English Festivals, 1947.*

WHITCOMBE, MRS H. P. *Bygone Days in Devon and Cornwall, 1874.*

WHITE, G. *The Natural History of Selborne, 1788.*

WILDE, F. S. *Ancient Curses, Charms and Usages of Ireland, 1890. Ancient Legends, Mystic Charms and Superstitions of Ireland, 1899.*

WIMBERLEY, L. C. *Folklore in English and Scottish Ballads, 1928.*

Worcestershire Notes and Queries.

WRIGHT, A. R. *English Folklore, 1928.*

WRIGHT, A. R. and LONES, F. E. *British Calendar Customs: England, 1936–9.* Three vols.

WRIGHT, E. M. *Rustic Speech and Folk Lore, 1913.*

WRIGHT, T. *Essays on Subjects connected with the Literature, Popular Superstitions and History of England in the Middle Ages, 1846.* Two vols.

YEARSLEY, MACLEOD. *The Folklore of Fairy-Tale, 1924.*

Yorkshire Notes and Queries.

INDEX